D1612299

THE PROHIBITION OF PROPAGANDA FOR
WAR IN INTERNATIONAL LAW

The Prohibition of Propaganda for War in International Law

MICHAEL G. KEARNEY

OXFORD
UNIVERSITY PRESS

OXFORD
UNIVERSITY PRESS

Great Clarendon Street, Oxford OX2 6DP

Oxford University Press is a department of the University of Oxford.
It furthers the University's objective of excellence in research, scholarship,
and education by publishing worldwide in

Oxford New York

Auckland Cape Town Dar es Salaam Hong Kong Karachi
Kuala Lumpur Madrid Melbourne Mexico City Nairobi
New Delhi Shanghai Taipei Toronto

With offices in

Argentina Austria Brazil Chile Czech Republic France Greece
Guatemala Hungary Italy Japan Poland Portugal Singapore
South Korea Switzerland Thailand Turkey Ukraine Vietnam

Oxford is a registered trade mark of Oxford University Press
in the UK and in certain other countries

Published in the United States
by Oxford University Press Inc., New York

British Library Cataloguing in Publication Data

Data available

Library of Congress Cataloging in Publication Data

Kearney, Michael.
The prohibition of propaganda for war in international law / Michael
Kearney.
   p. cm.
Includes bibliographical references and index.
ISBN–13: 978–0–19–923245–1 (alk. paper)
 1. War (International law)—Criminal provisions.   2. Freedom of
expression.   3. Propaganda, International.   4. Crimes against peace.
5. Aggression (International law)   I. Title.
   KZ5594.K43 2007
   341.6—dc22   2007034280

ISBN 978-0-19-923245-1

Foreword

Nations and governments are coming to realize that insufficient attention is being devoted to the deterrence of serious war crimes. Hitherto, the accent has been on trial and punishment after the event. No state crimes, whether genocide, crimes against humanity or war crimes are ever committed without prior propaganda aimed at securing popular support for the proposed illegal actions. This has been the experience of humankind since time immemorial. It has become more prominent and common with the growth and greater sophistication of modern means of communication.

In recent years, and especially following the establishment by the United Nations of the ad hoc international criminal tribunals for the former Yugoslavia and Rwanda, the laws of armed conflict, or humanitarian law, have attracted substantial public discourse. Hardly a day passes without media reference to war crimes and their consequences whether in domestic or international courts.

This timely book by Dr Michael Kearney examines in impressive detail the international law relating to propaganda for war. Propaganda for war as a form of criminal conduct has been largely ignored. However, the author forcefully argues that the legal basis for outlawing propaganda for war is to be found in existing international law. He relies in particular upon the provisions of Article 20 (1) of the International Convention on Civil and Political Rights. It is there provided that:

'(1) Any propaganda for war shall be prohibited by law.'

As Dr Kearney points out, a number of nations have inappropriately entered reservations with regard to this provision on the ground that it is or might reasonably be inconsistent with freedom of speech. That right is also expressly protected in the Convention. One finds in Article 19(2):

'Everyone shall have the right to freedom of expression . . .'

It follows, I would suggest, that the two rights are complementary and not in contradiction with each other. Indeed, this book convincingly demonstrates that propaganda for war should properly be regarded as criminal conduct and in no way be confused or conflated with freedom of speech. One needs only to refer to the Nazi propaganda that preceded and accompanied the Holocaust, or the broadcasts of Radio Télévision Libre des Mille Collines that preceded the genocide in Rwanda in the middle of 1994, to appreciate the distinction. No one could reasonably claim that the genocidal propaganda in either case was entitled to protection under the right to freedom of expression.

Decisions of the International Criminal Tribunal for Rwanda have made it clear that members of the media who indulge in such conduct might render themselves guilty of incitement to genocide. In 2003, Rwandan journalists were convicted of incitement to genocide for their role in founding and running the radio station RTLM. Navanethem Pillay, the presiding judge, said that Nahimana was 'fully aware of the power of words, and.... used the radio, the medium of communication with the widest public reach, to disseminate hatred and violence.' The station called on Hutus to attack named Tutsi targets. Two of those accused were sentenced to life imprisonment.

In the middle of 2009, the Assembly of States Parties, the governing body of the International Criminal Court, will meet in an attempt to find an agreeable definition of 'aggression.' If it is successful in this endeavour, aggression in all of its manifestations will become a crime within the jurisdiction of the Court. More likely than not, I would suggest, the definition will include incitement to aggression as a crime. In one way or another hate speech and propaganda for war is going to become a prominent issue on the international political and legal agenda. It is in this context that I commend Dr Kearney for devoting his doctoral thesis to the subject of propaganda for war. This book that grew out of that thesis will make an important contribution to the emerging debate. It is my hope and expectation that it will stimulate discussion and focus attention on this sorely neglected topic.

Richard Goldstone
Former Justice of the Constitutional Court of
South Africa and former Chief Prosecutor of the
International War Crimes Tribunals for the
former Yugoslavia and Rwanda.

Contents

Table of Cases

Introduction

Adopting the perspective that the 'most urgent problem of modern times is that of safeguarding peace, of eliminating war from the repertoire of man',[1] this book seeks to establish the meaning and scope of the prohibition of propaganda for war in international law. In 1958 John Whitton lamented the failure of the international lawyer to attend to 'the use of propaganda as an offensive weapon [...] at the same time that it has been given ever-increasing attention by the power politics school'.[2] Half a century later and these comments remain as relevant as they were at the height of the Cold War. That propaganda for war continues to be a central element in the preparation of war was demonstrated in the run-up to the 2003 invasion of Iraq. While that propaganda campaign was ultimately effective in achieving the requisite support necessary to initiate war, unprecedented and global popular opposition to the war was largely based on a rejection of the validity of the justifications proffered by what was frequently regarded as state propaganda for war.

Opposition to that war also drew significantly on the principles of international law and the purposes and principles of the Charter of the United Nations. In recent years the discourse of international law has entered the public consciousness to a degree hitherto unknown. Many of the distinct elements of the 'war on terror' such as the incarceration of prisoners at Guantanamo Bay, extraordinary renditions, torture, restrictions on civil liberties, and the use of force in international relations are increasingly being analysed and examined by the media and in public debate through the lens of international law.

The marked public concern as to the respect for international law coincides with an upsurge in awareness of the international framework for the protection of human rights. The significance of this development can be seen in comments such as those of the Attorney General of the United Kingdom in his advice to the Prime Minister Tony Blair on the legality of war against Iraq. Attorney General Goldsmith stressed therein that 'it must be recognised that on previous occasions when military action was taken on the basis of a reasonably arguable case, the degree of public and Parliamentary scrutiny of the legal issue was nothing like as great as it is today'.[3]

---

[1] Yuri Bobrakov, 'War Propaganda: A Serious Crime against Humanity', 31 Law and Contemp Probs 473 (1966) 473.

[2] John B Whitton, 'Radio Propaganda: A Modest Proposal', 52 AJIL 739 (1958) 739.

[3] Attorney General Goldsmith's Memorandum to the Prime Minister on Security Council Resolution 1441, 7 March 2003, para 30.

If two of the more significant developments in the opposition to the war on Iraq were the undermining of government propaganda for war (though ultimately unsuccessful in preventing the war) and a greater focus on international law, absent from both the public and academic discourse was an analysis of the status of the prohibition of propaganda for war in international law. That the broader public failed to make this connection is unsurprising given the paucity of academic scrutiny in this field. More than forty years ago John Whitton and Arthur Larson advocated that efforts be undertaken towards 'bringing the existence of the law of illegal propaganda to the consciousness of the people all over the world'.[4] Such efforts were deemed to be necessary on the grounds that:

It is quite possible that, if average people and even public leaders in various countries were asked about the law governing propaganda, nine out of ten would stare blankly and declare that they were not aware that there was any such law. Certainly a large part of official conduct around the world seems to be carried on as if the area were a legal vacuum.[5]

This state of affairs remains in the ascendancy today, when despite the exponential growth in the study of international law, the prohibition of propaganda for war has languished as a footnote in the academic literature. Bereft of any comprehensive analysis and subject to little if any sustained debate, the tangential location of the prohibition of propaganda for war in the discourse of international law has resulted in a situation where 'official conduct' continues to assume itself to be acting in a legal vacuum. Recent developments, however, suggest that a reappraisal of the prohibition of propaganda for war in international law may yet be pushed onto the international agenda. In 2006 a collective of non-governmental organizations (NGOs) and academic centres from the United States[6] submitted a shadow report to the Human Rights Committee which described the prohibition of propaganda for war as set forth in Article 20(1) of the International Covenant on Civil and Political Rights as 'implicitly recogniz[ing] that the condition of war jeopardizes the integrity and exercise of all of the political and civil rights elsewhere declared in the Covenant'.[7] It asserted that the USA, through the use of propaganda for war in the context of the 'war on terror' and the war on Iraq, 'contributed to violations, both here and abroad, of many other rights protected by this Covenant including articles 1, 2, 6, 7, 9,

---

[4] John B Whitton and Arthur Larson, *Propaganda: Towards Disarmament in the War of Words* (New York: Oceana Publications, 1964) 265.

[5] ibid.

[6] The International Women's Human Rights Law Clinic of the City University of New York School of Law, Women's International League for Peace and Freedom, United States Section, The Center for Constitutional Rights, Madre, International Federation for Human Rights (Fidh), Women's Environment and Development Organization (Wedo), National Lawyers Guild, American Humanist Association.

[7] Report on Failure of Compliance with Article 20 Prohibiting Propaganda for War prepared for the United Nations Human Rights Committee's eighty-seventh session for its review of the Second and Third Periodic Report of the United States of America under the International Covenant of Civil and Political Rights, June 2006.

10, 13, 14, 17, 19, 21, 24, 26 and 27'. The authors of the report stated that their purpose in filing this document with the Committee was to 'bring greater visibility and attention to the full significance and implications of the Covenant's prohibition of propaganda for war'. In undertaking to provide a comprehensive analysis of the meaning, scope, and application of the prohibition of propaganda for war in international law, this book shares those aims.

A. The Meaning of Propaganda for War

Both the words *propaganda* and *war* suffer from a distinct lack of definition for the purposes of international law, a quandary which, although significant, need not preclude a suitable understanding of the meaning of the term 'propaganda for war'. In his 1933 treatise *The Propaganda Menace*, Frederick Lumley discerned the etymological root of the word propaganda in the Latin:

It is from *propagatus*, perfect participle of *propagare*, which had reference to the very specific act of fastening down slips or roots of plants in such a way as to cause them to multiply and spread; in other words it had reference to the gardener's work of *forcing* growth among plants or vegetables. It also had reference to the forced breeding of animals. Gradually, as with hosts of other words, it came to have an abstract meaning and to signify all of the processes involved in the propagation of anything from a bit of silly gossip to the majestic doctrine of transubstantiation.[8]

Indeed, it is more usual for the origin of the word to be ascribed to the Sacra Congregatio de Propaganda Fide, a committee of cardinals founded in 1622 by Pope Gregory XV and charged with Catholic missionary work abroad.[9] *Black's Law Dictionary* defines propaganda as '[t]he systematic dissemination of doctrine, rumor, or selected information to promote or injure a particular doctrine, view or cause', or 'the ideas and information so disseminated'.[10] Whitton understood propaganda to mean 'the communication of facts, fiction, argument, and suggestion, often with the purposeful suppression of inconsistent material, with the hope and intention of *implanting* in the minds of the "target" audience certain prejudices, beliefs, or convictions aimed at persuading the latter to take some action serving the interest of the communicator'.[11]

---

[8] Frederick E Lumley, *The Propaganda Menace* (New York: D. Appleton—Century Company, 1933) 56.

[9] L John Martin, *International Propaganda: Its Legal and Diplomatic Control* (Minneapolis: University of Minnesota Press, 1958) 5. Adeno Addis, 'International Propaganda and Developing Countries', 20 Van J Transnat'l L 491 (1988) 491; Kenneth Macksey and William Woodhouse, *The Penguin Encyclopaedia of Modern Warfare: From the Crimean War to the Present Day* (London: Viking, 1991) 257.

[10] *Black's Law Dictionary* (7th edn).

[11] John B Whitton, 'Aggressive Propaganda', in M Cherif Bassiouni and Ved P Nanda (eds), *International Criminal Law*, vol i (Springfield, Ill: Charles C Thomas, 1974) 238–72, 239.

Neither is the word war itself frequently used in the context of international law, with aggression being the relevant term for the purposes of international criminal law and 'armed conflict' or 'use of force' employed by humanitarian lawyers. Each of these terms in turn remains the subject of heated definitional debates, and although these are of immense significance, the present book must proceed on the understanding, in particular as regards international criminal law, that while a definition of aggression is as yet not agreed upon, the principle at hand relates to a crime of incitement which should be developed in parallel with the drafting of the crime of aggression. As will become clear in the chapters to follow, the meaning of the word war in the term propaganda for war pertains only to wars of aggression in contravention of international law. These do not include wars of self-determination or collective self-defence or otherwise as provided for in the UN Charter.

As to whether the difficulty in defining *war* should preclude an analysis of the prohibition of 'propaganda for war' in international law, one must consider this book both to be aimed at contributing to the future development of international law, but also having regard to recent developments which affirm that the crime of aggression, war, may be subject to the jurisdiction of national tribunals, and thus propaganda thereto may also shortly be the subject of national judicial proceedings. Attorney General Goldsmith's advice to Tony Blair is again relevant in this regard, since it recognized that aggression is a crime under customary international law which automatically forms part of domestic law and '[i]t might therefore be argued that international aggression is a crime recognised by the common law which can be prosecuted in the UK courts'.[12] This opinion was subsequently affirmed by the House of Lords in *R v Jones, et al*, where the Court held that the crime of aggression constituted part of customary international law, with Lord Bingham considering that the crime did not 'lack the certainty of definition required of any criminal offence, particularly a crime of this gravity'.[13] Given that national courts are confident of identifying aggression, there is little doubt that they can also identify propaganda for wars of aggression, a point which will be returned to throughout the text.

It is not, however, the purpose of this study to suggest a general definition of either the word *propaganda* or *war*, but rather to understand each in the context of the phrase 'propaganda for war'. As noted by John Powell, '[t]he term "propaganda," as will be seen, cannot be given a universal definition, but only a situational context, if the current predicament is to be resolved'.[14] Since the bulk of efforts at formulating a prohibition of propaganda for war in international law occurred in the early decades of the Cold War, the proceedings of a seminar

---

[12] Attorney General Goldsmith's Memorandum to the Prime Minister on Security Council Resolution 1441, 7 March 2003, para 34.

[13] *R v Jones, et al* [2006] UKHL 16, para 19.

[14] John T Powell, 'Towards a Negotiable Definition of Propaganda for International Agreements Related to Direct Broadcast Satellites', 45 Law and Contemp Probs 3 (1982) 4.

on the issue held in the United States in 1966 provide a useful summary of the classic counter-interpretations of the meaning of propaganda for war, and of which specific forms of propaganda should be regulated by international law. Yuri Bobrakov, the Press Attaché of the USSR in Washington, stated that the term propaganda had 'rather a broad meaning, implying dissemination, or more specifically, purposeful dissemination, of certain information that is to produce upon its recipient a certain reaction which from the viewpoint of the disseminator is desirable',[15] and defined war propaganda to be both 'an incitement to war between states and [...] a means for preparing for aggressive war'.[16]

Richard Davies of the United States Information Agency understood propaganda, 'in its altogether neutral sense', to embrace 'informational, commentary, and feature materials dealing with the substance of international affairs, with the activities of the originating country that bear upon its relations with other states, and with the activities of other countries in the sphere of their relations with other states'.[17] The USA has generally opposed efforts to prohibit propaganda for war in international law, reasoning that the difficulties in distinguishing between permissible and impermissible propaganda present too great a threat to freedom of expression. Richard Falk, although accepting that incitement to war should be prohibited, justified the US approach by arguing that 'certain hostile propaganda' is of overall benefit since it 'help[s] to resolve international conflict by coercive competition without endangering the basic peace and security of the world, and deserve[s] to be tolerated in the interests of world order'.[18] Taking an overview of the different approaches, William O'Brien considered the limitation of international propaganda to arise not from a consensus of the 'international common good', but from the 'pragmatic necessities of coexistence in a dangerous world of conflict'. By this account, propaganda:

[...] that threatens to incite World War III would be judged impermissible—indeed, criminal—by all responsible members of the minimum world public order, whatever their ideological persuasion [but] less dangerous propaganda which thwarted progress in arms control and disarmament and pacific settlement of disputes might be considered permissible because its alleged truth and its ideological-political necessity outweighed the propagandists' concern for the minimum world public order.[19]

These statements provide a backdrop to the debates on the prohibition of propaganda for war, a key aspect of which is whether the term is limited to 'incitement to war' or whether it additionally encompasses propaganda which is antecedent

---

[15] Yuri Bobrakov, 'War Propaganda: A Serious Crime against Humanity', 473.

[16] ibid 475.

[17] Richard T Davies, 'The American Commitment to Public Propaganda', 31 Law and Contemp Probs 452 (1966) 455.

[18] Richard A Falk, 'On Regulating International Propaganda: A Plea for Moderate Aims', 31 Law and Contemp Probs 622 (1966).

[19] William V O'Brien, 'International Propaganda and Minimum World Public Order', 31 Law and Contemp Probs 589 (1966) 597.

to direct incitement to war but which serves either as a means of preparation for a future war, or perhaps to preclude peaceful settlement of disputes.

It should also be stated that while 'propaganda for war' is the formulation used in international human rights treaties, notably in Article 20(1) of the International Covenant on Civil and Political Rights, various terms have frequently been employed in a loose, overlapping fashion, a point which no doubt has further added to the confusion as to the meaning of 'propaganda for war'. Given its central position in the International Bill of Rights, the term propaganda for war will be used in this work, unless specific proposals or texts refer to other formulations such as 'war propaganda', 'propaganda for aggression', or 'war-mongering', in which case the relevant term will be used.

B. The Technique of Propaganda for War

Efforts to reach consensus on the definition of propaganda for war for the purposes of international law have been severely hampered by the inherent complexity of propaganda itself. Lumley considered 'cases of pernicious propaganda' to be fuelled by 'at least four major abuses of the laws of reasoning [...] suppression, distortion, diversion and fabrication'.[20] Whitton and Larson understood as the purpose of 'war-mongering' propaganda 'to implant in the minds of peoples a disposition or desire to engage in an international armed conflict'.[21] They suggest that:

At times its object is to produce a conviction that a nation must fight in self-defense, or fight a preventive war. Or the theme may be that war is necessary to serve some high moral cause, such as the need to save helpless people from oppression. The message may be the necessity of a great 'civilizing mission' as in the case of a colonial war.[22]

Whereas propaganda for war relies to a great extent on the selective and carefully orchestrated presentation of information and facts, the emphasis placed on shaping emotional responses to events is one of its core features. Lumley felt that no matter how highly literate or critical people may become, they will remain vulnerable to emotional manipulation since there will always be attachments to 'mother, home and country'.[23] His understanding of the role which propaganda would play in the modern world is worth considering at some length. Drawing on Harold Lasswell's observation that 'propaganda is a concession to the age', Lumley wrote:

Nobody now knows where the familiar boundaries are. Languages, trades, religions, political affiliations run out beyond the familiar state lines [...] With such staggering

---

[20] Frederick E Lumley, *The Propaganda Menace*, 116–17.
[21] John B Whitton and Arthur Larson, *Propaganda*, 62.
[22] ibid.
[23] Frederick E Lumley, *The Propaganda Menace*, 240–1.

immensities as the modern world shows us and as the future will more and more show, what instrumentality can ever hope to gather the people into wars except propaganda? The armies and navies and air services may be 'commanded' as of old. But the larger the population and the more complex its social life, the less it can be commanded. Immensity and complexity also mean a greater variety of allegiances, fewer universal formalities. What can cope with these except propaganda? Modern education is working steadily in the direction of more pronounced individuality. And what can cope with this except propaganda? It is true that modern education is steadily working towards more 'training in thinking'; but there is no thought or possibility of abolishing the emotions. Therefore it may be argued that, if we are to have wars in the future, and if we still have millions who can easily be made to fear, hope, love, and hate, and if we have ever more efficient journalists and press-agents—we shall have more propaganda.[24]

Chronicling the development of propaganda in military history, Kenneth Macksey and William Woodhouse claimed that 'as the people's insights are improved by education, they find it easier to recognise the subterfuge sometimes called "disinformation" '.[25] Nonetheless, it would appear that the central position which Lumley accorded to the shaping of emotions by propaganda is not misplaced. Propaganda continues to inhibit the development of rational thought or objective analysis by heightened emphasis on the emotive. Ian Burkitt has noted in this regard how propaganda for war against Iraq was directed towards manipulating emotional currents of anger, fear, and hope in the aftermath of 11 September 2001. He considers the deployment of such propaganda to be a reflection of Foucault's observation that power 'is a total structure of actions brought to bear upon possible actions: it incites, it induces, it seduces... [it is] a way of acting upon an acting subject or acting subjects'.[26] Burkitt traces 'the narrative of incitement to war' against both Afghanistan and Iraq as having been woven 'by drawing parallels from collective stories of history: from events already familiar to us'.[27] In linking the 2001 attacks to the attack on Pearl Harbor, and more particularly the response to that attack, he argues that the governments of the United Kingdom and the United States of America attempted:

[...] to build on these narratives and incite and seduce the public by manipulating the emotional response to September 11 in order to direct conduct. The narrative of war was used to construct the very idea of a 'war on terror' and to unify public opinion behind the various strategies designed to wage this war.[28]

---

[24] ibid 242.
[25] Kenneth Macksey and William Woodhouse, *The Penguin Encyclopaedia of Modern Warfare*, 257.
[26] Michel Foucault, 'The Subject and Power', in HL Dreyfus and P Rabinow (eds), *Michel Foucault: Beyond Structuralism and Hermeneutics* (Brighton: Harvester, 1982) 221. Cited in Ian Burkitt, 'Powerful Emotions: Power, Government and Opposition in the "War on Terror" ', 39 Sociology 4 (2005) 679, 683.
[27] Ian Burkitt, 'Powerful Emotions', 685.
[28] ibid 685.

This is not to say that propaganda is divorced from efforts at positing justifications for wars of aggression as rational and necessary actions. Burkitt has stressed that while support 'was elicited by attempting to incite powerful emotions', the governments also tried 'to induce people through persuasion', the most obvious example being the claims to have evidence that Saddam Hussein possessed weapons of mass destruction which could be used against them.[29] Propaganda for war is manifested as an appeal to both the emotions and the intellect. This duality is necessary if propaganda is to be effective in achieving its desired response. Attempts to 'incite, induce and seduce' are unpredictable since emotions have a complex logic,[30] and are more likely to carry conviction and to take the desired effect when linked to what is presented as an objective reality.

C. Freedom of Expression

As a prelude to his 'four freedoms' speech to the United States Congress in 1941, Franklin Roosevelt asserted that 'every realist knows that the democratic way of life is at this moment being directly assailed in every part of the world—assailed either by arms or by secret spreading of poisonous propaganda by those who seek to destroy unity and promote discord in nations that are still at peace'.[31] Two of the most pertinent 'essential human freedoms' to which Roosevelt's speech referred are freedom of speech and expression and 'freedom from fear'.[32] It is clear that he did not consider the former to extend to propaganda in violation of the latter; nurturing of fear with the aim of initiating aggression is a crucial aspect of propaganda for war, and it cannot be compatible with the protection of the right to freedom of expression.

The insistent reliance of states on their respect for the right to freedom of expression as a justification for the rejection of the prohibition of propaganda for war is a recurring theme in this study. It must be emphasized that the potential impact of the prohibition of propaganda for war on the right to freedom of expression is 'a very small fraction of the subject' in proportion to the total problem since it is the propaganda of states themselves, which wield the power to initiate war, rather than the individual, which must be of prime concern.[33] In this regard, the rejection of the prohibition on grounds of deference to the individual's rights to freedom of expression often appears as little more than an attempt

---

[29] Ian Burkitt, 'Powerful Emotions', See generally David Miller (ed), *Tell Me Lies: Propaganda and Media Distortion in the Attack on Iraq* (London: Pluto Press, 2004).

[30] ibid 689.

[31] 6 January 1941.

[32] Franklin D Roosevelt, 'Four Human Freedoms', 6 HRQ 3 (1984) 384.

[33] Arthur Larson, 'The Present Status of Propaganda in International Law', 31 Law and Contemp Probs 439 (1966) 443. Whitton also asserts that the cases of aggressive international propaganda which have created the greatest dangers have been 'organized, subventioned, and implemented by governments and governmental agencies'. John B Whitton, 'Aggressive Propaganda', 263.

by states to create a smokescreen to facilitate their ability to employ propaganda for war in a legal vacuum. Furthermore, limitations on the right to freedom of expression are specifically provided for in the International Bill of Rights as well as in regional human rights treaties and all national legal systems. Freedom of speech issues and controversies, particularly in relation to the law, have rarely ceased to be either topical or divisive and it remains of great difficulty in many societies, such as within the European Union, to precisely identify the true meaning of freedom of speech and its location amongst societal values. Conor Gearty, for example, is critical of the prevailing orthodoxy that freedom of expression is a sacrosanct right in the West, asserting that 'freedom of political speech has never existed properly in any liberal democratic society, that its foundational status in our culture is bogus, that its true place is as one of the essential myths with which liberalism has defended itself from socialism in the democratic era'.[34] The following chapters will demonstrate that since propaganda for war is by its very nature 'dominating, antidialogic and manipulative',[35] its prohibition, enforced in a judicious manner, is likely in fact to be a boon to the effective exercise and enjoyment of freedom of speech.

It is frequently the situation that when discussing the prohibition of propaganda for war states have failed to consider in any depth the responsibility of governments themselves for engaging in such propaganda, choosing to focus instead on the role of the mass media. This bias represents a purposeful incongruity by which states blame the medium by which propaganda for war is disseminated rather than the source. It may be argued that large media corporations have become so powerful that they can use their own initiative and means of production to disseminate propaganda for war which no government, particularly a beleaguered government in a state already torn by civil strife, could hope to counteract. While such a situation is possible, it is unlikely, though not strictly necessary, that such propaganda would be launched without at least the implicit support of a third state.

It may be further argued that a prohibition of propaganda for war is unnecessary since in most states, particularly those that respect freedom of the press, government propaganda would be severely curtailed and undermined by the 'fourth estate'. While the importance of the role of the media in this regard cannot be underestimated, the track record of the mass media with regard to challenging and undermining government propaganda for war does not always correlate well with the trust with which it is invested, not only by the general public, but also by leading academics and members of the governing elite.

Alex Carey considered the twentieth century to have been characterized by three developments of great political importance: 'the growth of democracy, the

---

[34] Conor Gearty, 'Protecting Political Speech at a Time of Perpetual War', The Austin Lecture delivered to the Association of Legal and Social Philosophy, 24 June 2005. See further Conor Gearty, *Principles of Human Rights Adjudication* (Oxford: Oxford University Press, 2005) 39–40.

[35] Adeno Addis, 'International Propaganda and Developing Countries', 492.

growth of corporate power, and the growth of corporate propaganda as a means of protecting corporate power against democracy'.[36] This corporate propaganda has long been interlinked with that of the state. Edward Herman and Noam Chomsky have repeatedly highlighted the manner by which the free market-place of ideas has been undermined by a mass media whose societal purpose is 'to inculcate and defend the economic, social and political agenda of privileged groups that dominate the domestic society and the state'.[37] Concurring with these views, Edward Said noted that the level of '[c]ooperation between the media and the state is quite unique to our time' and suggested that 'it's going to define politics in the future'.[38]

Other forms of expression such as racist hate speech, glorification of terrorism, and incitement to violence on discriminatory grounds have been prohibited in the national legislation of many states which otherwise continue to refuse to prohibit propaganda for war. While the specific arguments of States parties opposed to the International Covenant on Civil and Political Rights' prohibition of propaganda for war will be analysed herein, a typical example of this approach is to be found in the 2002 Best Practice Report on Freedom of Expression, Assembly, and Association of the Commonwealth Secretariat. In considering the mandatory limitations on the right to freedom of expression as set forth in Article 20 of the Covenant and Article 13(5) of the American Convention on Human Rights to prohibit any propaganda for war and expression that advocates national, racial, or religious hatred that constitute incitement to violence, hostility, or discrimination, the Secretariat states that it is of the opinion 'that given the crucial necessity to maintain harmonious relations among various groups in a pluralistic society and secure the personal safety of all, the prohibition of hate speech that constitutes incitement to violence, hostility and discrimination is acceptable'.[39] In continuing to stress the fundamental tenets of freedom of expression, it exhorts 'that no penalties should be imposed for hate speech unless there is proof of an intention to incite discrimination, hostility or violence'.[40] Rather than consider adopting a similar proviso with regards to propaganda for war, the

[36] Alex Carey, *Taking the Risk Out of Democracy: Corporate Propaganda Versus Freedom and Liberty* (Urbana: University of Illinois Press, 1997) 18. Hummel and Huntress, commenting long before the advent of the world wide web, also criticized the tendency 'toward greater and greater control of the media of mass propaganda by fewer and fewer great owners and publishers [which] is dangerous beyond any doubt, as dangerous, perhaps, as a corresponding growth of governmental control would have been'. William Hummel and Keith Huntress, 'The Nature and Media of Propaganda', in Nick Aaron Ford (ed), *Language in Uniform: A Reader on Propaganda* (New York: The Odyssey Press, 1967) 1–11, 11.
[37] Edward S Herman and Noam Chomsky, *Manufacturing Consent: The Political Economy of the Mass Media* (London: Vintage, 1994) 298.
[38] Gauri Viswanathan (ed), *Power, Politics and Culture: Interviews with Edward W. Said* (London: Bloomsbury, 2004) 64.
[39] Commonwealth Secretariat, *Freedom of Expression, Assembly and Association: Best Practice* (London, 2002) 11.
[40] ibid 12.

Report, noting that the provision is 'problematic', simply dismisses the relevant provisions without further discussion, asserting that '[e]ven though such speech may be undesirable and even deplorable, prohibition of mere propaganda would certainly be contrary to the spirit of the free marketplace of ideas essential to sustain democracy'.[41]

This dichotomy, and the refusal or failure to engage in any constructive debate as to how the provision may be interpreted and applied with due regard to the right to freedom of expression, frequently appears to denote a stance premised on the willingness of governments to restrict the speech of private individuals, whilst refraining from accepting any restriction on their own speech in the context of propaganda for war.

D. The Coming of Age of International Propaganda

History has recorded the use of propaganda since earliest times.[42] From biblical narratives to Hannibal's descent from the Alps trumpeting that 'he was not come to fight against Italians but on behalf of Italians against Rome',[43] propaganda has been central to military campaigns throughout the centuries. The French Revolution of 1789 has been identified as 'the beginning of world consciousness of international propaganda'.[44] In the period of instability that would unfold in its wake and the subsequent crystallization in the nineteenth century of the doctrine of non-intervention in the internal affairs of a state as a prescription of international law the legality of international propaganda began to be questioned.[45] Following the Revolution, in 1792 the French National Convention made an offer to come 'to the aid of all peoples who wish to recover their liberty'.[46] In a similar fashion to the protagonists of the later Bolshevik Revolution of 1917, the success of the French Revolution was believed to be conditional on spreading the revolutionary ideology to other countries. The United Kingdom condemned this action as the 'formal declaration of a design to extend universally the new principles of government adopted in France, and to encourage disorder and revolt in all countries, even those which are neutral'.[47] The ensuing 'guerre de propagande' resulted in the offer being repealed by the French National Convention in

---

[41] ibid.

[42] L John Martin, *International Propaganda*, 5–10; John B Whitton and Arthur Larson, *Propaganda,* 12–54; BS Murty, *Propaganda and World Public Order: The Legal Regulation of the Ideological Instrument of Coercion* (New Haven: Yale University Press, 1968) 1–11.

[43] Frederick E Lumley, *The Propaganda Menace,* 57. See also BS Murty, *Propaganda and World Public Order,* 2.

[44] L John Martin, *International Propaganda,* 6.

[45] Robert B Holtman, *Napoleonic Propaganda* (Baton Rouge: Louisiana State University Press, 1950).

[46] Arthur Larson, 'The Present Status of Propaganda in International Law', 441.

[47] ibid 441–2.

April 1793 in the face of hostilities from both the United Kingdom and the other European powers.[48]

The first form of propaganda which states sought to control through the mechanisms of international law was that disseminated by the agents of one state in the territory of another and which was intended to provoke civil unrest. Such propaganda frequently targeted ethnic or religious minorities, encouraging them to secede or to revolt against their governments, and was variously known as 'revolutionary propaganda' or 'subversive propaganda'.[49] At this juncture, hostile international propaganda was regarded as an international delinquency, an affront to the principle of non-intervention in the internal affairs of a sovereign state. Thus Éméric de Vattel could assert that 'it is in violation of the law of nations to call on subjects to revolt when they are actually obeying their sovereign, although complaining of his rule'.[50]

One of the earliest examples of a quasi-legal punishment of incitement to war is recorded as the 'Ambrister–Arbuthnot Affair' of 1818. During the war between the United States and the Seminole Indians in Florida, General Andrew Jackson captured an Englishman and a Scotsman fighting alongside the Seminoles in Spanish territory.[51] Jackson hastily convened a military court martial that found Arbuthnot guilty of the charge of 'exciting the Creek Indians to war against the United States' and ordered his execution.[52]

Political propaganda on the part of individuals and political networks was also widespread during the nineteenth century, with anarchists, communists, and other revolutionary ideologues seeking to inspire international solidarity and insurrection. Writing in 1869, Michael Bakunin announced that the International Workingmen's Association would 'spread its propaganda without regard for the susceptibilities of the bourgeoisie, so that every worker, emerging from the intellectual and moral torpor in which he has been kept, will understand his situation and know what he wants and what to do, and under what conditions he can obtain his rights as a man'.[53]

---

[48] Lawrence Preuss, 'International Responsibility for Hostile Propaganda against Foreign States', 28 AJIL 649 (1934) 654; Vernon B Van Dyke, 'Responsibility of States for International Propaganda', 34 AJIL 58 (1940) 59–62.

[49] See Hersch Lauterpacht, 'Revolutionary Activities of Private Persons against Foreign States', 22 AJIL 105 (1928); Hersch Lauterpacht, 'Revolutionary Propaganda by Governments', 13 Trans Grot Soc 143 (1928); Quincy Wright, 'Subversive Intervention', 54 AJIL 521 (1960); John B Whitton, 'Subversive Propaganda Reconsidered', 55 AJIL 120 (1961).

[50] Éméric de Vattel, *The Law of Nations or the Principles of Natural Law: Applied to the Conduct and to the Affairs of Nations and of Sovereigns* 3, trans Charles G Fenwick (Washington: Carnegie Institution of Washington, 1916), 131.

[51] Theodore S Woolsey, 'The Effect of the Unfriendly Act or Inequitable Conduct of the Citizen upon the Right to Protection', Am Soc'y Int'l L Proc 99 (1910) 104.

[52] Seymour D Thompson, 'Andrew Jackson and his Collisions with Judges and Lawyers', 31 Am L Rev 801 (1897) 810. See further Jonathan Lurie, 'Andrew Jackson, Martial Law, Civilian Control of the Military, and American Politics: An Intriguing Amalgam', 126 Mil L Rev 133 (1989) 136, fn. 13.

[53] Michael Bakunin, *Politique de l'Internationale* (Paris: Stock, 1911) vol v; reprinted in Sam Dolgoff (ed), *Bakunin on Anarchy* (London: George Allen & Unwin, 1973) 173.

Prior to 1914 state sponsored propaganda had primarily been directed at audiences in foreign countries. Propaganda began to be increasingly directed at domestic audiences during the First World War in response to the new forms of warfare and in recognition of the potential impact of the nascent modern communications technology and mass media on international relations.

Of great significance at this time was the realization by governments that in order to wage modern wars, the scale of which greatly surpassed anything experienced to that date, public opinion would have to be kept firmly behind the military effort. David Caron notes how during the descent into 'total war' between 1914 and 1918, '[t]echnology magnified the power of weapons [...] while mass propaganda demonized the intended targets'.[54] The increased destruction caused by war consequently led to a rise in 'popular suspicion of the purposes or wisdom of those who led their peoples to such slaughter',[55] a development which in turn necessitated more propaganda on the part of the state. Similarly, Whitton and Larson state that not long after the war began it became clear that modern warfare required the mobilization of the totality of the economic and industrial life of the nation. The greater sacrifices asked of the civilian population meant that the morale of the nation at war was of vital importance. Hence 'the attention given by all belligerents to the importance of propaganda, for if armies are mobilized by orders, it is not too much to say that civilians are mobilized by propaganda'.[56] Referring to the propaganda employed during the First World War, Harold Lasswell stated that civilian unity behind a government at war was 'achieved by the repetition of ideas rather than movements' since the 'civilian mind is standardized by news and not by drills'.[57]

This shift, from international propaganda aimed at inciting foreign audiences to propaganda directed at domestic audiences and intended to secure the requisite support necessary for the continuation of the First World War, marks the departure point for this study of the prohibition of propaganda for war in international law. Whilst revolutionary and subversive propaganda was to remain a tool of governments and non-state actors worldwide, international propaganda in the age of democracy was now as much concerned with influencing the thought, beliefs, and allegiances of domestic audiences as it had ever been with regard to foreign peoples. The role of propaganda in directing public opinion and manufacturing consensus has been predominantly discussed in relation to totalitarian states such as Nazi Germany or the USSR, yet recent decades have seen an upsurge in the analysis of the central role which propaganda—corporate, military, and patriotic—occupies in the Western liberal democracies. As Carey noted,

[54] David D Caron, 'War and International Adjudication: Reflections on the 1899 Peace Conference', 94 AJIL 4 (2000) 7.
[55] ibid.
[56] John B Whitton and Arthur Larson, *Propaganda*, 31.
[57] Harold D Lasswell, *Propaganda Technique in the World War* (New York: Alfred A Knopf, 1927) 11.

'propaganda plays an important role—and certainly a more covert and sophisticated role—in technologically advanced democratic societies, where the maintenance of the existing power and privileges are vulnerable to popular opinion'.[58]

Many of the propaganda techniques devised and applied during the First
World War are notable insofar as they resonate strongly with contemporary developments.[59] As noted by Mairín Mitchell, commenting in 1937, on comparisons
between English propaganda ascribing responsibility for 'atrocities' to the Irish
and Franco's propaganda against the Spanish Republicans, '[i]n a world to-day in
which the only certainty is change, and in which change is constant, it is strange
how conservative politicians are in their methods'.[60] Identifying a correlation
between the growth of democracy and the manipulation and control of public
opinion, Chomsky similarly noted that 'basic themes persist in different guise'.[61]

Censorship was widespread during the war and the United States, despite its
basic policy of encouraging the development of its domestic broadcasting system
by free enterprise, prohibited all private broadcasting from its entry into the war
in 1917 until 1919, both for reasons of national security and because of the fear
of the potential effects which hostile propaganda might have produced within its
own territory. On 5 August 1914 the United Kingdom cut the telegraph cables
between Germany and the United States, an event identified by Horace Peterson
as the first act of propaganda to be set in motion against the United States during the war, since 'the most effective instrument of propaganda, the news, was
suppressed at the most crucial time in the history of the war—the time when first
impressions were being made, when opinions were being established'.[62] All parties
to the conflict practised both direct and indirect control of the private press.[63]
W Philips Davison asserts that the Committee on Public Information, which

---

[58]　Alex Carey, *Taking the Risk out of Democracy* 12.

[59]　For further information and analysis of the techniques of propaganda see: Alex Carey, *Taking the Risk out of Democracy;* George N Gordon, Irving Falk, and William Hoddap, *The Idea Invaders* (New York: Hastings House Publishers, 1963); Jeremy Hawthorn (ed), *Propaganda, Persuasion and Polemic* (London: Edward Arnold Publishers, 1987); Harold D Lasswell, *Propaganda Techniques in World War I*; Frederick E Lumley, *The Propaganda Menace*; L John Martin, *International Propaganda*; HC Peterson, *Propaganda for War: The Campaign against American Neutrality, 1914–1917* (Norman: University of Oklahoma, 1939); Noam Chomsky, *Media Control: The Spectacular Achievements of Propaganda* (2nd edn, New York: Seven Stories Press, 2002); J William Fulbright, *The Pentagon Propaganda Machine* (New York: Vintage, 1971); Edward S Herman and Noam Chomsky, *Manufacturing Consent*; David Miller (ed), *Tell Me Lies*; Ben Novick, *Conceiving Revolution: Irish Nationalist Propaganda during the First World War* (Dublin: Four Courts Press, 2001); Nick Aaron Ford (ed), *Language in Uniform*; Robert Jackall, *Propaganda* (London: Macmillan, 1995).

[60]　Mairín Mitchell, *Storm Over Spain* (London: Secker, 1937) 194.

[61]　Foreword by Noam Chomsky in Alex Carey, *Taking the Risk out of Democracy*, p x.

[62]　Horace C Peterson, *Propaganda for War*, 12. For a critique of Peterson's analysis of the sig-
nificance of propaganda, see Casey's opinion that, '[e]nthralled by his major thesis, Professor
Peterson neglects the effect of a crisis event on the country's attitudes'. Ralph D Casey, 'The Press,
Propaganda, and Pressure Groups', 219 Annals of the American Academy of Political and Social
Science: The Press in the Contemporary Scene 66 (1942) 69.

[63]　Deian Hopkin, 'Domestic Censorship in the First World War', 5 Journal of Contemporary
History 4 (1970) 151.

oversaw US propaganda during the First World War, engaged in the bribery and subsidizing of newspapers and other information media in addition to the provision of facilities such as 'carefully constructed handouts' and office space, conducting tours, and providing special 'news scoops'.[64]

Beyond efforts at restricting the amount and content of information allowed into the public domain, First World War propaganda actively sought to create support for the governments' war effort. A key aspect of ensuring that public opinion was firmly behind the policy of continued war was to instil a sense of fear in the populace. An emphasis on a threat to the nation, either real or imagined, is a recurring motif in all records of propaganda for war. Lumley writes that if the state is to be assured of the public's support and willingness to work to aid military campaigns, then the public 'must be made to see clearly the far worse consequences of not doing so; it must be made afraid'.[65] Atrocity propaganda has proved to be one of the most successful ways of creating an atmosphere of fear, and during the First World War such propaganda—the accuracy of which was rarely an issue for the governments involved—was widely used.[66] Britain's worldwide machinery for the production and distribution of atrocity propaganda capitalized on disputed incidents such as the sinking of the *Lusitania* in order to influence the 'hearts and minds' of the public in both neutral and Allied countries.[67] Narratives of sexual violence and violations of family honour perpetrated by the enemy have become central to what Nicoletta Gullace describes as 'the creation of a gendered international language of 'just war' that has been indispensable in addressing western public opinion ever since [the First World War]'.[68] Amber Blanco White considered that the atrocity propaganda of the First World War:

[...] not only proved that one's behaviour was justified (if a nation is bestial and dangerous enough it becomes a simple duty to punish and curb it), but steeled men's hearts to

---

[64] W Philips Davison, 'Some Trends in International Propaganda', in L John Martin (ed), *Propaganda in International Affairs* 398 Annals of the American Academy of Political and Social Science 1 (1971) 3. For more contemporary manifestations of such activity see Laura Miller, John Stauber, and Sheldon Rampton, 'War Is Sell', in David Miller (ed), *Tell Me Lies*, 41.

[65] Frederick E Lumley, *The Propaganda Menace*, 230.

[66] Lumley provides a succinct analysis of the use of atrocity stories throughout history to appeal to fears upon which propagandists could capitalize. Frederick E Lumley, *The Propaganda Menace*, 382–4. For a case study of the use of Abyssinian atrocity stories by the Italian government to justify aggression against that country, see Francis O Wilcox, 'The Use of Atrocity Stories in War', 34 Am Pol Sci Rev 6 (1940) 1167.

[67] HC Peterson, *Propaganda for War*, 109–33. See further: *The Deportation of Women and Girls from Lille* (New York: George Doran Company, 1917); *The Crimes of Germany* (London: The Field & Queen, 1917); Gordon Williams, '"Remember the *Llandovery Castle*": Cases of Atrocity Propaganda in the First World War', in Jeremy Hawthorn (ed), *Propaganda, Persuasion and Polemic*; Ben Novick, *Conceiving Revolution*, 72–102.

[68] Nicoletta F Gullace, 'Sexual Violence and Family Honor: British Propaganda and International Law during the First World War', 102 American Historical Review 3 (1997) 715. John Stockwell reports that accusations in 1975 of Cuban soldiers in Angola raping women and pillaging had been fabricated by the CIA station in Kinshasa. John Stockwell, *In Search of Enemies: A CIA Story* (London: WW Norton, 1978) 194–5.

endure limitless suffering. The Allied troops were prepared to encounter ruthless and terrible foes, and to continue to fight against men who spitted babies on their bayonets and used priests for clappers in bells, until the politicians decided to end the struggle.[69]

Richard Delgado has asserted that, '[w]hen they deem it necessary to rouse rather than lull, governments may use fear-appeals and depictions of a terrifying enemy', a practice which, he suggests, 'may be a near-universal psychosocial activity'.[70] Summarizing the effectiveness of First World War atrocity propaganda, Lumley concluded thus:

And so citizens were made afraid; they were terrorized; in all countries they were frightened into feverish activity and every needed sacrifice. The methods were everywhere the same; to some extent the content was the same. But the differences in the propaganda of the several countries or the two sets of opposing forces gather mainly about the content.[71]

The significance of the development of the technology of modern mass media, though still in its infancy, was a vital aspect of First World War propaganda. Arthur Larson notes that 'for the first time in history, it became possible to exploit mob psychology without assembling the mob physically in one place'.[72] In the aftermath of the war, the rise to power of the Russian communists meant that the focus of most legal scholars continued to be on 'revolutionary propaganda' and 'subversive propaganda' rather than propaganda for war.[73] Legal discourse focused on state obligations to refrain from spreading hostile propaganda in other countries and state responsibility to prevent private organizations and individuals from engaging in such propaganda. The broad responsibility school of thought asserted that each state should be held accountable for individuals under its control who attempt to foment unrest or revolution in a foreign state. This theory is based on the obligation on all states to respect the independence of other nations, according to which, 'every state has the duty to prevent on its territory the commission of hostile and injurious acts against other states'.[74] The predominant view was that of the narrow responsibility school of thought as favoured by Hersch Lauterpacht among others, which was premised on the principle of non-intervention in the internal affairs of a state.[75] With regard to subversive propaganda, Lauterpacht concluded that whilst there was nothing in

---

[69] Amber Blanco White, *The New Propaganda* (London: Victor Gollancz, 1939) 19.

[70] Richard Delgado, 'The Language of the Arms Race: Should the People Limit Government Speech?', 64 BUL Rev 961 (1984) 969–70.

[71] Frederick E Lumley, *The Propaganda Menace*, 232.

[72] Arthur Larson, 'The Present Status of Propaganda in International Law', 440.

[73] Charles J Fenwick, 'The Use of the Radio as an Instrument of Foreign Propaganda', 32 AJIL 339 (1938) 341.

[74] John C Novogrod, 'Indirect Aggression', in M Cherif Bassiouni and Ved P Nanda (eds), *International Criminal Law*, i. 198–238, 215.

[75] Hersch Lauterpacht, 'Revolutionary Activities of Private Persons against Foreign States'; Vernon B Van Dyke, 'Responsibility of States for International Propaganda'; Quincy Wright, 'Subversive Intervention', 54 AJIL 521 (1960); John B Whitton, 'Subversive Propaganda Reconsidered', 120–2.

municipal legislation or in the principles of international law that justified the contention that states were bound to prevent international propagandizing by private individuals,[76] an act of subversive propaganda 'when emanating from the state as such, from its agents, or from bodies assisted by it, will constitute a clear violation of international law'.[77]

Difficulties in establishing the extent of state responsibility for propaganda of private individuals were compounded by the rise of states such as the USSR where governments acting through the intermediary of a political party or organization, engaged in activities which, if carried on directly by that government, would have been held to constitute an international delinquency. Lauterpacht foresaw difficulties in holding propagandists to account under international law since revolutionary governments whose success was to a large extent dependent upon the universal spread of their principles tended to concentrate functions otherwise fulfilled by private agencies in the hands of the state, resulting in 'the obliteration of the important distinction between official acts and those of a private character'.[78]

In an assessment of the 'organic connection' between governmental and party agencies in Russia, Germany, and China during the 1930s, Lawrence Preuss differentiated between governmental toleration and complicity, direct or indirect, in the initiation, encouragement, assistance, or promotion of 'propaganda or political movements which disturb the public order and security, and aim at the forceful overthrow of the constitutional or social order, of another state'.[79] He stated that while a government could tolerate such acts by private individuals, it might not engage in such activities 'through the intermediary of organizations which are subject to its direct or indirect control, although not possessing an official character in the legal sense'.[80] He asserted that there was no rule of international law obliging a state to prevent or punish hostile propaganda by private individuals against foreign states since 'international solidarity has not progressed so far as to produce a common agreement to prevent and punish hostile or revolutionary acts which fall short of the actual preparation, organisation or setting on foot of armed expeditions against another state'.[81] States which had legislated against private propaganda were, in his opinion, acting both under the threat of intervention that was likely to result from the potential hostile reaction of states claiming to be injured by such, as well as seeking to secure the benefits of reciprocal protection against political crime injurious to them, but committed abroad.[82]

[76] Hersch Lauterpacht, 'Revolutionary Propaganda by Governments', 144; BS Murty, *Propaganda and World Public Order*, 94.
[77] Hersch Lauterpacht, 'Revolutionary Propaganda by Governments', 143.
[78] ibid 144.
[79] Lawrence Preuss, 'International Responsibility for Hostile Propaganda against Foreign States', 668.
[80] ibid.
[81] ibid 649.
[82] ibid 651.

Several inter-war publicists also addressed the question as to whether propaganda that was outlawed among states at peace would also be outlawed between belligerents. Lauterpacht viewed such restrictions on the actions of belligerents as being incompatible with the fact that international law at the time permitted 'even the total annihilation of the enemy'.[83] Whereas Vattel had believed that the seducing of foreign subjects from their allegiance was to be resorted to only in a 'most just war' since it was not 'honourable, and consistent with the dictates of a good conscience', he did not believe that 'strict law' prevented a belligerent from sowing disaffection and treason among both the armies and population of an opponent.[84] Drawing on the practice of states during the First World War, Lauterpacht, while stressing that the principle of non-intervention in the internal affairs of a state remained the most absolute duty in international law, felt that the character of modern warfare meant that revolutionary propaganda by governments against belligerent states was permitted under international law.[85] He argued that during hostilities a neutral state was obliged to abstain from conduct harmful to a belligerent, including hostile propaganda, though there was no obligation to intervene if an individual under its jurisdiction indulged in such conduct.[86]

In reviewing the opinions of publicists up to the beginning of the Cold War, Whitton and Larson note that whilst they had questioned whether propaganda for war as disseminated by an individual was a *délit de droit de gens* and whether a state was under an obligation to suppress such behaviour, 'the important point for us here is that apparently these writers never questioned that an act of war propaganda if committed by the state, was a violation of the law of nations'.[87]

E. Chapter Outlines

Chapter 1 will consider the early development of the prohibition of propaganda for war in international law, outlining a range of bilateral treaties, non-governmental resolutions, and treaties and resolutions of the League of Nations, culminating with the 1936 Convention on the Use of Broadcasting in the Cause of Peace, each of which sought to establish that state sponsored propaganda for war constituted an illegal act in accordance with international law. It will also examine the judgments of the Second World War Tribunals, highlighting the emphasis which tribunals such as the International Military Tribunal at Nuremberg placed on individual criminal responsibility for propaganda for war when considering charges of Crimes against Peace.

---

[83] Hersch Lauterpacht, 'Revolutionary Propaganda by Governments', 152.
[84] Éméric de Vattel, *The Law of Nations or the Principles of Natural Law*, 300.
[85] Hersch Lauterpacht, 'Revolutionary Propaganda by Governments', 154.
[86] ibid 143–64; See further John B Whitton and Arthur Larson, *Propaganda*, 156–64.
[87] John B Whitton and Arthur Larson, *Propaganda*, 75.

The full impact and immensity of propaganda for war was perhaps only fully realized after the Second World War and from 1947 the prohibition of propaganda for war became a subject of sustained debate at the General Assembly of the United Nations. The repeated resolutions and declarations of the General Assembly condemning propaganda for war and affirming the duty on states to refrain from such propaganda will be examined in Chapter 2 and placed in the political context of the Cold War. Additional efforts at reaching agreement on the issue of state responsibility for propaganda for war within the United Nations framework will also be discussed.

The most significant provision of international human rights law concerning the prohibition of propaganda for war is Article 20(1) of the International Covenant on Civil and Political Rights, which forms a core part of the International Bill of Rights.[88] Many states have refused to give effect to this provision which requires that '[a]ny propaganda for war shall be prohibited by law', primarily on the grounds that 'propaganda for war' is not adequately defined, and that it constitutes an unacceptable threat to the right to freedom of expression. Chapter 3 consists of a detailed study of the *travaux préparatoires* to Article 20(1) which are essential in determining its meaning. The analysis is divided into three sections: The first two will consider the discussions in the first phase of the drafting history from 1947 to 1954 which took place primarily at the Commission on Human Rights. Section A will examine the drafting of the restrictions clause of the right to freedom of expression. Section B will consider the drafting of the provision prohibiting incitement to violence. Section C will consider the final phase of debates on both these provisions that took place at the Third Committee of the UN General Assembly meeting in New York in 1961. This study is essential to understanding the reasons why many states continue to reject the obligation upon States parties to the Covenant to prohibit propaganda for war by law. It also shows that the drafters understood the obligation upon states to be to prohibit not only incitement to war, but additionally speech which had as its purpose the creation of a climate of hatred and lack of understanding between the peoples of two or more countries, in order to bring them eventually to armed conflict.

Chapter 4 examines the manner by which the prohibition of propaganda for war has been interpreted and applied in the years since the Covenant's entry into force in 1976. It will set out examples of provisions of national legislation that states have enacted in order to give effect to Article 20(1). Reference will be had to the periodic reports of States parties to the Covenant, the comments of the Human Rights Committee, reservations and declarations entered into with regard to the provision, individual communications between the States parties and the Committee, and the academic literature on the subject. Several of the themes which have been noted above, such as the question of the compatibility

---

[88] Manfred Nowak, *U.N. Covenant on Civil and Political Rights: CCPR Commentary* (2nd edn, Kehl: NP Engel, 2005) p xix.

of the prohibition with freedom of expression and the responsibility of states for propaganda for war, will be fully examined in this chapter, with particular attention paid to the reservations and declarations which states have entered and the Committee's response thereto. This chapter will also consider the manner in which propaganda for war is regulated under the regional human rights instruments, the American Convention on Human Rights and the European Convention on Human Rights.

Turning to international criminal law, Chapter 5 will present the case for the inclusion of a distinct crime of direct and public incitement to aggression in the Rome Statute of the International Criminal Court. While the Second World War tribunals did not recognize a distinct crime of incitement to Crimes against Peace, such incitement was found by the International Military Tribunal at Nuremberg and the International Military Tribunal for the Far East to constitute the planning and preparation of crimes against peace. As the International Law Commission commenced drafting a Code of Offences Against the Peace and Security of Mankind, there was much support for the recognition of a crime of incitement to aggression. While an offence of direct incitement to aggression was set forth in the Commission's 1954 Draft Code, this was subsequently omitted from its 1996 Draft Code, a retrogressive step which requires examination.

The jurisprudence of the International Criminal Tribunals for the Former Yugoslavia and Rwanda provide much guidance on the criminalization of incitement to 'crimes of an international dimension'. Drawing on the case law concerning direct and public incitement to genocide, as well as incitement to war crimes and crimes against humanity, it will be demonstrated that the ad hoc International Criminal Tribunals have expressed the need for a reappraisal of the role of international criminal law in relation to incitement to the most serious international crimes, particularly when the individuals responsible for such incitement are closely aligned to state power. Finally, the Rome Statute of the International Criminal Court will be examined. Rather than commentating in any detail on the definition of the crime of aggression itself, it will be shown that the modes of commission, including non-inchoate incitement, currently provided for in the Rome Statute are inadequate for the purposes of incitement to aggression and that an inchoate crime of direct and public incitement to aggression should be included in the formulation of the crime of aggression which is currently being drafted for inclusion in the Statute.

1

The Roots of the Prohibition of Propaganda for War in International Law

A. The Prohibition of Propaganda for War in the Inter-War Years

The USSR's involvement in international political broadcasting was the cause of much international concern prior to the outbreak of the Second World War, prompting other states to invest increased efforts in the possible application of international legal mechanisms against hostile government propaganda. Two issues in particular impacted greatly upon the development of international treaties which could regulate international propaganda. The first was that the disseminators of propaganda were no longer the political radicals and agitators of the nineteenth century, but 'states themselves, acting through their public authorities, seeking to accomplish results antagonistic to the policy of the state in which the propaganda is being carried out'.[1] The second was the means by which propaganda was being disseminated. The slow process of political agitation carried out by pamphlets, leaflets, and posters in previous generations had been radically changed by radio, which allowed for continuous and immediate broadcasts to a huge audience. White considered these developments to have guaranteed political propaganda as the 'chief internal weapon of governments', one that was employed less to convince people that a particular course of action is right than to 'keep whole populations in a complete, and, it is apparently hoped, a perpetual emotional subjection'.[2] Philip Taylor has suggested the following three reasons as to why propaganda became a regular feature of international relations between the two world wars:

(1) a general increase in the level of popular interest and involvement in political and foreign affairs as a direct consequence of World War I; (2) technological developments in the field of mass communications which provided the basis for a rapid growth in propaganda as well as contributing towards the increased level of popular involvement in politics; and (3) the ideological context of the inter-war period, sometimes known as the 'European Civil War', in which an increased employment of international propaganda could profitably flourish.[3]

[1] Charles J Fenwick, 'The Use of the Radio as an Instrument of Foreign Propaganda', 341.
[2] Amber Blanco White, *The New Propaganda*, 11.
[3] Philip M Taylor, 'Propaganda in International Politics, 1919–1939', in KRM Short (ed), *Film and Radio Propaganda in World War II* (London: Croom Helm, 1983) 19–20.

The First World War had seen the application of a 'new agency of warfare':[4] modern mass communication technologies and combat in the skies. Rules concerning the use of wireless and air warfare during times of conflict were subsequently drafted at The Hague[5] and various international conferences were held in order to allocate radio waves to different states, several of which permitted the cutting of communication lines should the transmission of information appear as a threat to the security of the state.[6] With such propaganda now intrinsically linked to the state from which it emanated, as was the case with the USSR, efforts began to be focused at the international stage to regulate international propaganda.

i. Bilateral Treaties

The regulation of international propaganda in bilateral treaties can be traced back to a treaty signed between France and Russia in 1801, Article 3 of which bound the contracting states not to permit any of their subjects to carry on any correspondence, 'direct or indirect', with the internal enemies of the existing governments of the two states in order 'to propagate their principles contrary to their respective constitutions, or to incite disorders'.[7] Between world wars, similar clauses in bilateral treaties between the USSR and other states became commonplace. The best known of these, the peace treaty of Brest-Litovsk, was signed by Bolshevik Russia and the Central Powers of the First World War in 1918, Article 2 of which provided that the contracting parties would refrain from any 'agitation or propaganda against the Government or the public and military institutions of the other Party'.[8] Section V of the 1932 USSR–France Treaty of Non-Aggression obliged both parties 'to refrain from any action inclining toward incitement or encouragement of any kind of agitation, propaganda or attempts at intervention which have the aim of violating the territorial integrity of the other party or of changing by force the political or social structure of all or part of its territory'.[9] Such treaties were entered into as a result of demands that the USSR undertake to refrain from carrying on propaganda against the internal order of other states. In particular, states were fearful that once they recognized the USSR and established normal diplomatic relations, the Soviet's diplomatic missions would be used to disseminate revolutionary communist propaganda.[10]

---

[4] Manley O Hudson, 'The Development of International Law since the War', 22 AJIL 330 (1928) 335.

[5] Rules concerning the Control of Wireless Telegraphy in Time of War and Air Warfare. Drafted by a Commission of Jurists at The Hague, December 1922–February 1923.

[6] Article 29(1) and (2), The International Telecommunication Convention, 1947, UN Doc E/CN.4Sub 1/110, March 1950, 9.

[7] F de Martens, *Recueil de traités* [1817–1836] (St Petersburg, 1874–1909), vol vii [1800–1803], 387.

[8] The Peace Treaty of Brest-Litovsk, 3 March 1918.

[9] USSR–France: Treaty of Non-Aggression, reprinted in 27 AJIL 4 (1933) 174–6.

[10] Hersch Lauterpacht, 'Revolutionary Activities of Private Persons against Foreign States', 120–1.

The treaty between Saudi Arabia and Iraq of 2 April 1936 prohibited the use of subversive propaganda by either state,[11] whilst the treaty between Yugoslavia and Italy of 25 March 1937 bound each of the parties to refrain from assisting groups active in the dissemination of propaganda against the other party.[12] Vernon Van Dyke cites the agreements of 1867 and 1868 between Greece and Serbia to spread propaganda in Turkish territory as the only example of states formally contradicting the principle on which these other treaties rest.[13] The substance of these treaties indicates a reaction to the view expressed by publicists that states were under no obligation to prevent persons within their jurisdiction from engaging in hostile international propaganda, and suggests that bilateral treaties offered states protection from threatening propaganda for which international law as yet provided no defence.[14]

Of particular significance are the terms of a bilateral agreement which derived from the ultimatum delivered in 1914 to Serbia by Austria-Hungary. This ultimatum, which was to precipitate the First World War, had as its major objective 'to punish the Serbians for their long-continued irredentist intrigue and propaganda in Bosnia and Herzegovina'.[15] It demanded not only that Serbia cease all transnational propaganda against Austria-Hungary, but additionally required an end to such propaganda within the domestic sphere. Serbia was obliged to 'eliminate without delay from public instruction in Serbia [...] everything that serves, or might serve, to foment the propaganda against Austria-Hungary', and to 'remove from the military service, and from the administration in general, all officers and functionaries guilty of propaganda against the Austro-Hungarian Monarchy'.[16] Austria-Hungary further demanded that the Serbian government condemn all propaganda against Austria-Hungary and agree to rigorously prosecute persons engaged in spreading such propaganda either within Serbia or internationally.[17] Serbia accepted the former two demands, though restricting the application of the second to persons in the military service, and 'substantially agreed' to the latter.[18]

---

[11] LON TS, vol 174 (1937) 131.   [12] LON TS, vol 34 (1938) 331.

[13] ST Lascaris, 'La Première Alliance entre la Grèce et la Serbie (le traité de Voeslau du 14–26 août 1867),' *Le Monde slave*, NS 3 (1926) 430, 436; Cited in VB Van Dyke, 'Responsibility of States for International Propaganda', 59. For details of an alleged secret treaty between the USSR and Germany of 22 December 1917 permissive of certain propaganda directed toward Poland, see L John Martin, *International Propaganda*, 102.

[14] Governments were also wary of the threat posed to commercial considerations such as the protection of internal monopolies, while underdeveloped countries feared being overwhelmed by generalized foreign influences. Mavry Lisann, *Broadcasting to the Soviet Union: International Politics and Radio* (New York: Praeger, 1975) 3.

[15] John B Whitton, 'Aggressive Propaganda,' 241.

[16] Great Britain, Foreign Office, Collected Diplomatic Documents Relating to the Outbreak of the European War (1915) 5–8. Cited in Vernon B Van Dyke, 'Responsibility of States for International Propaganda', 62.

[17] Vernon B Van Dyke, 'Responsibility of States for International Propaganda', 66.

[18] Great Britain, Foreign Office, Collected Diplomatic Documents Relating to the Outbreak of the European War (1915) 506–14. Cited in Vernon B Van Dyke, 'Responsibility of States for International Propaganda', 66.

Larson claimed that despite accepting these terms, the Serbian government's propaganda continued so far as almost to seem to condone the assassination of Archduke Ferdinand and thus, 'as a result of nationalistic propaganda, a peaceful disposition of the controversies had already become virtually impossible'.[19]

ii. Non-Governmental Organizations

Contemporaneous to these developments, NGOs, recognizing that propaganda directed towards domestic audiences had become a destabilizing factor in the maintenance of peaceful international relations, sought to effect an even broader application of international law to hostile propaganda than that proffered by publicists and in bilateral treaties. Rather than being concerned with the protection of the state from the threat of external subversive propaganda, many NGOs directed their efforts towards ensuring world peace by advocating that international law should permit no form of propaganda for war.

Martin noted that the subject of avoiding international misunderstandings and the role of the press had been discussed at the First World Press Conference in Chicago in 1893 and considered NGOs to have played 'a leading role in urging the control of international propaganda, both as pressure groups and in laying the groundwork for action by governmental bodies'.[20] The International Broadcasting Union, an international organization of radio stations, adopted several resolutions in 1926 aimed at eliminating broadcasts prejudicial to good international relations, the principles of which were subsequently placed on the agenda of the League of Nations Advisory and Technical Committee for Communication and Transit.[21] In 1932, the Danish government held a conference attended by governmental press bureau, the League of Nations Secretariat and several independent news agencies. This conference endorsed the 'tribunal of honour' which had been established by the International Federation of Journalists in 1931 and whose aim was 'to pass on the worthiness of newspapermen guilty of publishing untrue or biased information to exercise their profession'.[22]

Several of the following examples were cited by Professor Vespasien Pella when compiling a list of proposals made by NGOs which called for propaganda for war to be declared a criminal offence.[23] The Inter-Parliamentary Union (IPU), representing members of national parliaments, prepared a draft resolution in 1914 recommending that states 'establish, by means of their legislation, efficacious penal sanctions, in order to prevent the wilful propagation, by means of the public press, of false or sophisticated news capable of compromising peaceful

[19] Arthur Larson, 'The Present Status of Propaganda in International Law', 440.
[20] L John Martin, *International Propaganda*, 66–7.
[21] ibid 78–9.
[22] ibid 67–8.
[23] A/CN.4/39: [1950] 2 YB ILC, 278.

relations between states'.[24] At its third conference in Geneva in 1932 at which twenty-seven countries were represented, the IPU passed a resolution urging its members to enact legislation by April 1933 for the punishment of persons 'inciting the country to war by writing, speech or any other form of publicity, or who, either by deliberately disseminating false news or false documents, or by fraudulent machinations, have disturbed international relations or increased the tension between certain countries'.[25]

At the first Conference of the International Bureau for the Unification of Criminal Law, an inter-governmental body—at Warsaw in 1927, delegates considered a proposal which stated that:

Quiconque dans un discours ou conférence publics ou par voie de propagation ou exposition publique d'une œuvre ou image aura tenté d'exciter l'opinion publique à la guerre d'agression, sera puni d'emprisonnement jusqu'à cinq ans.[26]

At a meeting attended by fourteen governments in 1930, the Bureau recommended the adoption in domestic legislation of provisions providing for the punishment of any person or persons 'conducting propaganda in public in favour of wars of aggression [...] provided such penalty exists in the law of the country against which the propaganda in favour of war was being conducted'.[27] In 1931 the Bureau adopted a resolution which urged the Secretary General of the League of Nations to convene an international conference with the goal of establishing 'une répression universelle de la propagande de guerre'.[28]

The 27th Universal Peace Conference, which met in Athens in 1927, passed a resolution intended to bring to the attention of governments the need for the inclusion in domestic criminal codes of 'offences against peace' including:

[...] le délit d'excitation directe de l'opinion publique en vue de promouvoir l'invasion du territoire d'un Etat étranger dont les frontières ont été reconnues par la communauté internationale, soit que cette excitation se poursuive par des conférences ou des discours prononcés en public, soit par la diffusion d'imprimés ou d'images tendant à cette fin.[29]

---

[24] Union Interparlementaire pour l'Arbitrage International, *Documents préliminaires*, XIXe Conférence, Stockholm, 19–21 August 1914 (Brussels, 1914) 55.

[25] L John Martin, *International Propaganda*, 67.

[26] 'Anyone who attempts to encourage public support of a war of aggression, by means of public address or conferences, or by distributing any work of art or picture will be sentenced to up to five years of prison' (author's translation). *Actes de Conférence*, 39–41: Cited in A/CN.4/39; [1950] 2 YB ILC p 341, para 124.

[27] (Author's translation); 'Quiconque fera une propagande publique pour inciter à la guerre d'agression sera puni de [...] La sanction ne sera applicable que sous réserve qu'une sanction pareille existe dans la législation du pays contre lequel a été dirigée l'incitation à la guerre.' LON, Quarterly Bulletin, vol II, no 8 (1930), 375: Cited in A/CN.4/39; [1950] 2 YB ILC, 342, para 125.

[28] 'universal suppression of propaganda for war' (Author's translation); *Actes de la quatrième conférence* 300: A/CN.4/39; Cited in [1950] 2 YB ILC, 342, para 125.

[29] '[...] direct incitement of public opinion to invade the territory of a state with internationally recognized borders is an offence, whether this incitement is induced by conferences, public discourse, the diffusion of publications or by images pursuing this objective' (author's translation); A/CN.4/39; [1950] 2 YB ILC, 342, para 125.

In 1931 the 28th Universal Peace Conference, meeting in Brussels, adopted a further Resolution calling on governments to honour their commitments under the Pact of Paris by prohibiting in their penal codes acts which, 'par la parole, par la plume ou par tout autre moyen analogue, incitent à la guerre'.[30] At the 3rd Conference of the Pan-European Union held at Basle in 1932, a resolution was adopted which advocated the criminalization of certain offences against universal peace, including 'la Propagande de guerre'.[31] Also in 1932, the Security Commission of the IPU adopted 'un projet de résolution' requesting national delegations to work towards the introduction of criminal legislation in each state, 'de dispositions permettant de châtier ceux qui auront incité l'Etat à la guerre par la plume, la parole ou tout autre moyen de publicité'.[32]

iii. The League of Nations

The issue of the regulation of propaganda for war was first brought to the attention of the League of Nations following the League's Advisory and Technical Committee adoption of recommendations made by the Office International de Radiophone prompting the Committee's decision to place on its agenda the question of the regulation of broadcasting and of propaganda by broadcasting.[33] In 1931 the Swedish government sent the Secretary General of the League a note raising concerns over the dissemination of false information, suggesting that the Special Committee Appointed to Frame a Draft General Convention to Improve the Means of Preventing War should include a provision requiring High Contracting Parties to undertake to endeavour 'to suppress all verbal or written propaganda designed to prevent a peaceful settlement of the crisis'.[34] The preliminary draft of this Convention declared that 'there are circumstances in which aggressive propaganda against a foreign power may take such offensive forms, and assume such a threatening character as to constitute a real danger to peace'.[35] The text of the Convention as adopted urged the League Assembly to address the issue of propaganda on the basis that 'aggressive propaganda against a foreign Power may, in certain circumstances, constitute a veritable threat to the peace of the world'.[36]

Poland, whose Penal Code provided for an offence of public incitement to a war of aggression, applicable if such incitement was also punishable under the

---

[30] ibid. 'through speech, writing or any other medium, incites to war' (author's translation).
[31] ibid.
[32] 'provisions providing for the punishment of persons who incite the state to war by writing, speech, or any other medium' (author's translation); ibid, *Bulletin interparlementaire*, February 1932, 73.
[33] 7 LON OJ 1191 (1926).
[34] L John Martin, *International Propaganda*, 69.
[35] LON VII Political (1931), Doc A.14.1931.VII.8, 32, 43; cited in John B Whitton, 'Aggressive Propaganda', 247 and L John Martin, *International Propaganda*, 69.
[36] ibid.

laws of the state against whom it was directed,[37] submitted a draft convention to the Disarmament Conference held in Geneva in 1932 which sought to establish individual criminal responsibility for incitement to war. The draft sought to obligate states to punish 'any person guilty of public incitement to war' or responsible for 'the projection of any film, and in general, any public performance, likely to disturb good relations between the peoples or to arouse hatred of foreigners'.[38] The significance of the role which public opinion could play within modern states was recognized in the proposals included in the Report of the Legal Committee of the Committee on Moral Disarmament. Headed by Pella, the Report proposed the adoption of an international convention which would obligate states to penalize the '[i]nciting [of] public opinion by direct public propaganda with a view to forcing the State to embark on a war of aggression',[39] the dissemination of 'false news, reports or of documents forged, falsified or inaccurately attributed to third parties, whenever such dissemination has a disturbing effect upon international relations and is carried out in bad faith', and a related offence of '[c]ausing prejudice to a foreign state by maliciously attributing to it acts which are manifestly untrue and thus exposing it to public resentment or contempt'.[40]

Efforts to control propaganda for war at the League of Nations were to continue apace, and in 1935 the legal committee at the League's Disarmament Conference defined 'war-mongering propaganda' for inclusion in a treaty on moral disarmament. Article 2(2) of this draft would have obliged States parties to adopt legislation calculated to penalize:

Direct public propaganda urging the state to be the first to commit, contrary to its international understandings, any one of the following acts:

  a) declaration of war upon another state;
  b) invasion by its armed forces, even without declaration of war, of the territory of another state;
  c) attack by its land, naval or air forces, even without declaration of war, upon the territory, vessels or aircraft of another state;
  d) naval blockade of the coasts or parts of another state;
  e) assistance, given to armed bands, organized in its territory, which have invaded the territory of another state, or refusal, in spite of the request of the invaded state, to take in its territory all possible steps to deprive the aforesaid bands of all assistance or protection.[41]

[37] Article 113 of Poland's Penal Code; A/CN.4/39; cited in [1950] 2 YB ILC 342, para 125.
[38] Minutes of the Political Commission, Disarmament Conference (1933), LON Pub, Disarmament. 1936. IX.8, 60.
[39] Report of the Legal Committee of the Committee on Moral Disarmament, 1933, LON Pub, Disarmament. 1935. IX. 4, 2, 701.
[40] Text proposed by the Legal Committee (Moral Disarmament), Conference for the Reduction and Limitation of Armaments, Conference Documents, vol ii (IX Disarmament. 1935. IX. 4), 702; cited in A/CN.4/39; [1950] 2 YB ILC 283.
[41] ibid.

Widespread opposition to these proposals among the liberal Western democracies, and particularly the United Kingdom, was premised on the basis that such regulations were synonymous with censorship. Nonetheless, as the main conference on moral disarmament itself ended without agreement, no direct action on the regulation of international propaganda resulted from these efforts.[42]

a. Convention on the Use of Broadcasting in the Cause of Peace (1936)

Whereas dangerous forms of international propaganda had been but one of many pressing issues discussed within the context of moral disarmament, the League's main contribution to the development of a prohibition of propaganda for war in international law was the Convention Concerning the Use of Broadcasting in the Cause of Peace, 1936.[43] In 1931 the Sixth Committee of the League Assembly commissioned a study by a League agency, the Committee on Intellectual Cooperation, on the use of international broadcasting in the cause of peace and for the promotion of international understanding. In 1933 the Assembly authorized the Committee to prepare a draft convention on propaganda and a preliminary draft convention for the use of broadcasting in the cause of peace which was submitted to all states, whether or not they were members of the League.[44] As a result of these initiatives the Convention on the Use of Broadcasting in the Cause of Peace was completed in September 1936 and entered into force on 2 April 1938.[45] Addressing delegates at the Inter-Governmental Conference for the Adoption of a Convention Concerning the Use of Broadcasting in the Cause of Peace, the Conference's President, Dr Raestad, had counselled that:

> Political broadcasting has enormous potentialities as a means of fomenting international discord [...] The underlying ideas of the draft convention are somewhat similar to those that induce Governments to renounce the use of certain means of destruction, which, though indubitably effective, cannot be limited in their action to the real objective.[46]

The Broadcasting Convention marks a radical initiative on behalf of the international community of states and was the first truly international treaty which bound States parties to restrict expression which constituted a threat to international peace and security. That the first article addressed the issue of subversive propaganda suggests that the fear of 'Fifth Columns' was to the fore of governments' concerns at this time. Article 1 required States parties to prohibit and stop

---

[42] John B Whitton, 'Aggressive Propaganda', 247.

[43] Convention Concerning the Use of Broadcasting in the Cause of Peace, Registered no 4319. LON TS, vol 186, 301; vol 197, 394, and vol 200, 557; 17 LON OJ 1438 (1936). Reprinted in 'International Convention Concerning the Use of Broadcasting in the Cause of Peace', 32 AJIL Sup 119 (1938).

[44] John B Whitton, 'Radio after the War', 22 Foreign Affairs 309 (1943–4) 314.

[45] 'International Convention Concerning the Use of Broadcasting in the Cause of Peace', 32 AJIL Sup 119 (1938).

[46] JD Tomlinson, *The International Control of Radio Communications* (Ann Arbor: Edwards Bros, 1945) 229.

the transmission within their territories of broadcasts 'of such a character as to incite the population of any territory to acts incompatible with the internal order or the security of a territory of a high contracting party'.[47]

Article 2 was the first provision of an international treaty to engage with the issue of propaganda inciting to war. Its scope may have been limited to 'broadcasts', as opposed to any other means of speech, but the principle was unequivocal insofar as the High Contracting Parties undertook to ensure 'that transmissions from stations within their respective territories shall not constitute an incitement either to war against another high contracting party or to acts likely to lead thereto'.[48] This provision represented a significant development insofar as it does not distinguish between the speech of the state or of private individuals, nor does it limit the application of the prohibition to either domestic or foreign audiences.

Articles 3 and 4 addressed 'false news', that 'particularly vicious and effective kind of communication', which Whitton and Larson perceived to be an integral part of propaganda for war.[49] Article 3 explicitly prohibits such broadcasts if they are 'likely to harm good international understanding the incorrectness of which is or ought to be known to the persons responsible for the broadcast' and requires that they be terminated at the earliest moment by the most effective means.[50] Article 4 set forth the obligation that particularly in times of crisis, the person responsible for the broadcast of information concerning international relations shall have thoroughly verified the accuracy of the material broadcast by all means within their power.[51] Article 5 sought to ensure that the new broadcasting technology be harnessed for the cause of peace by encouraging High Contracting Parties to share information—should they be so requested—which could be utilized by other national broadcasting services to 'promote a better

[47] 'Article 1. The high contracting parties mutually undertake to prohibit and, if occasion arises, to stop without delay the broadcasting within their respective territories of any transmission which to the detriment of good international understanding is of such a character as to incite the population of any territory to acts incompatible with the internal order or the security of a territory of a high contracting party.'

[48] 'Article 2. The high contracting parties mutually undertake to ensure that transmissions from stations within their respective territories shall not constitute an incitement either to war against another high contracting party or to acts likely to lead thereto.'

[49] John B Whitton and Arthur Larson, *Propaganda*, 65.

[50] 'Article 3. The high contracting parties mutually undertake to prohibit, and if occasion arises, to stop without delay within their respective territories any transmission likely to harm good international understanding the incorrectness of which is or ought to be known to the persons responsible for the broadcast. They further mutually undertake to ensure that any transmission likely to harm good international understanding by incorrect statements shall be rectified at the earliest moment by the most effective means, even if the incorrectness has become apparent only after the broadcast has taken place.'

[51] 'Article 4. The high contracting parties mutually undertake to ensure, especially in time of crisis, that stations within their respective territories shall broadcast information concerning international relations, the accuracy of which shall have been verified—and that by all means within their power—by the persons responsible for broadcasting the information.'

knowledge of the civilization and the conditions of life of his own country'.[52] The discretion as to whether to accept such requests and as to what matter of information should be so shared remained the prerogative of each party. Finally, Article 6 explicitly required that High Contracting Parties ensure that private as well as governmental broadcasting services operate in accordance with the principles set forth in Articles 1 to 4, thus confirming that the prohibition of incitement to war contained in the Convention was an absolute one from which no party was exempt.[53]

Delegates from twenty-eight countries had attended the Conference, and by the outbreak of the Second World War there had been thirteen ratifications[54] and nine accessions to the Convention.[55] A further fourteen states had entered signatures or accessions not yet perfected by ratification.[56] A declaration was entered by Belgium stating that the Convention did not affect the right to jam by its own means 'improper transmissions emanating from another country, insofar as such

---

[52] 'Article 5. Each of the high contracting parties undertakes to place at the disposal of the other high contracting parties, should they so request, any information that, in his opinion, is of such a character as to facilitate the broadcasting, by the various broadcasting services, of items calculated to promote a better knowledge of the civilization and the conditions of life of his own country as well as the essential features of the development of his relations with other peoples and of his contribution to the organization of peace.'

[53] 'Article 6. In order to give full effect to the obligations assumed under the preceding articles, the high contracting parties mutually undertake to issue, for the guidance of governmental broadcasting services, appropriate instructions and regulations, and to secure their application by these services. With the same end in view, the high contracting parties mutually undertake to include appropriate clauses for the guidance of any autonomous broadcasting organisations, either in the constitutive charter of a national institution, or in the conditions imposed upon a concessionary company, or in the rules applicable to other private concerns, and to take the necessary measures to ensure the application of these clauses.'

[54] States that ratified the Convention prior to 1 September 1939 are: Brazil, Denmark, Egypt, Estonia, France, Great Britain and Northern Ireland, India, Luxembourg, New Zealand, Norway, and Switzerland. Chile ratified the Convention 20 February 1940.

[55] States which acceded to the Convention are: Australia, Finland, Guatemala, Ireland, Latvia, New Hebrides, Salvador, Sweden, and Union of South Africa (including the Mandated Territory of South West Africa). The following British colonies also acceded: Burma, Southern Rhodesia, Aden Colony, Bahamas, Barbados, Basutoland, Bechuanaland Protectorate, Bermuda, British Guiana, British Honduras, British Solomon Islands Protectorate, Ceylon, Cyprus, Falkland Islands and Dependencies, Fiji, Gambia (Colony and Protectorate), Gibraltar, Gilbert and Ellice Islands Colony, Gold Coast ((a) Colony, (b) Ashanti, (c) Northern Territories, (d) Togoland under British Mandate), Hong Kong, Jamaica (including Turks and Caicos Islands and the Cayman Islands), Kenya (Colony and Protectorate), Leeward Islands (Antigua, Dominica, Montserrat, St Christopher and Nevis, Virgin Islands), Malay States ((a) Federated Malay States: Negri Sembiland, Pahang, Perak, Selangor; (b) Unfederated Malay States: Johore, Kedah, Kelantan, Perlis, Trengganu, and Brunei), Malta, Mauritius, Nigeria ((a) Colony, (b) Protectorate, (c) Cameroons under British Mandate), North Borneo (State of), Northern Rhodesia, Nyasaland Protectorate, Palestine (excluding Trans-Jordan), St Helena and Ascension, Sarawak, Seychelles, Sierra Leone (Colony and Protectorate), Somaliland Protectorate, Straits Settlements, Swaziland, Tanganyika Territory, Tonga, Trans-Jordan, Trinidad and Tobago, Uganda Protectorate, Windward Islands (Grenada, St Lucia, St Vincent), Zanzibar Protectorate as well as all French Colonies and Protectorates and Territories under French Mandate.

[56] Albania, Argentina, Austria, Belgium, Colombia, Dominican Republic, Greece, Lithuania, Mexico, Romania, Spain, Turkey, USSR, Uruguay.

a right exists in conformity with the general provisions of international law and with the Conventions in force'.[57] The Spanish delegate, representing a government attempting to prevent a fascist *coup d'état*, declared that Spain reserved the right 'to put a stop by all possible means to propaganda liable adversely to affect internal order in Spain and involving a breach of the Convention, in the event of the procedure proposed by the Convention not permitting of immediate steps to put a stop to such breach'.[58] The USSR entered a declaration which stated that pending the conclusion of the procedure set forth in Article 7 of the Convention for the settlement of disputes, it considered that 'the right to apply reciprocal measures to a country carrying out improper transmissions against it, insofar as such a right exists under the general rules of international law and with the conventions in force, is in no way affected by the convention'.[59]

Neither Spain nor the USSR was to ratify the Convention, and its effect was gravely limited by the fact that Germany, Italy, and Japan, states which were directing immense propaganda campaigns in the years prior to the Second World War, did not ratify. China did not sign the Convention whilst the United States, which was not a member of the League of Nations, neither attended the Inter-Governmental Conference nor signed the Convention. Whitton and Larson have argued that the United States was not opposed to the principle that propaganda for war was illegal, but chose not to ratify on the grounds that it did not control its private broadcasters and that broadcasts to foreign countries were a rarity at that time.[60]

BS Murty asserted that many states became party to the Convention because 'the vague character of the suggested treaty obligations [...] promised to leave untouched the liberty of the governments of states to shape policies'.[61] Martin highlighted several weaknesses in the Convention, noting that phrases such as 'incitement [...] to war' are not defined in the text, that obligations to ensure the accuracy of broadcasts are probably impossible to apply given the volume of broadcasts, and that, should disputes have come to arbitration, there had been no prescription made for penalties.[62] Whitton has rejected the latter point on the grounds that such reasoning would condemn most arbitration treaties,[63] yet acknowledged that those states which did ratify were 'in general states whose own broadcasting policy gave little cause for reproach'.[64]

During the Second World War, the Inter-American Neutrality Committee recommended that each state should decide the extent to which the principles of

---

[57] 'International Convention Concerning the Use of Broadcasting in the Cause of Peace', 32 AJIL Sup 119 (1938).
[58] ibid.
[59] ibid.
[60] John B Whitton and Arthur Larson, *Propaganda*, 70.
[61] BS Murty, *Propaganda and World Public Order*, 112.
[62] L John Martin, *International Propaganda*, 82.
[63] John B Whitton, 'International Propaganda', 72 Harv L Rev 396 (1958) 398.
[64] John B Whitton, 'Radio after the War', 314.

the Convention were in accord with the principles of neutrality, suggesting that since it was 'designed for a time of peace [...] it does not appear that they can have a strict application with respect to the duties of a neutral state in time of war'.[65] The Committee recommended that neutral states should prohibit all inhabitants of its territory from using 'any mechanical means of telecommunications for the purpose of sending to a belligerent, directly or indirectly [...] propaganda relative to the hostilities which may be considered contrary to its neutrality'.[66]

Despite such setbacks the Convention remained in place following the Second World War and in 1946 the Secretary General of the United Nations assumed the custodial functions set forth in the Convention.[67] The UN General Assembly subsequently recognized that the Convention '[c]onstituted an important element in the field of freedom of information'.[68] It requested States parties to declare whether or not they wished to transfer to the UN the functions which had been performed under the auspices of that Convention by the League of Nations.[69] Of the twenty-five States parties in 1960 no more than fifteen agreed to the transfer.[70] The General Assembly also instructed the UN Secretary General to prepare a draft protocol which would suggest new articles for inclusion in the Convention as might be necessitated for contemporary situations. These were to be based on the principle

that each High Contracting Party shall refrain from radio broadcasts that would mean unfair attacks or slanders against other peoples anywhere and in so doing conform strictly to an ethical conduct in the interest of world peace by reporting facts truly and objectively, and to provide that each High Contracting Party shall not interfere with the reception, within its territories of foreign broadcasts.[71]

The protocol was prepared and circulated to States parties, but as little support was forthcoming, the General Assembly subsequently abandoned all efforts at reviving the Convention.[72]

While commentators assertively described the Convention as dead law in the aftermath of the Second World War,[73] and little attention has been paid to it since that time, it is worthy of note that the most recent ratification of the Convention came on 1 December 1998 when Zimbabwe ratified by succession. Subsequent

---

[65] 'Telecommunications', 35 AJIL Sup 44 (1936); cited in L John Martin, *International Propaganda*, 84.
[66] ibid.
[67] GA Res 24(I), 12 February 1946.
[68] GA Res 841(IX), 17 December 1954.
[69] ibid.
[70] BS Murty, *Propaganda and World Public Order*, 112, fn 72.
[71] GA Res 841(IX), 17 December 1954.
[72] Eek Hilding, 'Principles Governing the Use of the Mass Media as Defined by the United Nations and UNESCO', in Kaarle Nordenstreng and Herbert I Schiller (eds), *National Sovereignty and International Communication* (Norwood, NJ: Ablex, 1979) 173–94, 188.
[73] Egon Schwelb, 'International Conventions on Human Rights', 9 ICLQ 654 (1960) 662–7; BS Murty, *Propaganda and World Public Order*, 109–13.

to the assumption of depositary functions by the Secretary General of the United Nations in 1946, six states acceded to the Convention,[74] and it was ratified by the Russian Federation on 3 February 1983 and by Czechoslovakia on 18 September 1984 with four additional states ratifying by succession.[75] Nonetheless during the 1980s the Convention was denounced by the Netherlands,[76] France,[77] Australia,[78] and the United Kingdom.[79]

The Broadcasting Convention is probably the most important indicator of the intention of states to control and prohibit propaganda for war under international law prior to the Second World War. W Fridemaan regarded the Convention as indicating a development in the traditional distinction between state and individual responsibility for acts of propaganda insofar as it suggests 'that governments in modern conditions may be held to be inevitably responsible for any international broadcasting that emanates from an organization of nationals'.[80] Summarizing the development of the prohibition of propaganda for war in international treaty law, Whitton stressed that whilst the Broadcasting Convention was ratified by few states and never applied, it represents 'a model, a kind of authoritative code of good conduct [...] Hence its historical significance and moral influence should not be underestimated.'[81] Although the Broadcasting Convention had little effect in averting the outbreak of the Second World War, it marks a watershed in the development of the prohibition of propaganda for war in international law, and as LF Luther notes, it should at least be remembered for the initiative shown by the League of Nations, which 'hammered out rules for maintaining peace, to be codified beside the longstanding rules for making war'.[82]

Although not referred to in any of the judgments of the Second World War Tribunals, the principles of the Convention, and in particular the obligation upon states to prevent any broadcasts which constitute an incitement either to war or to acts likely to lead thereto, were to be frequently cited in debates on the prohibition of propaganda for war at the Commission on Human Rights and in the General Assembly.

---

[74] Afghanistan, 8 February 1985; Bulgaria, 17 May 1972; the German Democratic Republic, 30 August 1984; the Holy See, 5 January 1967; Hungary, 20 September 1984; Lao Peoples Democratic Republic, 23 March 1966; and Mongolia, 10 July 1985. Afghanistan, Hungary, Mongolia, Czechoslovakia, the German Democratic Republic, and the USSR entered declarations to the effect that Article 14 of the Convention, concerning the application of the Convention to colonial and other dependent territories, had either been superseded by or had lost topicality due to the adoption by the General Assembly of the United Nations Declaration on the Granting of Independence to Colonial Countries and Peoples. GA Res 1514(XV), 14 December 1960.

[75] Cameroon, 19 June 1967; Malta, 1 August 1966; Mauritius, 18 July 1969; Zimbabwe, 1 December 1998.

[76] 11 October 1982.   [77] 13 April 1984.

[78] 17 May 1985.   [79] 24 July 1985.

[80] W Fridemaan, 'Hostile Propaganda', 50 AJIL 498 (1956) 499.

[81] John B Whitton, 'Aggressive Propaganda', 262.

[82] LF Luther, *The United States and the Direct Broadcasting Satellite: The Politics of International Broadcasting in Space* (New York: Oxford University Press, 1988) 64.

B. The Second World War Trials

The Charter and Judgment of the International Military Tribunal at Nuremberg (IMT) was to provide the basis for all subsequent discussions of propaganda for war at the United Nations. The judgment is critical insofar as the IMT's identification of the focal role of propaganda for war in the preparation of an atmosphere of war in which the Nazis were able to incite the German people to war was without precedent. The indictments, as well as the judgment of the IMT for the Far East at Tokyo and the indictments and judgment in the *Ministries* case, emphasize the means and methods of propaganda for war which had been employed by the axis powers in the preparation and launching of aggression, as well as in the perpetration of war crimes, crimes against humanity, and genocide.

i. The International Military Tribunal at Nuremberg

The Agreement for the Prosecution and Punishment of Major War Criminals of the European Axis, and Establishing the Charter of the International Military Tribunal was formally adopted by the United Kingdom, France, the United States, and the Soviet Union on 8 August 1945. The Charter of the International Military Tribunal was annexed to the Agreement,[83] and was subsequently adhered to by nineteen other states in an expression of support for the concept.[84] In October 1945 indictments were served on twenty-four Nazi leaders who were charged with crimes against peace, war crimes, and crimes against humanity. The *Trial of the Major War Criminals* ran for almost a year before judgment was delivered on 30 September and 1 October 1946.[85]

The indictment served on the defendants before the IMT claimed that through their use of propaganda, and their incitements to aggression, the accused were criminally responsible for crimes against peace. Count One charged the defendants with having been party to the common plan or conspiracy to commit crimes against peace, particularly in violation of Article 6(a) of the Charter, and Count Two charged the defendants with having committed crimes against peace. Article 6(a) defined crimes against peace as 'namely, the planning, preparation, initiation or waging of a war of aggression, or a war in violation of international treaties,

---

[83] Agreement for the Prosecution and Punishment of the Major War Criminals of the European Axis, and Establishing the Charter of the International Military Tribunal (IMT), Annexe, (1951) 82 UNTS 279.

[84] Australia, Belgium, Czechoslovakia, Denmark, Ethiopia, Greece, Haiti, Honduras, India, Luxembourg, the Netherlands, New Zealand, Norway, Panama, Paraguay, Poland, Uruguay, Venezuela, and Yugoslavia.

[85] International Military Tribunal (Nuremberg), Judgment and Sentences, 1 October 1946, reprinted in 41 AJIL 1 (1947) 172.

agreements or assurances, or participation in a common plan or conspiracy for the accomplishment of any of the foregoing'.[86]

Under Count One it was alleged that as part of the common plan or conspiracy the defendants had disseminated various doctrines which served the furtherance of the criminal plan and that the defendants had employed doctrinal techniques as part of the common plan or conspiracy in order to 'incite others to join in the common plan or conspiracy' to wage aggressive war.[87] By means of propaganda the accused had disseminated doctrines including the concept of the superiority of those of German ethnicity; the Leadership Principle (*Führerprinzip*); that war was a noble and necessary activity of Germans; and the idea that the leadership of the Nazi Party, as the sole bearer of the foregoing and other doctrines of the Nazi Party, was entitled to control each and every aspect of life. With regard to the defendants' acquisition of totalitarian control of Germany and the manner in which they had placed Germany on a military footing so as to accomplish their aim of waging aggressive war, the indictment alleged that a comprehensive 'propaganda framework' had been created:

In order to make the German people amenable to their will, and to prepare them psychologically for war, the Nazi conspirators reshaped the educational system and particularly the education and training of the German youth. The Leadership Principle was introduced into the schools and the Party and affiliated organizations were given wide supervisory powers over education. The Nazi conspirators imposed a supervision of all cultural activities, controlled the dissemination of information and the expression of opinion within Germany as well as the movement of intelligence of all kinds from and into Germany, and created vast propaganda machines.[88]

The indictment ascribed equal criminal responsibility to the defendants with regard to both generic propaganda which prepared the people for future wars, and propaganda intended to directly incite to specific wars of aggression. It describes how the former modes of propaganda had served the plans for aggression in the initial stages of the common plan or conspiracy but that at a critical juncture the purpose of propaganda shifted from preparation for war in general, to constituting a crucial element of preparation for specific acts of aggression:

When their expanding aims and purposes became finally so great as to provoke such strength of resistance as could be overthrown only by armed force and aggressive war, and not simply by the opportunistic methods theretofore used, such as fraud, deceit, threats, intimidation, fifth column activities, and propaganda, the Nazi conspirators deliberately planned, determined upon, and launched their aggressive war and wars in violation of

---

[86] Article 6(a) Agreement for the Prosecution and Punishment of the Major War Criminals of the European Axis, and Establishing the Charter of the International Military Tribunal (IMT), Annexe, (1951) 82 UNTS 279, 284.

[87] International Military Tribunal (Nuremberg), *Indictment*, Count One—The Common Plan or Conspiracy, I *Nazi Conspiracy and Aggression* (Washington: United States Government Printing Office, 1946) 17.

[88] ibid 21.

international treaties, agreements, and assurances by the phases and steps hereinafter more particularly described.[89]

It appears that the broader 'propaganda framework' which had been created to ensure that incitement to aggression could take full effect was regarded in the indictment as much a criminal act as the direct incitement to aggression itself. Even prior to the end of the war, the Soviet jurist AN Trainin had highlighted this 'propaganda framework', noting that after Hitler had seized power: '[p]reparations for aggression in Germany assumed a "total" character: army cadres were feverishly brought together, the whole of industry was militarised, a torrential and violent propaganda of aggression was carried on with the help of a special ministry of propaganda, armed bands ("Fifth Columns") were organized in other States for military purposes, and so on.'[90]

a. Propaganda for War as a Crime against Peace

The IMT considered the common plan or conspiracy to commit crimes against peace as applying to a period of twenty-seven years from the formation of the Nazi Party in 1919 to the end of the Second World War in 1945. Noting that plans had been made to wage wars as early as the first secret conference held by Hitler on 5 November 1937, and that 'the threat of war—and war itself if necessary—was an integral part of the Nazi policy',[91] the IMT found that, 'continued planning, with aggressive war as the objective, has been established without doubt'.[92] The final paragraph of Article 6 of the Charter provided that '[l]eaders, organizers, instigators and accomplices participating in the formulation or execution of a common plan or conspiracy to commit any of the foregoing crimes are responsible for all acts performed by any persons in execution of such plan'.[93] While the defendants were charged with participating in the formulation or execution of a common plan or conspiracy to commit all the crimes in the Charter,[94] the IMT held that the common plan or conspiracy charge was to be limited to the charge of preparing, initiating, and waging aggressive war, since the Charter defined only conspiracy to commit acts of aggressive war as a separate crime.[95] Thus an individual's activity or authority in the conspiracy to commit crimes against peace could not result in a finding of guilt unless the evidence demonstrated that he had had knowledge of the plans for aggression.

[89] International Military Tribunal (Nuremberg), *Indictment*, Count One—The Common Plan or Conspiracy, I *Nazi Conspiracy and Aggression* (Washington: United States Government Printing Office, 1946) 16–17.
[90] AN Trainin, *Hitlerite Responsibility under Criminal Law*, ed. A. Y. Vishinski, trans Andrew Rothstein (London: Hutchinson, 1945) 43.
[91] International Military Tribunal (Nuremberg), Judgment and Sentences, 1 October 1946, 187.
[92] ibid 223.
[93] Article 6, Agreement for the Prosecution and Punishment of the Major War Criminals of the European Axis, and Establishing the Charter of the International Military Tribunal (IMT), Annexe, (1951) 82 UNTS 279, 284.
[94] International Military Tribunal (Nuremberg), Judgment and Sentences, 1 October 1946, 172.
[95] ibid 222–4.

Francis Biddle, the US judge at Nuremberg, considered the charges of crimes against peace as having been directed against 'the politicians, military leaders, and industrialists who were responsible for unleashing war against a world at peace'.[96] Despite the indictment's emphasis on the central role which propaganda for war played in the preparations for and initiation of the Second World War, the Charter did not state that propaganda or incitement to any of the crimes set forth therein constituted a crime in itself. Nevertheless, it was in consideration of the defendants' responsibility for crimes against peace that the IMT was to consider and rule upon the various manifestations of propaganda which had resulted in wars of aggression.

As had been the case with the indictment, the judgment of the IMT stressed the central role which propaganda had played in the Nazi consolidation of power in Germany and in preparations for war. The IMT noted how the propagation of anti-Semitism and the theory of the 'master race', as well as the purging of internal dissidents, combined to ensure that the Nazi dominated plebiscite of 1934 placed full power over the German government in Hitler's hands. The weight placed by the Nazis on the indoctrination of youth was emphasized, with the judgment noting that, '[i]n the field of education, everything was done to ensure that the youth of Germany was brought up in the atmosphere of National Socialism and accepted National Socialist teachings'.[97] The IMT found that the Nazi government had 'endeavoured to unite the nation in support of their policies through the extensive use of propaganda',[98] which prepared the ground for the acceptance of war and the idea of 'German world supremacy'.[99] Whilst the use of radio towards this end has been described as 'one of the most pernicious accomplishments of the Nazi machine',[100] propaganda alone, without physical intimidation by means of state and mob violence, might never have afforded the Nazis the ability to acquire totalitarian control of Germany.[101] In this respect the judgment stressed that:

Through the effective control of the radio and the press, the German people, during the years that followed 1933, were subjected to the most intensive propaganda in furtherance of the regime. Hostile criticism, indeed criticism of any kind, was forbidden, and

---

[96] Francis Biddle, 'The Nurnberg Trial', 33 Virginia L Rev 6 (1947) 679, 689.

[97] International Military Tribunal (Nuremberg), Judgment and Sentences, 1 October 1946, 182.

[98] ibid.

[99] ibid.

[100] John B Whitton, 'Efforts to Curb Dangerous Propaganda', 41 AJIL (1947) 899.

[101] This propaganda framework was also applied in territories occupied by the German armed forces. At the post-war trial which found Dr Joseph Buhler guilty of war crimes and crimes against humanity, the Supreme National Tribunal of Poland held that through regulations in force from October 1939, control of the media by German forces during the occupation of Poland resulted in the elimination of the entire Polish press and that 'only those papers were allowed which carried German Propaganda'. The Trial of Dr. Joseph Buhler (Staatssekretär and Deputy Governor-General), Supreme National Tribunal of Poland, 17 June–10 July 1948, XIV Law-Reports of Trials of War Criminals 23.

the severest penalties were imposed on those who indulged in it. Independent judgment, based on freedom of thought, was rendered quite impossible.[102]

The IMT held that the Nazis had regarded war 'to be inevitable, or at the very least, highly probable',[103] and observing the role which propaganda and the crushing of dissent had to play as part of these preparations, considered that '[t]he German people [...] with all their resources were to be organised as a great political-military army, schooled to obey without question any policy decreed by the State'.[104]

Responsibility for the development and employment of some of the key aspects of Nazi propaganda for war were held to be contributory factors in the findings of guilt on charges of crimes against peace entered against the defendants Hess, Keitel, and Rosenberg. Rudolf Hess had been charged with crimes against peace for having promoted the accession to power of the Nazi conspirators, the consolidation of their control over Germany, and the promotion of the military, economic, and psychological preparations for war.[105] The IMT concluded that throughout the years of preparation for wars of aggression, Hess had supported Hitler's policy of vigorous rearmament in many speeches and relied upon his propaganda slogans—he 'told the people that they must sacrifice for armaments', repeating the phrase 'Guns instead of butter'[106]—as evidence of his guilt on the charges of crimes against peace.

Wilhelm Keitel had been Chief of Staff to the Minister of War from 1935 to 1938 and subsequently Chief of the High Command of the Armed Forces. In finding him guilty of crimes against peace the judgment referred to his responsibility for Nazi propaganda activities, noting that as part of the Nazi preparation for the aggression against Austria, in combination with Hitler he had 'continued to put pressure on Austria with false rumours, broadcasts and troop manoeuvres'.[107]

The indictment charged Alfred Rosenberg with having developed, disseminated, and exploited the doctrinal techniques of the Nazi conspirators, promoted the accession to power of the Nazi conspirators and the consolidation of their control over Germany, and promoted the psychological preparations for war.[108]

[102] International Military Tribunal (Nuremberg), Judgment and Sentences, 1 October 1946, 182.
[103] ibid.   [104] ibid 187.
[105] International Military Tribunal (Nuremberg), Indictment, Appendix A: Statement of Individual Responsibility for Crimes Set Out in Counts One, Two, Three and Four, 58.
[106] International Military Tribunal (Nuremberg), Judgment and Sentences, 1 October 1946, 276. Hess was found to have held prominent positions in the Nazi regime and that, as a result of his close relationship with Hitler, he 'must have been informed of Hitler's aggressive plans when they came into existence. And he took action to carry out these plans whenever action was necessary.' ibid.
[107] International Military Tribunal (Nuremberg), Judgment and Sentences, 1 October 1946, 281. In its determination of Kaltenbrunner's guilt the IMT noted that the Anschluss was not charged as an aggressive war though it was considered as an aggressive act. ibid 284.
[108] International Military Tribunal (Nuremberg), Indictment, Appendix A: Statement of Individual Responsibility for Crimes Set Out in Counts One, Two, Three and Four, 59.

Rosenberg was considered to having been the chief ideologist of the Nazi party and the judgment noted that he had developed and spread Nazi doctrines in newspapers which he edited as well as in numerous books. One particular book, *Myth of the Twentieth Century*, was found to have disseminated Nazi propaganda and ideology and had a circulation of over a million copies. In January 1934 Hitler appointed Rosenberg as his Deputy for the Supervision of the Entire Spiritual and Ideological Training of the Nazi Party. In January 1940 he was designated to set up the 'Hohe Schule', a Centre of National Socialistic Ideological and Educational Research, and organized the 'Einsatzstab Rosenberg' in connection with this task. The IMT held that Rosenberg had had knowledge of Hitler's intentions to wage aggressive war and, in taking these activities which constituted propaganda for war in conjunction with other actions concerning the formulation and execution of the administrative and military policies of the Nazis in occupied territories, found him guilty on the charge of crimes against peace.[109]

Several defendants whose propaganda activities might otherwise have seen them held criminally responsible on charges of crimes against peace were acquitted due to the failure to establish that they had been party to the common plan or conspiracy to wage aggressive war. Baldur von Schirach had had control over the Nazi dominated youth organizations throughout the Nazi consolidation of power in the 1930s and was charged with having promoted the psychological and educational preparations for war.[110] The IMT noted that von Schirach had used the Hitler *Jugend* to educate German youth 'in the spirit of National Socialism' and subjected them to an intensive programme of Nazi propaganda which 'placed particular emphasis on the military [...] the importance of return of the colonies, the necessity for Lebensraum and the noble destiny of German youth to die for Hitler'.[111] Despite his responsibility for the promulgation of such propaganda, von Schirach was acquitted as it was not proven that he had been involved in the development of Hitler's plan for territorial expansion by means of aggressive war, or that he had participated in the planning or preparation of any specific wars of aggression.[112]

Franz von Papen was indicted on both counts of crimes against peace.[113] As German Minister to Austria, a position he held from 1934 until 1938,[114] von Papen was active in trying to strengthen the position of the Nazi Party in Austria for the purpose of bringing about *Anschluss*. The IMT found that he had been involved with 'occasional Nazi political demonstrations, supported Nazi propaganda activities and submitted detailed reports on the activities of the Nazi

[109] International Military Tribunal (Nuremberg), Judgment and Sentences, 1 October 1946, 288.
[110] International Military Tribunal (Nuremberg), Indictment, Appendix A: Statement of Individual Responsibility for Crimes Set Out in Counts One, Two, Three and Four, 65.
[111] International Military Tribunal (Nuremberg), Judgment and Sentences, 1 October 1946, 309.
[112] ibid 310.
[113] International Military Tribunal (Nuremberg), Indictment, Appendix A: Statement of Individual Responsibility for Crimes Set Out in Counts One, Two, Three and Four, 63–4.
[114] International Military Tribunal (Nuremberg), Judgment and Sentences, 1 October 1946, 316.

Party, and routine reports relating to Austrian military defences'.[115] Although found not guilty since it had not been established that he had been party to Hitler's plan to occupy Austria by aggressive war if necessary, the IMT noted that rather than being offences which were considered to be criminal under the Charter, von Papen's 'intrigue and bullying' constituted 'offences against political morality'.[116]

b. *The Cases of* Streicher *and* Fritzsche

In the foregoing instances the defendants' development and dissemination of propaganda for war was one amongst several factors in the IMT's determination of criminal responsibility for crimes against peace. The cases against Streicher and Fritzsche differ in that both had been charged with crimes against peace exclusively on the basis of their speech and the influence they wielded over and through the media. Furthermore, this propaganda also provided the basis for additional charges of crimes against humanity in the case of Streicher,[117] and war crimes and crimes against humanity in the case of Fritzsche.[118]

The expression at issue in the *Streicher* case can be distinguished from the forms of propaganda previously discussed insofar as it was intended to incite the German public to hatred and violence against Jews, an identifiable ethnic group, rather than the promotion of acts of aggression against another state. Streicher was acquitted of charges of crimes against peace, the evidence having failed to establish that he had been closely connected with the formulation of the policies that led to war or that he had been connected with the conspiracy or common plan to wage aggressive war.[119] The IMT then focused on his propaganda and incitement in relation to the charges of crimes against humanity. Arguments before the IMT that the persecution of Jews or incitement thereto was a necessary preparation for aggressive war were unsuccessful since crimes against humanity, as defined by the Charter, had to be linked to the other charges of war crimes or crimes against peace.[120]

---

[115] International Military Tribunal (Nuremberg), Judgment and Sentences, 1 October 1946, 317.
[116] ibid 318.
[117] International Military Tribunal (Nuremberg), Indictment, Appendix A: Statement of Individual Responsibility for Crimes Set Out in Counts One, Two, Three and Four, 66.
[118] ibid 68. Article 6(b) of the Charter of the IMT defined war crimes as: 'violations of the laws or customs of war. Such violations shall include, but not be limited to, murder, ill-treatment or deportation to slave labor or for any other purpose of civilian population of or in occupied territory, murder or ill-treatment of prisoners of war or persons on the seas, killing of hostages, plunder of public or private property, wanton destruction of cities, towns or villages, or devastation not justified by military necessity.'
[119] International Military Tribunal (Nuremberg), Judgment and Sentences, 1 October 1946, 294.
[120] The temporal jurisdiction applicable to crimes against peace ranged from 1919 until 1945, whilst jurisdiction over crimes against humanity was restricted to events occurring after the Second World War officially began on 1 September 1939. See further Donna E Arzt, 'Nuremberg, Denazification and Democracy: The Hate Speech Problem at the International Military Tribunal', 12 NYL Sch J Hum Rts 689 (1995) 701.

Notorious for his anti-Semitic beliefs and persecution of Jews, Streicher had been both publisher and editor of *Der Stürmer*, an anti-Semitic weekly newspaper. Referring to his reputation as 'Jew baiter number one' the IMT held that, through speeches and publications, 'he infected the German mind with the virus of anti-Semitism and incited the German people to active persecution'.[121] His calls for the annihilation of Jews were held to be evident in *Der Stürmer* from at least 1938.[122] He published anti-Semitic propaganda through the medium of readers' letters as well as by his own hand in articles which demanded annihilation and extermination of Jews in unequivocal terms. The judgment noted that as the German armies occupied further territories Streicher intensified his efforts to incite Germans against Jews, describing the propaganda as 'poison [which] Streicher injected into the minds of thousands of Germans which caused them to follow the National Socialists' policy of Jewish persecution and extermination'.[123]

It was found that he had continued to write and publish this 'propaganda of death' with knowledge of the extermination of Jews in the areas of Eastern Europe occupied by the Nazis.[124] Although he had testified that he knew nothing of the mass executions of Jews, the IMT found that Streicher had continually received information on the progress of the 'Final Solution'.[125] Stressing the link between Streicher's writings and his knowledge of the persecution of Jews, the IMT drew upon the content of his writings, his knowledge of the ongoing persecution of Jews, and the timing of the publications to demonstrate that he had the requisite *mens rea* to be found guilty of incitement as a crime against humanity. The significance of this decision as regards propaganda for war is that, although Article 6(c) of the Charter which set forth the offence of crimes of humanity did not explicitly refer to incitement to such crimes as a criminal act in its own right,[126] the IMT concluded that 'Streicher's incitement to murder and extermination at the time when Jews in the East were being killed under the most horrible conditions clearly constitutes persecution on political and racial grounds in connection with war crimes as defined by the Charter, and constitutes a crime

---

[121] International Military Tribunal (Nuremberg), Judgment and Sentences, 1 October 1946, 294.
[122] ibid.
[123] ibid 294–5.
[124] ibid 295. This reference to crimes committed in Eastern Europe rather than in Germany has been interpreted as 'implicitly link[ing] the alleged crimes against humanity with war crimes'. Jamie F Metzl, 'Rwandan Genocide and the International Law of Radio Jamming', 91 AJIL 628 (1997) 637. Francis Biddle claimed that Streicher could also have been found guilty of war crimes for his incitement to violence against Jews, except that important evidence of his incitement was 'apparently secured after the Indictment was filed, and undoubtedly would have justified a finding of guilt on a charge of war crimes'. Francis Biddle, 'The Nurnberg Trial', 694.
[125] International Military Tribunal (Nuremberg), Judgement and Sentences, 1 October 1946, 295.
[126] Article 6(c) defined crimes against humanity as: 'murder, extermination, enslavement, deportation, and other inhumane acts committed against any civilian population, before or during the war; or persecutions on political, racial or religious grounds in execution of or in connection with any crime within the jurisdiction of the Tribunal, whether or not in violation of the domestic law of the country where perpetrated'.

against humanity'.[127] Accordingly, the IMT was in little doubt but that under the terms of the Charter Streicher had incurred individual criminal responsibility for crimes against humanity solely on account of his propaganda inciting to violence.

This finding that propaganda inciting to a criminal act under the Charter can also constitute a criminal act in itself would appear to be equally applicable to crimes against peace and to war crimes. Nevertheless, in the *Fritzsche* case, where the IMT had the clearest opportunity to declare that propaganda for war, ie propaganda inciting to crimes against peace, was a criminal act under the Charter, the failure to establish that the defendant had been party to the common plan or conspiracy resulted in his acquittal. Thus the IMT failed to specifically find propaganda inciting to war to be a criminal offence in a clear and direct manner.

Hans Fritzsche was charged on counts of crimes against peace, war crimes, and crimes against humanity.[128] He had been accused of disseminating and exploiting the principal doctrines of the Nazi conspirators, advocating, encouraging, and inciting the commission of war crimes and crimes against humanity, including particularly anti-Jewish measures, and the ruthless exploitation of occupied territories. When the agency of the German government which Fritzsche headed was incorporated into the Nazi Ministry of Popular Enlightenment and Propaganda in 1933 he joined the Nazi Party and moved to that ministry. In 1938 he was made director of the Home Press Division where he supervised 2,300 daily newspapers, and he was best known as a radio commentator, hosting his own programme, *Hans Fritzsche Speaks*.[129]

The judgment noted that early in his career Fritzsche had had no control of the formulation of propaganda policies and that he was merely a conduit to the press of the instructions handed him by the Reich Press Director, Otto Dietrich.[130] Towards the end of the war, however, Fritzsche became the sole authority for radio activities within the Ministry of Propaganda, formulating and issuing daily radio *paroles*, which accorded to the general political policies of the Nazi regime to all Reich Propaganda Offices.[131] In determining guilt on the charge of crimes against peace, the IMT stated that Fritzsche had directed the press to present to the people certain themes such as 'the leadership principle, the Jewish problem, the problem of living space, or other standard Nazi ideas'.[132] He was present at Goebbels's daily staff conferences in which he was instructed in the news and propaganda policies of the day and by 1943 he himself occasionally held these

[127] International Military Tribunal (Nuremberg), Judgment and Sentences, 1 October 1946, 296.
[128] International Military Tribunal (Nuremberg), Indictment, Appendix A: Statement of Individual Responsibility for Crimes Set Out in Counts One, Two, Three and Four, 68.
[129] International Military Tribunal (Nuremberg), Judgment and Sentences, 1 October 1946, 327.
[130] ibid. Dietrich's prosecution and acquittal in the *Ministries* case under Control Council Law no 10 is discussed below.
[131] ibid 327.
[132] ibid.

conferences, though the IMT considered that even then his only function was to transmit Goebbels's directives as communicated to him by telephone.[133] Despite having established Fritzsche's participation in the control and dissemination of propaganda, including his responsibility for a 'vigorous propaganda campaign [...] carried out before each major act of aggression',[134] he was found not guilty of crimes against peace. As in the cases of von Schirach, von Papen, and Streicher, the IMT held that Fritzsche had never 'achieved sufficient stature to attend the planning conferences which led to aggressive war', nor was 'there any showing that he was informed of the decisions taken at these conferences', thus his activities could not be said 'to be those which fall within the definition of the common plan to wage aggressive war as already set forth in this Judgment'.[135]

In determining Fritzsche's liability on the charges of crimes against humanity and war crimes the IMT again referred exclusively to his propaganda activities. While it found that he had broadcast 'definite anti-Semitism' in his speeches, it held that these 'did not urge persecution or extermination of Jews' and that there was no evidence that he was aware of the extermination of Jews in Nazi occupied Eastern Europe.[136] Fritzsche's responsibility in this regard may be distinguished on the facts from that of Streicher whom the IMT held to have been aware of the ongoing extermination of Jews. In that instance the IMT was satisfied that Streicher's knowledge provided the necessary element of causation in the definition of actionable incitement, namely, both inciting words and the actual physical implementation of their message. This 'direct' link between the impugned expression and the persecution of Jews was not present for Fritzsche. The IMT was 'not prepared to hold that [his speeches] were intended to incite the German people to commit atrocities on conquered peoples',[137] stating that:

It appears that Fritzsche sometimes made strong statements of a propagandistic nature in his broadcasts. But the Tribunal is not prepared to hold that they were intended to incite the German people to commit atrocities on conquered peoples, and he cannot be held to have been a participant in the crimes charged.[138]

Acquitting Fritzsche on all charges, the IMT concluded its analysis of his responsibility by stating that his aim had been 'to arouse popular sentiment in support of Hitler and the German war effort'.[139] Thus, Fritzsche was not held to have been responsible for direct incitement to war, but rather for a broader, less specific form of propaganda by which the conspiracy and acts of aggression were facilitated. This latter distinction, between propaganda directly inciting to a specific act of aggression and propaganda which rather creates a general warlike atmosphere, was subsequently to be the cause of significant dissonance during the drafting of the International Covenant on Civil and Political Rights' prohibition of propaganda for war.

---

[133] ibid 328.   [134] ibid 327.
[135] ibid 328.   [136] ibid.
[137] ibid.   [138] ibid.
[139] ibid.

Nikitchenko, the Soviet judge at Nuremberg, was particularly critical of this distinction and entered a Dissenting Opinion on the subject.[140] A critic of the conspiracy formula as applied by the IMT, Nikitchenko opposed the acquittal of Fritzsche on the grounds that the propaganda he had engaged in 'had a most basic relation to the preparation and the conduct of aggressive warfare as well as to the other crimes of the Hitler regime'.[141] Nikitchenko argued that the verdict's portrayal of Fritzsche as a secondary figure, merely carrying out the directives of Goebbels and Ribbentrop and of the Reich Press Director Dietrich, was flawed. He criticized the fact that the verdict did not mention that it was Fritzsche who until 1942 was the director de facto of the Reich Press and that, according to himself, he subsequently became the 'Commander-in-Chief of the German radio'.[142] In order to define the correct role which Fritzsche had played in the preparation of aggressive war, Nikitchenko stressed the importance which Hitler and his close associates, such as Goebbels, had attached to propaganda in general and to radio propaganda in particular, 'which was considered one of the most important and essential factors in the success of conducting an aggressive war'.[143]

Nikitchenko, no doubt aware of Trainin's commentary on the criminal nature of 'propaganda of aggression',[144] regarded such propaganda to be an invariable factor in the preparation and conduct of acts of aggression. Asserting that Fritzsche had been responsible for having trained the German public to accept obediently the criminal enterprises of German fascism, he described the machinations of Nazi preparations for aggression as having have been served by:

[…] a huge and well centralised propaganda machinery. With the help of the police controls and of a system of censorship it was possible to do away altogether with the freedom of the press and of speech […] The dissemination of provocative lies and the systematic deception of public opinion were as necessary to the Hitlerites for the realisation of their plans as were the production of armaments and the drafting of military plans. Without propaganda, founded on the total eclipse of the freedom of press and of speech, it would not have been possible for German Fascism to realise its aggressive intentions, to lay the groundwork and then to put to practice the war crimes and the crimes against humanity.[145]

The dissent noted that the primary method of propaganda employed by the Nazis was the dissemination of false information, a contention supported by reference to a passage from Hitler's *Mein Kampf*, which stated that:

[140] Office of United States Chief of Counsel for Prosecution of Axis Criminality, *Nazi Conspiracy and Aggression: Opinion and Judgement* (Washington: United States Government Printing Office, 1947).
[141] ibid 178.
[142] ibid 175.
[143] ibid.
[144] Trainin had signed the London Agreement for the establishment of the International Military Tribunal at Nuremberg on behalf of the USSR. See further Chapter 6 infra.
[145] Office of United States Chief of Counsel for Prosecution of Axis Criminality, *Nazi Conspiracy and Aggression: Opinion and Judgement*, 175.

With the help of a skilful and continuous application of propaganda it is possible to make the people conceive even of heaven as hell and also make them consider heavenly the most miserly existence.[146]

With regards to Fritzsche's responsibility for such propaganda, Nikitchenko argued that given the importance of propaganda to the Nazis it was inconceivable that Fritzsche, the Director of Radio Propaganda, who supervised radio activity of all the broadcasting companies and directed their propagandistic content, would have been considered a secondary figure. Noting that from 1942 until 1945, Fritzsche was not only Chief of the Radio Department of the Reich Ministry of Propaganda but also 'Plenipotentiary for the Political Organisation of Radio in Greater Germany':

As chief of the Press Section inside Germany it was also Fritzsche who was responsible for the activity of the German daily press consisting of 2,300 newspapers [...] Subsequently Fritzsche participated energetically in the development of the propaganda campaigns preparatory to the acts of aggression against Czechoslovakia and Poland. (Transcript, Morning, Session, 23rd January, 1946.) A similar active propaganda campaign was conducted by the Defendant prior to the attack on Yugoslavia as he himself admitted on oath in court. (Transcript, Morning Session, 23rd January, 1946.) [...] Fritzsche headed the German press campaign falsifying reports of Germany's aggressive war against France, England, Norway, the Soviet Union, the U.S.A., and the other States.[147]

Rejecting the IMT's assertion that Fritzsche was not informed of the war crimes and crimes against humanity perpetrated by the Nazis in occupied territories, Nikitchenko claimed that on the basis of the defendant's testimony he was satisfied that Fritzsche was fully aware of the fact that the Nazis were carrying out their decision to do away with all Jews in Europe and that he 'systematically preached the antisocial theory of race hatred and characterised peoples inhabiting countries victimised by aggression as "subhumans"'.[148]

Nikitchenko's dissent is significant in that it stressed the centrality of propaganda and the individuals responsible for its control in the preparation and planning of wars of aggression, and the necessity that such individuals be held responsible under international criminal law. In the light of the overall judgment there is little to suggest other than had Fritzsche been held to have been party to the conspiracy to wage aggressive war then his responsibility for having orchestrated a 'vigorous propaganda campaign [...] before each major act of aggression'[149] would have led to a finding of guilt on the charge of crimes against peace.

---

[146] ibid.
[147] ibid 176.
[148] ibid 177.
[149] International Military Tribunal (Nuremberg), Judgment and Sentences, 1 October 1946, 327.

ii. The *Ministries* Case

In order to give effect to the Moscow Declaration and the London Agreement, and to establish a uniform legal basis for war crimes prosecutions in Germany, the Allied Control Council adopted Control Council Law no 10 on 20 December 1945.[150] In the *Ministries* case, which was held in accordance with Control Council Law no 10, the defendants had been aligned 'with the central political and economic administration of the Third Reich at Berlin',[151] two of whom, Otto Dietrich and Ernst von Weizsaecker, were indicted on account of their participation in propaganda for war.

The prosecution's opening statement stressed that the defendants in this case were the 'men who transferred the plans and ideologies of the Third Reich into action', and who in their roles as civil servants

[...] entered upon a period such as was never accorded to them before. No longer did they have to consider parliamentary control because the German Reichstag was rendered impotent. No longer did they have to consider public opinion, because freedom of speech and assembly was trampled under foot and the press and radio became a chamber of mendacious echoes.[152]

The indictment charged Otto Dietrich, the State Secretary in charge of the Ministry of Propaganda and Public Enlightenment, with having been an 'active participant' in Hitler's seizure of power insofar as he, with others, had 'marshalled the [necessary] financial, political, psychological and propaganda support'.[153] He was also accused of having 'directed and controlled the use of press and propaganda organs to crush the development of any opposing political opinion'.[154] The indictment stated that the planning of the programme of aggression undertaken by the Nazis had included 'propaganda campaigns [...] launched to incite the German people to support the program of aggression',[155] and that Dietrich had 'created, formulated and controlled press and propaganda policies of the NSDAP [the Nazi Party] and of the German Government, both in furtherance of plans and preparations for aggression, and in the propaganda phases of the waging of these wars'.[156] The indictment stated that in furtherance of the planning and preparation of aggressive war, Dietrich, through the issuance of daily instructions, had:

---

[150] Control Council Law no 10, Punishment of Persons Guilty of War Crimes, Crimes against Peace and against Humanity, reproduced in Trials of War Criminals before the Nuernberg Military Tribunals, United States Government Printing Office, 1951, vol iii, XVIII.

[151] Opening Statement for the Prosecution, XII Trials of War Criminals before the Nuremberg Military Tribunals under Control Council Law No. 10 (1950), 137.

[152] ibid 138–9.

[153] Indictment, XII Trials of War Criminals before the Nuremberg Military Tribunals Under Control Council Law No. 10 (1950), 22.

[154] ibid.

[155] ibid 23.

[156] ibid 24.

[…] subordinated the entire German press to the political, diplomatic and military pur-pose of the Nazi leaders. By the falsification, distortion and perversion of news, and the extensive use of inflammatory propaganda, he so influenced and deceived the German people as to secure their support of the aggressive policies of the German Reich. He participated in the psychological planning and preparation of wars of aggression […] Before each aggressive act, press campaigns were initiated under the direction of the defendant Dietrich to weaken the prospective victims, provide spurious 'justification' for aggression, and prepare the German people psychologically for war.[157]

It was further alleged that prior to the invasion of Czechoslovakia, Dietrich had issued instructions to the press to 'play up' the alleged persecution of the Sudeten-German and Slovak minorities within Czechoslovakia and the 'anti-German politics' of the Prague government in order to secure public support for aggres-sion.[158] Another example of propaganda for war was cited in respect of the prepa-rations for aggression against Austria. The indictment asserted that '[i]n order to justify the invasion and give it a semblance of legality, a fictitious telegram concocted by Goering and Keppler was quoted by the German press to establish that the newly created Austrian puppet government had requested the presence of German troops to prevent disorder'.[159]

Dietrich and von Weizsaecker were charged with having designed the 'political, propaganda and diplomatic blueprint' for the war of aggression against Poland, with the intention of shifting the apparent responsibility for the war to the victims. The staging of border incidents and the publication of fabricated acts of terror-ism purported to have been executed by Poles on German nationals were exam-ples of propaganda for which they were charged with crimes against peace.[160] The indictment noted that whilst German public opinion had been 'nurtured' to ensure support for the Non-Aggression Pact which had been entered into with the USSR on 23 August 1939, in order to reverse this view, Dietrich had 'directed the press and propaganda agencies to renew anti-Soviet propaganda and to pre-sent the coming aggression against the Soviet Union as a "preventive war" for the defense of the Fatherland'.[161]

Given the emphasis placed on individual criminal responsibility for propaganda for war both in the indictment and throughout the proceedings of the *Ministries* case, the final judgments appear quite cursory in this respect. Before a finding of guilt could be made regarding crimes against peace it had to be established

[157] ibid 26.
[158] ibid 29.
[159] ibid 28.
[160] ibid 29–30. Other incidents noted in the indictment include the 'Venlo Incident' in which the defendant Schellenberg was accused of participating in the kidnapping of enemy and neutral nationals in order to fabricate a pretext for the invasion of the Low Countries, and the fabrication of atrocity stories that were alleged to have been committed against racial Germans in Yugoslavia and were publicized in the German press and propaganda organs under the supervision of Dietrich in order to serve as a pretext for invasion. ibid 30.
[161] ibid 31.

beyond a reasonable doubt that the defendant had knowledge of Hitler's plans for aggressive war.[162] The only evidence that Dietrich knew of Hitler's aggressive plans was that he had had control over the German and Nazi Party press. The Tribunal found that these had 'played the tune before and upon the initiation of each aggressive war, which aroused German sentiments in favour of them, and thus influenced German public opinion'.[163] The judgment recalled that Dietrich had served as Reich press chief and press chief of the Nazi Party during the entire period when the German aggressive wars were planned and initiated, and that he had been in constant attendance at Hitler's headquarters as a member of his entourage. However, despite having deemed it 'entirely likely' that he had had 'at least a strong inkling of what was about to take place', the Tribunal held that proof of guilt had not been shown beyond a reasonable doubt and thus acquitted Dietrich of crimes against peace.[164]

Whereas the defendant von Weizsaecker, who had served as State Secretary in the Foreign Service, was charged with crimes against peace in relation to acts of aggression against no less than eleven states, the question of his responsibility for propaganda was raised only as regards the act of aggression against Austria. The prosecution had asserted that von Weizsaecker's office had defrayed one-half of his propaganda expenses incurred by the Nazi Party in Austria, and that he had been aware in February 1938 that large quantities of Nazi propaganda materials were being shipped illegally into Austria from Germany. The Tribunal refused, however, to accept that the prosecution's submissions established the defendant's guilt, as the evidence had not established that he had had knowledge of Hitler's intention to invade Austria. In relation to his financing of, and logistical support for, Nazi propaganda in and against Austria, the judgment reflected the IMT's decision regarding von Papen when it stated that:

In the absence of Treaty obligations one may encourage political movements in another State, consort with the leaders of such movements, and give them financial or other support, all for the purpose of strengthening the movement which has an annexation as its ultimate purpose without violating international law. It is only when these things are done with knowledge that they are a part of a scheme to use force and to be followed, if necessary, by aggressive war or invasion that an offense cognisable by this Tribunal comes into being.[165]

Whilst it is clear from the *Ministries* case that propaganda for war was considered to be a criminal offence under the Statute when done with knowledge of plans for aggressive war, the final sentence of the excerpt from the judgment suggests that the Tribunal was prepared, obiter dicta at least, to consider such an offence to be an inchoate crime. Ultimately, the Tribunal held that no evidence was offered to substantiate a conviction for the defendants in a common plan or conspiracy to

---

[162] Judgment, XIV Trials of War Criminals before the Nuremberg Military Tribunals under Control Council Law no 10 (1950), 339.
[163] ibid 417.   [164] ibid.
[165] ibid 343.

wage wars of aggression and all the defendants charged thereunder, including von Weizsaecker and Dietrich, were acquitted.[166]

Familiar forms of direct incitement, as opposed to state sanctioned propaganda campaigns, were at issue in several of the Second World War Military Tribunals which convicted individuals for incitement as a means of commission of war crimes. Takashi Sakai was found guilty of war crimes and crimes against humanity by the Chinese War Crimes Military Tribunal which held that, 'in inciting or permitting his subordinates to murder prisoners of war, wounded soldiers, nurses and doctors of the Red Cross and other non-combatants [...] he had violated the Hague Convention concerning the Laws and Customs of War on Land and the Geneva Convention of 1929'.[167] Before a British Military Court at Venice, the German officer Kesselring was charged with 'being concerned in the killing as a reprisal of some 335 Italian nationals' in the Ardeatine Caves, and with 'inciting and commanding [...] forces [...] under his command to kill Italian civilians as reprisals in consequence of which a number of Italian civilians were killed'. The prosecutor put it to the Court that:

[...] the orders of 17th June and 1st July, were contrary to the laws and usages of war. The order of the 17th June was an incitement to the troops under the accused's command to commit excesses, and the prosecution obviously relies on the expression 'I will protect any commander,' etc. I say no more than that this is an incitement, but in the order of the 1st July the accused goes further and orders his troops to take reprisals and it is not until 24th September that he says 'this must stop.' That is the gravamen of this charge.[168]

The Court found the accused's orders to be a definite incitement to kill Italians and that the instances of indiscriminate killings of Italians by German troops were a direct consequence of these orders and he was found guilty on both charges.[169]

---

[166] ibid 435–6.

[167] *The Trial of Takashi Sakai*, Chinese War Crimes Military Tribunal, Nanking, 29 August 1946, III *Law Reports of Trials of War Criminals,* 7.

[168] *The Trial of Albert Kesselring*, British Military Court at Venice, Italy, 17 February–6 May 1947, VIII *Law Reports of Trials of War Criminals*, 11. In *The Trial of Major Karl Rauer and Six Others* by a British Military Court in 1946, German officers were charged with committing war crimes in that they were 'concerned in' the killing, contrary to the laws and usages of war, of Allied prisoners of war and had thereby violated Article 23(c) of the Fourth Hague Convention of 1907. In closing his case, the prosecutor pointed out that a man is deemed to intend the natural consequences of his acts and contended that the murder in these charges came about if not on direct orders then because the Kommandantur in the form of Rauer and Scharschmidt let their hostile views towards prisoners of war be known to their subordinates, who thereupon took action against the prisoners. He considered that the offence of incitement to murder came properly within the scope of the words 'were concerned in the killing', and cited in support Section 4 of the United Kingdom's Offences against the Person Act (1861), wherein incitement was defined as to solicit, encourage, persuade, endeavour to persuade, or propose to any person to murder any other person. The Court accepted these arguments and found all four officers guilty of being concerned in the killing of the prisoners. *The Trial of Major Karl Rauer and Six Others*, British Military Court, Wuppertal, Germany, 18 February 1946, IV *Reports of Trials of War Criminals*, 113–16.

[169] ibid 12. A further case concerning propaganda was heard by a US Military Commission in Shanghai following the German surrender in 1945. The Commission considered the activities

iii. The International Military Tribunal for the Far East

The International Military Tribunal for the Far East (the Tokyo Tribunal) was established by Special Proclamation of the Supreme Commander for the Allied Powers, General Douglas MacArthur, in furtherance of the commitment in the Potsdam Declaration of 26 July 1945 to try the major Japanese war criminals.[170] Whereas the United Nations General Assembly affirmed the principles of international law recognized by the London Charter and the judgment of the Nuremberg Tribunal, it merely took note of the similar principles adopted in the Tokyo Charter.[171]

The Tokyo Tribunal considered two charges in reference to crimes against peace: conspiracy to wage an aggressive war and actual waging of aggressive war. The charges specifically dealing with the planning and preparation stages of the crime were omitted as the Tribunal considered that they were included in the charge of conspiracy.[172] Murty considers that the Tokyo Tribunal gave greater importance to the facts relating to the use of propaganda as a means for preparation for aggression than the IMT at Nuremberg because of the adoption of a concept of conspiracy closer to that of the common law concept.[173]

The indictment alleged that in furthering the conspiracy 'to secure the domination and exploitation by the aggressive States of the rest of the world, and to this end to commit, or encourage the commission of, crimes against peace',[174] the accused psychologically prepared Japanese public opinion for aggressive warfare by establishing 'Assistance Societies', teaching nationalistic policies of expansion, disseminating war propaganda, and strictly controlling the press and radio.[175]

The prosecution alleged that the accused had used a 'propaganda framework' not dissimilar to the Nazis in their preparations for aggressive war which centred on the militarization of education, the control and dissemination of propaganda,

of Lothar Eisentrager and others, who were former employees of the German diplomatic mission in Japanese occupied China, which included 'the writing and transmission of propaganda to US troops' to be war crimes insofar as they amounted to 'military activities' undertaken in violation of the German Armistice agreement. UN War Crimes Cases, 14 (1947) 8. See further BS Murty, *Propaganda and World Public Order*, 195.

[170] Special Proclamation: Establishment of an International Military Tribunal for the Far East, annexed to the Judgment of the International Military Tribunal for the Far East, 4–12 November 1948, Annexe no A-4: The Potsdam Declaration of 2 August 1945, in setting forth the political and economic principles to govern the treatment of Germany in the initial control period as agreed by the United States, the United Kingdom, and Soviet Russia concerning Conquered Countries, had set as an aim in paragraph 3(III) '[t]o destroy the National Socialist Party and its affiliated and supervised organizations, to dissolve all Nazi institutions, to insure that they are not revived in any form, and to prevent all Nazi and militarist activity or propaganda'.
[171] GA Res 95(I), 11 December 1946.
[172] Judgment of the International Military Tribunal for the Far East, 4–12 November 1948, 32–3.
[173] BS Murty, *Propaganda and World Public Order*, 149.
[174] Judgment of the International Military Tribunal for the Far East, 4–12 November 1948, 46.
[175] ibid 46–7.

and the mobilization of the people for war. The prosecution summed up by saying:

[...] to enable the programs for economic, and military and naval preparations to be carried out and to be effectively used in accordance with the plans of the conspirators, it was necessary to prepare the Japanese people psychologically for war, so that they might feel it necessary and even come to desire it. This mission was accomplished through instruction in the schools, through use and control of all known media of propaganda and through the mobilization of the people into a single organization for purposes of propaganda and control.[176]

The Tribunal held the conspirators to have used propaganda and persuasion to win many to their side as part of their efforts to dominate the Japanese polity.[177] In tracing the gradual rise of the military to such a predominance in the government of Japan that no other organ of government could impose an effective check on the aggressive ambitions of the military, the Tribunal noted the preparation of 'virtually every segment of Japanese society for war, including the military, the civilian population, the educational system, the media, the economy and the essential industries'.[178] The Tribunal considered the individual responsibility of each of the accused in the light of its general findings with respect to the common plan or conspiracy to wage aggressive wars and the actual waging of aggressive wars.[179] Five of the accused, Araki, Hashimoto, Kido, Oshima, and Shiratori, were found guilty on Count One of conspiracy to commit crimes against peace in part due to their participation in propaganda inciting to aggression.

Sadao Araki was held to have been the leader of the conspiracy and was found to have advanced the army's policy of preparing for wars of aggression as a Cabinet member. The Tribunal held that after the conspiracy's early years—it was held to have commenced on 1 January 1928—he had acted mainly as a propagandist by stimulating a warlike spirit, by mobilizing Japan's material resources for war, and by giving speeches and controlling the press which incited and prepared the Japanese people for war.[180]

Kingoro Hashimoto, held to have been the principal actor in forming and executing the conspiracy, was found to have been outspoken in his views, initially advocating Japan's expansion in Manchuria by force and later advocating the use

---

[176] BVA Roling and CF Ruter (eds), *The Tokyo Judgement: The International Military Tribunal for the Far East (IMFTE) 29 April 1946–12 November 1948* vol ii (Amsterdam: APA—University Press, 1977) 759.

[177] Judgment of the International Military Tribunal for the Far East, 4–12 November 1948, 1139.

[178] ibid 83–520. See also Historical review of documents relating to aggression, Preparatory Commission for the International Criminal Court, Working Group on the Crime of Aggression, PCNICC/2002/WGCA/L.1, 24 January 2002, para 293.

[179] Historical review of documents relating to aggression, Preparatory Commission for the International Criminal Court, Working Group on the Crime of Aggression, PCNICC/2002/WGCA/L.1, 24 January 2002, para 324.

[180] Judgment of the International Military Tribunal for the Far East, 4–12 November 1948, 1146–7. See further BS Murty, *Propaganda and World Public Order*, 149.

of force against all Japan's neighbours to accomplish the aims of the conspiracy. The Tribunal held that his publications and societies were devoted to destroying democracy and establishing a form of government more favourable to the use of war for the achievement of Japan's expansion. Furthermore, it held that he had participated as a propagandist in the execution of the conspiracy, thus contributing to its success:

by inciting the appetite of the Japanese people for the possessions of Japan's neighbours, by inflaming Japanese opinion for war to secure these possessions, by his advocacy of an alliance with Germany and Italy which were bent on similar schemes of expansion, by his denunciation of treaties by which Japan had bound herself to refrain from the schemes of aggrandizement which were the aims of the conspiracy, and by his fervent support of the agitation for a great increase in the armaments of Japan so that she might secure these aims by force or the threat of force.[181]

Koichi Kido acted through his position as Education Minister to develop a 'strong warlike spirit in Japan'.[182] Hiroshi Oshima, the ambassador to Germany, was found to have been one of the principal conspirators and was held to have supported the proponents of war by articles in newspapers and magazines.[183] Finally, Toshio Shiratori the ambassador to Italy and advisor to Japan's Foreign Minister, was found to have supported the conspiracy by all means within his power. He was found to have carried on propaganda to prepare the way for a general alliance with Germany and Italy to support Japan's expansionist aims, wherein he advocated all the objects of the conspirators including that Japan should attack China and Russia, ally itself with Germany and Italy, take determined action against the Western powers, establish the 'New Order', and seize the chance offered by the war in Europe to advance to the south and attack Singapore.[184]

C. Summary

Telford Taylor, who served on the staff of United States Chief Prosecutor Robert Jackson at the IMT, and as Chief Prosecutor in the United States trials under Control Council Law no 10, considered one of the objectives of the IMT to be the establishment of a 'well-documented history of what we are convinced was a grand, concerted pattern to incite and coerce the aggressions and barbarities which have shocked the world'.[185]

[181] Judgment of the International Military Tribunal for the Far East, 4–12 November 1948, 1152.
[182] ibid 1171–3.
[183] ibid 1188–9.
[184] ibid 1199–201.
[185] Telford Taylor, *The Anatomy of the Nuremberg Trials: A Personal Memoir* (New York: Knopf, 1992) 54.

What is clear from the judgments of Nuremberg and Tokyo, as well as the judgment in the *Ministries* case, is that propaganda for war, or, as Murty described it, 'propaganda activity organized by the key policy-makers in a state, designed as a preparation for initiating a strategy of violence for purposes of aggression',[186] constituted an essential tool for the preparation of crimes against peace. Commenting upon the judgment of the IMT, Whitton and Larson noted that despite the acquittals of defendants such as von Schirach and Fritzsche, 'the crucial point is that [. . .] the Tribunal entertained no doubts of the existence of a rule against propaganda of a war of aggression'.[187] Biddle appears to have supported this argument when he stated that rather than opposing the fundamental principles of international law as adopted by the IMT, Nikitchenko's dissent primarily concerns 'the inferences that should be drawn from conflicting evidence'.[188] Nonetheless, and despite the repeated and solemn emphasis placed on the fundamental role of propaganda in creating a warlike atmosphere in Germany and in inciting to specific acts of aggression, the IMT's judgment failed to directly address the issue of incitement to aggression in as comprehensive a manner as it did incitement to crimes against humanity, a factor whose influence can be seen in the contrast between the centrality of the prohibition of direct and public incitement to genocide in the 1948 Genocide Convention[189] as well as contemporary international criminal law and the notable absence of debate around a parallel crime of incitement to aggression.

Furthermore, it is somewhat unclear from the judgment whether for propaganda for war to be criminal it was necessary that it directly incite to specific acts of aggression, or whether a defendant who had been a member of the conspiracy and who engaged in propaganda for war could have been held individually criminally responsible for propaganda which was directed at creating a warlike atmosphere conducive to the exercise in future of propaganda directly inciting to a specific act of aggression. While the *Fritzsche* decision may appear to have left this a moot point, the convictions of Hess, Keitel, and Rosenberg suggest that propaganda for war, even if not directly inciting to a specific act of aggression, but rather at the creation of a warlike atmosphere, constituted an international crime, a view which is in keeping with the significant emphasis placed on propaganda for war as a means of preparing for and launching war throughout the judgment. It would also appear that the Tribunal for the Far East, as with the IMT at Nuremberg, considered propaganda for war encompassing both propaganda intended to create a warlike spirit as a preparation for future wars and incitement to specific acts of aggression to be grounds for individual criminal responsibility for conspiracy to wage aggressive war.

[186] BS Murty, *Propaganda and World Public Order*, 238.

[187] John B Whitton and Arthur Larson, *Propaganda*, 81.

[188] Francis Biddle, 'The Nurnberg Trial', 696.

[189] Article III(c), Convention on the Prevention and Punishment of the Crime of Genocide, New York, 9 December 1948, 78 UNTS 277 (entered into force 12 January 1951).

The Charter and Judgment of the IMT was crucial in establishing the legitimacy and role of international law in the aftermath of the Second World War, and whereas the judgment may not have provided as clear a precedent as one might have desired as to the means by which international law should develop so as to combat propaganda for war, the combined jurisprudence of the Second World War Tribunals provided a clear warning to the newly established United Nations that propaganda for war had been a crucial aspect of the preparation and initiation of war without which the Second World War might not have taken place. As Pella was to note in this regard, '[l]e procès de Nuremberg offre lui aussi ample matière à méditation'.[190]

---

[190] A/CN.4/39, para 128; [1950] 2 YB ILC, 343.

2

Propaganda for War at the United Nations General Assembly

A. State Responsibility and Propaganda for War

The establishment of the United Nations, its Charter, and the Universal Declaration of Human Rights drew on the experiences of the League of Nations, the Second World War, and the judgments of the Second World War Tribunals, particularly the Charter and Judgment of the IMT at Nuremberg. Article II(4) of the UN Charter firmly established the illegality of aggressive war, providing that 'members shall refrain in their international relations from the threat or use of force against the territorial integrity or political independence of any state'.[1] The exceptions to this rule are the right to individual or collective self-defence, guaranteed in Article 51, and other measures consistent with chapter VII, as well as the right of all peoples to self-determination and independence. According to Quincy Wright, the Charter supported freedom of transnational communication to the extent that it is compatible with international peace and justice, a principle which was necessary 'to create the conditions for a peaceful, secure, free and just world'.[2] Whitton regarded the failure of the drafters of the Charter to directly address 'pernicious propaganda' to be surprising given the impact on international relations which propaganda had had prior to and during the Second World War.[3]

The Universal Declaration of Human Rights provides a universally recognized minimum standard of human rights, Article 19 of which set forth the right to freedom of expression: '[e]veryone has the right to freedom of opinion and expression; this right includes freedom to hold opinions without interference and to seek, receive and impart information and ideas through any media and regardless of frontiers.'[4] During the drafting of the Universal Declaration the USSR had made several proposals that racist propaganda as well as incitement to violence

---

[1] United Nations Charter, 26 June 1945, 59 Stat 1031, TS 993, 3 Bevans 1153, entered into force 24 October 1945.

[2] Quincy Wright, 'Freedom and Responsibility in Respect of Trans-National Communication', 44 Am Soc'y Int'l L Proc 95 (1950) 106.

[3] John B Whitton, 'Efforts to Curb Dangerous Propaganda', 899.

[4] GA Res 217A(III), 10 December 1948.

and to war should be prohibited thereunder.[5] Although these were not accepted, the USSR did succeed in adding to the right that '[a]ll are entitled to equal protection against any discrimination in violation of this Declaration' the guarantee of protection 'against any incitement to such discrimination' in Article 7.[6] Although no explicit limitations to the right to freedom of expression were set forth in Article 19, the drafters of the Universal Declaration recognized that no right is absolute, and Article 19 is tempered by Article 29(2) which provides that:

In the exercise of his rights and freedoms, everyone shall be subject only to such limitations as are determined by law solely for the purpose of securing due recognition and respect for the rights and freedoms of others and of meeting the just requirements of morality, public order and the general welfare in a democratic society.

Likewise, Article 30 declares that the rights set forth in the Universal Declaration may not be interpreted as implying any right to engage in any activity aimed at the destruction of these rights. The contemporary prohibition of propaganda for war set forth in the International Covenant on Civil and Political Rights is derived from these fundamental principles of international law, namely, that war is outlawed and that the principle of freedom of expression cannot be abused in order to violate the rights and freedoms of others.

While the UN Security Council has primary responsibility under the Charter for the maintenance of international peace and security, it has yet to adopt a resolution addressing propaganda for war. Article 39 of the Charter allows the Security Council to take the necessary action to deal with incidents, which do not exclude propaganda for war, which it considers to constitute a 'threat to the peace, breach of the peace or act of aggression'. Martin was sceptical that the Security Council would ever pass such a resolution, which he considered extremely unlikely since 'all states today are engaged in international propaganda'.[7] The General Assembly, however, has repeatedly dealt with the issue of propaganda for war since meeting for its second session in 1947.

i. General Assembly Resolutions

Before outlining the various General Assembly Resolutions condemning propaganda for war, reference must be made to the ideological and political divide of the Cold War which was to permeate all debates on the subject at the United Nations. Whereas the communist states, following the example of the USSR, were to the fore in advocating a prohibition of propaganda for war in international law, the liberal democracies, and particularly the United States and the United Kingdom, had little enthusiasm for such proposals. According to

---

⁵ AC.1/SR.7, 9.
⁶ Johannes Morsink, *The Universal Declaration of Human Rights: Origins, Drafting, and Intent* (Philadelphia: University of Pennsylvania, 1999) 65–72.
⁷ L John Martin, *International Propaganda*, 72.

Manfred Nowak this dichotomy had its roots in Marx's analysis of the French Declaration of the Rights of Man and Citizen of 1789 and the conflict between 'bourgeois and socialist human rights theory' which 'is most clearly manifested in the rights of political liberty (or communication) and in particular freedom of opinion and expression'.[8]

The tension between the United States and the USSR impacted heavily upon efforts to formulate by consensus a prohibition of propaganda for war at the United Nations. Fridemaan notes that the prevalence of propaganda throughout the early stages of the Cold War contributed substantially to the difficulty of reaching agreement on the role of international law in confronting propaganda for war:

[…] the organized dissemination of propaganda as a means of undermining the will to resistance and inciting disaffection against the hostile government became a major and integral part of military organization. Its relative significance has, if anything, increased in the period of 'cold war' which precludes direct armed action, but intensifies manoeuvring for political gains in foreign areas.[9]

Although the diametrically opposing stances taken by the two major superpowers may have shaped the early debates on the prohibition of propaganda for war, other voices were to emerge at the United Nations and contribute greatly to the debate. Samuel de Palmas observed in this respect that:

Current national concepts of freedom of the press or freedom of information, far from being characterized simply by the gap between the Soviet thesis of the state indoctrinated society and the democratic thesis of the society free to reach its own consensus on the basis of competing sources of news, are more accurately described as being ranged in a continuous ideological spectrum. This spectrum is bounded by the U.S.S.R. at one extreme and the United States at the other, with every country ranged between.[10]

At its first session in 1946, the General Assembly adopted a Resolution proposed by the Philippines calling for an international conference on freedom of information.[11] The Resolution's preamble recognized both the import of freedom of information and the threat which the abuse, restriction, or control of information could have on peaceful relations amongst and between states in asserting that while freedom of information 'is a fundamental right and the touchstone of all the freedoms to which the United Nations is consecrated' it required as an indispensable element 'the willingness and capacity to employ its privileges without abuse [and] the moral obligation to seek the facts without prejudice and to spread knowledge without malicious intent'.[12]

---

[8] Manfred Nowak, *U.N. Covenant on Civil and Political Rights: CCPR Commentary* (2nd edn), 438–9.

[9] W Fridemaan, 'Hostile Propaganda', 498.

[10] Samuel de Palma, *Freedom of the Press: An International Issue*, Department of the State Publication 3687 (1950) 17. Cited in John B Whitton and Arthur Larson, *Propaganda*, 241.

[11] GA Res 59(I), 14 December 1946.

[12] ibid.

On 18 September 1947, at the General Assembly's second session, the USSR proposed a draft resolution which condemned criminal propaganda for a new war as carried on by the United States, Turkey, and Greece.[13] The draft stated that this propaganda was a violation of the Charter, called on all nations to prohibit its circulation, and stressed the need for speedy implementation of General Assembly Resolutions dealing with the reduction of armaments and control of atomic energy.[14] On 27 October the Political and Security Committee of the General Assembly rejected a Venezuelan proposal to refer the matter to a subcommittee and the USSR proposal was rejected in a paragraph-by-paragraph vote.[15] There had been significant opposition to propaganda for war being acknowledged by the General Assembly as an international crime, exacerbated no doubt by the specific reference to individual states.[16] Australia, Canada, and France submitted a completely new Draft Resolution condemning all forms of propaganda which encouraged any aggression or threat to the peace, and urging each government to 'take appropriate steps within its constitutional limits' to promote propaganda leading toward friendly relations among nations.[17] The Committee adopted this Resolution on the same date.

Resolution 110(II) of 3 November 1947 entitled '[m]easures to be taken against propaganda and the inciters of a new war' was adopted unanimously.[18] The Resolution condemned 'all forms of propaganda, in whatsoever country conducted, which is either designed or likely to provoke or encourage any threat to the peace, or act of aggression'.[19] That the aim of this Resolution was the attainment of peace was confirmed by the preamble's statement that the principle had been derived from the UN Charter, whose purpose is 'to save succeeding generations from the scourge of war [...] and to practice tolerance and live together in peace with one another as good neighbours'.[20] In order to assuage liberal democracies' fears that in condemning such propaganda they were implicitly sanctioning state censorship, the second paragraph requested states to take proactive efforts at promoting 'by all means of publicity and propaganda available to them, friendly relations among nations based on the Purposes and Principles

---

[13] The USSR delegate who had submitted this proposal was Vishinski, who had edited AN Trainin's book *Hitlerite Responsibility under Criminal Law*, wherein the author advocated that 'propaganda for aggression' be recognized as an international crime.

[14] UN Doc A/BUR/86.

[15] UN Doc A/C.1/SR.86.

[16] Quincy Wright, 'The Crime of War-Mongering', 42 AJIL (1948) 128. See further L John Martin, *International Propaganda*, 71.

[17] 'General Assembly', 2 Int Org 1 (1948) 61.

[18] GA Res 110(II), 3 November 1947.

[19] In a note addressed to the US government, the USSR claimed that an article which appeared in the 17 May 1948 issue of *Newsweek*, discussing the role of US military bases abroad, was contrary to this Resolution. A formal protest was lodged with the US government and a similar protest was charged on the same day with the government of the Netherlands. See further Kazimierz Grzybowski, 'Propaganda and the Soviet Concept of World Public Order', 31 Law & Contemp Probs 479 (1966) 503–4.

[20] GA Res 110(II), 3 November 1947.

of the Charter'.[21] It further required states 'to encourage the dissemination of all information designed to give expression to the undoubted desire of all peoples for peace'.[22] A striking aspect of the language used in this Resolution is that the term propaganda is value-neutral, used to describe both positive and negative communications, suggesting that what was meant by propaganda was simply speech aimed at achieving a particular outcome.

Also at the second session of the General Assembly, Yugoslavia submitted a proposal that member states should adopt measures to prevent the dissemination 'of slanderous statements which were harmful to relations between states'.[23] At the behest of China, the heading 'slanderous information' was deleted and replaced by the phrase 'false or distorted reports'.[24] As adopted, Resolution 127(II) of 15 November 1947 invited member states to study such measures as may be taken at the national level to combat 'the diffusion of false and or distorted reports likely to injure friendly relations between states', and to submit reports on the matter to the Conference on Freedom of Information.[25]

General Assembly Resolution 381(V) of 17 November 1950 entitled '[c]ondemnation of propaganda against peace,' reaffirmed Resolution 110(II) and Resolution 290(IV) concerning the free exchange of information and ideas. Paragraph 2 declared that 'propaganda against peace' includes:

1. Incitement to conflict or acts of aggression;
2. Measures tending to isolate people from any contact with the outside world, by preventing the Press, radio and other media of communication from reporting international events, and thus hindering mutual comprehension and understanding between peoples;
3. Measures tending to silence or distort the activities of the United Nations in favour of peace or to prevent their peoples from knowing the views of other States Members.[26]

The text of this Resolution is notable insofar as the General Assembly recognized that the potential success of propaganda inciting to acts of aggression is greatly enhanced in an environment where the right to freedom of expression is gravely restricted. The judgment of the IMT at Nuremberg had been clear in this respect when it highlighted the means by which the Nazis had combined propaganda for war with repression of freedom of expression in the planning, preparation, and initiation of wars of aggression. This approach to the issue of the prohibition of propaganda for war in international law appears the most appropriate in that it not only ensures that the prohibition is not permitted to become a tool

---

[21] ibid, para 2(a).
[22] ibid, para 2(b).
[23] UN Doc A/445.
[24] 'General Assembly', 2 Int Org 1 (1948) 68.
[25] GA Res 127(II), 15 November 1947.
[26] GA Res 381(V), 17 November 1950.

for restricting the right to freedom of expression, but it is also likely to be most effective since it promotes an environment in which such propaganda is less likely to have the desired effect of inciting to war.

General Assembly Resolution 424(V) of 14 December 1950 on the Right to Freedom of Information condemned radio jamming and invited all governments to 'conform strictly to an ethical conduct in the interest of world peace by reporting facts truly and objectively'. The challenge of devising appropriate measures to deal with the dissemination of false and distorted information by both national and international information enterprises was referred by the General Assembly to the UN bodies studying the question of freedom of information in Resolution 634(VII) of 16 December 1952. The General Assembly's condemnation of propaganda for war was again reaffirmed in a 1954 Resolution entitled '[s]trengthening of peace through the removal of barriers to free exchange of information and ideas'.[27] This Resolution again stressed that there was no contradiction between prohibiting propaganda for war and respecting the individual's right to freedom of expression, suggesting in fact that both principles were necessary in order to strengthen the cause of peace. Likewise Resolution 819(IX) of 11 December 1954 which reaffirms Resolutions 110(II) and 381(V) reasserted the opinion of the General Assembly that the maintenance of barriers to the free exchange of information and ideas 'fosters the continuation of false and hostile propaganda against other States and peoples'.

From about 1950 many of the Soviet Bloc states enacted penal legislation prohibiting propaganda for war within their jurisdictions, an exercise that was intended to demonstrate internationally the viability in practice of a prohibition of propaganda for war in international law.[28] The USSR's Peace Defence Act of March 1951 provided that since 'war propaganda, in whatever form conducted, undermines the cause of peace, creates the danger of a new war and is therefore a grave crime against humanity [...] persons guilty of war propaganda shall be committed for trial as major criminals'.[29] Czechoslovakia issued the Act on

---

[27] GA Res 819(IX), 11 December 1954.

[28] The Supreme Soviet of the USSR on 12 March 1950 passed a law on the defence of peace which decreed '1. To recognise that war propaganda under whatever form it is made, undermines the cause of peace, creates the threat of a new war and is the gravest crime against humanity. 2. To bring to court persons guilty of war propaganda and to try them as having committed a most grave criminal offence.' See further Yuri Bobrakov, 'War Propaganda: A Serious Crime against Humanity', OC Giles, 'Judge-Made Crimes in Eastern Germany', 19 Mod LR 3 (1956) 313–15. Similarly, Section 2 of Albania's 1951 Law on the Defense of Peace provides that 'Whoever directly or indirectly [...] attempts to provoke an armed aggression of one state upon another; advocates the increase of armaments, the use of such weapons of mass destruction as the atom bomb, chemical and bacteriological weapons, and the like; advocates and propagates the doctrine of hatred among nations for the purpose of unleashing a new war; or commits any other acts aimed at the military and economic preparation of future aggression and causing in the minds of the people anxiety and fear of the possibility of a new war, shall be committing the crime of incitement to war and war propaganda.' Reprinted in 46 AJIL 3 (1952) 101.

[29] VOKS Bulletin, no 67 (1951), 5; New Times, 14 March 1951 (no 11), 1; reprinted in 46 AJIL Sup 34 (1952).

the Protection of Peace, the preamble of which noted that '[a]ware of the fact that the incitors of a new warfare augmenting the danger of war, are intensifying their propaganda of a new war and are turning to overt acts of aggression', and which declared as being criminal acts, 'attempts to disturb the peaceful communion of nations by inciting in any way whatsoever to war, by propagating war or otherwise supporting war propaganda'.[30] Nevertheless, many of the Western states were to view such laws as having less to do with the pursuance of peace than with the consolidation of the Soviet regimes and the continued repression of internal dissent.

ii. Draft Convention on Freedom of Information and the Press (1948)

Against the backdrop of these developments, efforts were under way at the Conference on Freedom of Information and the Press to reach agreement on a prohibition of propaganda for war. While the primary objective of the 1948 United Nations Conference on Freedom of Information and of the Press was to improve the means of sending information across national frontiers, it was also hoped that the intended Convention would 'combat forces which incite to war, by removing bellicose influences from media of information'.[31] The Resolutions passed by the General Assembly in 1947 directed against propaganda for war and false and distorted information[32] had been specifically referred to the Conference for attention.[33] The Sub-Commission on Freedom of Information and the Press, appointed by the Economic and Social Council, proposed that the Conference's agenda include 'the study of measures for counteracting the persistent spread of demonstrably false or tendentious reports which confuse the peoples of the world, aggravate relations between nations, or otherwise interfere with the growth of international understanding, peace, and security against a recurrence of Nazi, Fascist, or Japanese aggression'.[34] At the Conference itself a Resolution was adopted which:

Condemns solemnly all propaganda either designed or likely to provoke or encourage any threat to the peace, breach of the peace, or act of aggression, and all distortion or falsification of news through whatever channels, private or governmental, since such activities can only promote misunderstanding and mistrust between the peoples of the world and thereby endanger the lasting peace which the United Nations is consecrated to maintain.[35]

---

[30] Collection of Laws of the Czechoslovak Republic, no 165; *Bulletin de droit tchécoslovaque*, vol 9, no 1–2 (1 April 1950), 114; Reprinted in 46 AJIL Sup 34 (1952).

[31] John B Whitton and Arthur Larson, *Propaganda*, 70.

[32] GA Res 110(II), 3 November 1947; GA Res 127(II), 15 November 1947.

[33] John B Whitton, 'UN Conference on Freedom of Information and the Movement against International Propaganda', 43 AJIL (1949) 73.

[34] E/441, 5 June 1947; John B Whitton, 'Efforts to Curb Dangerous Propaganda', 901.

[35] UN Doc E/Conf 6/C.1/19.

This Resolution continued to assert that only a free press, that is, 'one free to seek and to disseminate the truth', could hope to counteract Nazi, fascist, or other propaganda of aggression or of racial, national, and religious discrimination,[36] thus again asserting the principle of the interdependency of both the prohibition of propaganda for war and the right to freedom of expression. Resolution 39 directed the Sub-Commission on Freedom of Information and of the Press to study the problems caused by the dissemination of false or distorted information, and also to recommend means to spread 'true information to counteract Nazi, Fascist or other propaganda of aggression or of racial, national and religious discrimination'.[37] Following the adoption of these Resolutions, the Inter-Parliamentary Union, meeting in Rome in September 1948, continued its efforts to encourage the prohibition of propaganda for war by adopting a Resolution which stated that:

Comme toute propagande en faveur de la guerre et toute incitation à l'agression constituent une menace pour la paix, vers le maintien de laquelle doivent tendre tous les efforts des Etats, il est du devoir des gouvernements de prendre des mesures efficaces afin d'assurer l'exécution des résolutions condamnant une telle propagande, adoptées à l'unanimité par la deuxième Assemblée générale des Nations Unies, en 1947, et par la Conférence pour la liberté de l'information, en 1948.[38]

In addition to adopting a draft article on the right to freedom of expression for inclusion in the Draft Covenant on Civil and Political Rights, the Conference adopted three Draft Conventions: the US sponsored Convention on the Gathering and International Transmission of News; the French sponsored Convention for an International Right of Correction; and the British sponsored Convention on General Principles of Freedom of Information. Although each of the Conventions and Resolutions were adopted by majority votes, the Communist Bloc refused to sign the Final Act of the Conference and employed obstructionist tactics at the Economic and Social Council, which subsequently had to submit the entire matter without action or recommendation to the General Assembly.[39] The approach adopted by the USSR during these negotiations was characterized by repeated accusations that the Western media was attempting to incite a war against the communist states. John Hazard noted two general themes which emerged from the negotiations. The first was a continuing communist propaganda drive 'to confuse world opinion by labelling the United States press in particular, and that

---

[36] John B Whitton and Arthur Larson, *Propaganda*, 200.

[37] ibid 201.

[38] 'As all propaganda in favour of war and incitement to aggression is a threat to peace, the maintenance of which must be the aim of all the States, governments must take efficient measures in order to ensure the implementation of all of the resolutions condemning war propaganda, which were unanimously adopted at the Second General Assembly of the United Nations in 1947, and at the Conference on Freedom of Expression in 1948' (author's translation). Cited in A/C.3/221, 3: A/CN.4/39; [1950] 2 YB ILC, p 343, para 128.

[39] John B Whitton and Arthur Larson, *Propaganda*, 201.

of several other Western states in general, as desirous of inciting a war against the Soviet Union'.[40] The second concerned communist claims that the United States' Convention was aimed at forming 'a solid foundation on which the newspaper monopolies of the United States and Great Britain could develop their plans of expansion'.[41]

The General Assembly adopted an amalgamation of the United States' and France's draft Conventions as the Convention on the International Transmission of News and the Right to Correction on 13 May 1949. The Convention's preamble stated that the contracting states desired 'to combat all propaganda which is either designed or likely to provoke or encourage any threat to the peace, or act of aggression'.[42] The purpose of the Convention was to provide a framework for a forum whereby false or inaccurate reports concerning international relations could be publicly corrected, although the preamble noted that 'it is not at present practicable to institute, on the international level, a procedure for verifying the accuracy of a report which might lead to the imposition of penalties for the publication of false or distorted reports'.[43]

The Sub-Commission was dissolved in 1952 but the General Assembly continued to pass several Resolutions concerning the right to freedom of information, including Resolution 634(VII) of 16 December 1952 which recommended that the UN bodies studying the question of freedom of information should consider appropriate measures for avoiding the harm done to international understanding by the dissemination of false and distorted information. Attempts had been made to shelve the entire idea of a Covenant on Freedom of Information and to replace it with a declaration on freedom of information, but in 1958 the General Assembly adopted a Resolution to proceed to a discussion of the text of the Draft Convention as formulated by the Committee on the Draft Convention on Freedom of Information.[44] At its fourteenth session in 1959, the Third

---

[40] John N Hazard, 'The Position of the Soviet Union in Respect to Trans-National Communication', 14 Am Soc'y Int'l L Proc 109 (1950) 109. Citing Samuel de Palma, 'Freedom of the Press: An International Issue', 21 Department of State Bulletin 541 (14 November 1949) 724, 733.

[41] John N Hazard, 'The Position of the Soviet Union in Respect to Trans-National Communication', 110.

[42] Convention on the International Right of Correction, 435 UNTS 191, entered into force 24 August 1962.

[43] ibid. A right of correction applies when a 'news dispatch' from one country is published and disseminated abroad and a contracting state contends that the report is false or distorted and 'capable of injuring its relations with other states'. In accordance with Article 3, the aggrieved state has the right to send a communiqué stating its version of the facts without comment or expression of opinion to the state within whose territory the dispatch is disseminated. Should a state receiving this communiqué fail to release it as soon as possible or at least within five days from date of its receipt to information agencies operating within its territory and to the headquarters of the medium whose correspondent authored the dispatch in dispute, if the headquarters are located within the territory of the country, Article 5 provides that the complainant state may refer the case to the International Court of Justice.

[44] GA Res 1313 C(XIII).

Committee of the General Assembly adopted the preamble and Article 1 of a Draft Convention which provided for a right to freedom of information.[45]

Draft Article 2 was adopted by the Third Committee in 1960.[46] This provision would have permitted States parties to restrict the right to freedom of information under the following circumstances:

1. The exercise of the freedoms referred to in Article 1 carries with it duties and responsibilities. It may, however, be subject only to such necessary restrictions as are clearly defined by law and applied in accordance with the law in respect of: national security and public order (*ordre public*); systematic dissemination of false reports harmful to friendly nations and of expressions inciting to war or to national, racial, or religious hatred; attacks on founders of religions; incitement to violence and crime; public health and morals; the rights, honor and reputation of others; and the fair administration of justice.

2. The restrictions specified in the preceding paragraph shall not be deemed to justify the imposition by any State of prior censorship on news, comments and political opinions, and may not be used as grounds for restricting the right to criticise the Government.[47]

The efforts to formulate a convention on freedom of information were destined to fail, however, an outcome which Whitton had predicted even prior to the convening of the first conference on freedom of information and the press in 1948. Referring specifically to radio propaganda, he doubted whether such an 'exceedingly complex and difficult problem' was to be dealt with 'as only a minor part of the vast subject of freedom of communications',[48] and proposed that a special conference, similar to that which had led to the adoption of the 1936 Broadcasting Convention, be devoted to this single matter. He cites two primary reasons in support of his views: first, since radio propaganda is a problem *sui generis*, to which all defences have proved inadequate, the drafting of treaty provisions for its regulation requires exclusive and intense preparation.[49] Secondly, he suggested that a conference with a specific focus on 'curbing the use of propaganda for aggression and war' would have a far greater chance of resolving the differences on the role of freedom of information and the press held by the USSR and the United States.[50] He had suggested that such a conference would provide a real opportunity for the two Cold War superpowers 'to labor together in the same cause'.[51]

Nonetheless, despite the fact that the Draft Convention on Freedom of Information was never ratified by the General Assembly, the adoption of draft Article 2 in 1960 was to prove extremely significant. The following year the Third Committee of the General Assembly held its final debates on the Draft Covenant

45 UN GAOR A/4341.
46 A/C.3/SR.1044, para 47. 50 : 5 with 19 abstentions.
47 A/C.3/SR.1044; UN Yearbook, 1960, 336.
48 John B Whitton, 'Efforts to Curb Dangerous Propaganda', 901.
49 ibid 902.
50 ibid.
51 ibid 903.

on Civil and Political Rights and took Article 2 as the starting point for negotiations on the right to freedom of expression. The drafting history of Article 20(1) of the International Covenant on Civil and Political Rights, which provides that '[a]ny propaganda for war shall be prohibited by law', closely reflects that of the immediate provision, and will be considered in detail in the next chapter. As noted by Elizabeth Downey, the centrality of the issue of the prohibition of propaganda for war to the General Assembly debates on human rights conventions demonstrates that at this juncture in the development of the international human rights framework, information, 'as a substantive issue of international law, had evolved from a purely political question to a question of human rights'.[52]

iii. Conference of the Eighteen-Nation Committee on Disarmament (1962)

A major agreement on the prohibition of propaganda for war was almost secured at the Conference of the Eighteen-Nation Committee on Disarmament in 1962. Had this agreement been realized, it would have represented a significant reconciliation of the positions of the Cold War superpowers who had taken opposing sides on this question since the establishment of the United Nations.[53] On 25 May 1962, the Committee of the Whole Conference unanimously adopted the following proposal which had been submitted by the USSR:

Recognizing that war propaganda in whatsoever form or country conducted which can provoke or encourage a threat to or breach of, the peace, is incompatible with the United Nations Charter and can lead to acts of aggression or war:

Recognizing that an end to such propaganda could facilitate the conclusion of an agreement on general complete disarmament:

1. Solemnly affirm their support for the United Nations General Assembly Resolution 110(II) which condemned 'all forms of propaganda, in whatsoever country conducted, which is either designed or likely to provoke or encourage any threat to the peace, breach of the peace, or act of aggression':

2. Condemn appeals for war and for the settlement of disputes between states by the use of force, and also statements to the effect that war is necessary or inevitable:

3. Affirm their conviction that in our day, war can no longer serve as a method of settling international disputes and their desire to educate the younger generation in this conviction and to promote the ideas of peace, mutual respect and understanding among the peoples:

4. Undertake to promote by every means at their disposal the widest possible circulation of news, ideas and opinions conducive to the strengthening of peace and friendship among peoples, and to extend cultural, scientific and educational relations with a view to

---

[52] Elizabeth A Downey, 'A Historical Survey of the International Regulation of Propaganda', 5 Mich YB Int'l Legal Stud 341 (1984) 347.
[53] Kazimierz Grzybowski, 'Propaganda and the Soviet Concept of World Public Order', 505.

better dissemination of the ideas of peaceful and friendly co-operation among states, and general and complete disarmament:

5. Call upon all states to adopt, within the limits of their constitutional systems, appropriate practical measures, including measures in a legislative form in the case of states which consider such form appropriate, with a view to giving effect to this declaration against war propaganda:

6. Call upon other states to support this declaration.[54]

The United States and the USSR both voted in favour of this Resolution, yet when the declaration was brought before the plenary session for adoption, the Soviet representative demanded changes to the text, ostensibly because of a West German demand for nuclear weapons and 'revanchist' propaganda for a change of frontiers during the intervening period.[55] The USSR requested that paragraphs 3–6 of the above text be replaced by the following:

Resolutely condemn all appeals for a preventative nuclear war as aggressive acts which conflict with the purposes and principles of the Charter of the United Nations and with the interests of maintaining peace, and which are incompatible with the honor and conscience of mankind:

Condemn propaganda for revanchism and for the revision of state frontiers in Europe which resulted from the Second World War as actions conflicting with the interests of peace and creating a threat to the security of the peoples:

Also condemn as being at variance with the United Nations Declaration on granting of independence to colonial countries and peoples, and as threatening universal peace, incitement to the use of force against peoples which have embarked on the course of national liberation and independent development:

Undertake within the shortest possible period and in any event not later than six months from the date of signature of this Declaration, to enact legislation, if it has not been previously enacted, declaring war propaganda in any form a grave crime against peace and humanity and providing for severe penalties against persons guilty of conducting such propaganda, including their immediate removal from all official posts, the loss of all ranks and titles and their criminal prosecution:

Call upon all other states to accede to this Declaration and to take similar measures in accordance with it.[56]

These proposed amendments, which are notable for introducing very specific examples of propaganda, requiring criminal prosecution for such propaganda, and removing all reference to encouraging the circulation of information in the cause of peace, were not surprisingly rejected by the representatives of the Western liberal democracies, and the Committee was not to revisit the issue.[57]

---

[54] Eighteen-Nation Disarmament Committee Document, ENDC/C.1/20, 25 May 1962. Reprinted in BS Murty, *Propaganda and World Public Order*, 235–6 and John B Whitton and Arthur Larson, *Propaganda*, 234–5.

[55] BS Murty, *Propaganda and World Public Order*, 236–7.

[56] Eighteen-Nation Disarmament Committee; Document, ENDC/PV/44, 29 May 1962. Reprinted in BS Murty, *Propaganda and World Public Order*, 237.

[57] BS Murty, *Propaganda and World Public Order*, 237.

As an example of 'demonstrative diplomacy', the USSR's sabotaging of a potential compromise text condemning propaganda for war suggests that it had been less driven towards reaching a consensus on the subject than it was in perpetuating its antagonistic conflict with the liberal democracies.[58]

iv. General Assembly Declarations

Following the adoption by the Third Committee of Article 20(1) of the draft Covenant on Civil and Political Rights in 1961, the General Assembly was to condemn propaganda for war in several far-reaching Declarations. Resolution 110(II) of 1947 was reaffirmed in the 1965 Declaration on the Promotion among Youth of the Ideals of Peace, Mutual Respect, and Understandings between Peoples.[59] Among the most important of the declarations adopted by the General Assembly is the Declaration on Principles of International Law Concerning Friendly Relations and Co-operation among States in Accordance with the Charter of the United Nations, which was adopted by consensus in October 1970.[60]

Following the adoption of the International Covenant on Civil and Political Rights in 1966, the terminology which had varied in General Assembly Resolutions, with the use of terms such as 'propaganda inciting to war', 'incitement to conflict or acts of aggression', and 'war propaganda', was standardized by the adoption of the term 'propaganda for war' as used in Article 20(1) of the Covenant. Thus, when the Czechoslovak delegate to the Special Committee on Principles of International Law Concerning Friendly Relations and Cooperation among States submitted a draft Resolution concerning the obligation that states refrain from the threat or use of force in international relations contrary to the United Nations Charter, paragraph 3 provided that:

Any propaganda for war, incitement to or fomenting of war and any propaganda for preventative war and for striking the first nuclear blow shall be prohibited. States shall take, within the framework of their jurisdiction, all measures, in particular legislative measures, in order to prevent such propaganda.[61]

While the drafting committee had difficulties in reaching consensus on whether the Declaration would elaborate upon propaganda for war,[62] the obligation that '[i]n accordance with the purposes and principles of the United Nations, states have the duty to refrain from propaganda for wars of aggression', was set forth in paragraph 3 of the Declaration's formulation of the prohibition of the threat or

---

[58] John B Whitton and Arthur Larson, *Propaganda*, 235.
[59] GA Res 2037(XX), 7 December 1965.
[60] GA Res 2625(XXV), 24 October 1970.
[61] UN Doc A/AC.119/L.6; Report of Special Committee, Doc A/5746, 19.
[62] Drafting Committee Paper no 10 and Corr 1, Report of the Special Committee, Doc A/5746, 16 November 1964, 51.

use of force. Robert Rosenstock considered the affirmation that states had a duty to refrain from propaganda for war to be 'a reflection of the understanding that for states to engage in war propaganda would be inconsistent with the Preamble of the Charter and the purposes of the United Nations as set forth in Article 1'.[63] He notes that there was widespread approval of the USSR's proposal to include this principle in the Declaration since it was deemed 'a useful and acceptable addition by others in light of the role war propaganda played in the late 1930s and 1960s in exacerbating tense situations'.[64]

Rosenstock stressed that the duty to refrain from propaganda for wars of aggression 'appears in the text subject to the express understanding that what is prohibited is state action, not individual conduct, the latter of which would involve issues of free speech'.[65] He notes that this assertion had never been challenged, a view confirmed by Dean Rusk who cites the US delegate's explicit statement during the drafting of the Declaration that the duty can apply only to governments 'since nations with strong guarantees of free speech and free press would face formidable constitutional issues if an attempt were made to enforce the obligation against individuals'.[66]

The final paragraph of the preamble to the 1978 Declaration on Preparation of Societies for Life in Peace noted the central role which respect for both the right to freedom of expression as set forth in the Universal Declaration and the prohibition of propaganda for war in the International Covenant on Civil and Political Rights has to play in the attainment of peace and the enjoyment of human rights. The Declaration again called upon all states to observe the principle that in accordance with the purposes and principles of the United Nations states have the duty to refrain from 'propaganda for wars of aggression'.[67] In order to implement the principles set forth in the declaration, states were asked to ensure that their educational and mass media policies 'incorporate contents compatible with the task of the preparation for life in peace of entire societies'.[68] The Declaration further required states to 'discourage and eliminate incitement to racial hatred, national or other discrimination, injustice or advocacy for violence and war'.[69] The Declaration was adopted by 138 votes without opposition although Israel and the United States abstained on the grounds that the prohibition of propaganda for wars of aggression implied an undue threat to freedom of expression.[70]

[63] Robert Rosenstock, 'The Declaration of Principles of International Law Concerning Friendly Relations: A Survey', 65 AJIL 4 (1971) 718.

[64] ibid.

[65] ibid. See generally the statement by Mr Gimer, the US delegate, at UN Doc A/S.6/SR.1180 (1970).

[66] Dean Rusk, 'The 25th U.N. General Assembly and the Use of Force', 2 Ga J Int'l & Comp L 19 (1972) 23–4.

[67] GA Res 33/73, I(3), 15 December 1978.

[68] ibid, II(a)(i).

[69] ibid, II(a)(ii).

[70] UN Press Release GA/5942 at 109 (1979); Louis B Sohn, 'The New International Law: Protection of the Rights of Individuals Rather than States', 32 Am UL Rev 1 (1982) 59.

This represented a retrogressive step on behalf of the United States which had accepted the obligation upon states to refrain from propaganda for war in supporting the Declaration on Friendly Relations. Following the adoption of that Declaration, Rusk, a former United States Secretary of State, had claimed that the duty to refrain from propaganda for war had little legal meaning in light of an absence of a definition of aggression and also expressed doubts as to 'the desirability or the efficacy of attempts to restrain international debate through law'.[71]

Despite the United States' concerns the General Assembly proceeded to adopt several further Declarations which expanded upon states' duties with regard to propaganda for war. The 1979 Declaration on International Co-operation on Disarmament urged all states, on the basis of the principles of the Charter, 'to take all appropriate measures, including legislative ones, to prevent and prohibit propaganda for war and the arms race'.[72] States were also urged to take 'vigorous measures, individually or collectively, to disseminate the ideals of peace, disarmament, co-operation and friendly relations between peoples'.[73] While these terms reflect the Czech draft proposal which has been noted above in relation to the Declaration on Friendly Principles, the immediate Declaration took a much more comprehensive stance, requiring not only that states take positive measures to prevent and prohibit propaganda for war, but that positive measures must also be taken to prevent and prohibit 'the dissemination of views asserting [the] necessity or usefulness on political, economic or other grounds' of war and the arms race.

The Declaration on the Inadmissibility of Intervention and Interference in the Internal Affairs of States adopted in 1981 stated that the principle of non-interference included the duty of states to abstain 'from any defamatory, campaign, vilification or hostile propaganda for the purpose of intervening or interfering in the internal affairs of other States'[74] and further provided for the right and duty of states to combat, 'within their constitutional prerogatives, the dissemination of false or distorted news which can be interpreted as interference in the internal affairs of other States or as being harmful to the promotion of peace, co-operation and friendly relations among States and nations'.[75] The most recent General Assembly Declaration to refer to propaganda for war is the 1987 Declaration on the Enhancement of the Effectiveness of the Principle of Refraining from the Threat or Use of Force in International Relations. It was declared therein that 'States have the duty not to urge, encourage or assist other States to resort to the threat or use of force in violation of the Charter'[76] and furthermore that 'in

---

[71] Dean Rusk, 'The 28th U.N. General Assembly and the Use of Force', 24.
[72] GA Res 34/88, II(f), 11 December 1979.
[73] ibid, II(g).
[74] GA Res 36/103, II(j), 9 December 1981.
[75] ibid, III(d).
[76] GA Res 44/22, I(4), 18 November 1987.

accordance with the purposes and principles of the United Nations, States have the duty to refrain from propaganda for wars of aggression'.[77]

The common thread running through each of the Resolutions and Declarations of the General Assembly concerning propaganda for war is that such propaganda represented an unacceptable threat to the purposes and principles of the UN Charter and the safeguarding of peace. While the repeated condemnation of propaganda for war in this respect is welcome, the net contribution to the development of international law was severely restricted by the failure of the UN to overcome the Cold War dichotomy of politico-military alliances. As noted by Cassese, 'basic problems remained unsolved, mainly because the great and middle-sized states were not prepared to discuss anew the central points of the existing system and risk upsetting the delicate balance that had been created, to their own advantage, in the application of the Charter rules'.[78]

B. Treaty and Other Condemnations of Propaganda for War

i. The Outer Space Treaty and Direct Satellite Broadcasting

With the rapid development of satellite technology during the Cold War, concerns grew regarding the potential of direct satellite broadcasting to disseminate unimpeded hostile propaganda to transnational audiences.[79] The UN Committee on the Peaceful Uses of Outer Space (COPUOS) was formed in 1958 to focus on developing workable international standards, policy, and law that would take into account such developing challenges and their potential threat to international peace. The following year, with the ever-increasing attention being paid to the exploitation of space by the United States and the USSR, the UN formalized COPUOS as a permanent body.[80] The General Assembly adopted the Declaration of Legal Principles Governing the Activities of States in the Exploration and Use of Outer Space in 1963.[81] Declaring that 'the exploration and use of outer space shall be carried on for the benefit and in the interests of all mankind', the preamble affirmed that

---

[77] GA Res 44/22, I(9).

[78] Antonio Cassese, *Violence and Law in the Modern Age* (Princeton: Princeton University Press, 1988) 40.

[79] See generally John T Powell, 'Towards a Negotiable Definition of Propaganda for International Agreements Related to Direct Broadcast Satellites' James Edwin Bailey, 'Current and Future Legal Uses of Direct Broadcast Satellites in International Law', 45 La L Rev 701 (1985); Jaqueline M Smith, 'Acceptance of Prior Consent as a Means of Regulating Direct Broadcast Satellites', 3 Emory J Int'l Dispute Res 99 (1988–9). For an analysis of the cultural and political impact of transnational satellite broadcasting see Naomi Sakr, *Satellite Realms: Transnational Television, Globalization and the Middle East* (London: IB Tauris, 2001).

[80] Colby C Nuttal, 'Defining International Satellite Communications as Weapons of Mass Destruction: The First Step in a Compromise between National Sovereignty and the Free Flow of Ideas', 27 Hous J Int'l L 389 (2005) 394.

[81] GA Res 1962(XVIII), 13 December 1963.

General Assembly Resolution 110(II) of 1947, which condemned 'propaganda designed or likely to provoke or encourage any threat to the peace', was applicable to outer space.[82] Concern that unrestricted broadcasting via new technology could damage states' interests led the French delegation to COPUOS in 1969 to suggest a comprehensive ban on propaganda which was 'likely to impair the maintenance of international peace or the domestic peace of States; to interfere in the internal affairs of foreign States; to be detrimental to the dignity of the individual or likely to encourage the violation of human rights and fundamental freedoms'.[83]

The preamble to the 1967 Outer Space Treaty again reaffirmed the application of General Assembly Resolution 110(II) to activities in outer space.[84] The treaty was permissive of transnational direct broadcasting of television signals but reaffirmed states' wishes that the transmission of information across international boundaries be subject to international law should it constitute a threat to or breach of the peace.[85] The General Assembly specifically appealed to the media of information in a 1968 Resolution to cooperate in combating propaganda for war.[86] At the third session of the COPUOS Working Group on Direct Satellite Broadcasting in 1970, the USSR proposed an international prohibition on 'broadcasts which are amoral or provocative in nature or which in any other matter tend to interfere with the national life of States'.[87] Japan proposed a more specific set of principles which would have prohibited propaganda for war, incitement to perform subversive acts against political institutions in the receiving country, slander against the national honour of the receiving country, and criticism of the international policies of the receiving country that interfere with domestic affairs.[88] The Working Group did not act upon either the Soviet or the Japanese proposals, yet it is worth highlighting that the Japanese proposal to prohibit propaganda for war in this forum contradicts the position which they have otherwise held since the drafting of the ICCPR.

---

[82] Although the preamble is not considered a binding element of a treaty, Article 31 of the Vienna Convention on the Law of Treaties states that the preamble of a treaty is to be considered in any attempt to divine the intent of the signatories as expressed in the body of the treaty.

[83] UN GAOR, Comm. On the Peaceful Uses of Outer Space, UN Doc A/AC. 105/62 (1969) 6.

[84] Treaty on Principles Governing the Activities of States in the Exploration and Use of Outer Space, Including the Moon and Other Celestial Bodies, 27 January 1967, 610 UNTS 205 (effective 10 October 1967).

[85] Article IV of the Outer Space Treaty provides that States parties shall not 'place in orbit around the Earth any objects carrying [...] weapons of mass destruction'. Nuttal asserts that although telecommunications satellites themselves are not weapons of mass destruction, nations have implicitly agreed that communication aimed at inciting violence is itself a weapon of mass destruction, and thus falls under the regulatory authority of the UN and the Outer Space Treaty. Colby C Nuttal, 'Defining International Satellite Communications as Weapons of Mass Destruction', 399.

[86] GA Res 2448(XXII), 19 December 1968.

[87] 1970 Soviet Draft Model Principles for the Use of Artificial Earth Satellites for Radio and Television Broadcasting, UN Doc A/AC.105/WG.3/CRP.1 (1970).

[88] Reports of the Working Group on Direct Broadcast Satellites: Comments Received from Governments, Specialized Agencies and Other Competent International Bodies, UN Doc A/AC.1 05/79, (1970) 7.

In 1974, the USSR presented revised draft principles to the fifth session of the Working Group on Direct Satellite Broadcasting which sought to prohibit:

any material which is detrimental to the maintenance of international peace and security, which publicizes ideas of war, militarism, national and racial hatred and enmity between peoples, which is aimed at interfering in the internal domestic affairs of other States, or which undermines the foundations of the local civilizations, culture, way of life, traditions or language.[89]

These proposals were rejected[90] and while propaganda for war was clearly stated to be incompatible with the peaceful uses of outer space, on the issue of the regulation of broadcasts by satellite, states, perhaps in response to the ever-changing developments in communications technology, have chosen to overlook the matter for the most part, preferring instead to focus their concern on the preservation of cultural integrity[91] and respect for national sovereignty.[92]

ii. The New World Information Order

During the 1970s many developing nations were clear in stating that the debate on the regulation of the new technologies of information and communication had to be considered in the context of the great disparity between rich and poor countries and were particularly anxious to avoid 'a kind of ideological occupation of satellite broadcasting by the superpowers'.[93] Such concerns were central to many of the Cold War debates on the regulation of propaganda. The lack of material resources to participate on an equal footing in the 'free market place of ideas' meant that many non-aligned states were to side against the liberal democracies' advocacy of minimal restrictions on freedom of information and expression. As Kenya noted at a COPUOS meeting in 1978:

In our view the existence of choices does not in itself guarantee freedom. In the current flow of information in the world, for instance, we have little access to the sources or say in

---

[89] Article IV, Principles Governing the Use by States of Artificial Earth Satellites for Direct Television Broadcasting, UN Doc A/AC.105/WG.3(V) CRP.I and Core I (1974).

[90] The USSR submitted similar proposals at the preparatory meetings of the 1974 Brussels Convention of 1974 (Convention Relating to the Distribution of Program-Carrying Signals Transmitted by Satellite, 21 May 1974, Article 3, UNTS 17949 (entered into force 25 August 1979)) which sought to prohibit the transmission by satellite of materials that are detrimental to international peace or security, publicize ideas of war, nationalism, or racial hatred, interfere with domestic affairs of countries, or undermine national laws, customs, and traditions. Carl Q Christol, 'The 1974 Brussels Convention Relating to the Distribution of Program-Carrying Signals Transmitted by Satellite: An Aspect of Human Rights', 6 J Space L 19 (1978) 31.

[91] See generally CM Dalfen, 'Direct Satellite Broadcasting: Towards International Agreements to Transcend and Marshal the Political Realities', 20 Uni Toronto LJ 366 (1970).

[92] See generally Jennifer Freeman, 'Toward the Free Flow of Information: Direct Television Broadcasting via Satellite', 13 J Int'l L & Econ 359 (1978–9).

[93] Frederick W Rockwood, '1973, the United Nations 27th Session: Direct Satellite Broadcasting', 14 Harv Int'l LJ (1973) 604.

the shaping and dissemination of that information. We have no existence in the present-day information world.[94]

In an effort to rectify the global imbalance in the control and means of communication, developments were undertaken by the non-aligned states (the Group of 77) to reshape the global communications environment. These states had begun to call for a New World Information Order which, it was hoped, would alter the world's communications framework by redirecting the flow of news and information between rich and poor countries.[95] In 1972, the United Nations Educational, Scientific, and Cultural Organization (UNESCO) passed a USSR sponsored resolution asking the Director General of the United Nations to prepare a draft declaration on 'the fundamental principles governing the use of the mass information media with a view to strengthening peace and international understanding and combating war propaganda, racialism and apartheid'.[96] The impetus for such a proposal came in part from Resolution 4.301 adopted at the 1970 UNESCO General Conference in Paris which addressed the role which information media should play in furthering international understanding and cooperation in the interests of peace and human welfare.[97] Paragraph 1 of the Resolution affirmed the inadmissibility of using information media for propaganda on behalf of war, racialism, and hatred among nations, and paragraph 2 invited all states to take the necessary steps, including legislative measures, to encourage the use of information media against propaganda on behalf of war, racialism, and hatred among nations.

Contemporaneous with the drafting of the New World Information Order, the principle that propaganda for war was prohibited under international law also found expression in the Helsinki Final Act.[98] In an attempt to consolidate a *détente* between the two Cold War superpowers, a conference on security and cooperation in Europe was attended by states from both power blocs, as well as non-aligned states. After several years of negotiations the Final Act of the Conference for Security and Cooperation in Europe concluded in Helsinki on 1 August 1975. The Helsinki Final Act addressed security and military issues as well as various aspects of economics, science, culture, and human rights which were of common concern to states on either side of the Cold War. The first section of the Final Act dealt with questions relating to security in Europe and included

[94] Doc A/AC.105/PV.184 (1978) 73. Cited in John T Powell, 'Towards a Negotiable Definition of Propaganda for International Agreements Related to Direct Broadcast Satellites', 21.
[95] See generally YV Lakshmana Rao, 'Propaganda through the Printed Media in the Developing Countries', in L John Martin (ed), *Propaganda in International Affairs* 398 Annals of the American Academy of Political and Social Science 93 (1971).
[96] Gen Conf Res 4.113, 17(1) UN UNESCO Resolutions/Recommendations at 70 (October–November 1972).
[97] Resolution 4.301, Records of the General Conference, Sixteenth Session, Paris, 12 October to 14 November 1970.
[98] Thomas Buergenthal and Alexandre Kiss, *La Protection internationale des droits de l'homme: précis* (Kehl: NP Engel, 1991) 87–91.

several principles which were to guide relations between participating states in the spheres of sovereign equality, the threat or use of force, non-intervention in internal affairs, and respect for human rights. Several provisions included in the Final Act were intended to give effect to these principles including a provision which required participating states to undertake:

To promote, by all means which each of them considers appropriate, a climate of confidence and respect among peoples consonant with their duty to refrain from propaganda for wars of aggression or for any threat or use of force inconsistent with the purposes of the United Nations and with the Declaration on Principles Guiding Relations between Participating States, against another participating State.[99]

Although the Helsinki Final Act did not create legal obligations *de novo*,[100] the inclusion of a reference to states' duty to refrain from propaganda for war is a notable statement of principle. Nonetheless, by permitting states to act upon this duty 'by all means which each of them considers appropriate', the Helsinki Final Act ensured that the longstanding political and ideological differences as to the practical application of the principle would not present an obstacle to the adoption of the overall accord.[101]

In 1978 the Declaration on Fundamental Principles Concerning the Contribution of the Mass Media to Strengthening Peace and International Understanding, to the Promotion of Human Rights and to Countering Racialism, Apartheid and Incitement to War was adopted by UNESCO.[102] This Declaration represented a symbolic step forward for many states who had spent the Cold War in the shadow of the two superpowers, but who wished to assert greater influence in the global communications network.[103] The Declaration's

---

[99] Article 1(b)(i), Conference on Security and Cooperation in Europe: Final Act, 1 August 1975. 14 ILM 1292 (1975).

[100] Buergenthal and Kiss maintain that rather than legal obligations, the Helsinki Final Act created a framework for cooperation whereby states affirmed a certain number of principles: 'il a créé un cadre de coopération permettant d'affirmer un certain nombre de principes.' Thomas Buergenthal and Alexandre Kiss, *La Protection internationale des droits de l'homme*, 87.

[101] On the question of the compatibility of radio jamming with the Helsinki Final Act, see Arie Bloed and Pascale de Wouters d'Oplinter, 'Jamming of Foreign Radio Broadcasts', in A Bloed and P van Dijk, *Essays on Human Rights in the Helsinki Process* (Dordrecht: Martinus Nijhoff, 1985) 163–80.

[102] 20 UNESCO Gen Conf, UNESCO Doc 20C/20 Rev (1978).

[103] In a Resolution adopted at the fourth meeting of the Inter-Governmental Coordinating Council for Information on Non-Aligned Countries in Baghdad in 1980, the sponsors of the NIIO stated that the concept was based on: '(a) the fundamental principles of international law, notably self-determination of peoples, sovereign equality of states and non-interference in internal affairs of other states, (b) the right of every nation to develop its own independent information system and to protect its national sovereignty and cultural identity, in particular by regulating the activities of the transnational corporations, (c) the right of people and individuals to acquire an objective picture of reality by means of accurate and comprehensive information as well as to express themselves freely through various media of culture and communication, (d) the right of every nation to use its means of information to make known worldwide its interests, its aspirations and its political, moral and cultural values, (e) the right of every nation to participate, on the governmental and nongovernmental level, in the intentional exchange of information under favourable conditions in

preamble recalls Article 19 of the Universal Declaration, Articles 19 and 20 of the International Covenant on Civil and Political Rights and Resolutions 110(II) and 127(II) adopted by the General Assembly in 1947. Article III states that the mass media, by 'disseminating information on the aims, aspirations, cultures and needs of all peoples', and by drawing 'attention to the great evils which afflict humanity, such as poverty, malnutrition and diseases', can contribute to the elimination of ignorance and misunderstanding between peoples, thus countering aggressive war, racialism, apartheid, and other violations of human rights which are 'spawned by prejudice and ignorance'.

While the Declaration did not introduce any new principles concerning the prohibition of propaganda for war, it raised significant issues regarding the concentration in the hands of the most powerful states of control and influence over the global media and communications systems, a factor which had played a crucial role in the decision of many non-aligned states to support the inclusion of the prohibition of propaganda for war in the International Covenant on Civil and Political Rights.[104] Furthermore, in using the term 'incitement to war', it was the first major United Nations document to break from the practice followed since the adoption of the ICCPR of using the term 'propaganda for war'. Following the MacBride Commission's report to the twenty-first UNESCO General Conference in Belgrade in 1980,[105] many Western states became extremely frustrated with the perceived challenges to their role in the international community which they regarded as 'another of Moscow's tactics to use [developing] countries to push for international legalization of its own authoritarian and restrictive concept of communication'.[106] For these reasons the United Kingdom and the United States officially withdrew from UNESCO in 1984.[107]

iii. United Nations Convention on the Law of the Sea

An interesting if rarely invoked provision of public international law concerning propaganda threatening the security of a state is to be found in Article 19 of the United Nations Convention on the Law of the Sea (UNCLOS). Article

---

a sense of equality, justice and mutual advantage, (f) the responsibility of various actors in the process of information for its truthfulness and objectivity as well as for the particular social objectives to which the information activities are dedicated.' See further Jonathan Graubart, 'What's News: A Progressive Framework for Evaluating the International Debate over the News', 77 Calif L Rev 629 (1989).

[104] Joel R Paul, 'Images from Abroad: Making Direct Broadcasting by Satellites Safe for Sovereignty', 9 Hastings Int'l & Comp L Rev 329 (1986) 340.

[105] UNESCO Doc 21 C/PRG.IV/DR. 8, at 5 C (1980).

[106] Adeno Addis, 'International Propaganda and Developing Countries', 498.

[107] The United Kingdom rejoined UNESCO in 1997. The United States rejoined in 2002 with President Bush declaring to the 57th session of the General Assembly that '[a]s a symbol of our commitment to human dignity, the United States will return to UNESCO. This organization has been reformed and America will participate fully in its mission to advance human rights and tolerance and learning.'

19(2)(d) of UNCLOS provides that the passage of a foreign ship shall be considered to be prejudicial to the peace, good order, or security of the coastal state if it engages in 'any act of propaganda aimed at affecting the defence or security of the coastal State'.[108] In accordance with UNCLOS, should a ship engage in such propaganda while in the territorial seas of a State party to the Convention, the state has the right to prevent such a ship from enjoying the right to innocent passage which provides that a ship of any nation may travel through the territorial waters of any coastal state. Reference to this provision is illustrative of the fact that states have continually considered the threat posed by hostile international propaganda to warrant regulation under international law.

The proceedings of the three conferences, which led to the adoption of UNCLOS, shed little light on the meaning of propaganda for the purposes of Article 19. The first conference was held in 1958 with a draft text prepared by the International Law Commission serving as the basis of negotiations. Article 15 of this draft addressed innocent passage but did not detail any particular acts which could result in a ship losing its right to innocent passage.[109] Coastal states wished to protect their military and economic interests and the conferences were dominated by debates as to whether military vessels could enjoy the right to innocent passage or whether fishing activities would negate this right.[110]

The first proposals that acts of propaganda could negate the right to innocent passage were submitted at the third Conference on the Law of the Sea in 1974 by non-aligned states. It was proposed that 'any act of propaganda affecting the defence or security of the coastal state' would constitute a violation of the right to innocent passage.[111] A working paper submitted by the Rapporteur General also proposed that '[a]ny act of propaganda affecting the security of the coastal State would render passage not to be innocent'.[112] At the Conference's sixth session in 1977, Article 19(2)(d) of a negotiating text proposed that passage would be rendered as not innocent by 'any act of propaganda aimed at affecting the defence or security of the coastal State'.[113] This text was retained in the

---

[108] Article 19(2)d, United Nations Convention on the Law of the Sea, adopted 10 December 1982, 1833 UNTS 397.

[109] 'Article 15(3): Passage is innocent so long as a ship does not use the territorial sea for committing any acts prejudicial to the security of the coastal State or contrary to the present rules, or to other rules of international law.' A/3159, UN Conference on the Law of the Sea, 209–21.

[110] Comments by Governments on the Draft Articles Concerning the Law of the Sea adopted by the International Law Commission at its Eight Session (Preparatory Document no 5). Doc A/Conf 13/5 and Add 1 to 4 [23 October 1957] para 6.

[111] Malaysia, Morocco, Oman, and Yemen: Draft Articles on Navigation through the Territorial Seas, Including Straits Used for International Navigation, Doc A/Conf 62/C.2/L.16. Article 3.2(f), 3rd Conference, vol iii (1974) 192.

[112] Statement of Activities of the Conference during its First and Second Sessions Prepared by the Rapporteur-General: Mr Rattray (Jamaica). Doc A/Conf 62/L.8/Rev 1, 3rd Conference, vol iii (1974) 93.

[113] Informal Composite Negotiating Text, Doc A/Conf 62/WP.10, 1977, 3rd Conference, vol viii (1976–7) 1.

Draft Convention[114] presented to the Conference at its tenth session in 1981, and subsequently included in the final text of UNCLOS.

Throughout the drafting process delegates had focused primarily on the applicability of the regime of innocent passage to military ships, rather than discussing specific acts which could negate the right to innocent passage. Given the repeated demands of many of the developing nations that the right of innocent passage should only be enjoyed by foreign warships that had either given prior notice to or received authorization to pass through coastal waters, it remains the case that the mere presence of a foreign warship in the territorial waters of another state may be construed as being an act of propaganda under Article 19(2)(d).

Such an incident arose in 2001 when an attempt by North Korean merchant ships to employ the right to innocent passage in the coastal waters of South Korea led to a stand-off with the South Korean navy. After having demanded that the merchant ships leave its territorial waters, South Korea finally acceded to their remonstrance that they were legitimately exercising the right to innocent passage. Coming at a time of tension between the two states, formally in a state of war, it has been suggested that the presence of North Korean ships could have been viewed as an act of propaganda which affected the peace and security of South Korea.[115] The possibility that the right of innocent passage could be manipulated for propaganda reasons had been noted at the 1976 Conference on the Law of the Sea where the United Arab Emirates asserted that no state should be permitted to violate the peaceful uses of the oceans 'by parading its maritime power in areas of tension'.[116]

iv. Bilateral Treaties

Although Martin assumed that after the Second World War, 'when the international propaganda activities of the majority of states were increased and regular propaganda programs became the accepted thing', no further bilateral treaties outlawing harmful international propaganda would be signed,[117] states have in fact continued to conclude agreements which attempt to regulate 'subversive' propaganda. In April 1948, India and Pakistan signed an agreement whereby each undertook to ensure that state organizations handling publicity and media 'refrain from and control' propaganda against the other state which was 'likely to inflame, or cause fear or alarm to, the population or a section of the population in either Dominion'.[118] Similar provisions are to be found in several peace

---

[114] Draft Convention on the Law of the Sea, Doc A/Conf 62/L.78. UN Conferences on the Law of the Sea, Official Records, 3rd Conference, vol xv (1976–7) 172.

[115] Stephen Kong, 'The Right of Innocent Passage: A Case Study on Two Koreas', 11 Minn J Global Trade 373 (2002).

[116] UN Conferences on the Law of the Sea, 3rd Conference, vol v (1976–7), 64, para 4.

[117] L John Martin, *International Propaganda*, 108.

[118] Section 2(iii)(a) and (b), UN Doc E/CN.4/Sub 1/105, 29. John B Whitton, 'International Propaganda', 398.

treaties signed during the Cold War. Article 5 of a bilateral agreement between Israel and Lebanon, signed 17 May 1983, provided that, '[c]onsistent with the termination of the state of war and within the framework of their constitutional provisions, the Parties will abstain from any form of hostile propaganda against each other'.[119] Article 3(2)(f) of the Agreement on Non-Aggression and Good Neighbourliness between South Africa and Mozambique of 16 March 1984 obliged the parties to 'eliminate and prohibit the installation in their respective territories of radio broadcasting stations, including unofficial or clandestine broadcasts, for the elements that carry out [...] violence, terrorism or aggression against the territorial integrity or political independence of the other'.[120] Article 5 further obligated the parties to 'prohibit within their territory acts of propaganda that incite a war of aggression against the other'.[121] Article II(10) of a 1988 Treaty between Afghanistan and Pakistan obliged each of the parties '[t]o abstain from any defamatory campaign, vilification or hostile propaganda for the purposes of intervening or interfering in the internal affairs of the other High Contracting Party'.[122] A further example of such bilateral agreements is the Gaza–Jericho Agreement signed by Israel and the Palestinian Liberation Organization (PLO) in 1994. Article XII, concerning relations between Israel and the PLO, sought to regulate hostile propaganda on the part of the signatories as well as private individuals and groups within their jurisdiction.[123] Paragraph 1 provided that each party 'shall seek to foster mutual understanding and tolerance and shall accordingly abstain from incitement, including hostile propaganda, against each other and, without derogating from the principle of freedom of expression, shall take legal measures to prevent such incitement by any organizations, groups or individuals within their jurisdiction'.[124]

C. Summary

Although the United Nations General Assembly clearly established the existence of a state obligation to refrain from propaganda for war, evidenced through repeated Resolutions and Declarations, enthusiasm for the principle was always weak on the

---

[119] Israel–Lebanon: Agreement on Withdrawal of Troops from Lebanon, 22 ILM 708 (1983).

[120] Agreement on Non-Aggression and Good Neighbourliness between the Government of the Republic of South Africa and the Government of the People's Republic of Mozambique, 23 ILM 282 (1984).

[121] ibid.

[122] Bilateral Agreement between the Republic of Afghanistan and the Islamic Republic of Pakistan on the Principles of Mutual Relations, in Particular on Non-Interference and Non-Intervention, 27 ILM 581 (1988).

[123] Toby R Unger, 'The Status of the Arts in an Emerging State of Palestine', 14 Ariz J Int'l & Comp L 193 (1997).

[124] Israel–Palestine Liberation Organization Agreement on the Gaza Strip and the Jericho Area, 33 ILM 622 (1994).

part of the Western liberal democracies, and appears to have completely dissipated since the collapse of the Soviet Union and the end of the Cold War. Following the adoption of the International Covenant on Civil and Political Rights by the General Assembly no new Resolutions were passed directly addressing propaganda for war, suggesting that many in the Assembly considered the Covenant and international human rights law as providing an adequate means of dealing with the issue.

3

The *Travaux Préparatoires* of Article 20(1) of the International Covenant on Civil and Political Rights

As the early sessions of the General Assembly were condemning propaganda for war through resolutions, the incorporation of a prohibition of propaganda for war in the International Bill of Rights was the subject of prolonged debate at the Commission on Human Rights and the Third Committee of the General Assembly. Article 20(1) of the International Covenant on Civil and Political Rights as adopted sets forth the obligation on States parties that, '[a]ny propaganda for war shall be prohibited by law'.[1]

Article 20 as a whole has been described as representing 'an alien element' in the system of the Covenant on the grounds that it does not set forth a specific human right but rather establishes limitations on other rights, particularly the Article 19 right to freedom of expression.[2] Difficulty in seeking to apply the provision has consistently revolved around definitional quandaries and the question of the meaning of the term 'propaganda for war'. Given the lack of relevant judicial or academic analysis, it is necessary in order to determine the meaning of the provision to turn to the *travaux préparatoires* of the Covenant. These not only provide a crucial resource for demystifying the 'alien' nature of this provision, but the discourse between the various delegations illustrates vividly the conflicting intentions brought to the drafting table by both the major power blocs in the Cold War and the non-aligned states. The positions adopted by many states during drafting, whether on ideological, political, or practical grounds, have proven to be of continuing significance, and the contemporary faultlines between States parties which accept or reject the provision remain closely linked to the geopolitical environment of 1961.

Over the fifteen years during which the Covenant was drafted myriad proposals and amendments concerning 'incitement to war', 'war propaganda', and

---

[1] International Covenant on Civil and Political Rights, Adopted and opened for signature, ratification and accession by General Assembly Resolution 2200A (XXI) of 16 December 1966, entry into force 23 March 1976, 999 UNTS 171.

[2] Manfred Nowak, *U.N. Covenant on Civil and Political Rights: CCPR Commentary* (2nd edn), 468.

'propaganda for war' were presented in relation to both Article 19 and Article 20 of the final document. In endeavouring to explain the rationale behind the different proposals and to determine the meaning of 'propaganda for war' this chapter will analyse the drafting process in three distinct sections. Sections A and B will focus on the initial phase of drafting, which took place primarily at the Commission on Human Rights (Commission) from 1947 until 1953. Section A will consider the ill-fated efforts of the communist states to have 'war propaganda' included as a ground for permissible restriction on the right to freedom of expression. Section B will analyse the tensions relating to the inclusion in the Draft Covenant of a prohibition of incitement to hatred and violence which was to provide the basis for the final text of Article 20. Section C concerns the seminal debates held at the sixteenth session of the Third Committee of the General Assembly, meeting in New York in 1961, which concluded with the adoption of the Covenant's prohibition of propaganda for war. When studying the progress of these debates it may be helpful to bear in mind Whitton and Larson's observation that '[t]rue democracy is founded on the freedom to propagandise, and the United Nations is the greatest forum for rival international propaganda the world has ever seen'.[3]

A. 'War Propaganda' as a Limitation to Freedom of Expression

i. Drafting Committee of the Commission on Human Rights (1947)

The Commission's Drafting Committee held its first session in June 1947 and forwarded a Draft Covenant which had been proposed by the United Kingdom for consideration by the Commission on Human Rights. The right to freedom of expression set forth in this draft was not an absolute right and provided that:

1. Every person shall be free to express and publish his ideas orally, in writing, in the form of art, or otherwise.
2. Every person shall be free to receive and disseminate information of all kinds, including facts, critical comment and ideas by books, newspapers, or oral instruction, and by the medium of all lawfully operated devices.
3. The freedoms of speech and information referred to in the preceding paragraphs of this Article may be subject only to necessary restrictions, penalties and liabilities with regard to: matters which must remain secret in the interests of national safety; publications intended or likely to incite persons to alter by violence the system of Government, or to promote disorder or crime; obscene publications; (publications aimed at the suppression of human rights and fundamental freedoms); publications injurious to the independence of the judiciary or the fair conduct of legal proceedings; and expressions or publications which libel or slander the reputations of other persons.[4]

---

[3] John B Whitton and Arthur Larson, *Propaganda*, 9.
[4] Article 9 of the draft submitted by the Drafting Committee set forth the right of freedom of expression. This was renamed Article 11 by the Commission. E/CN.4/21, Annexe G. E/CN.4/AC.3/SR.6, 2.

The manner in which restrictions on the right to freedom of expression should be formulated was to be a contentious issue throughout the drafting process. Preliminary discussions focused on whether the limitations clause should be a brief statement of general principles or whether it should be a full catalogue of specific limitations. In response to a criticism from Yugoslavia as to the number of restrictions set forth in paragraph 3, the Commission Chairman referred to a text submitted to him by the Coordinating Board of Jewish Organizations which had advocated the inclusion of restrictions on information and propaganda of a fascist nature.[5] He stated that this point should not be overlooked for fear that freedom of information may be interpreted as an encouragement to subversive propaganda.[6]

Of the limitations set forth in this draft article, both the reference to incitement to violence and the restriction located in brackets that 'publications aimed at the suppression of human rights and fundamental freedoms' were not to be protected under the right to freedom of expression are of particular note. The additional restrictions were neither surprising nor overly controversial since similar provisions were to be found in the domestic laws of most countries at this time. The principle that the right to freedom of expression should be tempered by the overriding aim of protecting human rights was to set the template for the debates on whether the draft Covenant should include a prohibition of propaganda for war, and was relied upon both by advocates and opponents of such proposals.

ii. Commission on Human Rights (1948)

The initial stages of drafting a Covenant on Civil and Political Rights overlapped substantially with efforts at drafting a Convention on the Right to Freedom of Information and the Press. Dr Charles Malik, the United Nations Rapporteur on Freedom of Information, proposed to the Working Group on a Convention for Human Rights that when the Commission referred the texts on the right to freedom of expression to the Sub-Commission on Freedom of Information, the following observations should be added:

The Commission on Human Rights resolves:

1. that freedom of expression and of information is, in its opinion, one of the most fundamental freedoms;
2. that this freedom must be included in a Convention on Human Rights;
3. that the Commission, having before it two texts on this subject, one submitted by the USA, and one by the UK, decides not to elaborate the final text of the Convention on this question until it hears the views of the Sub-Commission on Freedom of Information and of the Press and of the International Conference on Freedom of Information, and remits to these two texts for their consideration;

---

[5] E/CN.4/AC.3/SR.6, 3.　　　[6] ibid.

4. that, in their consideration, the above-mentioned two bodies should take into account the two Resolutions of the General Assembly on this question (Document A/C.1/228 'Measures to be taken against Propaganda and the Inciters of a new War' and Document A/C.3/180 'Slanderous Information');
5. that they should also consider the social, economic and political conditions which will render this fundamental freedom real.[7]

China supported this proposal, but requested that the text be supplemented by the submission of the Coordinating Board of Jewish Organizations.[8] The Rapporteur concurred and proposed an additional, sixth point which stated:

6. that they be requested also to consider the possibility of excluding from this freedom any publication or other media of public expression which aim to inflict injury, or incite prejudice or hatred, against persons or groups because of their race, language, religion or national origin.[9]

Paragraph 4 of the Rapporteur's proposal referring to the General Assembly Resolutions is of particular relevance since it demonstrates that the issue of propaganda for war was on the Commission's agenda from the very outset of the drafting process. The first five points of the proposal were adopted unanimously whilst the sixth was adopted with four votes in favour and one abstention.[10]

The initial drafting phase ended at the second session of the Drafting Committee in May 1948 with a brief discussion of the text of Article 17 on the right to freedom of expression which had been submitted to the Commission by the UN Conference on Freedom of Information. Article 17 provided that:

1. Every person shall have the right to freedom of thought and the right to freedom of expression without interference by governmental action; these rights shall include freedom to hold opinions, to seek, receive and impart information and ideas, regardless of frontiers, either orally, by written or printed matter, in the form of art, or by legally operated visual or auditory devices.
2. The right to freedom of expression carries with it duties and responsibilities and may, therefore, be subject to penalties, liabilities or restrictions clearly defined by law, but only with regard to:
   (a) Matters which must remain secret in the interest of national security;
   (b) Expressions which invite persons to alter by violence the system of government;
   (c) Expressions which directly incite persons to commit criminal acts;
   (d) Expressions which are obscene;
   (e) Expressions injurious to the fair conduct of legal proceedings;
   (f) Infringements of literary or artistic rights;
   (g) Expressions about other persons, natural or legal, which defame their reputations or are otherwise injurious to them without benefiting the public;
   (h) The systematic diffusion of deliberately false or distorted reports which undermine friendly relations between peoples and States.

---

[7] Working Group on Convention on Human Rights, E/CN.4/AC.3/SR.6, 5–6.
[8] ibid 6.   [9] ibid 6–7.
[10] ibid 7.

A State may establish on reasonable terms a right to reply or a similar corrective remedy.

3. Measures shall be taken to promote the freedom of information through the elimination of political, economic, technical and other obstacles which are likely to hinder the free flow of information.

4. Nothing in this Article shall be deemed to affect the right of any State to control the entry of persons into its territory or the period of their residence therein.[11]

The Chairman of the Drafting Committee noted that the Commission had previously postponed consideration of Article 17 until it had received the views of the Sub-Commission on the Freedom of Information and the Press and of the UN Conference on Freedom of Information.[12] The United Kingdom proposed therefore that the Drafting Committee should send the text of the Conference of Freedom of Information to the Commission, with the addendum that 'it had had no time to consider the article thoroughly'.[13] The USA agreed that limitations to the right to freedom of expression should be set forth in the Covenant, suggesting that if it were decided to list the specific limitations they would propose additional ones.[14] The USA did voice opposition to paragraph 2(h) concerning the dissemination of false news,[15] and although no explanation was proffered, the issue of whether false news published with the intention of disrupting international peace was to be addressed in the Covenant would resurface throughout the drafting process. The text of Article 17 did not refer directly to propaganda or incitement to war, but the principle that expression inciting to crime or violence was not protected under the right to freedom of expression can be deduced from subparagraphs 2(b) and (c) which permitted restriction of '[e]xpressions which invite persons to alter by violence the system of government' and '[e]xpressions which directly incite persons to commit criminal acts'. The USSR was not satisfied with the scope of these limitations since:

[…] the article as proposed would not prevent the enemies of the democratic order from working to undermine democracy and that human rights were therefore imperilled. The remnants of Nazism and fascism would have an opportunity to disseminate propaganda since there were no concrete provisions against such action. The article should specifically state the necessity for preventing propaganda by Nazis or fascists or propaganda based on racial or religious discrimination.[16]

Although the latter proposal to include provisions relating to the prohibition of discrimination in the article on freedom of expression met with little support, delegates of the USSR were to reintroduce it on several occasions during the

---

[11] E/CN.4/272, 3; Document E/800. (Reproduced as Annexe B to the report of the 3rd session of the Commission on Human Rights.)
[12] E/CN.4/AC.1/SR.26, 5.
[13] ibid 8.
[14] ibid 8–9.
[15] ibid 9.
[16] ibid 6 (Mr Pavlov).

drafting process. The French delegate, supported by his Chilean counterpart,[17] emphasized his country's determination to protect itself from a repeat of the suffering it had endured 'at the hands of the nazis and fascists', but felt that the terms 'Nazism' and 'Fascism' belonged in the past. He considered Article 17 to have made 'sufficient provisions for guarding against dangers such as those words had signified in the past as well as against dangers that might arise in the future'.[18] Similar sentiments had been aired during the debates on the drafting of the Universal Declaration of Human Rights, when the Canadian delegate asserted that '[t]he term "fascism" which had once had a definite meaning was now being blurred by the abuse of applying it to any person or idea which was not communist'.[19] Thus, without alteration by the USSR's comments, the Drafting Committee decided to submit to the Commission the text of Article 17 as had been proposed by the Conference on Freedom of Information.[20]

iii. Commission on Human Rights (1949)

The Commission's fifth session convened in 1949 with the Chairman highlighting amendments to Article 17 which had been submitted by France[21] and the USSR. The USSR's amendment was the first to include a reference to incitement to war and proposed that '[t]he use of freedom of speech and of the press for the purposes of propagating Fascism and aggression or of inciting war between nations shall not be tolerated'.[22] This proposal was quickly replaced and a subsequent amendment submitted by the USSR replaced the phrase 'propagating

---

[17] E/CN.4/AC.1/SR.26, 7.   [18] ibid 6 (Mr Ordonneau).
[19] Johannes Morsink, *The Universal Declaration of Human Rights*, 69.
[20] E/CN.4/AC.1/SR.26, 9.
[21] Text submitted by the Representative of France:
    '1. La parole est libre. Toute personne est libre d'exprimer et de publier ses idées par tout moyen de son choix.
    2. Toute personne est libre de recevoir et de diffuser des informations de toute espèce, notamment des faits, des appréciations critiques et des idées par le livre, le journal, l'enseignement oral ou tout autre moyen.
    3. Les libertés visées aux paragraphes précédents ne peuvent être soumises qu'aux restrictions, sanctions et responsabilités fixées par la loi pour la sauvegarde de l'ordre public, de la sécurité nationale et des bonnes mœurs et le respect des droits, de la réputation et des libertés d'autrui' (E/CN.4/272, 3).
[22] Text submitted by the Representative of the USSR:
    1. In accordance with the principles of democracy and in the interests of strengthening international co-operation and world peace, every person shall be guaranteed by law the right to the free expression of his opinions and, in particular, to freedom of speech and of the press, freedom of assembly and freedom of artistic representation. The use of freedom of speech and of the press for the purposes of propagating Fascism and aggression or of inciting war between nations shall not be tolerated.
    2. In order to ensure the right of the free expression of opinion for large sections of the peoples and for their organisations, State assistance and co-operation shall be given in providing the material resources (premises, printing presses, paper, and the like) necessary for the publication of democratic organs of the press' (E/CN.4/272, 3).

Fascism and aggression or of inciting war between nations' with the term 'war propaganda' to read:

In the interests of democracy, everyone shall be guaranteed by law the right of free expression of opinion, and in particular freedom of speech, of the Press and of artistic expression, provided that freedom of speech and of the Press is not used for war propaganda, for inciting enmity among nations, racial discrimination and the dissemination of slanderous rumours.[23]

Although there was minimal discussion of these proposals, the change effected by the USSR's deletion of the phrase 'inciting war between nations' was to prove of fundamental significance. The term 'war propaganda', although present in Resolutions of the General Assembly, was without precedent in an international legal instrument and its meaning was not specified by the USSR.

At this point in the Cold War Western capitalism was considered by the Soviets to be but the latest manifestation of fascism, and the stated purpose of the proposal was to check the activities of the Western media and specifically 'the warmongering propaganda and calumnies which were being made by a press serving the interests of the armaments industry'.[24] In replacing the distinct term 'incitement to war' with the broader term 'war propaganda', and advocating its inclusion in such a partisan manner, the USSR significantly limited the possibility that other delegates would look with favour on future proposals along the same lines. The failure to define 'propaganda' essentially meant that the Soviets had removed the term 'fascism' which had been criticized on definitional grounds, and replaced it with another term 'propaganda', which in the eyes of the West suffered from the exact same deficiencies in that it could be used by the Soviet states in order to manipulate human rights for repressive purposes.

The Commission voted at this point to follow the lead of the General Assembly which had postponed consideration of the Draft Convention on Freedom of Information by postponing consideration of Article 17 and the amendments submitted thereto until its next session for fear that the United Nations would draw up two separate texts on freedom of information.[25]

iv. Commission on Human Rights (1950)

The Commission returned to the discussion of the limitations clause of Article 17 at its sixth session, as well as an amendment proposed by Yugoslavia and a draft

---

[23] E/CN.4/220.

[24] E/CN.4/SR.120, 5. The USSR's delegate, Mr Pavlov, added that fascism could not be beaten by persuasion alone and that while 'the common sense and the intelligence of the popular masses were a powerful factor in the struggle against fascism, it had to be recognised that the campaigns for the propagation of distorted news which were being carried on in some countries in favor of so-called freedom of information and of the Press, sometimes prevented those factors from having full play, and enabled fascism to develop underground and manifest itself unexpectedly in all its strength'. ibid 8–10.

[25] ibid 3–4; 12:3 with 1 abstention.

proposed by the USA.[26] Amendments to the latter draft were also proposed by the UK,[27] France,[28] Egypt,[29] and India.[30] Yugoslavia's proposal guaranteed the right to freedom of expression provided it was not used for purposes including 'propaganda for aggression or war'.[31] Yugoslavia's delegate asserted that this amendment was based on 'a fundamental principle' necessary for the 'defence of democracy'[32] which flowed from the desire 'to prevent any attempt to create conditions favourable to a new world war'.[33] Warning the Commission that freedom of information lent itself to exploitation more than any other, he stated that if misused it 'could even run counter to the fundamental aim of the Charter, namely, the maintenance of peace'.[34]

The USA rejected this argument, accusing the Yugoslav amendment of being 'founded upon a concept of a society indoctrinated by the State',[35] and suggesting that since the national difficulties with propaganda which Yugoslavia was claiming to be suffering were temporary, and the Covenant was permanent, there was no need to include any such provision.[36] The US amendment proposed that a general limitations clause be adopted providing that the right to freedom of expression 'shall be subject only to such limitations as are pursuant to law and necessary for the protection of national security, public order, safety, health or morals, or the rights and freedoms of others'.[37] The USA also opposed a French proposal which included the phrase 'le respect des droits',[38] on the grounds that this might serve as an arbitrary basis for limiting freedom of information since governments would merely have to enact legislation designating any act as a crime in order to be able to prohibit or punish any expression relating to that act.[39]

Before voting on the US proposal delegates briefly discussed the meaning of the phrase 'public order' found in the French amendment. Although few delegations elaborated on the intersection between 'public order' or 'national security' and 'propaganda for war', several States parties which subsequently entered reservations and declarations to Article 20(1) of the Covenant, including France, were to claim that the concepts were closely related. These arguments, which we will return to in the next chapter, can be traced to the interpretation advanced by the French delegate, Professor René Cassin, who understood a prohibition of

---

[26] E/CN.4/365.   [27] E/CN.4/440.
[28] E/CN.4/438/Rev 1.
[29] Egypt's amendment, subsequently withdrawn, sought to add the following limitation to the right to freedom of expression: '[a]ny offence committed through the press against the person of a sovereign or the head of a foreign State and likely to impair the friendly relations existing between States.' E/CN.4/434. On the subject of defamatory propaganda against heads of state see BS Murty, *Propaganda and World Public Order*, 222–30 and John B Whitton and Arthur Larson, *Propaganda*, 147–56.
[30] E/CN.4/424.   [31] E/CN.4/220.
[32] E/CN.4/SR.162, para 18 (Mr Jevremovic).
[33] ibid, para 37.
[34] E/CN.4/SR.166, para 59.
[35] E/CN.4/SR.163, para 38.
[36] ibid, para 46.
[37] E.CN.4/365.
[38] 'respect for law'; E/CN.4/433.
[39] E/CN.4/SR.162, para 11.

propaganda for war as being unnecessary since the aim of such a provision could be achieved by reference to 'public order'. He considered the French amendment to be adequate in this regard since 'it was unquestionable that in a genuinely democratic society a state of peace was indispensable for national security, and anything which threatened peace could only be considered as running counter to public order'.[40] This interpretation was opposed by Yugoslavia which argued that the phrase 'national security' would not prevent the dissemination of information for purposes of propaganda for war, and that neither could such general terms as 'public order' and 'national security' offer the necessary guarantees.[41] As will be seen when analysing the interpretation of the prohibition of propaganda for war in the following section, Cassin's idealism has yet to be achieved in practice by the liberal democracies which continue to rely upon his interpretation to justify their refusal to fulfil their obligations under Article 20(1).

As debate continued, the US proposal, revised by a United Kingdom amendment,[42] was unanimously adopted.[43] This provided:

3. The right to seek, receive and impart information and ideas shall be subject only to such limitations as are provided by law and necessary in the interests 1) of national security, public order, safety, health and morals 2) and for protection of the rights, freedoms or reputations of others.[44]

The Commission then turned its attention to India's amendment which sought to add to the limitations clause of the UK amendment[45] an 'essential'[46] provision to permit the restriction of expression 'for the prevention of spreading deliberately false or distorted reports which undermine friendly relations between peoples and States'.[47] The Western states were broadly opposed to such a provision and the USA, claiming that the Draft Covenant 'already contained a general statement on freedom of expression and a list of general exceptions, which covered all possible general cases',[48] saw a paradox in the Indian proposal insofar as it would require censorship, that 'weapon of totalitarianism',[49] in order to determine what the true facts were. The United Kingdom acknowledged the threat posed by false and distorted reports but also stressed that the adoption of the Indian amendment would require unacceptable censorship.[50] It did suggest that

---

[40] E/CN.4/SR.166, para 63 (Mr Cassin).
[41] E/CN.4/SR.167, para 17.
[42] E/CN.4/SR.165, para 105.
[43] E/CN.4/SR.167, para 22.
[44] ibid, para 23.
[45] E/CN.4/365.
[46] E/CN.4/SR.167, para 26 (Mrs Mehta).
[47] E/CN.4/424.
[48] E/CN.4/SR.167, para 27.
[49] ibid, para 41.
[50] The United Kingdom's delegate warned that, 'in the effort to eliminate that danger, all information on foreign countries would have to be made subject to censorship, thus destroying the very freedom which the Covenant sought to safeguard'. ibid, para 35.

such proposals could be discussed in relation to the draft provision on the prohibition of incitement to violence, but not in the context of the right to freedom
of expression for fear that it 'could be interpreted to prevent the free discussion of
foreign relations and foreign policy, matters which the UK felt should be open to
debate by the public'.[51]

France[52] and the USA[53] suggested that while the Indian proposal was out of
context with the Draft Covenant, it could be more appropriately discussed in
relation to an instrument such as the Convention on the International Right of
Correction,[54] and that the General Assembly might decide to introduce further
safeguards of freedom of information in a separate convention. Denmark considered the term 'public order' in the approved text to cover the limitations proposed
by India and considered any further limitations to be 'superfluous'.[55] Australia
also considered India to have submitted a valid case and, whilst agreeing in principle that it called for some kind of action, asserted that such a provision would be
almost impossible to enforce by law.[56]

Lebanon challenged these states to suggest some positive means of eliminating false and distorted reports and slanderous information media.[57] Yugoslavia
considered the Indian proposal to be in harmony with the spirit of the UN
Charter, particularly Article 1.[58] It further claimed that censorship in this regard
was irrelevant, pointing out that while the amendment did not specify who was
to determine the truth or falsity of reports, neither did Article 17 stipulate who
was to determine what was necessary for the protection of 'public order' or other
stated restrictions, but that 'obviously the same criterion would apply'.[59] India's
delegate persevered in her efforts to have the proposal adopted and rejected suggestions that it would require the institution of a form of censorship, arguing that
'not only the press, but the radio, cinema and individuals should be prevented
from spreading deliberately false and distorted information [and] be made to realise their responsibility for maintaining peace in the world'.[60] Nevertheless, when
the Chairman put the Indian amendment to the vote, it was narrowly rejected
6:5 with four abstentions.[61] The Chairman then put to the vote Article 17,
amended as a whole, paragraph 2 of which read:

---

[51] Ms Bowie, E/CN.4/SR.162, para 34.
[52] E/CN.4/SR.167, para 46.
[53] ibid, para 42.
[54] Convention on the International Right of Correction, 435 UNTS 191, entered into force
24 August 1962.
[55] E/CN.4/SR.167, para 36.
[56] ibid, para 48.
[57] ibid, para 38, (Mr Malik).
[58] ibid, paras 31–2.
[59] ibid, para 44.
[60] ibid, para 47.
[61] ibid, para 51.

The right to seek, receive and impart information and ideas carries with it special duties and responsibilities and may therefore be subject to certain penalties, liabilities and restrictions, but these shall be such only as are provided by law and are necessary for the protection of national security, public order, safety, health and morals, or of the rights, freedoms or reputations of others.[62]

This formula was adopted 13:0 with 2 abstentions.[63] The United Kingdom abstained from the vote despite being in agreement with much of the text, partly because the limitations set forth in paragraph 2 were overly broad.[64] India compromised and supported the vote but expressed the hope that a provision prohibiting the spread of deliberately false or distorted reports might yet be included in the Covenant.[65]

Yugoslavia also abstained from voting on Article 17 as a whole, both on the grounds that general phrases such as 'public order' and 'national security', which cast 'a deplorable shadow on the entire Covenant', were open to abuse, and because the provision did not adequately frame the right to freedom of expression and information as a collective right.[66] Requesting a vote be taken on his proposal, the delegate of Yugoslavia highlighted the frequent tendency of great powers to use their overwhelming resources to limit the freedom of smaller states and make them subservient.[67] He claimed that Yugoslavia, as well as many other states, 'had been the victim of repeated aggression by more powerful States and was forced to make strenuous and constant efforts to safeguard its national existence and preserve its independence'.[68] The Yugoslav proposal for an alternative text of Article 17 which would have included 'propaganda for aggression or war'[69] as a limitation to the right to freedom of expression received little support and was rejected 5:1 with 8 abstentions.[70] Australia explained its vote against the proposal by stating that whilst not in opposition to its principles, the text was not 'suitable for inclusion in the Covenant and did not provide an effective substitute for the basic text just adopted'.[71] Chile had been opposed to the Yugoslav proposal to replace the terms 'national security' and 'public order' with a specific reference to what it termed 'incitement to war', on the grounds that previous proposals along these lines had been politically motivated campaigns 'of slander against the

---

[62] Doc E/1681, Article 14.

[63] E/CN.4/SR.167, para 55.

[64] ibid, para 62. The second ground related to paragraph 1 which provided for the right to '[f]reedom of opinion without interference'. The United Kingdom found this provision to be very difficult to achieve in practice. Similar sentiments were aired by the USA which voted in favour but reserved the right to study further the phrase 'without governmental interference'. ibid, para 59. France also voted in favour, but agreed with the United Kingdom 'that governmental interference was sometimes necessary'. ibid, para 65.

[65] ibid, para 63 (Mrs Mehta).

[66] ibid, para 58.   [67] ibid, para 69.

[68] ibid, para 70.   [69] E/CN.4/220.

[70] E/CN.4/SR.167, para 71; It was defeated 5:1 with 8 abstentions.

[71] ibid, para 72.

democratic press'.[72] As the debates wore on, the Chilean delegation was nonetheless to become one of the strongest, most coherent, and rational advocates of the inclusion in the Covenant of a prohibition of propaganda for war.

The question of where the threat of propaganda might come from was not discussed in any detail, and it was generally assumed that the press and the media were the primary instigators of propaganda for war. This is a crucial aspect of discussions on the prohibition of propaganda for war in international law. Since it is the state which has traditionally conducted the most effective propaganda campaigns, permitting governments to restrict the right to freedom of expression in order to prevent propaganda for war was seen by many as paradoxically bolstering the state's ability to conduct such propaganda. The delegate of the Philippines, for example, opposed the Indian amendment due to concerns that it would accord governments greater ability to employ censorship and control over the media in order to disseminate negative propaganda. Citing the fact that the first measure taken by the Japanese occupying forces in the Philippines during the Second World War had been to suppress all newspapers, he stated that '[r]ecent history seemed to indicate that freedom of information was most effectively abused by the propaganda machine of the State when the State overstepped its powers and encroached on the freedom of individuals'.[73] Given the opposition on freedom of expression grounds to the inclusion of a prohibition of propaganda for war in the Covenant, it is necessary to consider delegates' statements in light of the above paradox. The central issue here, as with all other provisions of international law, is holding the state to account for its obligations to ensure the protection of human rights. Once again the subject of propaganda for war was removed from the Commission's agenda, and at the second reading of the Draft Covenant on Human Rights, Article 17 was renamed Article 14.[74]

v. Third Committee of the General Assembly (1950)

The USSR, supported by Poland,[75] the Ukrainian SSR,[76] and the Byelorussian SSR,[77] each of which spoke of the need to ensure that propaganda inciting to

---

[72] E/CN.4/SR.163, para 33.

[73] E/CN.4/SR.167, para 49.

[74] E/CN.4/SR.200.

[75] Poland's delegate stated that Article 14 required a clause stressing the peaceful nature all information should have in order to 'counteract propaganda of aggression, and national, religious and racial hatred'. A/C.3/SR.290, para 5.

[76] The delegate of the Ukrainian Soviet Socialist Republic stated that the Draft Covenant should help to strengthen democracy and peace and should struggle against fascism and warmongering, and criticized the draft's omission of any reference to propaganda for Nazism, fascism, or racist views, which he argued should be prohibited, as should also any incitement to war and enmity between nations. A/C.3/SR.291, para 12.

[77] The delegate of the Byelorussian Soviet Socialist Republic stated that the rights proclaimed in Article 14 would be useless if not supplemented by a limitation prohibiting their enjoyment 'by

war was prohibited under the Covenant, kept the issue of 'war propaganda' on the drafting programme by reintroducing the proposal it had made at the Commission in 1949 to insert the following sentence into Article 14:

In the interests of democracy, everyone shall be guaranteed by law the right of freedom of expression of opinion, and in particular freedom of speech, of the Press and of artistic expression, provided that freedom of speech and of the press is not used for war propaganda, for inciting to enmity among nations, racial discrimination and the dissemination of slanderous rumours.[78]

Yugoslavia agreed with what had been said by the representatives of Poland and the Ukrainian SSR but challenged them to actually implement such ideals in their relations with Yugoslavia since, 'without such application, they were just empty words'.[79] El Salvador sought to balance the opposing views on the subject, warning that while laws against abuse of the freedom of the press were justified, they 'must always be invoked against the offender himself, never against the Press as an institution'.[80]

Although there was little focused debate on the question of propaganda for war, the delegate of Lebanon raised fundamental questions concerning the right to freedom of expression and the limitations which the Covenant would permit states to place on that right. Highlighting the threat posed to democracy and human rights by propaganda, he directed the Committee's attention to the role of propaganda as an instrument of state power and control over the individual. Referring to Nazi Germany, 'where propaganda had succeeded in convincing everybody that there was a state of emergency in which any restriction was permitted',[81] he asserted that limitations on the right to freedom of expression would be ineffective in combating propaganda since they accorded the state the potential power to control the flow of all information. Criticizing the phrase 'reasonable and necessary' in Article 14, he considered such a broad term as sufficient to enable a state to violate human rights with absolute impunity. He also claimed that the sole reason for the violation of human rights in vast regions of the world was that 'propaganda had convinced the populations that their country was in a state of emergency'.[82] He saw in the state structure the most potent threat to human rights and stressed that restrictions on the right to freedom of expression, even in the guise of a prohibition of propaganda for war, would not help the human rights

---

those who would use them against the interests of democracy and for the purposes of inciting to hatred and propaganda for a new war'. A/C.3/SR.291, para 59.

[78] A/C.3/SR.289, para 36.
[79] A/C.3/SR.291, para 23.
[80] ibid, para 60.
[81] A/C.3/SR.289, para 6.
[82] ibid, para 6.

situation, since only the maximum freedom of expression would be effective in combating the propaganda of the state.

Brazil asserted that difficulty in reaching consensus over the definition of particular words or phrases should not be allowed to derail efforts to include necessary restrictions, as '[p]recision of language was not perhaps of primary importance, since governments possessing clearly drafted constitutions were not always those which showed most respect for fundamental human rights and freedoms'.[83] Noting that agreement on the definition of propaganda was not the only way of ending the threat of propaganda, Brazil's delegate argued that the overall development of political education and the good faith of governments were essential elements in the establishment of a system in which the rights and freedoms in the Covenant would be respected.[84]

vi. Third Committee of the General Assembly (1952)

Frustration with the slow pace of drafting was apparent at the Third Committee's sixth session in 1952. Introducing a joint Draft Resolution,[85] France noted that all efforts made to improve the position regarding freedom of information, particularly the work of the UN Conference on Freedom of Information held at Geneva in 1948, had had no tangible result, despite all countries being in agreement as to the importance and urgency of the matter.[86] Similarly, Mexico stressed that the right to freedom of information should not be permitted to become a dead letter, 'but should receive, as it were, an infusion of new life at each session'.[87] Saudi Arabia acknowledged that distinguishing propaganda—which 'might either be positive, in the form of dramatization or exaggeration, or negative, as a conspiracy of silence'[88]—from genuine news was difficult, but nevertheless it was not impossible, since 'all that was necessary was the exercise of the moral sense'.[89] The Czechoslovak delegate highlighted the principles underlying General Assembly Resolution 110(II) to assert that it was a right, 'and even a duty, to disseminate true information with a view to strengthening co-operation and friendship among peoples, maintaining peace and counteracting plans for war'.[90] Concluding this discussion, Syria's delegate, drawing on the prolonged experience of UN discussions of the rights to freedom of information and expression, wishfully suggested 'that in future, politics as far as possible be banished from the discussions on Freedom of Information'.[91]

[83] A/C.3/SR.289, para 24.
[84] ibid.
[85] A/C.3/L.227/Rev 1.
[86] A/C.3/SR.412, para 67.
[87] A/C.3/SR.414, para 11.
[88] ibid, para 62 (Mr Baroody).
[89] ibid.
[90] A/C.3/SR.415, para 48.
[91] ibid, para 50.

vii. Commission on Human Rights (1952)

At this stage in the drafting process, while delegates were generally agreed on the formula in which the positive right to freedom of expression would be set forth, they remained divided on the issue of how the permitted limitations to this right were to be worded. The issue which shaped almost the entirety of this phase of the debate was the question of 'war propaganda' and how or whether the Draft Covenant was to approach it. Although the UK,[92] Egypt,[93] and Yugoslavia[94] submitted amendments, the latter two of which contained proposals to permit states to restrict expression which would damage friendly relations between states and propaganda for war, discussions focused on the proposals submitted by the USSR and France.

The USSR warned that, '[b]y recognising the theoretical right to hold any opinion, the article as it stood might be used by some persons as a justification for propaganda for war, racial hatred and all fascist and nazi doctrines'.[95] It proposed replacing Article 14 with a text which essentially repeated that submitted to the Third Committee of the General Assembly in 1950 which would have provided that the right to freedom of expression could only be enjoyed 'under conditions ensuring that freedom of speech and of the Press are not exploited for war propaganda'.[96] The delegate asserted that '[i]f freedom of expression was enjoyed under such conditions, the war psychosis which now existed in various countries was bound to come to a stop'.[97]

This proposal, as well as the other amendments, was unacceptable to the USA. Eleanor Roosevelt, the US delegate, stated that most of the proposed amendments were less satisfactory than the text of Article 14 adopted by the Commission in 1950. She accused the Egyptian amendment of being a means for legalizing censorship and control of the press,[98] and that of the USSR as being 'tantamount to complete [state] control of the press'.[99] The USA was not proposing that there

---

[92] E/CN.4/L.144/Rev 1.

[93] E/1992, Annexe III, Section A, 32. Egypt's delegate, Azmi Bey, said that this would place such limitations to the right of freedom of expression as were necessary 'for the maintenance of peace and friendly relations between the States, which was one of the objectives set out in the Charter'. E/CN.4/SR.320, 3.

[94] E/1992, Annexe III, Section A, 32. The Yugoslav delegate stated that this amendment contained only penalties, liabilities, and restrictions necessary for the suppression of all propaganda in favour of aggression and discrimination, and which might only be imposed 'as were strictly necessary for the protection of the purposes of the Charter and the principles of the Universal Declaration of Human Rights'. E/CN.4/SR.320, 3.

[95] E/CN.4/SR.320, 4 (Mr Morozov).

[96] 'In the interests of democracy everyone must be guaranteed by law the right to the free expression of opinion; in particular, to freedom of speech, of the Press, and of artistic representation, under conditions ensuring that freedom of speech and of the Press are not exploited for war propaganda, for the incitement of hatred among the peoples, for racial discrimination and for the dissemination of slanderous rumours.' E/CN.4/L.125.

[97] E/CN.4/SR.320, 4.

[98] ibid 6–7.

[99] E/CN.4/SR.321, 7.

be no permitted limitations on the right to freedom of expression, however, and distinguished between limitations on grounds such as 'national security', which were considered as being an acceptable function of government, and propaganda for war or 'slanderous rumours', which were considered to accord the state unnecessary and dangerous power over expression. The communist states saw this distinction as evidence of US hypocrisy. They would repeatedly charge the USA with opposing proposals that freedom of expression be limited in order to prevent propaganda for war on the grounds that the USA itself wanted a free rein to continue engaging in such propaganda against communist states.

In this regard Poland noted that international agreements had been concluded in the past to prohibit the use of the press for immoral purposes, and that since the USA itself was a signatory of Conventions prohibiting the dissemination of obscene publications, Poland's delegate wondered how it could consider such publications 'more dangerous than war propaganda, the incitement of hatred among the peoples, racial discrimination and the dissemination of slanderous rumours, or how it could consent to the suppression of the former but not of the latter'.[100] He further asserted that the limitations already set forth in Article 14, such as 'public order' and 'national security', were 'extremely vague terms' constituting a serious threat to the freedom of the press, while those in the USSR's amendment merely 'precluded the possibility of the press being used for immoral purposes harmful to the welfare of mankind'.[101] He concluded by citing an example of 'dangerous propaganda' disseminated in the US press: 'An American periodical', he claimed, 'had recently published a map to show American people how easily Poland could be conquered by the US in the event of a new war; no such propaganda appeared in the Polish Press.'[102]

The delegate of the USSR also argued that the limitations for which the USA had voted 'were more comprehensive than the four restrictions contained in the USSR proposal',[103] and that the USA, which claimed to be the champion of freedom of the press, 'was the advocate of increased international tension, war propaganda and hatred, and of curbs on freedom in order to protect the monopolies and big business'.[104] Referring to a 'disgraceful campaign of war propaganda [which] had been unleashed in the US press',[105] he said the comments of the US delegate served to highlight the unwillingness of both the USA and other states to implement General Assembly Resolution 110(II) condemning propaganda and incitement to war. Finally, Yugoslavia pointed out that the USA had accepted 'an enumeration of cases in which freedom of information might be limited that was tantamount to authorising censorship and the suppression of

---

[100] E/CN.4/SR.321, 5–6.   [101] E/CN.4/SR.322, 3.

[102] E/CN.4/SR.321, 6.   [103] ibid 12–13.

[104] ibid. It was further claimed that the USA was opposed to any restrictions aimed at the maintenance of peace and good international relations because the US media was itself 'engaging in war propaganda detrimental to good international relations'. E/CN.4/SR.320, 8–9.

[105] E/CN.4/SR.321, 12–13.

freedom of information',[106] and that the Yugoslav amendment merely proposed to make freedom of information subject to the purposes and principles of the United Nations, 'precisely in order to prevent any possibility of the misuse of State control for anti-democratic purposes'.[107]

Egypt sympathized with such criticisms, noting that while it understood the traditional desire of the USA to maintain the absolute freedom of the press, 'nevertheless that country had renounced isolationism in order to become an international power and its traditional conception of freedom of the press should be adjusted accordingly, since it must take the requirements of international society into account'.[108] The USA failed to make comprehensive arguments in support of its position, and did not address the charges of hypocrisy or of 'warmongering' made by the communist states.

Introducing the French proposal, Cassin stated that although in favour of a general text, France was keen to address the threats posed by the exploitation of freedom of expression for goals contrary to the aims and purposes of the United Nations. The French proposal provided that:

> The exercise of the rights provided for in the foregoing paragraph carries with it special duties and responsibilities. It may therefore be subject to certain restrictions, but these shall be such only as are provided by law and are necessary, (1) for respect of the rights or reputations of others, (2) for the protection of national security or of public order, or of public health or morals.[109]

Reminding the Commission that the experience of the pre-war years had proved the danger of stifling criticism of other nations in the interest of maintaining peace and fostering friendly relations, he argued that full freedom must be granted under the Covenant in order to draw attention to all threats to the peace of an internal or external character.[110] It was stated that this proposal highlighted the importance of reaffirming and respecting freedom of expression while simultaneously avoiding any impairment of the rights and reputations of individuals.[111] Secondly, he stressed that the 'national community as a whole' must be protected against any incitement by the press to violate public order, morals, and national security and that respect for public policy, both national and international, had to be ensured by stipulating that the press and other methods of information should respect the purposes and principles of the United Nations. Lastly, it was emphasized that the proposed limitations were not tantamount to prior censorship, and that there was:

> [...] all the difference in the world between such censorship and a warning to the journalists responsible that, if they violated certain rules, they would lay themselves open to penalties such as the obligations to issue corrections, actions for slander, and criminal prosecutions

---

[106] E/CN.4/SR.320, 10.   [107] ibid 10.
[108] ibid 13–14.   [109] E/2256, Article 16(3).
[110] E/CN.4/SR.321, 11–12.   [111] E/CN.4/SR.320, 12.

in serious cases. In short the freedom of the press must be proclaimed, but at the same time the responsibilities incumbent upon journalists must be made quite clear.[112]

The French proposal received much support from the liberal democracies, which, although opposed to specific limitations on the right to freedom of expression, recognized the necessity of the state not being precluded from limiting speech which it considered as a threat to its security. Australia, for example, while wary of adding further limitations, was prepared to accept either the French or the UK text,[113] or possibly a composite of the two, 'since they avoided generalisation and provided relatively narrow limitation'.[114] The approach of the liberal democracies was succinctly described in the response of the United Kingdom to a question posed by India as to 'whether it was the intention of the UK that there should be no limitation on the right of expression'.[115] The United Kingdom's delegate stated that his nation, as one of a group of Western European countries, approached the issue of freedom of expression 'in the light of its history and tradition'.[116] The elements in the United Kingdom's formulation,[117] he said, were familiar to the courts and generally applicable to all individuals, whereas the USSR formulation contained vague new criteria which had never served as guides for the application of legal sanction. He regarded the aims sought by the USSR as being best achieved by improving the general level and standard of the press in a democratic society rather than by negative legislation.[118]

In seeking to find a compromise which the majority of United Nations members would accept, Lebanon stated that the three factors which complicated the drafting of the provision were 'the importance assumed by information media and the extent of their influence on public opinion in modern times; the fact that those media were unequally distributed among the various countries; and thirdly, the difference between the concept of information in Communist and non-Communist countries'.[119] The delegate of Lebanon found the wording of Article 14 to be 'most satisfactory', but asserted that the terms of each of the USSR, Yugoslav, Egyptian, and French amendments were 'vague and extremely dangerous, since they set the State up as supreme arbiter of what was or was not

---

[112] E/CN.4/SR.320, 12.
[113] E/CN.4/L.144/Rev 1.
[114] E/CN.4/SR.321, 4.
[115] ibid 13 (Mrs Mehta).
[116] ibid 13–14.
[117] E/CN.4/L.144/Rev 1. This provided that '[t]he exercise of the freedom to receive and impart information and ideas since it carries with it duties and responsibilities, may be subject to such conditions and limitations as are prescribed by law and are necessary in the interests for the protection of national security, or public safety, for the prevention of disorder or crime, for the protection of health and morals, for the protection of the reputation or rights of others, for preventing the disclosure of information received in confidence or for ensuring the fair and proper conduct of judicial proceedings.'
[118] E/CN.4/SR.321, 13–14.
[119] E/CN.4/SR.320, 12.

allowed'.[120] He considered the introduction in the USSR amendment of the notion of 'democracy', which was interpreted in diametrically opposite ways in different countries, as enabling 'the State to suppress all individual liberties, including freedom of expression'.[121] He made similar arguments against the inclusion in the Covenant of the notions of 'war propaganda' and 'hatred among the peoples'.[122] He stated that although he understood the terms borrowed from the Charter used in the Yugoslav amendment, Lebanon was opposed to their inclusion in Article 14 since:

[…] they could not be left at the mercy of those who might be interested in interpreting them contrary to what was intended. Furthermore, those terms were used in article 1 of the Charter to express the ideals of the UN, whereas in the Yugoslav amendment they were being used as limitations on freedom of information. To take them out of their context would be dangerous.[123]

The Chinese delegate (representing the government-in-exile in Taiwan) took a contrasting approach to the issue, premising the desirability of limitations on the right to freedom of expression on the need to protect the state from hostile external influences. He counselled the leaders of 'free countries' to recognize that the unwise use of freedom of information could lead to their own destruction, and that the use of the various media of information 'to create prejudice, intolerance and disrespect for the social order and political institutions of other States, particularly with a view to undermining the existing government, could be interpreted as an abuse of freedom of information'.[124] The idea that limitations on freedom of expression were a means of protecting the state and not primarily of protecting human rights themselves appears to have been a strong undercurrent in the approach of the liberal democracies and may be contrasted with the approach of the communist states, which, although also primarily concerned with the consolidation of the state, nonetheless emphasized the idea that certain categories of speech should be restricted in order to protect the collective right to peace.

At this juncture the various amendments were put to a vote. The Chairman put the USSR amendment to the vote in several parts.[125] A roll-call vote on the words 'in the interests of democracy' was rejected.[126] Two more votes on the amendment were rejected before the USSR's proposal as a whole was taken off the agenda.[127]

---

[120] ibid 13.   [121] ibid.
[122] ibid.   [123] E/CN.4/SR.321, 11.
[124] ibid 3.   [125] E/CN.4/SR.322, 7.
[126] 3:13 with 2 abstentions. (In favour: Poland, Ukrainian SSR, USSR; against: Australia, Belgium, Chile, China, Egypt, France, Greece, Lebanon, Pakistan, Sweden, UK, USA, Uruguay; Abstaining: India, Yugoslavia.)
[127] A vote on whether the phrase 'everyone must be guaranteed by law the right to the free expression of opinion' should be adopted was rejected 7:9 with 2 abstentions. (In favour: Egypt, Lebanon, Pakistan, Poland, Ukrainian SSR, USSR, Uruguay; Against: Australia, Belgium, Chile, China, Egypt, France, Greece, Sweden, UK, USA; Abstaining: India, Yugoslavia.) A vote taken by roll-call on the remainder of the amendment, beginning with the words, 'everyone must be

Paragraphs 1 and 2 of the original text of Article 14[128] which set forth the right to freedom of expression were then adopted by the Commission.[129] The Yugoslav[130] and Egyptian[131] amendments to paragraph 3 were defeated,[132] prompting the USSR to express regret 'that the limitations on freedom of speech and the press aimed at preventing warmongering, hatred among peoples, racial discrimination and the spreading of slanderous rumours had been rejected'.[133] Finally, the French amendment to Article 14(3) was put to the vote and was adopted 8:6 with 3 abstentions[134] and Article 14 as a whole was adopted 12:3 with 3 abstentions.[135]

viii. Summary

After six years of drafting, the formula of the right to freedom of expression as adopted by the Commission in 1952 contained no reference to 'war propaganda', 'incitement to war', or 'propaganda for war'. During this phase of drafting, proposals that the right to freedom of expression could be restricted in order to prevent propaganda for war were confined—with the exception of communist Yugoslavia—to states from the Soviet Bloc. Rather than attempt to create a consensus about the necessity of the international community confronting propaganda for war in the Covenant, the Soviets adopted a confrontational approach, lambasting the press and government of the USA as the nerve centre of dangerous international propaganda. Whitton had noted a similar tendency during the 1948 Convention on Freedom of Information and the Press:

> The Eastern Bloc took advantage of this additional opportunity to accuse Americans of imperialism, press monopoly and racial discrimination, and to attack our press for irresponsibility and war-mongering. Apparently they hoped in this way to keep the spotlight from their own deficiencies and cause division among the non-Communist powers.[136]

---

guaranteed by law the right to freedom of speech, of the press', was also rejected 4:12 with 2 abstentions. E/CN.4/SR.322, 8.

[128] E/1992.

[129] Paragraph 1 was adopted 12:0 with 6 abstentions. Paragraph 2 was adopted 14:3 with 1 abstention. E/CN.4/SR.322, 10.

[130] E/1992, Annexe III, Section A, 32.

[131] E/1992, Annexe III, Section A, 32.

[132] The Yugoslav amendment was rejected 4:8 with 6 abstentions. (For: Chile, Egypt, Uruguay, Yugoslavia; against: Australia, Belgium, China, Greece, Lebanon, Sweden, UK, USA; abstaining: France, India, Pakistan, Poland, Ukrainian SSR, USSR.) E/CN.4/SR.322, 10. Egypt's amendment was rejected 6:8 with 4 abstentions. E/CN.4/SR.322, 11.

[133] ibid 12.

[134] ibid 13. The summary records do not record the voting pattern other than that Belgium and Egypt abstained, Australia voted in favour, and both the USSR and the UK opposed.

[135] ibid. The delegates of the USSR and Poland stated that they had voted against Article 14 because the USSR amendment, with its limitations on freedom of speech and of the press aimed at preventing propaganda for war, had been rejected. E/CN.4/SR.322, 14.

[136] John B Whitton, 'UN Conference on Freedom of Information and the Movement against International Propaganda', 76.

The manner in which the communist states employed the term propaganda during the drafting of the covenant had a similar effect on the delegates of the Western democracies. They came to understand communist proposals regarding 'war propaganda' as being targeted at practically anything disseminated by the US press, thus obviating their support for any such proposals. Ralph Casey noted that using the term 'propaganda' in a moralistic sense only confuses its meaning more.[137] For the Western democracies, which could not but view the Soviets' proposals as being a manifestation of communist morals and an anathema to their own liberal principles, there was little prospect of accepting the inclusion of such limitations on the right to freedom of expression in the Covenant.

Nonetheless, the Western democracies, as frequently pointed out by the communist states, were fully supportive of allowing the right to freedom of expression to be restricted on grounds such as 'public order' and 'national security'. While the French delegate stated that 'war propaganda' fell within the ambit of 'expression' which could be restricted on grounds of national security, there had been little vocal support for this idea and at any rate such an interpretation would essentially preclude any possibility of the government itself being held to account for engaging in such propaganda, a factor which had been central to the General Assembly's Resolutions against propaganda for war.

This aspect of the discourse had been highlighted by the Lebanese delegations which had repeatedly advocated that there be no permitted limitations to the right to freedom of expression, asserting that such limitations constituted a threat to human rights by facilitating state propaganda campaigns and state control of information. The role of the state in the dissemination of propaganda for war had been consistently overlooked by the other delegates, an omission which remains of immense significance to the effectiveness of the prohibition of propaganda for war in international law. Whereas the communist states focused primarily on the private 'Hearst Press' of the West, typical of the stance of Western delegates was the comment by the USA that 'the Commission must realise, that any curbs placed upon journalists would also apply to lawyers, artists, teachers and similar professionals, as article 14 dealt with all forms of expression'.[138] The exclusion from almost all of the debates of the necessity of restricting the speech of the state itself in order to protect human rights is a significant characteristic of the discussions recorded in the *travaux préparatoires*.

---

[137] Ralph D Casey, 'The Press, Propaganda, and Pressure Groups', 66.
[138] E/CN.4/SR.321, 7. Mr Beer, the representative of the International League for the Rights of Man, felt that the distinctions between the journalist and the ordinary citizen that were being drawn by several delegates during the drafting process were fallacious since '[j]ournalists were not a separate category of human beings, but merely the agents of other people who could not obtain information at first hand and could not, for one reason or another, express themselves'. He did not, however, elaborate upon the role and responsibility of the state in the dissemination of propaganda for war. E/CN.4/SR.321, 9.

B. The Prohibition of Incitement to Hatred and Violence

Each of the proposals as to the formulation of the right to freedom of expression contained limitations which had been framed as permissive rather than obligatory. The insertion into the Draft Covenant of an obligatory prohibition of propaganda for war was a consequence of the debates on the requirement to prohibit incitement to violence which had been running parallel to but distinct from those on the right to freedom of expression. A key aspect of these debates was the issue of whether it was sufficient for the Covenant to prohibit not just incitement to violence, but also the hate speech which, although falling short of direct incitement, was considered to be a necessary antecedent to successful incitement. Similar issues were to arise in the case of propaganda for war, with many delegates considering it necessary not only to prohibit incitement to war, but also the antecedent propaganda which created the atmosphere in which incitement to specific wars of aggression could take effect.

i. Commission on Human Rights (1947)

Following the rejection of a USSR proposal to add a new paragraph on the prohibition of discrimination to draft Article 19 which would have made the 'advocacy of national, racial and religious hostility'[139] a criminal act,[140] France proposed an alternative amendment to replace the last sentence of Article 19 with the following text:

Every person, regardless of office or status, shall be entitled to equal protection under the law and shall be protected by the law against any arbitrary discrimination and against any incitement to such discrimination in violation of this Declaration.[141]

Following the successful adoption of this amendment,[142] the Commission considered China's proposal to add a new paragraph to Article 19 providing that '[a]ny advocacy of national, racial or religious hostility, designed to provoke violence, shall be forbidden under the law of the State'.[143] The United Kingdom suggested that since this discussion concerned limitations on the right to freedom of expression, there should be no further discussion of these amendments

[139] The USSR's proposal read: '[a]ny advocacy of national, racial and religious hostility or of national exclusiveness or hatred and contempt, as well as any actions establishing a privilege or a discrimination based on distinctions of race, nationality or religion, constitute a crime and shall be punishable under the law of the State.' E/CN.4/SR.34, 9.

[140] Ibid. 4:10 with 7 abstentions. The Chilean delegate was opposed on the grounds that the USSR text placed unnecessary power into the hands of the state which he saw as 'the chief threat to the rights of the individual', while Eleanor Roosevelt did not think that such a law could be applied in practice, curiously citing as a precedent the failure of the prohibition laws in the USA. E/CN.4/SR.34, 10.

[141] E/CN.4/SR.35, 11.
[142] 11:1 with 4 abstentions.
[143] E/CN.4/SR.35, 11.

and that they should be remitted for consideration to the Sub-Commission on Freedom of Information and the Press and to the International Conference on Freedom of Information.[144] Australia felt that the text of the Chinese amendment might throw Article 19, which was intended to deal with discrimination, 'out of balance', and suggested that since it contained a new idea it should be embodied in a separate article.[145] China agreed to this proposal and asked that the text of the amendment should be inserted immediately after the article prohibiting discrimination since it related to one aspect of discrimination.[146] The amendment in the form of a new article was then adopted by the Commission.[147] The French and Chinese amendments were merged to form a distinct provision and a new draft Article 21 provided that '[a]ny advocacy of national, racial or religious hostility that constitutes an incitement to violence shall be prohibited by the law of the state'.[148]

ii. Commission on Human Rights (1948)

When Article 21 came up for discussion at the second session of the Drafting Committee of the Commission, the Chair, speaking as the US delegate, stated that she felt that it was 'better to err on the side of too great freedom of speech' than to include any further restrictions on the right to freedom of expression.[149] She considered that the problem of incitement was best treated by individual self-discipline, 'rather than by the enactment of laws which played into the hands of those who would attempt to restrict freedom of speech entirely'.[150] The United Kingdom supported this view and advocated the deletion of Article 21.[151]

The USSR sought to broaden the scope of Article 21 and proposed that the words 'to violence' be omitted from the text, since 'true democrats could not but be anti-fascist and anti-Nazi, and were therefore obliged to combat such theories'.[152] Chile took a similar approach and proposed that the wording be changed to read '[a]ny advocacy of national, racial or religious hostility that constitutes an incitement to violate the liberties and rights mentioned in this Covenant shall be prohibited by the law of the State'.[153] The Union of South Africa and the United Kingdom were opposed to the provision as a whole and when the USSR called

---

[144] ibid 7.
[145] ibid 11.
[146] ibid 12.
[147] ibid. 7 : 2 with 7 abstentions.
[148] Document E/600. The subject of incitement to discrimination remained on the agenda of the draft article on the prohibition of discrimination, which was to become Article 26 of the final Covenant until eventually withdrawn at the Commission's eighth session in 1952. E/CN.4/SR.327, 14, E/CN.4/SR.328, 3.
[149] E/CN.4/AC.1/SR.28, 2–3.
[150] ibid 2–3.
[151] ibid 3.
[152] ibid (Mr Pavlov).
[153] ibid 4.

for a vote on whether Article 21 should be retained in the Draft Covenant it was defeated.[154]

iii. Commission on Human Rights (1949)

The subject returned to the Commission's agenda with a new USSR amendment to the original text of Article 21.[155] This amendment omitted any reference to incitement to violence, providing that:

The propaganda in whatever form of Fascist-Nazi views and the propaganda of racial and national superiority, hatred and contempt shall be prohibited by law.[156]

The USSR said that this formula was based on the experience acquired by mankind after many years of hard and bitter struggle against fascism in which '[m]illions had perished because the propaganda of racial and national superiority, hatred and contempt, had not been stopped in time'.[157] Yugoslavia asserted that since propaganda 'inciting to murder and arson' was prohibited by national legislations, and that fascist-Nazi views and propaganda of racial and national superiority constituted a similar crime at the international level, '[n]o person advocating such criminal views should be allowed the protection of the Covenant'.[158] The United States was opposed to this formula, and cited the jurisprudence of the US Supreme Court in support of the argument that the principle of democracy was better served by allowing individuals to create disputes and dissent than by suppressing their freedom of speech.[159]

France pursued a middle ground between the two superpowers and whilst agreeing with the USSR that where freedom of speech was abused to provoke criminal acts it should be curbed, noted the difficulty of determining where use became abuse. Cassin recommended that a more general wording than that in the USSR text which referred to 'Fascist-Nazi views' should be adopted,[160] and proposed that the words 'and violence' be included so that Article 21 would read: '[a]ny advocacy of national, racial or religious hostility that constitutes an incitement to violence and hatred shall be prohibited by the law of the state.'[161]

---

[154] E/CN.4/AC.1/SR.28, 3 : 1 with 1 abstention.

[155] Document E/800; E/CN.4/SR.123, 4.

[156] E/CN.4/223.

[157] E/CN.4/SR.123, 4.

[158] E/CN.4/SR.123, 5 and E/CN.4/SR.123/Corr 1.

[159] E/CN.4/SR.123, 5. According to Farrior the case in question is most likely *Terminiello v Chicago*, 337 US 1 (1949). Stephanie Farrior, 'Molding the Matrix: The Historical and Theoretical Foundations of International Law Concerning Hate Speech', 14 Berkeley J Int'l L 3 (1996) 27, fn 125. Mr Pavlov of the USSR responded to the US comments by highlighting the Dissenting Opinion recorded by the minority in the Supreme Court, which, he argued, amounted to an objection to allowing freedom for the dissemination of fascist views. E/CN.4/SR.123, 5.

[160] E/CN.4/SR.123, 6 (Mr Cassin).

[161] E/CN.4/365 (and Document E/1371). E/CN.4/SR.123, 6.

As with the draft Article on the right to freedom of expression, the Commission decided to postpone a vote on this proposal until the General Assembly had considered the results of the Convention on Freedom of Information.[162] Concluding the debate, the USSR criticized the tendency to postpone consideration of one article after another since the discussion on Article 21 had made it possible for all members to express their views concerning the freedom to be allowed for propaganda of racial and national superiority, and a vote could be taken forthwith.[163]

iv. Commission on Human Rights (1950)

France reintroduced its amendment at the Commission's sixth session,[164] asserting that it was more moderate than the USSR's proposal[165] since it 'did not seek to promote the adoption of preventative and censorship measures', but rather left governments free to choose the means by which they might prohibit certain kinds of harmful propaganda.[166] Distinguishing between draft Article 17 on the right to freedom of expression[167] and the immediate provision, France stressed that while the role of the press as a medium for incitement would be dealt with by the Draft Convention on Freedom of Information, there were other media of propaganda and that the Covenant 'should contain provisions to prohibit them, irrespective of the scope to be given to article 17'.[168] Although there was little further comment on the other media of incitement, or on the sources of such expression, it would appear from the overall drafting that the French delegate was considering private individuals or organizations rather than the state in this regard. The USA was to reiterate its desire that Article 21 be deleted,[169] 'since any criticism of public or religious authorities might all too easily be described as incitement to hatred and consequently prohibited'.[170]

The delegate of Lebanon was broadly opposed to the principle set forth in Article 21 and feared that the French proposal represented 'peace at any price'.[171] Conditioning any support for the proposal on an assurance that its adoption would not be liable to restrict the possibility of expressing the truth, he argued that '[t]ruth stood above national peace' and that '[i]t would be a serious mistake to introduce a provision into the Covenant prohibiting in effect the scientific

---

[162] E/CN.4/SR.123, 6. 5:3 with 4 abstentions.
[163] ibid.
[164] E/CN.4/365 (and Document E/1371).
[165] E/CN.4/223.
[166] E/CN.4/SR.174, para 21.
[167] E/CN.4/272, 3; Document E/800.
[168] E/CN.4/SR.174, para 23. India supported the principle of Article 21 but thought that it should not stand as a separate article, but should be incorporated into Article 17 on freedom of expression. E/CN.4/SR.174, para 32.
[169] ibid, para 24.
[170] ibid, para 25.
[171] ibid, para 34.

and objective utterance of truth, which was the best guarantee of human progress'.[172] While the suggestion that truth is more important than 'national peace' is a provocative statement, he added that should the reference to 'incitement to hatred' be deleted, he would consider supporting the proposal.[173] These statements are interesting since this is the first time that the Lebanon's delegate had given his views on the issue of 'incitement to violence'. Although he had opposed all other limitations to the right to freedom of expression for fear that they would serve the state as opposed to the enjoyment of human rights, his contemplation of a proposal prohibiting incitement to violence suggests that such a provision represented an exceptional measure which he regarded as positive for the protection of human rights. The French delegate responded to these comments by asserting that:

Realities should be faced squarely. On one side were those who wished to silence free men, and on the other, those who wished to permit full freedom of expression for the purpose of incitement to hatred and violence.[174]

It was noted that that while freedom of the press was recognized in France, punishment for incitement to violence was also provided for under French law, and the French delegate signalled his willingness to amend the proposal so as to make a clear distinction between objective studies of a scientific nature and pure propaganda. In this regard, 'the works of Gobineau, which gave a predominant role in the Germanic race but were in the nature of a scientific study, should not be confused with the newspaper "*Der Stürmer*" which incited to murder'.[175] In seeking support for the French proposal, it was stated that '[b]etween the two extremes of authoritarianism and unlimited freedom which would make it possible to interfere with the freedoms of others, the French amendment represented a middle course; it recognised both the right to freedom and the obligation to respect the rights and freedoms of others'.[176]

Several of the liberal democratic states gave guarded support to the idea of prohibiting incitement to violence, whilst remaining opposed to the proposal's reference to incitement of hatred. Australia said that the problem which the French draft was endeavouring to resolve might be met by the adoption of a formula prohibiting incitement to violence on religious grounds or grounds of national origin, which 'would serve as a useful indicator of the limits which freedom of expression must observe'.[177] The United Kingdom also considered the phrase 'advocacy of national, racial or religious hostility' to be appropriate for inclusion under the general heading of incitement to violence since the legislation of the United Kingdom, as of other countries, envisaged circumstances which might give rise to violence and provided for the punishment of incitement to violence.[178]

---

[172] E/CN.4/SR.174, para 36.   [173] ibid, para 44.
[174] ibid, para 45.   [175] ibid, para 47.
[176] ibid, para 48.   [177] ibid, para 67.
[178] ibid, para 62.

Several delegates attempted to provide clarity on the meaning of the words found in the various amendments. The Lebanese delegate stated that whilst he understood that the word 'advocacy' in the proposed text should be understood to mean systematic and persistent propaganda, he felt further clarification should be given.[179] Regarding the term 'incitement to violence', he felt that the word 'violence' was certainly appropriate, but that 'it would be very difficult to define incitement to violence'.[180] The USA stated that drawing a distinction between the terms 'advocacy' and 'incitement', or differentiating between the various shades of feeling ranging from 'hatred to ill-feeling and mere dislike', was 'inherently difficult' and 'likely to be exploited by totalitarian States for the purpose of rendering the other articles null and void'.[181] The post-Second World War peace treaties with Hungary, Bulgaria, and Romania were cited in this regard, and it was claimed that while they had required the safeguarding of basic human rights and fundamental freedoms for all people in those countries, the clause permitting suppression of fascism and hostile propaganda had 'provided a loophole for those seeking to ignore their obligations and enabled them to consider themselves justified in their attitude'.[182]

Chile, opposed to the addition of limitations on the right to freedom of expression other than those found in Article 17, warned that use of the word 'advocacy' could justify censorship,[183] and considered the word 'incitement' to be too vague, and the words 'violence or hatred' too general.[184] Greece stated that the word 'propagande' in the text proposed by France should have been translated into English by the word 'propaganda' rather than 'advocacy'.[185] The United Kingdom disagreed, stating that the word 'advocacy' was the proper legal term since the widely used word 'propaganda' was both vague and derogatory.[186] China approved of the 'constructive' French text but rejected the words 'Fascist-Nazi' in the USSR text on the grounds that these words designated ideologies which could be given different names and therefore had no place in the Covenant.[187]

---

[179] ibid, para 37.

[180] ibid, para 38.

[181] ibid, para 26.

[182] ibid, para 29. Egon Schwelb notes that '[i]n the Peace Treaty of 1947 the Allied Powers, including the United Kingdom and the United States, imposed on Hungary the obligation not to permit Fascist-type organisations conducting propaganda, including revisionist propaganda hostile to the United Nations'. Egon Schwelb, 'The International Convention on the Elimination of All Forms of Racial Discrimination', 1022. Similar provisions had appeared in the peace treaties with Bulgaria, Finland, Italy, and Romania, as well as in the 1955 State Treaty with Austria. See further Stephanie Farrior, 'Hate Propaganda and International Human Rights Law', in Monroe E Price and Mark Thompson (eds), *Forging Peace: Intervention, Human Rights and the Management of Media Space* (Edinburgh: Edinburgh University Press, 2002) 69–103, 77–8.

[183] E/CN.4/SR.174, para 56.

[184] ibid, para 61.

[185] ibid, para 54.

[186] ibid, para 65.

[187] ibid, para 49.

Belgium, which had earlier advocated the deletion of Article 21 in its entirety,[188] considered propaganda per se as being neither intrinsically good nor bad, but rather a notion whose desirability depended on the end towards which it was intended. Concerns as to national defence prompted a query as to whether the expression 'any advocacy of national [...] hostility'[189] in the French draft 'would prevent a country from engaging in internal propaganda with a view to arming for defence'.[190] Lebanon's delegate said that he did not regard such a formula as being applicable to situations of self-defence and that he 'would approve of incitement to violence when it was used in order to forge weapons of defence'.[191] Not surprisingly, this was among the few principles upon which delegates were to achieve consensus throughout the drafting process.

Although France had proposed that its amendment be voted on in parts in order to allow the Commission to register its opinion on the question,[192] at the close of the session a US proposal to delete both the French and USSR amendments was adopted.[193] Nonetheless, the sustained debate on the meaning of 'incitement to violence' and the role that the Covenant could or should play in this regard (aided perhaps by the absence of the Soviet Bloc states from this session of debates) ensured a swift return of the issue of incitement to violence to the Commission's agenda.

v. Commission on Human Rights (1953)

At its ninth session the Commission debated a proposal submitted by the Sub-Commission on Prevention of Discrimination and Protection of Minorities for a new article providing that:

Any advocacy of national, racial or religious hostility that constitutes an incitement to violence shall be prohibited by the law of the State.[194]

The communist states, along with several Latin American countries, were dissatisfied with this text's omission of any reference to 'incitement to hatred'. Poland claimed that it did not go to the root of the evil but merely tackled its consequences, since it implied that 'propaganda advocating exclusiveness, hatred and contempt, would not call for legal action, provided it was not directly conducive

---

[188] Arguing that Article 21 was 'dangerous and likely to lead to abuses' Belgium did not think that it came within the scope of the Draft Covenant. E/CN.4/SR.174, para 31.

[189] 'Any advocacy of national, racial or religious hostility that constitutes an incitement to violence or hatred shall be prohibited by the law of the State.' E/CN.4/365 (and Document E/1371).

[190] E/CN.4/SR.174, para 52.

[191] ibid, para 38 (Mr Malik).

[192] ibid, para 22.

[193] 7:4 with 3 abstentions. E/CN.4/SR.175, para 22. Although the Summary Records do not indicate the voting pattern, the following delegations were in attendance: Australia, Belgium, Chile, China, Denmark, Egypt, France, Greece, India, Lebanon, United Kingdom, Uruguay, Yugoslavia, and the United States of America.

[194] Document E/2256, 54; E/CN.4/L.269.

to violence'.[195] Recalling the widespread use by the Nazi regime of nationalist and racist propaganda, he stated that under the Sub-Commission's text, it would be virtually impossible to draw the line accurately between propaganda and incitement to violence,[196] and proposed it be amended to read:

Any advocacy of national or racial exclusiveness, hatred and contempt or religious hostility, particularly of such a nature as to constitute an incitement to violence, shall be prohibited by the law of the State.[197]

While the substance of this proposal would be adopted as Article 20(2) of the final draft of the Covenant, the distinction made by Poland's delegate between speech—propaganda—which creates an enabling environment for violence, and speech which directly incites to violence, is notable in that similar views were expressed in the final debates on the distinction between propaganda for war and 'incitement to war'. This distinction was again referred to by Yugoslavia when highlighting General Assembly Resolution 421(V), which stated 'that in the drafting of the covenant account should be taken of the Purposes and Principles of the Charter of the United Nations and that these Purposes and Principles should be consistently applied and assiduously protected'.[198] Yugoslavia argued that the provision must be directed, not just against incitement to violence, but also against 'all propaganda that constituted incitement to hatred and intolerance in every sphere'.[199]

Chile concurred with these views[200] and proposed inserting the words 'hatred and' between the phrase 'that constitutes an incitement to' and the word 'violence'.[201] Arguing that the least the Commission could do was 'to take action against propaganda inciting not only to actual violence, but also to hatred, which was at the root of the violence',[202] it was asserted that it was not a case of drawing a distinction between advocates of individualism on the one hand, and those of state intervention on the other, but rather:

[...] of accepting the fact that contemporary conditions showed that the defence of democracy could not be left with the individual, even though it was on him, in the last analysis, that the essence of democracy depended. Intervention by the State was essential if the democratic way of life was to survive.[203]

---

[195] E/CN.4/SR.377, 4.
[196] ibid.
[197] E/CN.4/L.269 (emphasis in original).
[198] GA Res 421(V), Section B, para 3(c).
[199] E/CN.4/SR.377, 6.
[200] Chile would not support the Sub-Commission's proposal as it dealt only with incitement to violence and left the door open to all forms of intolerance, 'consequently render[ing] no service to the cause of tolerance'. ibid 14.
[201] E/CN.4/L.270. This represented a radical shift from Chile's opposition to the initial USSR proposal on this issue presented to, and rejected by, the Commission in 1947 which the Chilean delegate opposed on the grounds that the USSR text placed unnecessary power into the hands of the state which he saw as 'the chief threat to the rights of the individual'. E/CN.4/SR.34, 10.
[202] E/CN.4/SR.378, 11.
[203] E/CN.4/SR.377, 13.

Speaking at length on the problem of hate propaganda, and pre-empting Chile's support for the prohibition of propaganda for war at the final debates of the Third Committee in 1961, he described it as 'a weapon of mass psychological penetration that could arouse national, racial or religious enmity'.[204] Citing the work of 'certain psychologists', he noted that 'the masses' were especially receptive to negative doctrines of hatred, and that racial hatred, 'once aroused, unleashed the worst instincts and succeeded in making racial extermination or the use of cremation ovens appear logical and natural'.[205] He warned that incitement to hatred gave birth to a collective psychosis that allowed the justification of violence and crime, and felt that 'modern scientific methods' made it possible to specify the instances in which propaganda was particularly dangerous, in which case, 'the principle of *laisser-faire* was indefensible, and there must be provision for recourse to the law'.[206] He argued that since limitations on the exercise of the Draft Covenant's right to freedom of expression were recognized as necessary for reasons of public order, public health, or morals, delegates 'would surely agree that advocacy of hostility and incitement to violence were in the present age as great a menace to humanity as threats to public health or order'.[207] Uruguay added that 'it was quite clear that the draft article submitted by the Sub-Commission in no way affected the rights of citizens to criticise, but merely forbade anything which might constitute incitement to violence'.[208]

The United Kingdom and Australia repeated their concerns about the inclusion of concepts such as 'hatred' and 'hostility' in the Covenant, and warned that a positive requirement on states 'to take repressive action', even if limited by the criterion of incitement to violence, might result in violations of the right to freedom of expression, since each government could interpret in its own way what degree of transgression constituted incitement to violence.[209] Australia asserted that the UN Charter emphasized the 'practice' of tolerance, which could be achieved primarily through means other than legislation,[210] and saw in the proposal a danger which 'might be worse than the evil it sought to remove'.[211] The United Kingdom, though previously having accepted the term 'advocacy' as being a 'proper legal term',[212] now claimed that the notion of advocacy was in fact not defined. Averring that 'advocacy' might be well intentioned but overstep the bounds of the permissible, that it might be misguided, or that it might simply be foolish,[213] it was argued that it was impossible to express those shades of meaning in a text.[214]

Criticizing the opposition of the liberal democracies to his earlier proposal on this subject, the delegate of the USSR aptly noted that '[c]ertain delegations were

[204] E/CN.4/SR.378, 12.
[205] ibid 12.
[206] ibid.
[207] ibid 13.
[208] E/CN.4/SR.379, 7.
[209] E/CN.4/SR.377, 9–10.
[210] ibid 7.
[211] ibid.
[212] E/CN.4/SR.174, para 65.
[213] E/CN.4/SR.379, 6.
[214] ibid.

in the habit of expressing warm support for a principle, of declaring, for example, that propaganda was an evil and contrary to the principles of the Charter, and then of asserting that they were none the less unable to vote in favour of a concrete proposal aimed at eradicating the very evils they condemned'.[215] He curtly concluded by supposing that the next logical step would be to 'deny the usefulness of legislation as a means of ensuring law and order in society'.[216]

France was in favour of the Sub-Commission's text but agreed that thorough consideration should be accorded the amendments of Poland[217] and Chile,[218] which to all extents and purposes reproduced the French amendment rejected by the Commission in 1950.[219] While acknowledging the difficulties involved in drawing the line between lawful and unlawful propaganda,[220] the French delegate responded to the Australian criticisms by stating that:

[…] it was clear that countries could not be left defenceless against propaganda which constituted an incitement to violence […] The Commission must not, however, blind itself to the fact that to transform the state of mind of a nation was a laborious task and, moreover, not solely a matter for the legislator, since what was required was a revolution not merely in legislation but also in national ways of thought.[221]

He asserted that the word 'prohibited' did not mean, a priori, that a government should set up a system to stifle freedom of expression, adding that a criminal prohibition was not strictly required, since a religious or other group which was the object of propaganda constituting an incitement to violence could sue the authors of such propaganda for damages in the civil courts.[222]

Egypt stated that not all forms of propaganda were impermissible, citing as an example propaganda for the enlightenment of public opinion as employed by national liberation movements. It proposed the insertion in either of the texts, after the word 'violence', of the words 'not aiming at the achievement or protection of the rights recognised in this Covenant'.[223] This was subsequently retracted, however, as was an earlier statement that it would be wise 'to amplify the text so as to make clear that incitement to violence should be prohibited unless it was required for the protection or realisation of the rights enunciated in

---

[215] E/CN.4/SR.377, 10.

[216] ibid.

[217] 'Any advocacy of national or racial <u>exclusiveness, hatred and contempt</u> or religious hostility, <u>particular of such a nature</u> as to constitute an incitement to violence, shall be prohibited by the law of the State.' E/CN.4/L.269 (emphasis in original).

[218] 'Insert the words "hatred and" between the phrase "that constitutes an incitement to" and the word "violence".' E/CN.4/L.270.

[219] E/CN.4/SR.377, 13.

[220] E/CN.4/SR.379, 9 (Mr Cassin).

[221] E/CN.4/SR.377, 12.

[222] E/CN.4/SR.379, 10. Pakistan's delegate concurred with this observation and stated that whilst he also understood the term prohibition to include penalties, he did not consider it as involving censorship. E/CN.4/SR.379, 12.

[223] E/CN.4/L.271; E/CN.4/SR.378, 13.

the draft Covenants',[224] on the grounds that it would be detrimental to the cause of human rights, and detract from the value of the Covenant, to link the attainment of lawful objectives with hatred and violence.[225] Pakistan asserted at this point that the whole object of the provision was to prohibit propaganda in one country inciting to violence against another.[226]

Following these discussions, the Polish amendment was voted upon in two parts, and both were rejected.[227] The Chilean amendment was adopted, however,[228] and the Article as a whole, reading, '[a]ny advocacy of national, racial or religious hostility that constitutes an incitement to hatred and violence shall be prohibited by the law of the State',[229] was adopted 11 : 3 with 3 abstentions.[230]

The USA, supported by Australia, stated that while it would not have opposed the Sub-Commission's original text, it had voted against the Chilean amendment because of the inclusion of the term 'and hatred' on the grounds that it admitted the possibility of government censorship, and might therefore lead to the destruction of certain fundamental freedoms.[231] Likewise, the United Kingdom stated that it had opposed the amendment because if the word 'hatred' was an alternative, then it was open to the objections which he had already made and which the US representative had expressed, while if it was an addition, it modified in an entirely new way the conception of incitement to violence well known to the law of his own and many other countries.[232]

vi. Summary

The drafting history of what would become enshrined as Article 20(2) of the Covenant reveals a provision which, although rejected on several occasions and deleted from the draft, was to doggedly return to become one of the core principles of the international human rights framework. Stemming from the fundamental concept of non-discrimination, the initial proposal of France, which would have required the law of the state to protect individuals from any incitement to discrimination,[233] was immediately amended by China which advocated placing

---

[224] E/CN.4/SR.378, 7.
[225] E/CN.4/SR.379, 4.
[226] ibid 12.
[227] The Polish amendment read '[a]ny advocacy of national or racial exclusiveness, hatred and contempt or religious hostility, particularly of such a nature as to constitute an incitement to violence, shall be prohibited by the law of the State'. The first part was rejected 9 : 3 with 5 abstentions. The second part was rejected 11 : 3 with 3 abstentions. E/CN.4/SR.379, 13.
[228] ibid 13. 8 : 5 with 4 abstentions.
[229] ibid 14.
[230] In favour: Pakistan, Philippines, Poland, Ukrainian SSR, USSR, Uruguay, Yugoslavia, Chile, Egypt, France, India. Against: UK, USA, Australia. Abstained: Sweden, Belgium, China. (This is an extremely rare example of any of the Nordic states not actively opposing a proposed limitation on freedom of expression.)
[231] E/CN.4/SR.379, 14.   [232] ibid.
[233] E/CN.4/SR.35, 11.

a positive obligation upon states to prohibit by law 'hostility that constitutes an incitement to violence'.[234] Despite being deleted from the draft on two occasions, the scope of the Article as adopted in 1953 was expanded to additionally prohibit incitement to hatred, an element which was to draw sustained criticism from the United Kingdom and the USA. The influence of the delegates of Chile and France, who were instrumental in securing support for the provision, can be contrasted with the failure of the USSR to secure any support for its contemporaneous efforts with regard to the issue of 'war propaganda' in the Article 19 debates. It is clear from the drafting of this provision that many delegates were extremely concerned with the power of propaganda to undermine fundamental human rights by facilitating an environment conducive to incitement to violence thus whereas several delegations were hesitant in granting states undue leeway in restricting freedom of expression on grounds such as national security or public order, they were to conclude that a prohibition of incitement to hatred and to violence should be an essential element of the draft Convention, a shift which paved the way for the adoption also of the prohibition of propaganda for war.

C. The Prohibition of Propaganda for War

Following the conclusion of the first phase of the drafting process, delegates meeting at the ninth session of the Third Committee in 1954 remained divided on the formulation of draft Articles 19 (freedom of expression) and 26 (prohibition of incitement to hatred and violence). At this juncture the limitation clause of draft Article 19 provided that:

The exercise of the rights provided for in the foregoing paragraph carries with it special duties and responsibilities. It may therefore be subject to certain restrictions, but these shall be such only as are provided by law and are necessary, (1) for respect of the rights or reputations of others, (2) for the protection of national security or of public order, or of public health or morals.[235]

Draft Article 26 provided that '[a]ny advocacy of national, racial or religious hostility that constitutes an incitement to hatred and violence shall be prohibited by the law of the State'.[236] The communist states remained critical of the omission of any reference to 'war propaganda' in draft Article 19, with Poland recommending that '[i]t should be stipulated in article 19 of that draft that no one might exercise his right of freedom of expression in defiance of the principles of the United Nations, especially to engage in war propaganda, to arouse hostility between the nations, to encourage racial discrimination or to spread false

---

[234] Document E/600.
[235] Document E/2256, Article 16(3).
[236] E/CN.4/SR.379, 14.

information likely to jeopardize international co-operation'.[237] The delegate of the Byelorussian SSR challenged the 'purely artificial division of human rights' advanced by the delegates of the United Kingdom, the USA, Australia, Belgium, and France.[238] In her opinion, since it was obvious that if the prohibition of incitement to national hostility 'were not extended to peoples or nations, it could not be enjoyed by the individuals who formed part of these peoples or nations', it was essential to include a prohibition of 'war propaganda' in the Draft Covenant.[239]

In contrast, Argentina's delegate considered Article 26 to seriously threaten the principle of freedom of information. He stated that while most members would condemn the advocacy of hostility of any kind, he doubted whether they could be defined with sufficient precision for an international treaty, warning that 'such a prohibition would entail acceptance of totalitarian control over all forms of expression'.[240] Canada's delegate was also opposed to Article 26, considering that it was 'superfluous and inconsistent with other provisions of the draft Covenant'.[241] She stated that it was impractical to define 'incitement to hatred and violence', and moreover that the purpose of the article was achieved by Article 19.[242]

The opinions of these delegations changed little in the years between 1954 and the final debates on draft Articles 19 and 26 which took place in 1961. A crucial development which took place in the intervening years was the large numbers of former colonies and newly independent states which had joined the United Nations and which had begun to participate actively in the development of the norms of international human rights law. By approaching the question of whether the Covenant should include a prohibition of propaganda for war with a less confrontational attitude than the Soviet Bloc states had, and by clearly linking it

---

[237] A/C.3/SR.571, para 26. The USSR reasserted that the Draft Covenant should include a reference to 'war propaganda' in addition to the inadmissibility of using the rights enumerated against the interests of international cooperation based on mutual respect for the rights of states. A/C.3/SR.565, para 32; A/C.3/SR.576, para 31. A/C.3/SR.571, para 26. Czechoslovakia considered the text of Article 19 to be incomplete since it did not incorporate the principles of General Assembly Resolution 110(II). The delegate stated that 'certain statesmen were devoting all their efforts to war propaganda, even at that very moment, when nations were endeavouring to improve their relations', and therefore an explicit prohibition of such propaganda in the Covenant was a necessity and of equal importance to the prohibition of any advocacy of national, racial, or religious hostility. A/C.3/SR.569, para 14.

[238] A/C.3/SR.575, para 3.

[239] ibid. Mrs Us, the delegate of the Byelorussian SSR, argued that the liberal democracies were opposed to the inclusion of 'some of the most progressive provisions' of the Draft Covenant such as the prohibition of discrimination and incitement to national hostility in draft Article 26 on the grounds that it was a collective right. The Byelorussian SSR favoured the inclusion of provisions such as 'the prohibition of war propaganda, of incitement to hostility among nations, of racial discrimination and dissemination of slanderous information and the prevention of the use of the right of association for the establishment of organizations of a fascist and anti-democratic character'. A/C.3/SR.575, para 8.

[240] A/C.3/SR.568, para 15.

[241] A/C.3/SR.570, para 4.

[242] ibid.

to the overall aims and purposes of the UN Charter, the non-aligned states revitalized what up to this point had appeared to be a discarded proposal.

i. Article 19(3): War Propaganda

The Third Committee took the text of Articles 1 and 2 of the Draft Convention on Freedom of Information[243] previously adopted at its fourteenth and fifteenth sessions in 1960 as the departure point for the final phase of debates on the limitations clause of the draft right to freedom of expression. These texts represented the most recent opinions on the matter held in the United Nations,[244] and while Article 1 set forth the right to freedom of expression, Article 2 provided that:

1. The exercise of the freedoms referred to in Article 1 carries with it duties and responsibilities. It may, however, be subject only to such necessary restrictions as are clearly defined by law and applied in accordance with the law in respect of: national security and public order (*ordre public*); systematic dissemination of false reports harmful to friendly relations among nations and of expressions inciting to war or to national, racial, or religious hatred; attacks on founders of religions; incitement to violence and crime; public health and morals; the rights, honor and reputation of others; and the fair administration of justice.

2. The restrictions specified in the preceding paragraph shall not be deemed to justify the imposition by any State of prior censorship on news, comments and political opinions, and may not be used as grounds for restricting the right to criticise the Government.[245]

India presented an amendment to Article 19(3), which essentially reproduced Article 2(1) of the Draft Convention on Freedom of Information, thereby providing that it would be permissible for states to restrict expressions 'inciting to war'.[246] Brazil then proposed that the terms 'systematic dissemination of false reports harmful to friendly relations among nations and of expressions inciting to war or to national, racial, or religious hatred; attacks on founders of religions; incitement to violence and crime' in the Indian amendment be replaced with the words 'including the prevention of war propaganda'.[247] Reminding the Committee that 'war propaganda' was already regarded as a crime in the legislation of many countries including Brazil, and was clearly condemned under international law, Brazil's delegate asserted that if the waging of war was illegal, 'then propaganda inciting to war must certainly also be inadmissible'.[248] He stated that

---

[243] UN Doc A/4341 and Doc A/4636.

[244] A/C.3/SR.1070, para 29.

[245] UN Yearbook, 1960, 336. A/C.3/SR.1044.

[246] A.C.3/L.919; A/C.3/SR.1070, para 30. The texts differed only with regard to the first sentence. Mr Baroody, Saudi Arabia's delegate, approved of the Indian amendment and emphasized that the delegations which had been in favour of that wording, and therefore of the restrictions it mentioned, were no less determined than the other delegations to defend and safeguard freedom of information. A/C.3/SR.1070, para 32.

[247] A/C.3/L.920.

[248] A/C.3/SR.1071, para 5 (Mr Mello).

if this amendment were adopted, Brazil would consider Article 26 on incitement to violence to be redundant and would propose its deletion.[249]

The USSR proposed a similar amendment which would have permitted the restriction of freedom of expression as necessary 'for the prevention of war propaganda, incitement to enmity among nations, racial discrimination, and the dissemination of slanderous rumours'.[250] Although considering the Indian amendment to have certain positive elements, notably the clause excluding the systematic dissemination of false reports and of expressions inciting to war, and praising the reference to 'war propaganda' in the Brazilian amendment,[251] the USSR nevertheless asserted that the formulation in its text was clearer and more explicit.[252]

The broad support for the inclusion in the Covenant of a prohibition of incitement to violence, apparent from the Commission debates noted above, combined with the hostile attitude of many states to the term 'war propaganda', would suggest that a consensus on this subject might have been reached had the term 'incitement to war' been retained over the term 'propaganda for war'. This view is accentuated by the fact that when the General Assembly had voted on Article 2 of the Draft Convention on Freedom of Information in 1960, only the Nordic states had voted against the provision, with the consistent critics of proposals concerning propaganda for war such as the United Kingdom, Canada, Belgium, and the United States having abstained.[253]

The reason that this approach was not advocated by the Soviet Bloc or other states may be divined from the meaning of 'war propaganda' as expounded upon by Soviet jurists who had distinguished it from incitement to war, stating that whereas 'war propaganda' is very close to incitement to war 'it does not coincide with it'.[254] In the legal system of the USSR 'war propaganda' differed from incitement to war in that it need not have contained a 'direct call to war', and entailed criminal responsibility, 'also where there is no direct call to war against a specific state; a general call to aggression is enough for the notion of propaganda'.[255] Bulgaria shared this understanding, stating that the core of the dispute concerned 'the prevention of war propaganda, *including* the dissemination of slanderous rumours which undermined relations between States, and incitement to national, racial or religious hatred'.[256]

---

[249] A/C.3/SR.1071, para 6.   [250] A/C.3/L.921.

[251] The USSR did not approve, however, of the reference to 'class prejudice' contained therein. A/C.3/SR.1071, para 21.

[252] A/C.3/SR.1071, para 20.

[253] Article 2 of the Draft Convention on Freedom of Information was adopted in December 1960, 50:5 with 19 abstentions. A/C.3/SR.1044, para 47. The Nordic states which had opposed the provision's adoption were Denmark, Finland, Iceland, Norway, and Sweden.

[254] VD Men'shagin and PS Romashkin (eds), *Sovetskoe Ugoluvnie Pravo* [Soviet Criminal Law], Special Part (Moscow, 1957) 536–7. Cited in John B Whitton and Arthur Larson, *Propaganda*, 157, fn 120.

[255] ibid.

[256] A/C.3/SR.1074, para 5 (emphasis added).

Several delegations had, like Brazil, suggested that should Article 19(3) permit the restriction of speech which constituted war propaganda then Article 26 on the prohibition of incitement to violence would no longer be necessary. This further suggests that 'war propaganda' represented a composite of different forms of incitement to violence, of which war was the most grievous outcome. Mali for example argued that provisions relating to propaganda for war and hatred among people were more appropriate in Article 19 on the grounds that they would have a broader field of application than in Article 26.[257] This was supported by Ghana which understood it to serve 'the same purpose as article 19'.[258]

The Chilean delegate led the proposals that 'the modern phenomenon of propaganda' could be dealt with most strongly in draft Article 26 rather than Article 19. He suggested that the two distinct problems of protecting the right to freedom of expression and of prohibiting incitement to enmity and discrimination should be dealt with in separate articles. In order that the underlying connection between the two principles involved would be clearly seen, he recommended placing Article 26 immediately after Article 19, and renumbering it as Article 20.[259] Asserting that in contemporary society, 'information—both in its sources and the means used for its dissemination—was in the hands not of individuals but of groups, parties, the State, etc',[260] he said that if the prohibition was to be made absolute it should not be listed among the restrictions provided for in Article 19, which was otherwise couched in basically positive terms allowing states an option to impose restrictions, but in Article 26 which required states to prohibit certain forms of propaganda, on the grounds that:

Propaganda, good or bad, was one of the features of modern society, the inevitable counterpart of the free expression of ideas and opinions. The problem which it undeniably represented, however, should be dealt with, not in article 19, but in article 26, which treated the matter in a clear and forceful manner.[261]

Nonetheless, Chile acknowledged that for the purposes of the Covenant it might be difficult to define 'propaganda', and suggested that if the words 'incitement to violence' in Article 26 were replaced by the words 'incitement to violence and war', then the delegates of Brazil and the USSR might be satisfied and withdraw their amendments.[262]

Pakistan[263] and Senegal,[264] sharing the view of those who felt that war propaganda was too great an evil to be given only passing mention in the Covenants, also advocated the retention of Article 26, suggesting that the ideas embodied in the Brazilian and Soviet amendment be incorporated therein rather than in Article 19. Likewise, the Philippines advocated that those

[257] A/C.3/SR.1075, para 31.　　[258] A/C.3/SR.1072, para 11.
[259] A/C.3/SR.1071, para 22.　　[260] A/C.3/SR.1072, para 21.
[261] ibid, para 24.　　　　　　　[262] ibid.
[263] A/C.3/SR.1073, para 43.　　[264] ibid, para 57.

restrictions on the right to freedom of expression necessary 'for the purpose of safeguarding international peace and security' should be set out in Article 26.[265] Austria agreed that the need to prevent war propaganda, incitement to enmity among nations, racial discrimination, and the dissemination of slanderous rumours should find a place in the Draft Covenants, but also regarded these provisions as being distinct and unconnected to the right to freedom of expression.[266] The delegate of the United Arab Republic was of similar opinion, also opining that Article 26 should immediately follow Article 19 as the two texts were 'not contradictory and there was no duplication. They were complementary and both were designed to promote international peace and understanding.'[267] Placing the stance taken by many of the non-aligned and developing countries in context, he stated that their position regarding global media was 'all the more difficult as their opinions and actions were often misinterpreted or distorted either as a result of a lack of interest, if the crisis was not acute enough to threaten the peace, or out of a desire to serve the interests of a given group'.[268]

The USSR, although distinguishing between the permissive nature of the restrictions on Article 19 and the obligatory nature of Article 26, continued to advocate the inclusion of 'war propaganda' as a permitted restriction to the right to freedom of expression, stressing that its amendment was not intended to replace Article 26.[269] It is notable that despite its repeated statements that 'war propaganda' was illegal, a danger to peace, and contrary to the purposes and principles of the United Nations, at no point did the USSR advocate that it should be subject to a mandatory prohibition rather than a permissive restriction.

Commenting on this discrepancy, Uruguay's delegate stated that such restrictions would be more suitably mentioned in Article 26 since '[f]ar from being weakened thereby, as the USSR representative feared, such restrictions would rather be strengthened, since article 26 imposed a strict restriction on States'.[270] Expressing his support for the prohibition of war propaganda, though dubious as to the practicality of the proposed amendments, he discerned a divide between those delegations 'which wanted article 19 to establish definitions of, and guarantees for,

---

[265] A/C.3/SR.1072, para 39.

[266] A/C.3/SR.1074, para 40.

[267] A/C.3/SR.1073, para 25.

[268] ibid, para 20. Chile noted in this regard that 'it was essential to bear in mind that many countries possessed very limited media of information and consequently had to rely on the information systems of the highly advanced nations. Countries inhabited by 70 per cent of the world's population did not satisfy the minimum requirements for information media established by UNESCO.' A/C.3/SR.1078, para 11.

[269] The USSR's delegate, Mr Sapozhnikov, noted that, 'while article 19 provided only that the exercise of the right to freedom of expression might be subject to certain restrictions, obviously at the discretion of individual States, article 26 laid down a specific obligation to prohibit harmful propaganda'. A/C.3/SR.1071, para 23.

[270] A/C.3/SR.1072, para 40.

rights they considered absolutely fundamental', and on the other, 'those which wished to convert it into a list of restrictions designed to protect the State from human freedom'.[271] He claimed that such divisions had been apparent 'ever since human rights had first been discussed [...] because they involved two different ideological outlooks'.[272] He considered that physical actions—the propaganda of the deed—in addition to print or press campaigns, could constitute war propaganda. Uruguay considered the dissemination of war propaganda to be a criminal act which should be set forth in a distinct article, but asked who was to decide where it began, since '[t]o advocate the dropping of atomic bombs was obviously war propaganda but what of the unilateral resumption of nuclear tests?'[273]

Asserting that '[t]here appeared to be a tendency in the Soviet Union to regard all unpalatable information as propaganda',[274] the USA considered the changes proposed by India and Brazil to be unnecessary since 'propaganda and prejudice could be overcome only by the freest possible flow of information making the facts available to the people'.[275] The USA proceeded to submit an amendment which was based on a merger of subparagraphs 1 and 2 of Article 2 of the Draft Convention on Freedom of Information, but minus the terms 'systematic dissemination of false reports harmful to friendly nations and of expressions inciting to war or to national, racial, or religious hatred; attacks on founders of religions; incitement to violence and crime', precisely those which Brazil had termed 'war propaganda'.[276]

The US draft reintroduced the prohibition of prior censorship which the other delegates had omitted to comment upon, and is notable for the retention of the clause 'to prevent incitement to violence by fostering national, racial or religious hatred'. This was a significant compromise on the part of the USA, which explained that the verb 'prevent' had been used 'to preclude any interpretation that would open the door to prior censorship'.[277] Claiming that by incorporating this amendment into Article 19, the Committee would be promoting consistency

[271] A/C.3/SR.1075, para 2.

[272] ibid.

[273] ibid, para 4.

[274] A/C.3/SR.1074, para 18.

[275] A/C.3/SR.1071, para 12. Sweden considered the proposed limitations in the Indian amendment to be unsuitable for 'clear and precise definition'. A/C.3/SR.1073, para. 50. The Turkish delegate also noted his unease with the language of the Indian amendment, claiming that '[i]t would be difficult for a judicial authority to decide whether false reports had been disseminated systematically or not. Were they not to be condemned if they had been disseminated unsystematically?' A/C.3/SR.1075, para 12.

[276] The US text of Article 19(3) read '[t]he above-mentioned rights shall not be subject to any restrictions except those which are provided by law, are necessary to protect national security, public order (ordre public), public health or morals or the rights and freedoms of others, to prevent incitement to violence by fostering national, racial or religious hatred, and are consistent with the other rights recognized in this Covenant. However, these limitations shall not be deemed to justify the imposition by any State of prior censorship of news, comments and political opinions and may not be used as grounds for restricting the right to criticize the Government.' A/C.3/L.925.

[277] A/C.3/SR.1074, para 20.

in the various articles, the US delegate stated that this clause was intended to combat hate-mongers and hate-propaganda groups and its inclusion 'indicated that the methodical defamation by which the Nazis had come to power had not been forgotten in her country, any more than it had in other parts of the world'.[278] She concluded by stating that this clause 'overlapped sufficiently with the Soviet proposal concerning prevention of war propaganda to obviate the necessity for including such a separate concept in the third paragraph'.[279]

The USSR objected, stating that the US text was too narrowly construed since if only those ways of fostering national, racial, or religious hatred which constituted an incitement to violence were to be condemned, the text of Article 19 would be inadequate for the protection of human rights.[280] Poland expressed surprise at the opposition aroused by the proposed prohibition of war propaganda, 'for nobody seemed to fear that the Covenants would be too lengthy as a result of the repeated—and very appropriate—references to the restrictions relating to public order and to public health and morals in a democratic society'.[281]

Rather than dealing directly with this growing groundswell of support for a prohibition of war propaganda, the USA, joined by states such as Belgium, issued clumsy rejoinders to such arguments when it remained open to them to attempt to direct the discussions away from 'war propaganda' towards the clearer formulation of 'incitement to war'. Belgium made the assertion that '[t]he question [of restrictions] was thus not one of censorship, but of the degree of restriction of freedom of expression necessary for the preservation of morals in a civilised State'.[282] Likewise, the USA stated that 'in speaking of alleged censorship of publicity on radio and television, the Soviet representative seemed to have confused censorship and restraint [since] to prevent misleading publicity from being broadcast could not be considered a form of censorship'.[283] Read in combination these arguments appear both weak and obtuse, particularly in light of the grave nature of the topic being discussed, and no doubt compounded the difficulty of many non-aligned states in accepting the US view as to the role which international law had to play with regard to speech which had the potential to ignite a third world war.

In an attempt to secure a compromise agreement, Indonesia proposed, as a substitute for the three amendments, a formula to be added at the end of paragraph 3 which would have permitted restriction of expression 'for securing peaceful and neighbourly relations among nations and races'.[284] Cambodia expressed similar sentiments and urged the Committee to insert the phrase 'in conformity with the principles of a democratic society and with the spirit of the Charter' after

[278] A/C.3/SR.1074.
[279] ibid.
[280] ibid, para 36.
[281] A/C.3/SR.1073, para 29.
[282] A/C.3/SR.1075, para 14.
[283] A/C.3/SR.1076, para 26.
[284] A/C.3/L.923/Rev 2 (an earlier draft had read 'or peaceful co-existence between nations and races' A/C.3/L.923); A/C.3/SR.1072, para 49.

the words 'and are necessary' in Article 19(3). Such wording it was claimed would suffice to place the restrictions in a clearer and more positive context.[285]

When Chile formally proposed that immediately after considering Article 19 the Committee should take up the debates on Article 26, which would then become Article 20,[286] the Chair agreed and it was so decided.[287] This decision resulted in a shift in the tempo of the debates. The USA withdrew its proposal, while Brazil withdrew its amendment[288] and proceeded to submit an amendment to Article 26.[289] India was prepared to accept the original text of Article 19, but 'in view of the importance to all countries, including those of Latin America, of maintaining peace and preventing war propaganda',[290] associated itself with Indonesia in proposing the addition, at the end of paragraph 3—subject to which India was willing to withdraw its earlier amendment—of the phrase '[f]or the promotion of peace and friendly relations among peoples and nations'.[291]

Two relevant amendments remained before the Committee: those of the USSR and the amendment co-sponsored by Indonesia and India. Chile was willing to accept the original text of Article 19 without difficulty,[292] but was not convinced by the arguments in favour of the amendment submitted by India and Indonesia.[293] Noting that under the terms of Article 19(3), states 'would not be bound to adopt provisions to promote the cause of peace',[294] Chile asserted that only in 'an article such as the present article 26 could the desire of all delegations to further the cause of peace be expressed'.[295] Similarly, the Moroccan delegate felt that the Indian and Indonesian amendment might be better placed in Article 26, since it 'imposed a definite prohibition, it served the purposes of the amendments better than did article 19, which merely offered to Governments certain possibilities'.[296] At this point the Chairman recalled that it had been agreed that, subject to the approval of the other members of the Committee, Article 26 might contain a mention of propaganda for war *or* incitement to war, as well as of incitement to racial discrimination and national enmity.[297] As the debates neared a

---

[285] A/C.3/SR.1074, para 32.
[286] A/C.3/SR.1073, para 46 (Mr Casaneuva).
[287] ibid, para 49.
[288] A/C.3/L.920.
[289] A/C.3/L.930; A/C.3/SR.1076, para 7. An amendment submitted by eleven Latin American States (A/C.3/L.926 and Add 1. Argentina, Chile, Colombia, Costa Rica, Ecuador, Guatemala, Nicaragua, Panama, Peru, Uruguay, and Venezuela) which had not been discussed was also withdrawn on the understanding that they would support the original text of Article 19 and that the references to propaganda for war thus withdrawn would be reconsidered in relation to the new Article 20. A/C.3/SR.1076, para 5.
[290] A/C.3/SR.1076, para 10.
[291] A/C.3/L.923/Rev 2.
[292] A/C.3/SR.1076, para 33.
[293] ibid, para 34.
[294] ibid.
[295] ibid, para 35.
[296] ibid, para 40.
[297] ibid, para 41.

conclusion, Yugoslavia's delegate suggested that by inserting in paragraph 3, after the word 'restrictions', the words 'compatible with the principles and purposes of the Charter of the United Nations', the Committee would have created the advantage not only of expressing the idea contained in the amendment of India and Indonesia, but also of covering all the points in regard to such matters as racial enmity and propaganda for war contained in the various amendments.[298]

Before proceeding to the results of the voting on the various proposals, it may be useful to reflect on a dialogue between the delegates of the United Kingdom and the USSR which aptly indicates the level to which Cold War tensions were impacting upon the ability of the United Nations to draft a core instrument of international human rights law. The delegate of the United Kingdom considered that the USSR amendment, though 'based on universally recognised principles, seemed to cover too wide a field in too loose a way',[299] pointing out that it would permit governments to forbid the dissemination of practically any opinion by calling it a 'slanderous rumour'.[300] Intent perhaps on undermining the high moral stance of the USSR, she added that recent statements made by the USSR Premier, Mr Khrushchev, on the nuclear strength of the USSR might be interpreted by some countries as 'war propaganda', which 'was presumably not the intention of the Head of the Soviet Government, since the Constitution of his country prohibited such propaganda'.[301] She claimed that such examples demonstrated the difficulty in defining the terms used in the USSR amendment which her delegation would not therefore be able to support. The USSR delegate responded by claiming that 'Mr Khruschev had simply stated that anyone rash enough to launch a war against the Soviet Union or one of the socialist countries must expect to bear the consequences of his action. A statement of that kind could not, in good faith, be described as "war propaganda".'[302]

By this stage it was apparent that by shifting the proposals related to propaganda for war to the new Article 20, there remained little dispute over the remaining provisions of Article 19.[303] The Peruvian delegate added that although freedom of expression 'prevented the abuse of authority and was an indispensable means of counteracting propaganda',[304] his delegation was prepared, as was that of Panama,[305] to consider the Brazilian amendment concerning war propaganda in connection with Article 26.[306] The Chairman invited the Committee to vote on the three paragraphs of Article 19 and the amendments thereto. Paragraph 1 was adopted unanimously and paragraph 2 was adopted 88:0 with 1 abstention.

---

[298] A/C.3/SR.1076, para 48.   [299] ibid, para 20.
[300] ibid.   [301] ibid.
[302] ibid, para 29.
[303] Thus the delegate of Congo (Leopoldville) said that he would vote against the amendments of the USSR and India and Indonesia, rather than abstain, 'purely out of its desire to avoid any unnecessary overloading of article 19 and in the hope that the proposed amendments would be examined when article 26 came up for discussion'. A/C.3/SR.1077, para 9.
[304] A/C.3/SR.1077, para 30.
[305] ibid, para 40.   [306] ibid, para 33.

A roll-call vote was taken on the Indian and Indonesian amendment to paragraph 3[307] and it was rejected 343 : 44 with 13 abstentions.[308] The Chairman next invited the Committee to vote on the first part of the USSR amendment[309] up to and including the words 'racial discrimination'. The amendment was rejected 25 : 42 with 23 abstentions.[310] The Chairman decided, in view of that result, not to put the second part of the amendment to the vote. Paragraph 3 was adopted 71 : 7 with 12 abstentions. Article 19 as a whole, as drafted by the Commission in 1952, was adopted 82 : 1 with 7 abstentions.[311]

ii. Article 20(1): Propaganda for War

The USA opened this final phase of debate on the question of propaganda for war by repeating its view that whereas the advocacy of national, racial, or religious hostility constituting an incitement to violence 'could be, and ought to be, forbidden, and [that] she was therefore in sympathy with the spirit of the article', the phrase 'incitement to hatred' could undermine the right to freedom of expression, and thus the article 'in its present wording [. . .] should be deleted from the Covenant'.[312] This distinction between the prohibition of incitement to violence, and incitement to other forms of hostility such as hatred, which were considered by many to be at the root of such violence, was to be the definitive issue in the Committee's seminal debate on propaganda for war. The debates were to turn on two distinct understandings of 'war propaganda'. The first would have prohibited only that form of propaganda which incites to war, while the second, broader interpretation would also encompass propaganda which was regarded as creating the 'atmosphere' necessary for incitement to war to be effective.

The first amendment to be discussed was Brazil's proposal to insert the phrase 'including war propaganda' between the words 'violence' and 'shall be prohibited', so that Article 26 would read:

Any advocacy of national, racial or religious hostility that constitutes an incitement to hatred and violence, including war propaganda, shall be prohibited by the law of the State.[313]

---

[307] A/C.3/L.923/Rev 2.

[308] A/C.3/SR.1077, para 55.

[309] A/C.3/L.921.

[310] A/C.3/SR.1077, para 57.

[311] ibid, para 58. Article 19(3) 'The exercise of the rights provided for in paragraph 2 of this article carries with it special duties and responsibilities. It may therefore be subject to certain restrictions, but these shall be such only as are provided by law and are necessary, (1) for respect of the rights or reputations of others, (2) for the protection of national security or of public order, or of public health or morals.'

[312] A/C.3/SR.1078, para 6.

[313] A/C.3/L.930. This was subsequently revised to read '[a]ny advocacy of national, racial or religious hostility that constitutes an incitement to hatred and violence, including war propaganda, shall be prohibited. This prohibition shall be incorporated in the law of the State.' A/C.3/L.930/Rev 1.

Brazil considered Article 26 to be incomplete as it stood since, 'while it stipulated provisions to be included by States in their domestic laws, it did not lay down any international legal rule such as might possibly serve as a basis for international legal machinery designed to guarantee the protection of human rights'.[314] In supporting this proposal,[315] Chile's delegate attempted to draw a distinction between propaganda and information by stressing, 'propaganda began when a medium of communication surrendered its function of informing or instructing disinterestedly and started to serve a specific end'.[316] He noted that 'organised propaganda' played a preponderant role in shaping public opinion 'even in the great democratic Powers of today, which exalted individualism and freedom of opinion'.[317] Acknowledging that propaganda was difficult to define precisely, he said that it 'could in general be regarded as the art of influencing public opinion through the deliberate and systematic dissemination of information tending to affect the emotions',[318] and asserted succinctly that:

It did not proliferate opinions or stimulate the power of judgement but levelled out ideas and controlled the attitudes of individuals and groups. Paradoxically, propaganda often drew upon genuine information, but never in such a way as to provoke a clash of ideas.[319]

Nor did he consider the lack of an accepted legal definition justification for the dismissal of the issue,[320] stating that the need for legal provisions concerning propaganda could hardly be questioned in the aftermath of 'Hitlerism', which 'had conditioned people to commit the most atrocious crimes'.[321] In support of the proposal he cited as legal precedents:

[T]he action of the League of Nations; the judgements of the Nuremberg Tribunal, some of which had been rendered in cases involving solely the dissemination of Nazi propaganda; the two historic decisions of the General Assembly contained in resolution 110(II), entitled 'Measures to be taken against propaganda and the inciters of a new war' and resolution 381(V) entitled 'Condemnation of propaganda against peace'; the draft Convention on Freedom of Information, which dealt with the question of propaganda in some detail; and, the provisions on propaganda contained in the laws and constitutions of many States.[322]

In response to the query put by the Danish delegate during the discussions on Article 19 as to 'who was to decide what was and was not war propaganda',[323] the Chilean delegate assumed that this role would be played by national courts, and conveyed his delegation's wishes that Article 26 'should end with the words "shall be prohibited by the law" rather than "shall be prohibited by the law of the State", for in that way the matter of implementation would be placed firmly in the hands of the legislatures and the courts'.[324] Malaya suggested that if 'war

---

[314] A/C.3/SR.1079, para 3.   [315] A/C.3/SR.1078, para 15.
[316] ibid, para 8.   [317] ibid, para 10.
[318] ibid, para 12.   [319] ibid.
[320] ibid, para 13.   [321] ibid, para 14.
[322] ibid.   [323] A/C.3/SR.1074, para 27.
[324] A/C.3/SR.1078, para 15.

propaganda' meant expression constituting an incitement to hatred and violence then the words 'including war propaganda' should be inserted after the word 'hostility' rather than after the word 'violence'.[325]

Nonetheless, Brazil's proposal was replaced by a revised joint amendment, the 'nine-power amendment', submitted by the non-aligned states of Brazil, Cambodia, Ghana, Guinea, Iraq, Mali, Morocco, the United Arab Republic, and Yugoslavia, which read:

> Any advocacy of national, racial or religious hostility that constitutes an incitement to hatred, discrimination and violence, as well as war propaganda, shall be prohibited. This prohibition shall be incorporated into the law of the State.[326]

A crucial distinction between the nine-power amendment and that of Brazil is that whereas the latter prohibited advocacy of hostility that constitutes an incitement to violence 'including' war propaganda, the former dissociated war propaganda from the elements of national, racial, or religious hostility by providing for the prohibition of incitement to violence, '*as well as* war propaganda'. This is a wider-reaching formula which consolidated the movement towards expanding the concept of 'war propaganda' beyond expression directly inciting to war.

This intention was confirmed by the Brazilian delegate who explained that 'war propaganda' meant 'the repeated and insistent expression of an opinion for the purpose of creating a climate of hatred and lack of understanding between the peoples of two or more countries, in order to bring them eventually to armed conflict'.[327] He asserted that this was an intention 'which any court should be able to establish as easily as it established animus injuriandi or animus defendendi in criminal law'.[328] Recalling that General Assembly Resolution 110(II) condemning war propaganda had been adopted unanimously, he expressed his regret towards the change of attitude revealed by the statements of the United Kingdom and the USA.[329] Concerning linguistic discrepancies between the various texts, Brazil's delegate requested the Secretariat to try to bring the English, French, and Spanish texts of his delegation's amendment into line. The first used the word 'advocacy' and the other two the words 'propagande' and 'propaganda'. He suggested the word 'propaganda' for the English text, or the words 'manifestatión' and 'manifestación' for the other two texts.[330]

A new 'concise four-power amendment' was submitted by Saudi Arabia, the Philippines, Lebanon, and Thailand.[331] This text was the first to use the phrase 'propaganda for war', which had been included without any suggestion that it had a different meaning from 'war propaganda'. It proposed that:

> Any propaganda for war and any advocacy of national, racial and religious hatred inciting to violence shall be prohibited by law.[332]

---

[325] ibid, para 21.
[326] A/C.3/L.930/Rev 2.
[327] A/C.3/SR.1079, para 2 (Mr Mello).
[328] ibid (emphasis in original).
[329] ibid, para 4.
[330] ibid, para 5.
[331] ibid, para 60.
[332] A/C.3/L.932.

Varying interpretations were applied to this text. Saudi Arabia, a sponsor of the proposal, hoped that it 'might provide a partial remedy for the cold war, in which propaganda was in fact the principal weapon', and suggested that '[p]erhaps that is why those using it were afraid of being deprived of it'.[333] It also stated that it was intended to restrain states by law 'from advocating the overthrow of other governments through hostile propaganda'.[334]

The liberal democracies shared the Greek view that this formulation meant that 'propaganda for war was really only a form of incitement to violence'.[335] The US delegate expressed interest in achieving 'an appropriate wording' of Article 26,[336] and made a striking compromise by indicating support for the four-power amendment and in particular the phrase 'inciting to violence', which as the core of the amendment was regarded as solving the difficulties of the USA. This amendment, she felt, set out the principle the USA supported 'in a straight-forward and lucid manner [...] while not leaving the way open for abuse'.[337] Italy's delegate also said that the principle of Article 26 should become a rule of law in every state,[338] but as her delegation was unhappy with using so vague a term as 'propaganda', asked whether the sponsors of the various amendments might not find a basis for discussion in the following text, '[a]ny advocacy of national, racial and religious hatred that constitutes incitement to violence and war shall be prohibited by law'.[339] Although still concerned that Article 26 could be used to facilitate unwarranted restrictions on the right to freedom of expression, the delegate of the Netherlands confirmed that his delegation was prepared to cooperate with the majority of the Commission by not opposing its adoption.[340] Similarly, the United Kingdom's delegate stated that she was not now pressing for the deletion of Article 26, but that her inability to vote for the article remained unchanged.[341]

Several other delegates made comments at this point which differ considerably from the position advanced by the liberal democracies. India's delegate expressed his approval that in the 'nine-Power amendment' and the 'four-Power amendment', the question of propaganda for war had been dissociated from the concept of 'violence', thus removing the possibility that Article 26 could not be invoked before the outbreak of war.[342] The Chilean delegate found the Spanish text of the

---

[333] A/C.3/SR.1078, para 18 (Mr Baroody).
[334] ibid.
[335] A/C.3/SR.1081, para 73.
[336] A/C.3/SR.1080, para 19.
[337] ibid.
[338] A/C.3/SR.1081, para 65.
[339] ibid, para 66.
[340] ibid, para 15.
[341] A/C.3/SR.1080, para 17.
[342] ibid, para 2. The Saudi delegate, commenting on the meaning of advocacy of hostility inciting to hatred or violence, stated that the proposal did not require violence before the prohibition could be enforced and interpreted the phrase 'inciting to violence' as clearly referring to 'propaganda and advocacy which were of a nature to incite to violence and not which had incited to violence'. A/C.3/SR.1080, para 20.

'four-Power amendment' to be unsatisfactory, as it appeared to condemn war propaganda only if it incited to violence. That, he claimed, was entirely redundant, 'for such propaganda itself constituted an incitement to violence', although an appeal to national, racial, or religious hatred, on the other hand, could only be punishable if it was coupled with incitement to violence.[343] The Chilean delegate suggested that it was the idea of 'incitement to violence' that introduced a juridical element into propaganda, and such incitement should be duly condemned, as in the 'four-Power amendment', which he considered 'more logical and more likely to rally unanimous support' than the nine-power amendment.[344]

Refuting claims that propaganda for war was impossible to define, the Iraqi delegate stated that world public opinion was sufficiently conscious and sufficiently developed 'to recognise such propaganda when it appeared',[345] and noted that not a single delegation had spoken against the principles set forth in Article 26 and the amendments.[346] The delegate of the Philippines warned that the destructive power of modern armaments was so great that it was no longer possible to accept the risk of a war merely in order to safeguard freedom of expression and considered Article 26 to sanction 'the right to life and the right to live in peace with one's neighbours'.[347] Cambodia's delegate stated that he was not surprised by the shift in the attitude of the United Kingdom and the USA, given that 'those delegations had realised that there was no possibility of their point of view being accepted and that it was in their own interest to support the text that was closest to it'.[348]

The Congo's (Leopoldville) delegate considered Article 26 in its present form to be totally ineffective since propaganda was 'undeniably difficult to define', though he regarded the formula 'incitement to violence' to be a clear and precise notion which could be prohibited by the UN.[349] Pakistan favoured the adoption of the expression 'propaganda for war' which appeared in the 'four-Power amendment' since it considered the term 'war propaganda' used in the 'nine-Power amendment' to be too vague.[350] Indonesia's delegate considered peace to mean 'not merely the absence of war, but also the absence of any propaganda likely to lead to an arms race',[351] and suggested that Article 26 be drafted as follows: '[a]ny propaganda for war, and any advocacy of national, racial or religious hostility inciting to intolerance, discrimination or violence shall be prohibited by law.'[352]

The Chairman then drew the Commission's attention to the 'sixteen-Power amendment'.[353] The text had been prepared by a working group consisting of the sponsors of the 'nine-Power amendment' and the 'four-Power amendment',

---

343 A/C.3/SR.1081, para 42.
344 ibid, para 40.
345 ibid, para 55.
346 ibid, para 58.
347 ibid, para 23.
348 ibid, para 60.
349 A/C.3/SR.1079, para 41.
350 A/C.3/SR.1081, para 48.
351 ibid, para 1.
352 ibid, para 80.
353 A/C.3/L.933.

both of which had now been withdrawn, as well as other interested delegations and sought to dissociate the prohibition of 'propaganda for war' from incitement to violence in order to ensure that both the antecedent propaganda for war, in addition to direct incitement to war, fell within the meaning of the term.[354] This amendment read as follows:

1. Any propaganda for war shall be prohibited by law.
2. Any advocacy of national, racial or religious hatred that constitutes incitement to discrimination, hostility or violence shall be prohibited by law.[355]

Brazil's delegate stated that since there seemed to be a very strong feeling in the Committee that a clear condemnation of propaganda for war be made, the sponsors of the joint amendment had decided to devote a separate initial paragraph to the matter.[356] He explained that the words 'prohibited by law' meant that the actions covered by the article would be prohibited by the domestic law of the countries acceding to the Covenant.[357] The Yugoslav delegate repeated these statements,[358] and described how on each occasion that his country had been subject to acts of aggression, the aggression had been preceded 'by propaganda aimed at creating war psychosis, intolerance and hatred among peoples'.[359] He asserted that moving the reference to propaganda for war into a separate paragraph served to meet the objections of those delegations 'which had regarded the linking of propaganda for war with incitement to violence as implying the possibility of [permitting] war propaganda which did not incite to violence'.[360]

The US delegate felt that this text had unduly broadened the meaning of 'propaganda for war' beyond direct incitement to war. She said that she would have been able to accept the expression 'propaganda for war' only if it had remained linked, as in the 'four-Power amendment', with the precise legal concept of incitement to violence.[361] She again stated that the term 'propaganda for war' was ill defined and could lead to abuses of the right to freedom of expression,[362] enquiring as to whether media reporting the 'explosion of a high-power bomb [...] could be accused of engaging in war propaganda'.[363] Cyprus also preferred the four-power text since it made the prohibition of propaganda for war dependent on incitement to violence, thus reducing the risk of abuse.[364] The delegate of Ecuador was

[354] Brazil, Cambodia, Congo (Leopoldville), Ghana, Guinea, Indonesia, Iraq, Lebanon, Mali, Morocco, Philippines, Poland, Saudi Arabia, Thailand, United Arab Republic, and Yugoslavia. A/C.3/SR.1082, para 1.
[355] A/C.3/L.933.
[356] A/C.3/SR.1082, para 3.
[357] ibid, para 7.
[358] ibid, para 13.
[359] A/C.3/SR.1079, para 11.
[360] A/C.3/SR.1082, para 10.
[361] A/C.3/SR.1083, para 15.
[362] ibid, para 16.
[363] ibid, para 17.
[364] A/C.3/SR.1082, para 18.

unhappy with the 'broad drafting' of paragraph 1, but stated that he would support the amendment if the words '[a]ny propaganda that incites to war' were substituted for '[a]ny propaganda for war'.[365] The French delegate was highly critical of the fact that the phrase 'propaganda for war' had not been suggested until such a late stage in the drafting and accurately noted that 'its definition would present serious difficulties when the time came for the practical and legal application of the article'.[366] Uruguay's delegate had similar misgivings as to the definition of 'propaganda', since it was understood by some as 'the simple act of communicating information' while to others 'it was an evil in itself', and in his opinion, at most the word could be said to describe 'a certain breadth of dissemination of information, as distinct from communications between individuals'.[367]

India recalled that it had suggested the formula 'inciting to war' in its proposal on Article 19(3) but that delegates such as those of the USA had felt that this would unduly restrict freedom of information. Refusing to accept that 'propaganda for war' was a vague expression, it asserted that the 'sixteen-Power amendment' was not imprecise, as the goal aimed at was clear. It was not for the Committee to interpret the text, the delegate noted, as that would be the task of the national courts.[368] Towards the conclusion of the debate, Saudi Arabia stated that:

[...] in modern times propaganda represented a weapon in the service of State policy in nearly all the industrialised countries of the world, and that it must not be confused with freedom of information [...] In the present day, the masses were too beset by daily economic cares to be capable of arriving at a genuinely informed opinion: they were conditioned by the big press agencies which told them what to think; only the privileged class engaged in non-manual professions was able to resist such propaganda [...] War propaganda was extremely well organised today and delegations must not persist in a position taken up ten years earlier [...]. [369]

The USSR asked for a roll-call vote on the sixteen-power amendment, even if a separate vote were to be taken on the two paragraphs.[370] The Committee adopted

---

[365] ibid, para 19.

[366] A/C.3/SR.1083, paras 11–12. Mr Bouquin, the French delegate, also expressed concern that placing Article 26 after Article 20 would destroy the harmonious whole presented by Articles 24, 25, and 26 of the Draft Covenant, in addition to undermining the freedoms laid down in Article 19. A/C.3/SR.1083, para 7.

[367] ibid, para 21. The delegate of Japan, whilst agreeing that all propaganda for war should be prohibited (A/C.3/SR.1083, para 29), stated that she was unable to vote for the article solely because its wording remained vague and imprecise and because she felt that it could be invoked to suppress freedom of information. A/C.3/SR.1083, para 30.

[368] ibid, para 34.

[369] ibid, para 36. Concluding the debates in the Third Committee, the delegate of Congo (Leopoldville) acknowledged that, while the fear expressed by several delegations that excessive restrictions might be placed on freedom of expression 'was a most praiseworthy expression of concern', he did not think it justified, nor supported by conclusive arguments. Drawing on analogy, he stated that it was as logical to restrict freedom of expression by prohibiting propaganda for war as to restrict individual liberty by prohibiting murder and theft. A/C.3/SR.1083, para 45.

[370] ibid, para 51.

a Malian proposal that they should proceed immediately to a vote, and the Chair stated that delegations that wished to do so could explain their votes after the voting.[371] This proposal was adopted,[372] but aroused much bitterness on behalf of several delegations. The Committee was invited to vote on the two paragraphs of the 'sixteen-Power amendment'.[373] Paragraph 1 of this amendment was adopted 53 : 21 with 9 abstentions.[374] A vote on the phrase 'to discrimination, hostility or' in paragraph 2 was also adopted,[375] and paragraph 2 as a whole was adopted 50 : 18 with 15 abstentions.[376] The Chairman then put to a roll-call vote Article 26 as a whole, in the form of the 'sixteen-Power amendment', and it was adopted 52 : 19 with 12 abstentions.[377]

D. Summary

As the drafting of Article 20 drew to a close, there had been two distinct positions taken on the question of the prohibition of propaganda for war. On the one hand were those states which, although dubious as to the wisdom of including the term 'propaganda for war' in the Covenant, were willing to compromise and accept its inclusion on the understanding that it was to be interpreted as 'incitement to war'. The majority of states, considering such a restrictive interpretation to be far from adequate in light of the dangers posed by propaganda for war which fell

---

[371] A/C.3/SR.1083, para 48.

[372] ibid, para 54. 44 : 19 votes with 10 abstentions.

[373] A/C.3/L.933.

[374] A/C.3/SR.1083, para 55. In favour: Yemen, Yugoslavia, Afghanistan, Albania, Brazil, Bulgaria, Burma, Byelorussian SSR, Cambodia, Cameroun [Cameroon], Central African Republic, Ceylon, Chad, Chile, Congo (Brazzaville), Congo (Leopoldville), Cuba, Czechoslovakia, Dominican Republic, Ethiopia, Ghana, Guinea, Haiti, Hungary, India, Indonesia, Iraq, Israel, Lebanon, Liberia, Libya, Mali, Mexico, Morocco, Nicaragua, Niger, Nigeria, Pakistan, Peru, Philippines, Poland, Romania, Saudi Arabia, Spain, Sudan, Thailand, Togo, Tunisia, Ukrainian SSR, USSR, United Arab Republic, Upper Volta, Venezuela.
Against: Argentina, Australia, Belgium, Canada, Denmark, Ecuador, Federation of Malaya, Finland, France, Iceland, Ireland, Italy, Japan, the Netherlands, New Zealand, Norway, Sweden, Turkey, UK, USA, Uruguay.
Abstaining: Austria, China, Colombia, Cyprus, Greece, Iran, Panama, Portugal, South Africa.

[375] ibid, para 57. 43 : 21 with 19 abstentions.

[376] ibid, para 58.

[377] ibid, para 59. In favour: Dominican Republic, Ethiopia, Ghana, Guinea, Haiti, Hungary, India, Indonesia, Iraq, Israel, Lebanon, Liberia, Libya, Mali, Mexico, Morocco, Nicaragua, Niger, Nigeria, Pakistan, Peru, Philippines, Poland, Romania, Saudi Arabia, Sudan, Thailand, Togo, Tunisia, Ukrainian SSR, USSR, United Arab Republic, Upper Volta, Venezuela, Yemen, Yugoslavia, Afghanistan, Albania, Brazil, Bulgaria, Burma, Byelorussian SSR, Cambodia, Cameroun [Cameroon], Central African Republic, Ceylon, Chad, Chile, Congo (Brazzaville), Congo (Leopoldville), Cuba, Czechoslovakia.
Against: Denmark, Ecuador, Federation of Malaya, Finland, Iceland, Ireland, Italy, Japan, the Netherlands, New Zealand, Norway, Sweden, Turkey, UK, USA, Uruguay, Australia, Belgium.
Abstaining: France, Greece, Iran, Panama, Portugal, South Africa, Spain, Argentina, Austria, China, Colombia, Cyprus.

short of direct incitement to a specific war, succeeded in overcoming substantial opposition and securing the adoption of a much broader provision.

Similar differences had arisen with regards to the drafting of Article 20(2), with many states which had accepted the necessity of prohibiting incitement to violence, remaining opposed to the prohibition of incitement to hatred. In both Article 20(1) and Article 20(2), the final outcome was the adoption of a provision which obliged states to prohibit not only incitement to war or violence, but also certain forms of speech which were considered to be antecedent to incitement to violence. In the case of the prohibition of propaganda for war, this explains why the majority of the Third Committee was unwilling to accept a prohibition of incitement to war only. It was felt that a provision which was limited to prohibiting incitement to war would have little chance of securing a lasting peace and preventing future conflicts. A precedent for the prohibition of such propaganda may be found in General Assembly Resolution 381(V) on the '[c]ondemnation of propaganda against peace' which was noted in the previous chapter.[378] Therein the General Assembly had not only condemned incitement to war but also restrictions on freedom of expression intended to prevent understanding between peoples, as well as measures aimed at distorting the activities of the United Nations in favour of peace. The inclusion in the International Bill of Rights of a similar obligation on states was premised on the principle that peace is more than the absence of war, and required that states take positive measures in line with the Charter to ensure its realization. It is also in keeping with the judgment of the IMT at Nuremberg which considered illegal propaganda to constitute not just incitement to specific wars, but also the creation of a warlike atmosphere in which such incitement could take root. Given the widely accepted view that propaganda for war posed an immense obstacle to the upholding of the purposes and principles of the UN Charter the adoption of Article 20(1) was considered essential in order to secure and maintain world peace.

Despite the heated debates and the persistent criticisms that 'propaganda' lacked any acceptable definition, there were few attempts at clearly outlining the meaning of either the term 'war propaganda' or 'propaganda for war'. It appears that most delegates who had been in favour of the provision were satisfied that when such propaganda arose they, or their national judiciary, would have little problem in identifying it. This may explain why the term 'propaganda for war' could replace 'war propaganda' at such a late stage in the drafting process with so little critical comment.

---

[378] GA Res 381(V), 17 November 1950. Paragraph 2 condemned:

'1. Incitement to conflict or acts of aggression;

2. Measures tending to isolate people from any contact with the outside world, by preventing the Press, radio and other media of communication from reporting international events, and thus hindering mutual comprehension and understanding between peoples;

3. Measures tending to silence or distort the activities of the United Nations in favour of peace or to prevent their peoples from knowing the views of other States Members.'

It is clear that there are two distinct elements to 'propaganda for war'. The first concerns 'incitement to war'. Since Brazil had introduced the term 'war propaganda' into the final phase of debates and had been party to the drafting of all but one of the proposals considered in relation to draft Article 26, it is apt that the Brazilian delegate had provided the clearest explanation of the second element, when he declared that it meant 'the repeated and insistent expression of an opinion for the purpose of creating a climate of hatred and lack of understanding between the peoples of two or more countries, in order to bring them eventually to armed conflict'.[379] Although the liberal democracies were staunchly opposed to accepting an obligation to prohibit such forms of propaganda, this interpretation was carried by the weight of the non-aligned states. Their stance in this regard was plainly put by the delegate of the Cameroon when he stressed that '[t]he nations which had recently thrown off the yoke of colonialism and those which were still under some form of servitude had great need of the safeguards afforded by article [20]'.[380]

[379] A/C.3/SR.1079, para 2 (Mr Mello).
[380] ibid, para 35.

4

The Prohibition of Propaganda for War in International Human Rights Treaties

A. The International Covenant of Civil and Political Rights

Given the conflicting hopes and fears which accompanied the adoption of Article 20(1) of the International Covenant on Civil and Political Rights[1] and the significance of the principle in question, the paucity of academic analysis of the interpretation and application of the provision is remarkable. Even during the Cold War, when efforts to regulate international propaganda by law attracted significant attention from scholars, commentary on the provision rarely went beyond an acknowledgement that it was an 'encouraging development in the direction of growth of conventional law',[2] or that it signified 'ample evidence of the deep concern of the international community with respect to the dangers of hostile international communications'.[3] This trend continues to prevail and the prohibition of propaganda for war has merited little more than a cursory reference in many more recent publications with notable exceptions including Karl Partsch,[4] Dominic McGoldrick,[5] and Manfred Nowak who considers propaganda for war to constitute 'intentional, well-aimed influencing of individuals by employing various channels of communication to disseminate, above all, incorrect or exaggerated allegations of fact. Also included thereunder are negative or simplistic value judgements whose intensity is at least comparable to that of provocation, instigation, or incitement.'[6] The spirit of the principle has been lauded by authors such as Rhona Smith who considers the restriction set forth in Article 20 as being of 'paramount importance to the realization of the purposes

---

[1] International Covenant on Civil and Political Rights, Adopted and opened for signature, ratification and accession by General Assembly Resolution 2200A (XXI) of 16 December 1966, entry into force 23 March 1976, 999 UNTS 171.

[2] BS Murty, *Propaganda and World Public Order*, 266.

[3] John B Whitton, 'Aggressive Propaganda', 248.

[4] Karl J Partsch, 'Freedom of Conscience and Expression, and Political Freedoms', in Louis Henkin (ed), *The International Bill of Rights: The Covenant on Civil and Political Rights* (New York: Columbia University Press, 1981) 209–45.

[5] Dominic McGoldrick, *The Human Rights Committee: Its Role in the Development of the International Covenant on Civil and Political Rights* (Oxford: Clarendon, 1991) 480–97.

[6] Manfred Nowak, *U.N. Covenant on Civil and Political Rights*, 472.

of the United Nations itself',[7] and Paul Sieghart who identified the fundamental objective of the United Nations—international peace and security—as being expressed positively in Article 28 of the UDHR and negatively in Article 20(1) of the Covenant.[8]

It is worth repeating at this juncture that throughout the drafting of the provision few delegations departed from the orthodox assumption that it was the press and other media which presented the greatest threat to world peace through the use of propaganda for war. The role of the state and the responsibility of governments themselves for instigating and promoting propaganda for war were mentioned by only a handful of delegations, despite the fact that it is governments who are in a position to wield the force of propaganda for war most efficiently. This overriding emphasis on the restriction of the speech of individuals and the corresponding neglect of the responsibility of government and state actors for propaganda for war has prevailed since the entry into force of the Covenant.

i. Provisions of National Law Giving Effect to Article 20(1)

Article 20(1) requires that 'propaganda for war' be prohibited by law, but does not specify whether criminal or other forms of responsibility are required. The *travaux préparatoires* suggest that there was a widely held assumption that a penal provision would be the most suitable and perhaps the only effective means of giving effect to the obligation. Although there had been little sustained discussion on this point, Italy explained its vote against the provision on the grounds that it 'threatened the structural balance of the draft Covenant, the essential purpose of which was to safeguard human rights, and not to legislate against crime'.[9] Christian Tomuschat, a former member of the Human Rights Committee, has described Article 20 as the main example of that category of Covenant rights which require that penal statutes be enacted in order to safeguard specific rights or goods of exceptional vulnerability.[10] A review of provisions of national law by which States parties have given effect to the prohibition demonstrates a strong inclination towards prohibiting propaganda for war through criminal rather than civil legislation. Nowak posits that a criminal prohibition is necessary since 'it is clear that in the event of a heightened threat of war, States will hardly be able to make do without criminal sanctions if they are to enforce this prohibition'.[11] However, given that propaganda for war encompasses more than

---

[7] Rhona KM Smith, *Textbook on International Human Rights* (2nd edn, Oxford: Oxford University Press, 2005) 289.

[8] Paul Sieghart, *The International Law of Human Rights* (Oxford: Clarendon Press, 1983) 372.

[9] A/C.3/SR.1084, para 14.

[10] Christian Tomuschat, 'National Implementation of International Standards on Human Rights', Can Hum Rts YB 31 (1984-5) 45.

[11] Manfred Nowak, *U.N. Covenant on Civil and Political Rights*, 474.

direct incitement to war it may be incorrect to suggest that legislation other than penal legislation may be of little consequence, particularly when applied against individuals or groups who may have little influence upon their society. Given the concerns about the impact of the prohibition on the right to freedom of expression, significant consideration should be given towards restricting the application of penal legislation to the most grievous cases of propaganda for war. Most states favour penal legislation to give effect to the Article 20(2) obligation to prohibit incitement to violence, yet these two provisions may be distinguished by the scale of the violence against which each is directed, the latter form of violence being far less difficult to bring about by private individuals or groups given that the power to initiate wars of aggression lies predominantly in the hands of the state only.

Partsch has remarked that a provision explicitly mentioning 'propaganda for war' is not necessary so long as 'the act of propagating war comes under a general prohibitory clause in the penal or other law'.[12] Given the lack of a generally accepted definition of 'propaganda for war', states have consequently employed a variety of terms when taking action to give effect to the provision. Just as a variety of terms were used during the drafting process, examples of terms used in national legislation include 'incitement to war', 'war propaganda', and 'propaganda for aggression'.

Considering the stress which the USSR placed on the subject of propaganda for war during the drafting process, it is not surprising that the majority of states which have criminal legislation prohibiting propaganda for war were once within the communist sphere of influence. In its first periodic report to the Committee, the USSR, retaining its preferred phrase 'war propaganda' as opposed to 'propaganda for war', noted its constitutional provision that '[i]n the USSR war propaganda is banned'.[13] A law entitled 'The Defence of Peace' stated that 'war propaganda', no matter what form it might take, was a criminal offence since it undermines the cause of peace and creates the threat of another war and was therefore an 'extremely serious crime against humanity'.[14]

Similar provisions were cited in the initial periodic reports of Czechoslovakia and the German Democratic Republic, prompting the Committee to ask for further details as to the exact terms of the legislation as '[t]he relevant text would not only be useful for the Committee, but might also be helpful to Governments which had thus far been reluctant to make war propaganda a punishable act'.[15] Illustrative commentaries on how communist states were implementing the prohibition were not forthcoming. Czechoslovakia merely stated, '[t]he aim

[12] Karl J Partsch, 'Freedom of Conscience and Expression, and Political Freedoms', 228.
[13] Article 28: CCPR/C/1/Add 22, 21. The 1977 Constitution of the USSR is reprinted in 4 Rev Socialist L 57 (1978). It should be noted that 'the prohibition of war propaganda' was included in the official 'Syllabus on International Law for Law Faculties of Universities and Juridical Institutes' in the USSR. WS Butler, 'The Teaching of International Law in the USSR', 8 Rev Socialist L 183 (1982) 190.
[14] ibid.
[15] Mr Tomuschat, CCPR/C/SR.65, 3. See also CCPR/C/SR.67, 12.

of that law was to encourage understanding and co-operation between States, with a view to establishing peace and effective human rights'.[16] The German Democratic Republic stressed the link between propaganda for war and propaganda for fascism, noting that, under the Penal Code, proceedings could be initiated against anyone engaging in propaganda for a war of aggression or other aggressive acts.[17] Graefrath, also a Committee member, cited Article 89 of the Penal Code of the German Democratic Republic as an example of legislation that does give effect to Article 20(1):

A person who makes propaganda for a war of aggression, another aggressive act or use of nuclear weapons or other means of mass extermination for aggressive purposes or calls for the violation of international agreements which service the preservation and consolidation of peace or, in this context, incites towards the persecution of supporters of the peace movement, uses force against such persons on account of their activities, persecutes them or causes them to be persecuted, is liable for imprisonment of from two to eight years.[18]

By prohibiting not only incitement to war, but also what may be termed 'propaganda against peace', in addition to persecution of the anti-war movement, this example corresponds with the broadest interpretation of the prohibition of propaganda for war advanced by the drafters of Article 20(1). Many States parties that were once part of the Soviet Bloc have retained similar, if less far-reaching, legislation. Armenia's Constitution prohibits the exercise of rights and freedoms 'for purposes of [...] propaganda for violence and war',[19] and its Criminal Code provides that 'propaganda for war, in whatever form it may be conducted, shall be punished'.[20] Similarly, Moldova's Constitution requires the prohibition of incitement to war and aggression,[21] while its Criminal Code stipulates that war propaganda of any kind shall be punished by imprisonment.[22] Azerbaijan's Criminal Code provides for an offence of disseminating war propaganda in any form,[23] and that of the Kyrgyz Republic prohibits 'any form of advocacy of war'.[24] Latvian criminal law prescribes liability for public incitement to commence a war of aggression or a military conflict.[25] Under civil law, the publication of information which is a state secret or any other secret specifically protected by law that incites to violence and advocates war,[26] the dissemination of propaganda for war

---

[16] CCPR/C/SR.66, 8.
[17] CCPR/C/SR.68, 9–10.
[18] B Graefrath, 'How Different Countries Implement Standards on Human Rights', Can Hum Rts YB 3 (1984–5) 10. Graefrath had been appointed to the Committee by the German Democratic Republic.
[19] Article 48: ICCPR/C/92/Add 2 (1), para 212.
[20] ibid, Article 66.
[21] Article 32(3): ICCPR/C/MDA/2000/1 (1), para 549.
[22] ibid, para 550: Article 68.
[23] Article 64: ICCPR/C/AZE/99/2 (2), para 499.
[24] Article 65; ICCPR/C/113/Add 1 (1), para 425.
[25] Article 77: CCPR/C/LVA/2002/2, para 274.
[26] ibid, para 277: Article 7 of the Law 'On Press and Other Mass Media'.

at meetings, processions, and pickets,[27] and the broadcast of programmes which include an incitement to cause war or a military conflict are prohibited.[28] Estonia's Criminal Code defines propaganda for war in any form as a crime against the state,[29] while in Slovakia any propaganda for war is a criminal offence justified on the grounds of safeguarding peace.[30] The Polish Penal Code prohibits public incitement to initiate a war of aggression.[31] Russia's Criminal Code penalizes planning, preparing for, embarking on, or conducting a war of aggression, as well as public incitement to embark on a war of aggression.[32] Russian Criminal Law further prescribes liability for public incitement to commence a war of aggression or a military conflict.[33] Ukraine's Penal Code provides that 'public calls for an aggressive war or a decision to unleash a military conflict are punishable by imprisonment'.[34] Romania has asserted that, in the light of the recommendations and comments of the Committee, propaganda for war is considered one of the most serious offences under the domestic Penal Code and is therefore listed alongside genocide under the title 'Crimes against peace and humanity'.[35]

The Penal Code of the former Yugoslavia provided for an offence of 'advocacy of or incitement to aggressive war',[36] and similar provisions have also been retained in the penal codes of several of the independent Balkan states. The Criminal Code of Serbia and Montenegro prescribed a prison term for 'advocating war or for war mongering activities that are considered to be criminal offences'.[37] Similarly, the Croatian Criminal Code provides that 'whoever calls or instigates a war of aggression shall be punished by imprisonment from one to ten years',[38] an offence which has been clarified by the inclusion of a definition of aggression in the Criminal Code.[39] In Slovenia, '[p]ropaganda for war and incitement to national, racial or religious hatred which would mean the encouragement of discrimination, enmity or violence are sanctioned in the Penal Code as criminal acts'.[40] The initial periodic report of Bosnia and Herzegovina notes that in accordance with

---

[27] ibid, para 278: Article 10 of the Law 'On Meetings, Processions and Pickets'.

[28] Article 17 of the Law 'On Radio and Television': CCPR/C/LVA/2002/2, para 279.

[29] Article 69: CCPR/C/81/Add 5, para 168.

[30] Act No 165/1950 Coll; CCPR/C/81/Add 9, para 77.

[31] Article 117(3): CCPR/C/POL/2004/5, para 340.

[32] Articles 353 and 354: CCPR/C/RUS/2002/5.

[33] ibid, Article 77.

[34] CCPR/C/UKR/6, para 302: Article 63. Article 3 of the Act on Printed Mass Media (the Press) prohibits the publication in the mass media of propaganda for war. ICCPR/C/UKR/99/5 (5), para 508.

[35] Title XI: ICCPR/C/95/Add 7(4).

[36] Article 152: CCPR/C/1/Add 23, para 22.

[37] CCPR/C/SEMO/2003/1, para 520.

[38] Article 157(4): ICCPR/C/HRV/99/1(1), para 461.

[39] ibid, para 462.

[40] CCPR/C/74/Add 1, para 53. Slovenia continued to inform the Committee that: 'There are no instances of such crime in the Republic of Slovenia, although in the territory of certain other states of former Yugoslavia war is raging [...].'

the Constitution and the Criminal Code, 'calling and motivation' for war is a criminal act punishable by up to ten years' imprisonment.[41]

Propaganda for war is prohibited under Vietnam's Penal Code as well as by the Law on the Press and the Law of Publication.[42] The Law on Education contains provisions prohibiting 'educational activities aimed at distorting the State's guidelines, policies, and law, destroying the national unity, inciting violence, propagandizing for aggressive war'.[43]

Examples of such legislation are less commonly reported by other States parties. The Moroccan Penal Code stipulates that 'any propaganda for war is prohibited by law'.[44] Kenya's Penal Code expressly prohibits any propaganda for war either directly or indirectly, and requires a mandatory life sentence for the offence.[45] Although Cameroon claimed to have adopted 'an extremely severe position against any persons guilty of incitement to war',[46] there are no references to the relevant legislation included in its periodic reports.[47]

Of the Western European States parties a Monaco Ordinance dating from 1910 states that expression which incites to theft, murder, pillaging, or war shall be punished.[48] Under the title of 'crimes against peace', the Portuguese Penal Code provides that any person who, publicly and on several occasions, is guilty of incitement to hatred against a people for the purpose of starting a war is liable to imprisonment,[49] and under the heading of 'crimes against the state', includes the crime of the performance of actions likely to bring about war.[50] Article 26 of the German Basic Law (*Grundgesetz*) provides that 'acts leading to and undertaken with intent to disturb peaceful relations between nations' shall be unconstitutional and punishable as an offence.[51] Section 80 of the Criminal Code (*Strafgesetzbuch*) sets forth an offence of preparation for a war of aggression which causes danger of a war involving Germany.[52] In accordance with Section 80(a) 'everyone who in public, at assemblies or by distribution of pamphlets incites to aggressive war will be liable to imprisonment'.[53]

---

[41] CCPR/C/BIH/1, para 225.
[42] ICCPR/C/VNM/2001/2 (2), paras 216–19.
[43] ibid, para 220.
[44] ICCPR/C/115/Add 1 (4), para 163.
[45] Chapter 63 in Section 44: CCPR/C/KEN/2004/2, para 164.
[46] CCPR/C/63/Add 1, para 87.
[47] CCPR/C/102/Add 2.
[48] Article 16 of the Ordinance of 3 June 1910: ICCPR/C/MCO/99/1 (1), para 152.
[49] CCPR/C/PRT/2002/3, para 20.2.
[50] ibid, Article 236: para 20.3.
[51] CCPR/C/1/Add 18, 26.
[52] '§ 80 Vorbereitung eines Angriffskrieges
Wer einen Angriffskrieg (Artikel 26 Abs. 1 des Grundgesetzes), an dem die Bundesrepublik Deutschland beteiligt sein soll, vorbereitet und dadurch die Gefahr eines Krieges für die Bundesrepublik Deutschland herbeiführt, wird mit lebenslanger Freiheitsstrafe oder mit Freiheitsstrafe nicht unter zehn Jahren bestraft.'
[53] '§ 80a Aufstacheln zum Angriffskrieg
Wer im räumlichen Geltungsbereich dieses Gesetzes öffentlich, in einer Versammlung oder durch Verbreiten von Schriften (§ 11 Abs. 3) zum Angriffskrieg (§ 80) aufstachelt, wird mit Freiheitsstrafe von drei Monaten bis zu fünf Jahren bestraft.' For further details of German penal

Austrian law does not prohibit propaganda for war per se and while the state places a strong emphasis on its obligations under Article 20(2), Austria's periodic reports do not detail legislative or other initiatives taken to satisfy Article 20(1). The sole provision mentioned in Austria's 2006 periodic report which may be considered to fall within the ambit of Article 20(1) is Article 320 of the Criminal Law Code (Prohibited Support to Parties in Armed Conflicts), which prohibits advocating support at public meetings in favour of a party 'during a war or an armed conflict in which the Republic of Austria is not involved, or upon an imminent risk of such a war or conflict'.[54]

Several periodic reports refer to legislation which prohibits specific groups, notably political parties and media outlets, from engaging in propaganda for war. Macedonia's Constitution provides that 'programmes and activities of associations of citizens and political parties may not be directed towards [...] encouragement or incitement to military aggression',[55] and the Law on Broadcasting declares impermissible 'programmes of broadcasting companies which are directed towards [...] encouragement or incitement to military aggression, or stirring up national, racial or religious hatred and intolerance'.[56] In Azerbaijan, the founding and activity of political parties having propaganda for war as their aim or modus operandi is prohibited by law.[57] Lithuania's Law on Political Parties stipulates that political parties the activities of which include war propaganda or advocacy of discrimination, or which violate human rights in any other way, are prohibited.[58] Tanzania reports that although propaganda for war is not specifically prohibited under domestic law, refugees 'are informed that no kind of military training or propaganda for genocide or war shall be entertained while on Tanzanian soil'.[59] It is clear from this survey that while several States parties have narrowly interpreted Article 20(1) and prohibited incitement to war only, the majority of states which have enacted legislation to give effect to Article 20(1) have adopted a broader interpretation. Nonetheless, there are scant examples available of individuals having been prosecuted under domestic legislation prohibiting propaganda for war.

A large number of States parties claim to have satisfied the obligation of Article 20(1) by committing themselves to the object of peace, either through their constitutions, domestic legislation, or international pledges, without having enacted specific legislation concerning propaganda for war. Colombia recognized this

provisions on incitement to hatred and violence see Section 130 of the Crime Prevention Act. CCPR/C/84/Add 5, para 130.

[54] CCPR/C/AUT/4, para 339.
[55] Article 20(3): ICCPR/C/74/Add 4(1), para 419.
[56] ibid.
[57] Article 4, The Political Parties Act: CCPR/C/81/Add 2, para 108.
[58] Article 2: CCPR/C/81/Add 10 (1), para 132.
[59] ICCPR/C/83/Add 2(3), para 116. Reporting under the heading of Article 20, Benin notes that political parties are required 'to prohibit, in their programme and activities, [...] the incitement to or use of violence in all its forms' implying that this includes propaganda for war. Article 4(1): CCPR/C/BEN/2004/1/Add 1, para 95.

distinction when, after suggesting that the prohibition is implicit in its constitutional provision that 'peace is a right and a mandatory duty',[60] it conceded that its legal system reflected the obligation only 'indirectly, incompletely and imperfectly'.[61]

The Committee declared that such general commitments failed to satisfy the obligation set forth in Article 20(1) when commenting in 1981 on the substance of Italy's first periodic report. Italy had relied on the peremptory nature of the declaration as a fundamental principle in the Italian Constitution that 'Italy repudiates war as an instrument of offence against the liberty of other persons and as a means of settling international disputes' to argue that there was no further requirement to promulgate a specific law prohibiting propaganda for war.[62] The Committee stated that repudiation of war 'was not [...] quite the same thing as the prohibition of war propaganda',[63] confirming that since 'a specific law against war propaganda was required [...] Italy had, consequently, not complied with article 20'.[64] The Italian government failed to reply to these comments,[65] and to date has not enacted legislation prohibiting propaganda for war. Tomuschat considered the incorporation of a treaty into national law as being only the first step of implementation and that the enactment of penal statutes prohibiting propaganda for war was a requisite second stage of implementation.[66] Likewise, Graefrath stated that Article 20 required special legislation to be enacted since a simple transformation of the treaty into domestic law did not constitute adequate implementation of the obligations contained therein.[67]

Many states continue to rely on general commitments in order to claim that they are in compliance with the provision. Examples include Gabon, which maintains that since its Constitution reserves the right to declare war to the National Assembly, it has satisfied the requirements of Article 20(1).[68] Syria reports that '[a]dvocacy of a war of aggression is prohibited as a matter of principle since it would constitute interference with a view to changing the Constitution of another State and violating the rights of the latter's citizens, which would be incompatible

[60] CCPR/C/103/Add 3, para 296.

[61] ibid, para 300.

[62] The state report further asserted that if cases of such propaganda occurred, they would be subject to all the penalties laid down in the Penal Code for the various forms they might assume and that this interpretation of the Italian Constitution was 'in full accord with article 19 paragraph 1 of the Covenant'. CCPR/C/6/Add 4, para 83.

[63] Mr Graefrath: CCPR/C/SR.257, para 33. See also Mr Hanga: CCPR/C/SR.257, para 42. Hanga had been appointed to the Committee by Romania.

[64] Mr Sadi: CCPR/C/SR.257, para 73; Mr Koulishev: CCPR/C/SR.258, para 31. Koulishev had been appointed to the Committee by Bulgaria.

[65] CCPR/C/SR.258.

[66] Christian Tomuschat, 'National Implementation of International Standards on Human Rights', 46.

[67] B Graefrath, 'How Different Countries Implement Standards on Human Rights', 10.

[68] CCPR/C/128/Add 1, para 41: Article 49.

with Syria's public policy as can be inferred from its general legal provisions'.[69] Egypt relies on its constitutional obligation to follow a foreign policy premised on making every effort to 'achieve peace, based on justice, for our world' as evidence of its observance of Article 20(1).[70] Kuwait also cites its constitutional commitment to peace and the repudiation of wars and its policy of rejecting propaganda for war as evidence that it has satisfied Article 20(1),[71] as does Sudan.[72]

Sri Lanka has claimed that it is in compliance with Article 20(1) insofar as '[t]he Directive Principles of State Policy and Fundamental Duties under the Constitution of Sri Lanka state that it is the duty of every person to defend the constitution and the law, and to further the national interest and to foster national unity (Article 28)'.[73] Senegal has cited its signature of the Charter of the Organization of African Unity as satisfying the obligation,[74] while Nepal claims that as a member of the United Nations, it has accepted the Charter's prohibition of the threat of and use of force, and thus is vigilant with regard to the prevention of propaganda for war within its territory.[75] Similarly, Yemen refers as evidence of its implementation of the obligation to a constitutional provision by which '[t]he State affirms its adherence to the Charter of the United Nations, the Universal Declaration of Human Rights, the Pact of the League of Arab States and the generally recognized rules of international law'.[76] Thailand has suggested that since its Constitution provides that the state 'shall promote friendly relations with other countries',[77] any propaganda for war is consequently an illegal act in Thailand.[78] Japan refers to the renunciation of war 'as a sovereign right of the nation' in its Constitution as evidence of its satisfaction of Article 20(1)'s obligation, whilst further claiming that 'it is almost inconceivable that any propaganda for war could actually be carried out'.[79] It has stated that, 'should there emerge a danger of a harmful effect of propaganda in future, legislative measures would be studied, as the occasion demands, with careful consideration for freedom of expression'.[80] Finally, and indicative of the forlorn status of Article 20(1), Jordan has announced that whereas there is no legislation prohibiting propaganda for war, it has gone some way towards satisfying the obligation since 'there is no legislation which promotes or encourages war'.[81]

---

[69] CCPR/C/SYR/2004/3, para 193.
[70] CCPR/C/EGY/2001/3, para 501.
[71] CCPR/C/120/Add 1, para 246.
[72] CCPR/C/SDN/3, para 299.
[73] ICCPR/C/LKA/2002/4.
[74] CCPR/C/6/Add 2, 21.
[75] CCPR/C/74/Add 2, para 47.
[76] CCPR/C/82/Add 1, para 84: Article 5.
[77] CCPR/C/THA/2004/1, para 485: Section 74.
[78] ibid, para 486.
[79] ICCPR/C/115/Add 3(4), para 181.
[80] ibid, para 182.
[81] CCPR/C/1/Add 55, 5.

ii. The Obligation on States Parties to Refrain from Propaganda for War

In observing that 'international law is at its strongest when dealing with the liability of a state for the state's own act', Whitton and Larson stressed that 'it is the propagandistic activities of states themselves that hold the greatest potential peril for international relations'.[82] Throughout the drafting of Article 20(1), delegates focused almost exclusively on the role of the press in disseminating propaganda for war, and although several stressed that the provision must, of necessity, apply not only to journalists but to each individual, few commented on the role played by the state in the dissemination of propaganda for war. China (Taiwan) had abstained from the final vote on this account, asking 'how the law of the State could prohibit war propaganda when the State itself was the offender'.[83] Nowak discerns the obligation in Article 20(1) to be primarily one of state responsibility to fulfil and protect at the horizontal level: 'thus states are obliged from engaging in "official" state propaganda and to prohibit any propaganda for war by private persons or semi-state media.'[84] Although the text of Article 20(1) is itself unambiguous insofar as it requires that 'any propaganda for war', without distinction as to the actor involved, 'shall be prohibited by law', this section will demonstrate that it does in fact set forth an obligation which requires the enactment of legislation prohibiting propaganda for war not only on the part of private individuals and other non-state actors but also on government officials and the state itself.

In discussing the nature of the rights set forth in the Covenant, Louis Henkin noted that international agreements, while creating rights and duties for the States parties, may also give the individual 'rights against his society under international law'.[85] He draws on Article 20 as an example of such a provision of international human rights law, emphasizing that while the Covenant creates an international duty upon the states to prohibit propaganda for war, there is also a right in other States parties to have the prohibition enacted.[86]

The Committee clearly affirmed that the obligation in Article 20(1) was to apply to governments in addition to private individuals when discussing Canada's first periodic report in 1979. Therein the Canadian government noted that:

There is no law prohibiting propaganda in favour of war. An individual or organization may, therefore, legally disseminate such propaganda. The Government of Canada cannot do so, however, without breaking the commitments it made by signing the Convention.[87]

[82] John B Whitton and Arthur Larson, *Propaganda*, 60.
[83] A/C.3/SR.1082, para 26.
[84] Manfred Nowak, *U.N. Covenant on Civil and Political Rights*, 473.
[85] Louis Henkin, 'International Human Rights as Rights', 1 Cardozo L Rev 425 (1979) 440.
[86] ibid, 440, fn 49.
[87] CCPR/C/1/Add 43 (vol i), 86–7.

The Committee responded to this 'serious omission'[88] by asserting that the government had not met its obligations in full[89] since 'States had a duty to enact legislation prohibiting not only State agencies but also individuals from making propaganda for war'.[90] Confirming that Article 20(1) 'applied not only to Governments but to every citizen of a country',[91] the Committee stated that:

[H]owever commendable [the] statement of principle, it needed to be accompanied by concrete legal provisions. The question was whether there was any procedure to which a citizen could resort if he felt that the Government was disseminating propaganda in favour of war.[92]

Canada's subsequent periodic report claimed that since the government did not disseminate propaganda for war, citizens need not concern themselves with this type of question.[93] It further suggested that 'if the government did disseminate propaganda in favour of war, citizens would rely on the provisions of the Protocol and submit a communication to the Committee'.[94] The Committee was critical of the government's failure to enact the requisite legislation, and pointing to the guidance provided in the General Comments on Articles 6, 19, and 20 of the Covenant, asked why 'Canada had made no efforts in an area of such vital concern to mankind as a whole'.[95]

Canada responded by stating that, 'even if such provisions were not explicitly contained in the Canadian Charter, the Canadian Government and people were fully aware of the problems of war, the arms race and disarmament. Canada was prepared to take the necessary steps to fulfil its obligations under article 20.'[96] Such general assertions on the part of the government are typical of many States parties who, whilst giving general assurances that they respect the principle that propaganda for war should be prohibited, refrain from actually legislating on the matter. Although the government stated that a fuller report on the issue would be forthcoming, this was not to be the case. While Canada has not reneged on the principle advanced in its first report, it has not followed the Committee's recommendations on the matter and the issue has not been raised in any communication between the parties since.[97]

In a comparison of the Canadian Charter of Rights and Freedoms and the Covenant, WS Tarnopolsky argued that while there was no requirement in either the Covenant, international law, or the Canadian Constitution that an

[88] CCPR/C/SR.206, para 39: Mr Sadi.
[89] CCPR/C/SR.207, para 3: Mr Movchan (appointed to the Committee by the USSR).
[90] ibid, para 27: Mr Koulishev.
[91] CCPR/C/SR.205, para 62: Mr Hanga.
[92] CCPR/C/SR.206, para 8: Mr Bouziri.
[93] CCPR/C/1/Add 62 1983, 80.
[94] ibid.
[95] CCPR/C/SR.560, paras 31 and 42: Mr Movchan.
[96] ibid, para 45.
[97] CCPR/C/51.Add 1, CCPR/C/SR.1010-13, CCPR/C/64.Add 1, CCPR/C/103/Add 5, CCPR/C/SR.1737-8.

exact copy of the Covenant be included in the Canadian Charter, the absence of provisions giving effect to Article 20 from national laws constituted a violation of the Covenant.[98] He considered it reasonable to argue that a prohibition of propaganda for war in accordance with Article 20(1) constituted an appropriate limitation on other rights under Section 1 of the Canadian Charter.[99] The Constitutional Court of South Africa has made a similar finding. Section 16(1) of the Constitution of South Africa provides that everyone has the right to freedom of expression,[100] while Paragraph (2) states that the right does not extend to

  (a) propaganda for war;
  (b) incitement of imminent violence; or
  (c) advocacy of hatred that is based on race, ethnicity, gender, or religion, and that constitutes incitement to cause harm.

Jeremy Sarkin recounts how the African National Congress had advocated the inclusion of these restrictions on the grounds that they were a necessary addition to the 'reasonable and justifiable' limitations of rights provided for in the Constitution's limitations clause.[101] In 2002 the Constitutional Court held that the three categories of expression enumerated in Section 16(2), including 'propaganda for war', are 'expressed in specific and defined terms' and that the provision adequately 'defines the boundaries beyond which the right to freedom of expression does not extend'.[102]

Responding to the widespread failure of States parties to provide sufficient information on the relevant national legislation and practice concerning the implementation of Article 20, the Committee issued General Comment 11 in 1983.[103] Therein the Committee stressed that:

For article 20 to become fully effective there ought to be a law making it clear that propaganda and advocacy as described therein are contrary to public policy and providing for an appropriate sanction in case of violation [and] that States parties which have not yet

[98] WS Tarnopolsky, 'A Comparison between the Canadian Charter of Rights and Freedoms and the International Covenant on Civil and Political Rights', 8 Queens LJ 211 (1982–3) 231. This view is also taken by Freeman and van Ert who consider Canada to have violated Article 20(1) by failing to implement the obligation in Canadian law. Mark Freeman and Gibran Van Ert, *International Human Rights Law* (Toronto: Irwin, 2004) 224–5.
[99] WS Tarnopolsky, 'A Comparison between the Canadian Charter of Rights and Freedoms and the International Covenant on Civil and Political Rights', 215.
[100] Section 16(1): 'Everyone has the right to freedom of expression, which includes—(a) freedom of the press and other media; (b) freedom to receive or impart information or ideas; (c) freedom of artistic creativity; and (d) academic freedom and freedom of scientific research.'
[101] Jeremy Sarkin, 'The Drafting of South Africa's Final Constitution from a Human-Rights Perspective', 47 Am J Comp L 67 (1999) 81. On the limitations clause of the South African Constitution see further Richard J Goldstone, 'The South African Bill of Rights', 32 Tex Int'l L J 451 (1997) 460–4.
[102] *Islamic Unity Convention v Independent Broadcasting Authority and Others*, (CCT36/01) 2002 (4) SA 294; 2002 (5) BCLR 433; [2002] ZACC 3 (11 April 2002), para 35.
[103] General Comment 11, Article 20 (1983), UN Doc HRI\GEN\1\Rev 1 at 12 (1994), para 1.

done so should take the measures necessary to fulfil the obligations contained in article 20, and should themselves refrain from any such propaganda or advocacy.[104]

By this the Committee clearly asserts that legislation is required which declares propaganda for war to be contrary to public policy. According to the Committee, States parties are themselves required to refrain from any propaganda for war, a requirement which is evident both from the Covenant itself and the relevant Resolutions and Declarations of the General Assembly, until such time as they have fulfilled the obligation to enact legislation prohibiting both government and state officials as well as private individuals from engaging in any propaganda for war.

Further confirmation of this obligation is found in General Comment 29 on Article 4 of the Covenant relating to derogations.[105] Issued in 2001, it is the most recent General Comment to reference Article 20(1). Therein the Committee stressed that the Covenant's derogation provision does not mean that other articles in the Covenant may be subjected to derogations at will, even where a threat to the life of the nation exists. Paragraph 13 of the Comment provides several 'illustrative examples' of those provisions of the Covenant that are not specifically listed in Article 4(2) as provisions from which no derogation is permissible, but of which, in the Committee's opinion, there are elements that cannot be made subject to lawful derogation under Article 4. Paragraph 13(e) stated in this regard that:

No declaration of a state of emergency made pursuant to article 4, paragraph 1, may be invoked as justification for a State party to engage itself, contrary to article 20, in propaganda for war, or in advocacy of national, racial or religious hatred that would constitute incitement to discrimination, hostility or violence.[106]

The International Commission of Jurists also found Article 20 to be a non-derogable right which should be included in Article 4(2),[107] while Nowak considers that the significance of General Comment 29 may properly be regarded as lying in 'the express recognition that certain essential rights of the human being and his or her dignity that are particularly endangered in emergency situations may not be restricted in any circumstances'.[108]

A comparative analysis of Article 20(1) and Article 13 of the Migrant Workers Convention adopted by the General Assembly in 1990[109] further augments this

---

[104] ibid, para 2.

[105] General Comment no 29; States of Emergency (Article 4), UN Doc ICCPR/C/21/Rev 1/Add 11 (2001).

[106] ibid, para 13(e).

[107] International Commission of Jurists, *States of Emergency: Their Impact on Human Rights* (Geneva,1983) 440.

[108] Manfred Nowak, *U.N. Covenant on Civil and Political Rights*, 95.

[109] International Convention on the Protection of the Rights of All Migrant Workers and Members of their Families, GA Res 45/158, Annexe 45 UN GAOR Supp (no 49A) at 262, UN Doc A/45/49 (1990), entered into force 1 July 2003.

principle. Article 13 of the Migrant Workers Convention provides for the right to freedom of expression for migrant workers and members of their families and paragraph 3 holds that States parties may limit the right to freedom of expression of migrant workers on four grounds. Subparagraphs (a) and (b) reproduce the restrictions found in Article 19 of the Covenant. Subparagraphs (c) and (d) permit contracting parties to place restrictions on the right to freedom of expression as are provided by law and are necessary 'for the purpose of preventing propaganda for war' and '[f]or the purpose of preventing any advocacy of national, racial or religious hatred that constitutes incitement to discrimination, hostility or violence'.[110]

Article 13(3)(a) differs from Article 20(1) in that it provides for a permissible limitation which the state can place on the right to freedom of expression as opposed to an obligatory one. This distinction is notable since it suggests that propaganda for war, when engaged in by private individuals and particularly by such a precarious category as migrant workers, is not considered to pose as great a threat to international peace as when engaged in by the state itself. Considering the sources examined thus far, particularly the *travaux préparatoires*, it is apparent that had the drafters of the Covenant not intended that states would be required to enact legislation curtailing their own ability to engage in propaganda for war, then the term 'propaganda for war' would have been set forth as a permissible restriction on the right to freedom of expression in Article 19(3) of the Covenant using a similar formula to that used in the Migrant Workers Convention.

Instances of States parties enacting legislation which specifically provides that public officials are liable to prosecution for propaganda for war are uncommon. In Tajikistan, public incitement of a war of aggression is punishable by a fine, while 'the same acts, when committed by use of the media or by persons holding government positions, are punishable by deprivation of liberty for between 7 and 10 years with suspension of the right to hold certain posts or engage in certain activities for up to five years'.[111] The Georgian Criminal Code categorizes as criminal

---

[110] '2. Migrant workers and members of their families shall have the right to freedom of expression; this right shall include freedom to seek, receive and impart information and ideas of all kinds, regardless of frontiers, either orally, in writing or in print, in the form of art or through any other media of their choice.
3. The exercise of the right provided for in paragraph 2 of the present article carries with it special duties and responsibilities. It may therefore be subject to certain restrictions, but these shall only be such as are provided by law and are necessary:
    (a) For respect of the rights or reputation of others;
    (b) For the protection of the national security of the States concerned or of public order (ordre public) or of public health or morals;
    (c) For the purpose of preventing any propaganda for war;
    (d) For the purpose of preventing any advocacy of national, racial or religious hatred that constitutes incitement to discrimination, hostility or violence.'
[111] CCPR/C/TJK/2004/1, para 250: Article 396(2). The periodic report notes that between 1999 and 2003, no criminal proceedings were brought under these provisions, 'since none of the offences in question was committed'.

offences 'public incitement to the conduct of a war of aggression, including through the media or committed by a person holding State political office'.[112] In this instance state political office is defined so as to include the President, members of Parliament, members of the Georgian government, members of the supreme representative bodies, and the heads of the government institutions of the autonomous republics.[113] A comparison of the periodic reports of the Ukrainian Soviet Socialist Republic and post-communist Ukraine highlights the necessity for legislation prohibiting both government officials as well as private individuals from engaging in propaganda for war. The first periodic report submitted by the Ukrainian Soviet Socialist Republic noted the existence of criminal liability for engaging in war propaganda, but continued to assert that '[t]here are in the Republic no classes or social groups which are interested in unleashing a war; and there are therefore no cases of war propaganda'.[114] In a periodic report submitted to the Committee following the collapse of the Soviet Bloc, Ukraine conversely noted that:

The legislative foundation for prohibition of war propaganda was noted in previous periodic reports as having existed in the Ukraine even earlier [than independence], both in the Constitution and in the laws. However, this did not prevent the communist regime from engaging in propaganda and real acts for the furnishing of so-called 'international assistance', including military assistance through weapons and military advisers—or through direct aggression.[115]

iii. The Misinterpretation of 'War'

Several States parties have sought to restrict the scope of Article 20(1) by misinterpreting 'war' in order to suit their own ends. One example is that of states restricting the application of the prohibition to propaganda exposing the state to an external threat of aggression, and not propaganda directed towards initiating aggression by that state against others. Instances of such legislation include the Jamaican Treason Felony Act which provides that:

If any person or persons whosoever [...] move or stir any foreigner or stranger with force to invade this Island, and shall express, utter, or declare, by publishing any printing or writing, or by open and advised speaking, or by any overt act or deed, such compassing, imaginations, inventions, devices, or intentions, or any of them, every person so offending shall be guilty of felony.[116]

Similarly, under the Albanian Penal Code propaganda which exposes the state to the 'eventuality of the intervention of foreign states' is punishable by law.[117]

---

[112] ICCPR/C/GEO/2000/2 (2), para 468: Article 405.
[113] ibid, Article 1(3).
[114] Article 65: CCPR/C/1/Add 34, 23.
[115] CCPR/C/95/Add 2, para 168.
[116] ICCPR/C/42/Add 15 (2), para 102: Section 3.
[117] CCPR/C/ALB/2004/1, para 1006: Article 211.

Israel has limited the scope of Article 20(1) to apply only against 'friendly states' by a penal provision providing that '[a] person who, by making a speech in a public place or at a public gathering or by publishing any writing, endeavours to incite hostile acts against the government of a friendly State is liable to imprisonment for three years'.[118] The Republic of Korea sets forth an offence of agitating to commence hostilities or propagating war against the Republic in conspiracy with a foreign country, or of propagating war between other states in violation of neutrality orders.[119]

It is more usual that States parties, in reporting on measures ostensibly taken to implement Article 20(1), describe the enactment of legislation which greatly expands upon the meaning of 'war'. In this regard reference should be had to India's claim that in order to give effect to Article 20(1) the Indian Constitution provides that 'the State can impose restrictions on the freedom of speech and expression in the interests of friendly relations with foreign States'.[120]

It is submitted that in order to protect the right to freedom of expression, legislation enacted to give effect to Article 20(1) must be clearly delineated to apply only to propaganda for wars of aggression, and not expanded to a concept as broad and nebulous as friendly relations between states without any reference to war. This issue had been addressed by the Committee when considering the first periodic report submitted by the Federal Republic of Germany. The report referred to a provision of the Criminal Code which provided that anyone who in public or at assemblies or by distribution of pamphlets incites to aggressive war would be liable to imprisonment. This provision was premised on Article 26(1) of the Basic Law, which provided that 'acts tending to and undertaken with intent to disturb peaceful relations between nations' shall be unconstitutional and made a punishable offence.[121] While the Federal Republic of Germany was praised by the Committee for having prohibited propaganda for war in accordance with the Covenant,[122] one member asked how the reference to 'peaceful relations between nations' could be reconciled with the activities of Radio Free Europe broadcast from Munich into the Soviet Bloc.[123] The Committee has similarly criticized the offence in Slovakia's Criminal Code of disseminating 'false information abroad which harms the interest' of Slovakia, on the grounds that it is 'so broadly phrased as to lack any specificity' and likely to be in violation of Article 19(3).[124]

---

[118] ICCPR/C/81/Add 13(1), para 166: Penal Law 5737-1977. The periodic report also notes that under the standard of *mens rea* defined in Israeli Penal Law, this prohibition will apply not only to a person who clearly intends to incite to war, but also if that person is merely indifferent or careless regarding the possibility that such hostilities might occur.

[119] CCPR/C/114/Add 1, para 210.

[120] ICCPR/C/76/Add 6 (3), para 103.

[121] CCPR/C/A/Add 18, 26.

[122] CCPR/C/SR.94, para 21: Mr Koulishev.

[123] CCPR/C/SR.94, para 4: Mr Movchan.

[124] CCPR/C/79/Add 79, para 22. A periodic report submitted by the Republic of Korea noted the enactment of legislation under Article 19 of the Covenant which prohibited 'praising, encouraging and propagating anti-State organizations and producing or distributing materials for the benefit of

The *travaux préparatoires* give no suggestion that 'war' was to be understood as anything other than wars of aggression between states in violation of international law. Other forms of propaganda inciting to manifestations of violence such as civil war, rebellion against the government, or violence against the person were either prohibited under Article 20(2) or were grounds for permissible limitations on the right to freedom of expression in Article 19(3). Nonetheless, a tendency has arisen to alter the purpose of Article 20(1) by interpreting 'war' in an extremely broad manner. Of particular concern is the shift towards interpreting 'war' to mean any violence or threat of violence from within the state, or from non-state actors, which is directed against the state structure itself. Should the focus of the provision be permitted to be placed on restricting the speech of non-state actors within a state which is perceived to constitute a threat to the government, Article 20(1) loses its *raison d'être*, and consequently serves as little more than a fourth paragraph to Article 19. It is essential to identify and to confront this trend since, as had been repeated throughout the drafting by the liberal democracies, governmental abuse of the prohibition of propaganda for war with the aim of suppressing internal dissent is likely to have severe repercussions on the individual's ability to enjoy the right to freedom of expression.

Several States parties have failed to acknowledge the distinction between civil war and wars of aggression when reporting under the rubric of Article 20(1). Chile's Penal Code not only restricts the meaning of war by providing for the punishment of anyone who induces a foreign power to declare war on Chile,[125] but the State Security Act concomitantly expands the meaning in a different direction by providing for the punishment of anyone who provokes civil war, 'or the propagation by means of the spoken or written word of theories conducive to the violent overthrow of the social order'.[126] Morocco's Penal Code makes it an offence for 'any Moroccan or foreign national, who, through hostile acts [...] exposes Morocco to a declaration of war'[127] and prohibits 'any act designed to provoke civil war by arming or inciting the people to take up arms against one another, or to cause devastation, massacres and looting'.[128] In reporting on measures taken to implement Article 20(1) Mauritius stated that the offences of 'stirring up war against the State' and of 'stirring up civil war' are punishable by death, while the offence of '[i]nciting citizens to rise up in arms' is punishable by death and forfeiture of property.[129]

---

an anti-State organization', particularly on behalf of organizations agitating for 'violent revolution' or the overthrow of 'the free and democratic system'. CCPR/C/114/Add 1, paras 204-6. The Committee declared this legislation to be unreasonably wide since the Covenant does not permit restrictions on the expression of ideas merely because they coincide with those held by an enemy entity or may be considered to create sympathy for that entity. CCPR/C/79/Add 114, para 9.

[125] ICCPR/C/95/Add 11 (4), para 213; CCPR/C/CHL/5, para 256: Article 106.
[126] CCPR/C/CHL/5, para 256.
[127] CCPR/C/115/Add 1, para 163.
[128] ibid, para 164.
[129] CCPR/C/64/Add 12.

There is little authority to suggest that propaganda inciting to manifestations of violence other than to wars of aggression was intended to be prohibited under Article 20(1). Venezuela has explained to the Committee that whereas the provision of its Criminal Code characterizing 'propaganda for war or incitement of war' as a crime refers explicitly to 'civil war', this formulation is resultant from the fact that the state has not been involved in an international war since independence, and it has assured the Committee that the provision is interpreted as a general prohibition concerning the crime of propaganda for war in its general sense.[130]

Nowak has stated that internal armed conflicts, or 'civil wars', were not meant to fall within the scope of Article 20(1)'s application, 'so long as they do not develop into an international conflict'.[131] Similarly, Partsch interprets the term 'war' as meaning only 'war of aggression'.[132] McGoldrick notes that the working groups which drafted General Comment 11 worked for two years on the definition of war. Proposals that 'war' should not be interpreted broadly to include 'not only open conflicts between two or more countries but also any direct or indirect armed intervention in another country for any reason' were rejected.[133] The General Comment as adopted used the language found in General Assembly Resolution 110(II),[134] asserting that the prohibition 'extends to all forms of propaganda threatening or resulting in an act of aggression or breach of the peace contrary to the Charter of the United Nations'.[135] Although the Committee's statement that '[t]he prohibition applies [...] whether such propaganda or advocacy has aims which are internal or external to the State concerned'[136] may suggest that there are grounds for arguing that propaganda for internal armed conflicts is also prohibited by Article 20(1), such an interpretation would be flawed. By this statement the Committee intended to confirm that States parties were obliged to prohibit all 'propaganda for war' without distinction as to whether the propaganda in question was intended to incite domestic or foreign audiences. The Committee also confirmed, as had been stressed during the drafting of Article 20(1), that the provision does not prohibit 'advocacy of the sovereign right of self-defence or the right of peoples to self-determination and independence in accordance with the Charter of the United Nations'.[137] McGoldrick has

---

[130] CCPR/C/VEN/98/3(3), para 301: Article 144.

[131] Manfred Nowak, *U.N. Covenant on Civil and Political Rights*, 473.

[132] Karl J Partsch, 'Freedom of Conscience and Expression, and Political Freedoms', 227. Jayawickrama also asserts that ' "[w]ar" is understood in the sense of any act of aggression or breach of the peace contrary to the Charter of the United Nations'. Nihal Jayawickrama, *The Judicial Application of Human Rights Law: National, Regional and International Jurisprudence* (Cambridge: Cambridge University Press, 2002) 720.

[133] CCPR/C/SR.429, para 57: Mr Bouziri. Cited in Dominic McGoldrick, *The Human Rights Committee*, 481, fn 13.

[134] GA Res 110(II), 3 November 1947.

[135] General Comment 11, Article 20 (19th session, 1983), UN Doc HRI\GEN\1\Rev 1 at 12 (1994), para 2.

[136] ibid.

[137] ibid.

noted that an earlier draft which would have permitted 'propaganda' in favour of self-determination had been replaced with 'advocacy' in favour thereof so as to 'maintain the subtle distinction of the drafters',[138] a distinction which confirms the contemporary derogatory nature of the word propaganda.

The meaning of 'war' was further clarified in the discourse between the Committee and several of the States parties which have entered reservations and declarations to Article 20(1). France issued a declaration of understanding with regard to the meaning of the word 'war' (*guerre*), to the effect that it meant war in contravention of international law.[139] The Committee held that 'the general prohibition on war propaganda has to be seen in conjunction with article 51 of the Charter of the UN and the right to legitimate self-defence',[140] and approved this interpretation without objection, considering it to be 'extremely judicious from the legal point of view since it distinguished from just and unjust wars'.[141] A similar clause is found in Thailand's declaration which affirms 'that Thailand shall interpret the term "war" to be a "war" under international law, which does not include the war as a result of self defense'.[142] Finland, whose reservation will be considered in some detail below, remarked to the Committee that the wording of the provision was far from specific, asking 'to what kind of war did it refer?'[143] In Finland's view, and the Committee did not disagree, 'since the term "aggression" had been defined by the United Nations, [...] it was obvious that article 20, paragraph 1, must refer only to propaganda for aggressive war, which should be penalized'.[144]

Despite these authorities, many States parties persevere in citing legislation concerned exclusively with the protection of national security or public order when reporting on their implementation of Article 20(1), either independent of, or in addition to, legislation directly concerned with 'propaganda for war'. Indeed, several States parties have suggested that simply by prohibiting paramilitary or terrorist organizations they have fulfilled their obligations under Article 20(1). In this regard Italy referred to its ratification of the International Convention against the Recruitment, Use, Financing and Training of Mercenaries to claim that it had fulfilled its obligations under Article 20(1),[145] and Portugal (Macau) referred the Committee to the Penal Code's prohibition of 'armed, military type, militarized or paramilitary associations and organizations which adopt Fascist ideology'.[146] Spain's first periodic report noted that its Penal Code prohibited 'illegal propaganda' aimed at the violent overthrow of the legal, political, social,

---

[138] Dominic McGoldrick, *The Human Rights Committee*, 436, citing CCPR/SR.447, para 3.
[139] CCPR/C/2/Rev 4, 20.
[140] CCPR/C/SR.440, para 33: Mr Ortega.
[141] ibid, para 46: Mr Hanga.
[142] CCPR/C/THA/2004/1, para 3(e).
[143] CCPR/C/2/SR.30, para 46.
[144] ibid.
[145] ICCPR/C/103/Add 4 (4), para 171.
[146] ICCPR/C/70/Add 9 (3): Article 46(4).

or economic order or directed against the unity of the state.[147] In response to the Committee's question as to whether propaganda for war was prohibited by law,[148] Spain stated that while the Penal Code did not deal with the matter specifically, it could be regarded as falling within the scope of 'illegal propaganda',[149] further illustrating the manner by which many states have understood Article 20(1) as providing security to the state as opposed to protecting the individual from the scourge of wars of aggression.

The 1996 state report of Nigeria, submitted by what was then the Federal Military Government, claimed that Nigeria had acted in direct compliance with the provisions of Article 20 by passing decrees such as the 'Treasonable and Other Offence Decree No. 1 of 1986 under which a coup tribunal has been set up for trial of coup plotters'.[150] Libya proclaimed that propaganda for war is prohibited by law,[151] yet the Penal Code is cited only with regard to the prescription of penalties 'for stirring up intercommunal strife through public incitement to hatred or contempt of any group of persons in a manner that poses a threat to communal stability and security'.[152] Guatemala's Criminal Code provides for the punishment of anyone who, 'in public or by any broadcasting medium, formally and directly incites rebellion or sedition or gives instructions for these to be carried out'.[153] Cyprus's periodic reports state that the relevant provisions of the Criminal Code, with regard to the prohibition of propaganda for war, concern the '[p]reparation of war or warlike undertaking',[154] inciting to mutiny,[155] and '[e]ncouraging violence and promoting ill will'.[156] Syria has also interpreted Article 20(1) to apply to incitement to civil war or intercommunal strife,[157] and additionally notes that the applicable law imposes severe penalties on all acts of terrorism and the perpetrators, accomplices, participants, and instigators thereof.[158] Hong Kong, following the approach adopted while under the United Kingdom's responsibility, has also interpreted propaganda for war to mean propaganda directed against the government only. While the criminal law does not specifically prohibit the distribution of propaganda for war, Hong Kong states that 'if such propaganda, or its manner of presentation, were such as to bring the sovereign Government into hatred or contempt or generally to create disorder, discontent or disaffection, it might

---

[147] CCPR/C/4/Add 5.
[148] CCPR/C/SR.142, para 34: Mr Koulishev.
[149] CCPR/C/SR.143, para 42.
[150] CCPR/C/92/Add 1, para 158.
[151] CCPR/C/102/Add 1, para 295.
[152] CCPR/C/102/Add 1, para 298: Article 318.
[153] CCPR/C/GTM/99/2, para 341: Article 389.
[154] CCPR/C/94/Add 1(3), para 240: Article 40.
[155] ibid, Article 42.
[156] ibid, Article 51.
[157] CCPR/C/SYR/2004/3, para 192: Article 298.
[158] ibid, para 193.

amount to sedition under the current law, at least if there was an intention to provoke a breach of the peace'.[159]

Although Peru has not prohibited propaganda for war, the government asserts with regard to Article 20(1) 'that in the field of violence we have made a great step forward and this represents an important beginning, so that we will be able in the future to carry on legislating on the outstanding issues'.[160] Taking an extremely broad interpretation of Article 20 as a whole, the government described how:

[...] in its desire for pacification, [it] published Decree Law No. 25475, which stipulates in its article 2, that anybody who provokes, creates or maintains a state of anxiety, terror or fear among the population or part of the population [...] which may cause damage or serious disturbance of the peace or affect international relations or the security of the State and society, shall be punished with imprisonment for not less than 20 years.[161]

Likewise, Cambodian legislation cited as satisfaction of Article 20(1) is concerned solely with the prevention of terrorism and civil war.[162] Such an approach is also found in the most recent report of the Democratic Republic of Congo, which refers only to the constitutional provision that '[a]ll Congolese have the right to peace and security. No sector of the national territory may be used as a base for subversive or terrorist activities against any other State.'[163] While the prohibition of propaganda for war in Macedonia's constitutional and civil law has been cited previously, the Criminal Code includes a wide range of additional offences which are claimed to be giving effect to Article 20(1). Thus propaganda for war is interpreted to include acts 'perpetrated by a person who, with the intention of endangering the constitutional order or security of the Republic of Macedonia, publicly or by spreading leaflets calls for or instigates direct perpetration' of crimes ranging from 'acknowledging occupation' to the murder of state authorities and espionage.[164] Madagascar purports to prohibit propaganda for war, and taking account of 'the extremely serious nature of incitement to war [...] does not hold back from imposing the death penalty on those found guilty'.[165] In

---

[159] China (Hong Kong)—ICCPR/C/HKSAR/99/1(1), para 377; CCPR/C/HKG/2005/2, para 269. China is not a State party to the ICCPR but has assumed responsibility for reporting on the implementation of the Covenant in relation to the Hong Kong Special Administrative Region.
[160] CCPR/C/83/Add 1, para 289.
[161] ibid, para 286.
[162] CCPR/C/81/Add 12, paras 303–4.
[163] CCPR/C/COD/2005/3, para 216: Article 53.
[164] CCPR/C/74/Add 4(1), para 421. Under the criminal code such acts 'are perpetrated by a person who, with the intention of endangering the constitutional order or security of the Republic of Macedonia, publicly or by spreading leaflets calls for or instigates direct perpetration of the crimes in article 307 (acknowledging occupation), article 308 (endangering independence), article 309 (murder of representatives of the highest State authorities), article 310 (kidnapping representatives of the highest State authorities), article 311 (violence against representatives of the highest State authorities), article 312 (armed rebellion), article 313 (terrorism), article 314 (diversion), article 315 (sabotage), article 316 (espionage) and article 317 (disclosing a State secret). A prison sentence of three months to five years is foreseen for the offence.'
[165] CCPR/C/MDG/2005/3, paras 316–17.

considering the relevant provision of the Criminal Code, however, Malagasy law appears to exclude wars of aggression insofar as it refers only to attempts 'to incite civil war by arming citizens or inhabitants against one another'.[166]

Although the Committee has rarely commented on the propriety of States parties' expansion of the meaning of 'war', two instances included in Algeria's periodic report in 1998 should have given rise to concern. The first concerned the questioning of journalists who were alleged to have published 'as an advertisement' a call for disobedience and sedition. Algeria found this expression to have 'threatened the security of the state' and understood it as a call for civil war in violation of Article 20(1).[167] The second instance concerned the publication of a pamphlet held to have 'licentiously insulted' a sector of the government with the intention of creating a split in society which 'would, in effect, have been disastrous, not only for the survival of the machinery of State, but also for the unity of the country'.[168] In response the Committee requested that Algeria review its numerous restrictions on the right to freedom of expression concerning material interpreted as sympathy for, or encouragement of, subversion which gravely prejudiced the right of the media to inform the public and the right of the public to receive information, so as to protect fully the right to freedom of thought and opinion and freedom of expression as guaranteed under Articles 18 and 19 of the Covenant.[169] It failed, however, to comment on the propriety of reporting on this matter under the rubric of Article 20, rather than of Article 19 which would have been the proper basis for discussion since it would have been correctly located as a matter of national security or public order rather than of war of aggression.

The comments of Ireland, explaining before the Committee why it had been deemed necessary to reserve the right to postpone the introduction of legislation prohibiting propaganda for war, are notable for their construction as to the meaning of 'war' in Article 20(1). Ireland explained that the reservation 'had been motivated by a concern that approval of an insurrectionary war against apartheid, support of Islamic jihad, or the endorsement of a peace-enforcement initiative like that mounted in Kosovo or Bosnia should not be criminalized or come within the definition of propaganda for war'.[170] This recognition that, for the purposes of Article 20(1), the meaning of 'war' does not extend to 'wars' of national liberation such as the struggle against the apartheid regime in South Africa, the support of non-state actors which use violence against a state, or humanitarian intervention—assuming it is in accordance with the UN Charter—is a position consistent with the *travaux préparatoires* and the interpretation advanced by the Committee.

---

[166] CCPR/C/MDG/2005/3, para 318: Article 91. Under Malagasy law the above penalties are doubled where the offence is committed by a public official in the performance of his or her duties. Para 321.

[167] CCPR/C/101/Add 1(2), para 168.

[168] ibid, para 169.

[169] CCPR/C/79/Add 95, para 16.

[170] CCPR/C/SR.1846, para 20.

iv. Reservations and Declarations

The Covenant's regime of reservations, interpretative declarations, and derogations permits States parties to alter their duties, subject to certain limitations,
under the Covenant and the two Optional Protocols.[171] Reservations and declarations can be made by states upon ratification of the Covenant and serve
either to render the pertinent provisions non-binding or to partially reduce the
effect of a certain guarantee.[172] According to the Committee, the purpose of this
regime is to maximize the amount of ratifications to a treaty by encouraging
states which consider that they have difficulties in guaranteeing all the rights in
the Covenant to nonetheless accept the generality of obligations in that instrument.[173] In General Comment 24, the Committee distinguished declarations
from reservations, stating that:

> If a statement, irrespective of its name or title, purports to exclude or modify the legal
> effect of a treaty in its application to the State, it constitutes a reservation. Conversely,
> if a so-called reservation merely offers a State's understanding of a provision but does
> not exclude or modify that provision in its application to that State, it is, in reality, not a
> reservation.[174]

Article 19(3) of the Vienna Convention on the Law of Treaties[175] stipulates that
where a reservation is not prohibited by a treaty or falls within the specified
permitted categories, a state may make a reservation provided it is not incompatible with the object and purpose of the treaty. While the Committee can give
its opinions on the compatibility of reservations with the Covenant, its views
have no legal force. Nevertheless, the Committee remains the pre-eminent inter-
preter of the Covenant and since its decisions, therefore, are strong indicators of
legal obligations, 'so rejection of those decisions is good evidence of a State's bad
faith attitude to its ICCPR obligations'.[176] The Committee has clearly indicated
that many 'reservations' are both ineffective and incompatible with the object

---

[171] Optional Protocol to the International Covenant on Civil and Political Rights, Adopted and
opened for signature, ratification, and accession by General Assembly Resolution 2200A(XXI)
of 16 December 1966, entry into force 23 March 1976, in accordance with Article 9: Second
Optional Protocol to the International Covenant on Civil and Political Rights, aiming at the
abolition of the death penalty. Adopted and proclaimed by General Assembly Resolution 44/128
of 15 December 1989.

[172] See generally Robert Jennings and Arthur Watts (eds), *Oppenheim's International Law*, vol i,
parts 2–4 (9th edn, London: Longman, 1996) 1240–7.

[173] General Comment no 24: Issues relating to reservations made upon ratification or accession
to the Covenant or the Optional Protocols thereto, or in relation to declarations under article 41 of
the Covenant: (1994). ICCPR/C/21/Rev 1/Add 6, para 4.

[174] ibid, para 3.

[175] The Vienna Convention on the Law of Treaties. Adopted on 22 May 1969 and opened for
signature on 23 May 1969 by the United Nations Conference on the Law of Treaties. Entry into
force on 27 January 1980, in accordance with Article 84(1). UNTS vol 1155, 331.

[176] Sarah Joseph, Jenny Schultz and Melissa Castan, *The International Covenant on Civil and
Political Rights: Cases, Materials and Commentary* (Oxford: Oxford University Press, 2000) 14.

and purpose of the Covenant, thus having 'no impact on the actual extent of the reserving State's ICCPR obligations'.[177]

Following the adoption of the Covenant, AH Robertson assumed that the 'far-reaching' nature of Article 20, combined with the fact that few legal systems actually prohibited propaganda for war and incitement to discrimination in express terms, would mean that ratification of the Covenant would necessitate legislation or reservations in this respect.[178] There have been thirteen reservations[179] and five declarations[180] submitted with regard to Article 20(1), and all but the most recent declaration, submitted by Thailand, have been on behalf of Western liberal democracies. The geopolitical imbalance reflected in the group of states which choose to enter reservations is not surprising since the majority of the liberal democracies voted against the adoption of the provision at the Third Committee of the General Assembly in 1961.[181] Austria, Cyprus, Greece, and Portugal abstained from the final vote and the single Western European government to vote in favour of the provision was Franco's dictatorship in Spain, which, along with France, was to abstain from voting on Article 20 as a whole.[182] The effect of having so many States parties, including several with respected records in promoting the advancement of international human rights mechanisms, refusing to accept the validity of the obligation set forth in Article 20(1) has been a key factor in the sidelining of the provision to date. These states, which are frequently to the fore in criticizing others for failing to implement their obligations under international human rights law and which profess a commitment to an international community premised on the purposes and principles of the United Nations, have, in concert, discounted and abandoned a provision which may yet emerge as a decisive element in the struggle against war.[183]

Although concern as to the threat posed to the right to freedom of expression by Article 20(1) is the common thread linking each of the reservations and declarations, the existence of several distinct approaches to the issue allow for a subdivision into three categories. The first includes Australia, the United Kingdom, New Zealand, Liechtenstein, Switzerland, France, and Ireland. Rather than outright rejections of Article 20(1), these states have reserved the right not

[177] Sarah Joseph, Jenny Schultz and Melissa Castan, *The International Covenant on Civil and Political Rights: Cases, Materials and Commentary* (Oxford: Oxford University Press, 2000) 620.
[178] AH Robertson, 'The United Nations Covenant on Civil and Political Rights and the European Convention on Human Rights', 43 Brit YB Int'l L 21 (1968–9) 40.
[179] Australia, Denmark, Iceland, Ireland, Liechtenstein, Malta, the Netherlands, New Zealand, Norway, Sweden, Switzerland, United Kingdom, United States of America.
[180] Belgium, Finland, France, Luxembourg, Thailand.
[181] A/C.3/SR.1083, para 55.   [182] A/C.3/SR.1083, para 59.
[183] It should be further noted that, in 1975, the year prior to the entry into force of the Covenant, fourteen of the eighteen states which entered reservations or declarations (Belgium, Denmark, Finland, France, Iceland, Ireland, Liechtenstein, Luxembourg, Malta, Norway, Sweden, Switzerland, the United Kingdom, and the United States of America) had signed the Helsinki Final Act, Article 1(b)(i) of which recognized a duty 'to refrain from propaganda for wars of aggression'. Conference on Security and Cooperation in Europe: Final Act, 1 August, 1975. 14 ILM 1292 (1975).

to introduce any further legislation, arguing that pre-existing public order legislation was adequate to achieve the aims of the provision. Although Ireland merely postponed the introduction of legislation giving effect to Article 20(1), it is still to be considered in this group. The second category includes Belgium, Luxembourg, Malta, the Netherlands, and the United States of America, each of which has entered outright reservations to Article 20(1) on the grounds that the provision was inherently incompatible with the right to freedom of expression. The final category consists of the Nordic states of Denmark, Finland, Iceland, Norway, and Sweden. While these states also entered outright reservations, a greater level of discourse between the various governments and the Committee on the matter justifies a separate analysis.

a. Australia, New Zealand, The United Kingdom, Liechtenstein, Switzerland, France, and Ireland

Although none of these states has demonstrated any real commitment towards satisfying the obligation set forth in Article 20(1), they have not formally rejected the principle in its entirety. The Commonwealth countries of the United Kingdom, Australia, and New Zealand entered reservations to the effect that they interpret Article 20 as consistent with Articles 19, 21, and 22, Australia and the United Kingdom stating that, 'having legislated with respect to the subject matter of the article in matters of practical concern in the interests of public order (*ordre public*), the right is reserved not to introduce any further legislative provision on these matters'.[184] New Zealand maintained that it had already legislated in the area of public order with regard to Article 20(2) and, consequently, 'having regard to the right of freedom of speech', reserved the right not to introduce further legislation with regard to Article 20.[185]

Australia felt that to restrict propaganda for war in times of peace would be 'too severe' a restriction on the right to freedom of expression.[186] It continued to note that where there 'has been a clear necessity for restriction of the right in the public interest, or for reasons of international diplomacy, Commonwealth governments have prohibited or suppressed propaganda'.[187] Australia provided as an example the prohibition during the Second World War of propaganda by 'enemy aliens' and the subjection of some forms of communication to censorship.[188] In several communications to the Committee, Australia has cited further examples of

---

[184] Australia, CCPR/C/2/Rev 3, 934: United Kingdom, CCPR/C/2/Rev 3, 961.
[185] New Zealand, CCPR/C/2/Rev 3, 956.
[186] CCPR/C/14.Add 1, para 360.
[187] ibid, para 361.
[188] CCPR/C/AUS/98/3, para 1046. Roger Douglas argues that the Second World War created a climate in which the repression of *anti-war* propaganda became both politically feasible and politically expedient in Australia. Roger Douglas, 'Law, War and Liberty: The World War II Subversion Prosecutions', 27 Melbourne Uni L Rev 65 (2003). Concerning a similar situation in the USA see Geoffrey Stone, 'Free Speech in World War II: "When are you Going to Indict the Seditionists?" ', 2 Int'l J Const L 2 (2004) 334.

legislation which it claims has gone some way towards satisfying the obligation set forth in Article 20(1). These include legislation permitting the Federal
Courts 'to have associations declared unlawful which by propaganda advocate
or encourage the overthrow by force or violence of the established government of
the Commonwealth or of a State or of any other civilized country or of organized
government',[189] and the Crimes (Foreign Incursions and Recruitment) Act 1978
which prohibits the recruitment and training within Australia of persons proposing to engage in hostile activities in foreign countries.[190] These examples demonstrate that Australia has also skewed the meaning of Article 20(1) by reporting
on measures intended to protect national security and public order rather than
prohibiting propaganda for wars of aggression. Moreover, in claiming that its
experience with censorship implies adherence to Article 20(1), Australia is relying
upon the very activities on which its opposition to the adoption of the provision
during the drafting process was founded.

Throughout its exchanges with the Committee, the United Kingdom has
maintained that despite having entered a reservation to Article 20(1), propaganda
for war was nevertheless subject to legislative restrictions. It claimed that such
propaganda could constitute a violation of the Public Order Act 1936: 'if the
propaganda or its manner of presentation, was such as to bring the sovereign or
government into hatred or contempt, or generally to create disorder, discontent
or dissatisfaction, it may amount to sedition [...] or if intended to cause a breach
of the peace.'[191] The government also claimed that even if the rights set forth in
Article 20 were not reflected by such provisions, 'there was nevertheless not at the
present time any practical need for further legislation'.[192] New Zealand adopted
a similar stance, stating that 'depending on the nature of the propaganda and its
presentation, it may well constitute an offence against public order or a breach of
the peace under existing New Zealand law'.[193]

This emphasis on public order legislation fails to satisfy the Article 20(1) obligation in that propaganda for war as engaged in by state and government officials
would actually be portrayed as being in defence of public order and national security. To suggest that the object of Article 20(1) can be achieved simply through
public order legislation is incorrect in light of the intentions of the drafters and the
reality of propaganda for war. René Cassin of France had advanced the view that
the prohibition of propaganda for war fell within the scope of public order legislation during the drafting of the provision. Although this interpretation had been
rejected by the majority of the Third Committee, as evidenced by the adoption of
an explicit prohibition of propaganda for war, it has nonetheless been retained by
the liberal democracies. In advancing his interpretation of public order, Cassin
had in mind a truly democratic society in which no government would engage

---

[189] CCPR/C/42/Add 2, para 504.   [190] CCPR/C/AUS/98/3, para 1049.
[191] CCPR/C/Add 17, 23.   [192] ibid.
[193] CCPR/C/10/Add 6, para 257.

in propaganda for war. By delimiting the scope of the prohibition of propaganda for war to individuals or groups which threaten public order, governments are in effect absolving themselves, and individuals serving their aims, from any accountability for engaging in propaganda for war and thus implicitly reserving the right of the government to engage in propaganda for war under domestic law.

The Committee refused to accept that public order legislation went any considerable way towards satisfying the obligation set forth in Article 20(1) and considered the rationale for the reservations, namely the protection of the right to freedom of expression, as signifying an incorrect interpretation of the Convention. It asserted that not only was Article 20(1) fully consistent with the rights set forth in Articles 19, 21, and 22, but that it 'might be necessary for the protection of [these] rights'.[194] This was further affirmed in General Comment 11 which states that the obligations set forth in Article 20 'are fully compatible with the right of freedom of expression as contained in article 19, the exercise of which carries with it special duties and responsibilities'.[195] Noting that the periodic reports of Australia and the United Kingdom mentioned different kinds of prohibitions that had been deemed necessary to ensure respect for Articles 19, 21, 22, such as legislation concerned with sedition and treason, the Committee noted that 'since all those prohibitions related to various forms of propaganda, demonstrations etc., it did not appear impossible or unnecessary to take similar action in the case of article 20'.[196] The Committee also asked why, since domestic legislation prohibited defamation or slander and, in the case of New Zealand, incitement to war against that country, 'propaganda for war was not prohibited as well'.[197]

Members of the Committee expressed doubts as to the validity of these reservations. It was asserted that since propaganda for war had been prohibited under the Covenant and 'had been condemned as a crime under international law',[198] Australia's reservation was contrary to the Covenant since '[u]nless article 20 was treated as mandatory it would be meaningless'.[199] Similarly, New Zealand was asked whether, in light of the 'many events [which] had occurred in the world since the ratification', the reservation would be withdrawn with a view to the strict implementation of Article 20.[200]

Each of these states remain opposed to accepting the obligation to prohibit propaganda for war by law, repeatedly asserting that there is no necessity for such a prohibition within their jurisdictions.[201] New Zealand responded to the

---

[194] CCPR/C/SR.403, para 22: Mr Graefrath.
[195] General Comment 11, Article 20 (1983), UN Doc HRI\GEN\1\Rev 1 at 12 (1994), para 2.
[196] CCPR/C/SR.403, para 22: Mr Graefrath.
[197] CCPR/C/SR.482, para 41: Mr Graefrath.
[198] CCPR/C/SR.402, para 23: Mr Vallejo.
[199] ibid.
[200] CCPR/C/SR.482, para 27: Mr Vallejo.
[201] Heyns and Viljoen have noted, with regard to Australia, that 'little opposition to the maintenance of the reservation is apparent'. Christof Heyns and Frans Viljoen, *The Impact of the United Nations Human Rights Treaties on the Domestic Level* (The Hague: Kluwer, 2002) 55.

Committee's criticisms by stating that legislation affecting freedom of expression was enacted only when there was a clear need for it and, while claiming that there was no problem of propaganda for war in New Zealand at that time, added that should such a problem arise, the need for legislation making war propaganda a specific offence might be reconsidered.[202] Australia was to make similar statements, asserting that it 'would only be prepared to prohibit propaganda of this nature if a clear need for such action arose'.[203] The United Kingdom explained that the absence of provisions prohibiting propaganda for war was due to the 'specific difficulties' of introducing such provisions into the criminal law.[204] It was also stated that having had regard to General Comment 11, it had decided not to introduce 'the kind of legislation which article 20 seemed to require' on the grounds that 'since war propaganda was not a problem in the UK, there was no need to formulate laws on that subject'.[205]

Both Switzerland[206] and Liechtenstein[207] have entered reservations to the effect that they reserve the right 'not to adopt further measures to ban propaganda for war, which is prohibited by article 20, paragraph 1'. Switzerland has not informed the Committee of measures which it has already taken to address propaganda for war,[208] with the Committee pointing out that the large number of reservations entered by Switzerland mean that it has not fully recognized and implemented the Covenant.[209] Liechtenstein has claimed that whereas its criminal law does not contain an explicit provision concerning the prohibition of 'war propaganda', the obligation is satisfied by 'a wide range of thematically related provisions'.[210] Examples cited include an offence of undertaking to change the constitution of a foreign state or cause the secession of territory belonging to a foreign state through the threat of violence while in Liechtenstein, while under the State Security Act, printed materials calling for acts of violence are prohibited.[211] Such examples fail to satisfy the obligation to prohibit propaganda for war, a shortcoming which Liechtenstein has acknowledged, stating that, '[a]lthough all of these provisions aim to prevent the stirring up of violent conflict, it cannot be claimed with certainty that these provisions are sufficient to satisfy article 20

---

[202] CCPR/C/SR.487, para 47.
[203] CCPR/C/AUS/98/3, para 1048.
[204] CCPR/C/SR.70, 12.
[205] This position was reiterated in several of the UK's periodic reports, without any response by the Committee. CCPR/C/Add 17, 23, CCPR/C/95/Add 5, para 248; CCPR/C/UK/99/5. At one point the government argued that the UK was 'actually confronted with problems due to attempts from within the UK to overthrow the governments of certain countries. But in that area as well it was very difficult to take effective measures because of the problems of definition and application.' CCPR/C/SR.597, para 42.
[206] CCPR/C/2/Rev 3, 957.
[207] ibid 951.
[208] CCPR/C/CH/98/2.
[209] CCPR/C/SR.1537, para 48: Mr El Shafei.
[210] CCPR/C/LIE/2003/1, para 4.
[211] ibid.

paragraph 1 of the Covenant'.[212] The reason given for the failure to satisfy the provision in full is the absence of a generally recognized definition of the term 'war propaganda'.[213] At this juncture it is necessary to stress that despite the clear text of the Covenant, a plethora of States parties, as well as the Committee itself, persist in using the term 'war propaganda' interchangeably with 'propaganda for war'. While it has been noted that national legislation giving effect to the provision need not necessarily contain the term 'propaganda for war', steps towards reaching consensus on the meaning of Article 20(1) would be greatly facilitated by a common adherence to the actual text of the provision.

Rather than reserve the right not to introduce any further legislation with regard to Article 20(1), France's declaration simply stated that 'legislation in this matter is adequate'.[214] Following the submission of France's first periodic report[215] the Committee asked how Article 20(1) was being interpreted.[216] It was put to France that since its declaration and the periodic report claimed that its legislation is adequate, why was it that 'the legal formalities could not be abandoned and a law adopted prohibiting propaganda for war as the UNGA continued to call for, year after year, in resolutions adopted unanimously'?[217] The reply of the French delegate was little more than an obtuse statement confirming that he agreed that the UN Charter took precedence over the Covenant.[218] Recent French periodic reports simply repeat these comments with the additional statement that 'French law, which penalizes the vindication of war crimes, is in keeping with the intentions of article 20'.[219] Such claims do little justice to the purpose of Article 20(1), yet the Committee has failed to challenge France any further on the issue of the prohibition of propaganda for war, focusing instead, as is the case with the majority of state's reports, on steps taken with regard to Article 20(2).

Ireland's reservation can be distinguished by the fact that the government indicated that it fully accepted and would implement, as far as possible, the principle set forth in Article 20(1). Nonetheless, it reserved 'the right to postpone consideration of the possibility of introducing some legislative addition to, or variation of, existing law until such time as it may consider that such is necessary for the attainment of the objective of paragraph 1 of article 20'.[220] In this respect, since it does not seek to exclude or modify the legal effect of the treaty in its application to the state, but rather offers an understanding—or perhaps a lack of understanding—of the provision, it should properly have been entered as a declaration. Following submission of its second periodic report,[221] the Irish representative acknowledged that the reservation, 'which was admittedly hard to defend', had been entered 'because Ireland had experienced difficulty in formulating a specific offence capable of adjudication at the national level in such a form as to reflect

[212] ibid, para 6.
[213] ibid.
[214] CCPR/C/2/Rev 3, 942.
[215] CCPR/C/22.Add 2 1982.
[216] CCPR/C/SR.440, para 15: Mr Vallejo.
[217] CCPR/C/SR.441, para 55.
[218] CCPR/C/SR.445, para 72.
[219] CCPR/C/76/Add 7, para 311.
[220] CCPR/C/2/Rev 3, 947.
[221] CCPR/C/IRL/98/2.

general principles of law recognized by the community of nations as well as the right of freedom of expression'.[222] He nevertheless expressed confidence that 'capable draftsmen would produce a satisfactory solution'.[223]

b. *Belgium, Luxembourg, Malta, the Netherlands, and the USA*

The declarations entered by Belgium[224] and Luxembourg[225] proclaim that they do not consider themselves obligated to enact legislation in the field covered by Article 20(1), and that Article 20 as a whole shall be applied taking into account the rights to freedom of thought and religion, freedom of opinion and freedom of assembly and association proclaimed in Articles 18, 19, and 20 of the Universal Declaration of Human Rights and reaffirmed in Articles 18, 19, 21, and 22 of the Covenant. It would appear that both these declarations are in fact reservations since they purport to exclude the entire provision from the states' obligations under the Covenant.

Following the submission of Belgium's first periodic report the Committee referred the government to General Comment 11, with one member asserting that the declaration 'amounted to non-observance of the Covenant, since all States were required to enact such legislation'.[226] Since that point, Belgium has not added any further comment on its declaration and the dialogue between the government and the Committee has been confined to issues relating to Article 20(2).[227] The Committee also responded to the receipt of Luxembourg's first periodic report by asking the government to consider withdrawing its declaration since 'the world conscience had developed over the years in the direction of condemning war between peoples, and all states should now apply the principle of condemning any incitement to war'.[228] The fact that many other Western states had entered similar reservations was described as a source of great concern, and the government was asked why it had made the declaration, and to expand upon its attitude to the prohibition of propaganda for war.[229] Luxembourg explained that the declaration had been entered because of concern as to the right of freedom of expression, and also because 'the text did not seem to state clearly whether a law was necessary in general or whether legislation should be on a case-by-case basis'.[230] It would seem clear from all other sources reviewed that a general law was required under Article 20(1) rather than the enactment of legislation on any other basis, but the Committee failed to clarify the issue at this point, simply

[222] CCPR/C/SR.1846, para 20.
[223] ibid.
[224] CCPR/C/2/Rev 3, 938.
[225] ibid 951.
[226] CCPR/C/SR.822, para 48: Mr Movchan.
[227] CCPR/C/57/Add 3 1991, para 181; CCPR/C/SR.1142-43; CCPR/C/94/Add 3, para 272; CCPR/C/79/Add 99; CCPR/C/BEL/2003/4; CCPR/C/SR. SR.1706-7.
[228] CCPR/C/SR.628, para 28: Mr Vallejo.
[229] ibid, para. 40: Mr Movchan.
[230] CCPR/C/SR.632, para 24.

requesting that the declaration should be withdrawn since respect for freedom of expression 'should not go to the length of precluding the prohibition of war, the very negation of life'.[231]

The Netherlands entered a reservation simply noting that it 'does not accept the obligation set out in this provision'.[232] The reservation applied to the Netherlands only and not to its colonies or dependent territories, and it was noted that the government of the Netherlands Antilles would be submitting a bill for the inclusion in the criminal code of a prohibition of propaganda for war,[233] an anomaly which perhaps suggests concerns regarding the emergence of independence movements in the colonies which might advocate war against The Hague. In its first periodic report the Netherlands stated that:

[I]t is extremely difficult to formulate a statutory prohibition of propaganda for war in such a way that excessive infringements of freedom of expression are avoided. A criminal provision would have to be worded so that it related only to the use of armed violence in conflict with international law. The question is then what sort of violence as such is meant, and this question does not appear to lend itself to adjudication by domestic courts.[234]

As to the question of what sort of violence is meant to be prohibited by Article 20(1), it has been clearly shown to be wars of aggression. Nowak maintains that difficulties with the meaning of war should not be considered an undue obstacle to the application of Article 20(1):

Since the offence of propaganda for war does not require that a war actually take place, it is only of minor importance as to when armed aggression reaches the degree of intensity constituting a war. Instead, what is decisive is that the propaganda aims at creating or reinforcing the willingness to conduct a war of aggression.[235]

The drafters of Article 20(1) had envisaged that the provision would be interpreted and applied in practice by the national courts. As stressed by Chile during the concluding stages of drafting: 'the matter of implementation would be placed firmly in the hands of the legislatures and the courts.'[236] The Netherlands noted that the reservation had also been prompted by concerns that 'trials on this matter would soon take on a political nature, which should be avoided in general'.[237] Similar sentiments were expressed by Norway which argued that 'even if the prohibition were restricted to wars of aggression, it would be problematic for the Public Prosecutor and the courts to decide who should be considered the

[231] ibid, para 39: Mr Ndiaye (appointed to the Committee by Senegal). Subsequent periodic reports have made no reference to Article 20(1). CCPR/C/57.Add 4 1991; CCPR/CO/77/MLI.
[232] CCPR/C/2/Rev 3, 954.
[233] CCPR/C/10/Add 5, 11.
[234] CCPR/C/2/Add 2.
[235] Manfred Nowak, *U.N. Covenant on Civil and Political Rights*, 473. Furthermore, although a definition of aggression has yet to be settled upon in international law, it remains open to governments to adopt a suitable definition in national legislation.
[236] A/C.3/SR.1078, para 15.
[237] CCPR/C/2/Add 2.

aggressor in any given conflict'.[238] As has been emphasized in the Introduction, national courts in cases such as *R v Jones* before the UK's House of Lords[239] have signalled their ability and willingness to pronounce judgment on cases concerning the crime of aggression, and it would appear that the refusal of States parties to accept that the national judiciary are capable of determining whether a particular expression constitutes propaganda for war appears to be premised less on rational legal analysis than it is on the political sensitivities of governments themselves.

The United States' reservation to Article 20(1) proclaims that the provision 'does not authorize or require legislation or other action by the United States that would restrict the right of free speech and association protected by the Constitution and laws of the United States'.[240] In dialogue with the Committee the USA asserted that Article 20 in its entirety conflicted with its constitutional guarantee of free speech. Affirming that the government would not introduce such restrictions, the USA expressed the opinion 'that other States should do so only where absolutely necessary'.[241] A declaration was also entered wherein the view was expressed that States parties to the Covenant 'should wherever possible refrain from imposing any restrictions or limitations on the exercise of the rights recognized and protected by the Covenant, even when such restrictions and limitations are permissible under the terms of the Covenant'.[242] Whereas this view is very relevant to Article 19, Article 20 actually obliges the prohibition of propaganda for war rather than permitting states to restrict such propaganda.

The first periodic report of the USA asserted that '[u]nder the First Amendment, opinions and speech are protected categorically, without regard to content. Thus, the right to engage in propaganda for war is as protected as the right to advocate pacifism.'[243] It added that not all speech is protected under the Constitution since 'fighting words' that insult or provoke violence as well as speech intended and likely to cause imminent violence may be constitutionally restricted 'so long as regulation is not undertaken with respect to the speech's content'.[244] In light of this statement, it appears that the comment equating the right to engage in propaganda for war with the right to advocate pacifism is not wholly accurate since the former may constitute an incitement to violence and therefore may be constitutionally restricted were it intended and likely to cause imminent violence, an outcome which could hardly be said to arise regarding the advocacy of pacifism.

The final state in this category is Malta. Whereas Malta has entered a reservation affirming that it reserved the right 'not to introduce any legislation for

[238] CCPR/C/SR.846, para 20.
[239] *R v Jones, et al* [2006] UKHL 16.
[240] CCPR/C/2/Rev 3, 963; CCPR/C/USA/3, paras 330–1.
[241] CCPR/C/SR.1401, para 14.
[242] CCPR/C/2/Rev 3, 952.
[243] CCPR/C/81.Add 4, para 597.
[244] ibid, para 598.

the purposes of article 20',[245] the government has made the claim that 'Malta made no reservation regarding this article in the sense that it interprets article 20 consistently with the rights confessed by articles 19 and 21 of the Covenant but reserves the right not to introduce any legislation for the purposes of article 20.'[246] There have been no further explanations or communications on the subject of the reservation between Malta and the Committee.

c. The Nordic States

Iceland,[247] Norway,[248] Denmark,[249] Sweden,[250] and Finland[251] have long presented a united front in opposing the obligation to prohibit propaganda for war as set forth in the Covenant. This stance is essentially premised on the belief that the prohibition constitutes an unacceptable threat to the right to freedom of expression as provided for in national[252] and international law.[253] Nonetheless, Finland has recently broken with this position by enacting legislation intended to give effect to Article 20(1), a development which will be discussed following a consideration of the communications between the Committee and the other Nordic states.

The Committee considered Iceland's justification for its reservation to be invalid from 'a legal standpoint'.[254] It was put to Iceland that on the one hand it was defending its Constitution which restricted the right to freedom of expression more so than the Covenant, while on the other it had entered a reservation to

---

[245] CCPR/C/2/Rev 4, 29.

[246] CCPR/C/68.Add 4 1993, para 52.

[247] 'Article 20, paragraph 1, with reference to the fact that a prohibition against propaganda for war could limit the freedom of expression. This reservation is consistent with the position of Iceland at the General Assembly at its 16th session.' CCPR/C/2/Rev 3, 946.

[248] Norway acceded to the ICCPR 'subject to reservations to [...] article 20, paragraph 1'. CCPR/C/2/Rev 3, 956.

[249] 'Reservation is further made to Article 20, paragraph 1. This reservation is in accordance with the vote cast by Denmark in the XVI General Assembly of the United Nations in 1961 when the Danish Delegation, referring to the preceding article concerning freedom of expression, voted against the prohibition against propaganda for war.' CCPR/C/2/Rev 3, 941.

[250] 'Sweden reserves the right not to apply the provisions [...] of article 20, paragraph 1, of the Covenant.' CCPR/C/2/Rev 3, 957.

[251] 'With respect to article 20, paragraph 1, of the Covenant, Finland declares that it will not apply the provisions of this paragraph, this being compatible with the standpoint Finland already expressed at the 16th United Nations General Assembly by voting against the prohibition of propaganda for war, on the grounds that this might endanger the freedom of expression referred in article 19 of the Covenant.' CCPR/C/2/Rev 3, 941.

[252] CCPR/C/10/Add 4 1981, para 58 (Norway); CCPR/C/SR.635, para 33 (Sweden).

[253] CCPR/C/1/Add 51, 36 (Denmark); CCPR/C/64/Add 11, para 125; CCPR/C/DNK/99/4, para 202. There are significant similarities in the additional Nordic reservations. For example a reservation to Article 10(3) concerning the obligation to segregate juvenile offenders from adults was also entered by each Nordic state. See further Jakob Moller and Alfred de Zayas, 'Optional Protocol Cases Concerning the Nordic States before the United Nations Human Rights Committee', 55 Nordic J Int'l L 398 (1986).

[254] CCPR/C/SR.391, para 49: Mr Movchan.

Article 20(1) on the behest of protecting freedom of expression.[255] The Committee asked Sweden to reconsider enacting a law regarding Article 20(1) since '[o]ther countries had adopted such laws, which did not restrict freedoms any more than a law against slander, for example'.[256]

The frustration of some members of the Committee with the position adopted by the Nordic states is illustrated in a remarkable comment by Committee member Mr Movchan which was characteristic of the ideological tête-à-tête which frequently found expression in the Committee during the Cold War. Movchan, who had been appointed to the Committee by the USSR, relied upon the assumption that 'all religions prohibited war' to query, '[h]ow was it that Norway, a country having a State religion, had no law banning war propaganda?'[257] Referring to the failure of the Norwegian Parliament to enact legislation prohibiting propaganda for war, he stated that 'no reservation to Article 20 could be made on the basis of article 19'[258] and asked the Norwegian representatives to draw their government's attention to:

[T]he fact that, with all due respect, the reservation to article 20 on the basis of article 19 had no legal justification. That was because war, as history had taught, ran counter to the life of man, without which he had no rights, including civil and political rights. Article 20, therefore, was the logical outcome of article 19 and attested to the strong stance of the United Nations that there was no place in the world for war.[259]

Norway responded by stating that if it 'could have banned war by enacting legislation, it would have long since done so', and although considering the enactment of such legislation not to be a 'realistic approach', reassured the Committee that it 'would continue to make every reasonable effort to further the cause of peace'.[260]

Iceland[261] and Sweden[262] have claimed that since there was no propaganda for war being disseminated within their jurisdictions, there was no reason to enact specific legislation prohibiting it. Nonetheless, Iceland cited several provisions of its Penal Code which it felt 'would likely cover such propaganda if it occurred'.[263] These included the offences of inciting rebellion to change the Constitution through violence, and of attempting, through violence, threat of violence or other coercion, to bring the Icelandic state, or a part thereof, under the control

---

[255] CCPR/C/SR.391. Mr Graefrath, noting the ban on advertisements for alcohol and tobacco products, 'regretted that there was no similar ban on war propaganda or advertisements recruiting mercenaries'. CCPR/C/SR.392, para 12.

[256] CCPR/C/SR.638, para 27: Mr Movchan; CCPR/C/SR.638, para 33: Mr Graefrath.

[257] He continued by asking whether '[i]n doing so had it not acted counter to the Norwegian Constitution by acting against the State religion? Members of the Committee espousing communist thinking believed it had.' CCPR/C/SR.302, para 31.

[258] CCPR/C/SR.302, para 31: Mr Movchan.

[259] ibid.

[260] ibid, para 41.

[261] CCPR/C/46/Add 5, para 326.

[262] CCPR/C/SR.636, para 19.

[263] CCPR/C/46/Add 5, para 327.

of a foreign power.[264] Similarly, Sweden affirmed that since '[t]here was absolutely no doubt that the activities of groups that advocated war should be exposed and punished', its Penal Code contained provisions concerning the application of penalties for that purpose.[265] It is apparent therefore, that these states interpret the provision in the manner earlier critiqued, by omitting any consideration of governmental propaganda for war by focusing on private individuals only, and also by confronting propaganda for violence directed against the state as opposed to war between states.

Iceland's second periodic report concluded that '[i]t can hardly be possible to discuss inciting Iceland to war or other military involvement with other States, considering that Iceland has no military'.[266] Whilst accepting that 'Iceland was certainly not a potential aggressor, and a warmonger in that country would be simply ridiculous', the Committee stressed the importance of Article 20(1) being implemented and applied as a matter of international responsibility. It suggested that positive steps in this direction by Iceland would set a good example since 'the problem certainly arose in other countries, particularly in the context of the current deplorable arms race, where advocacy of the stockpiling of weapons might be regarded by some as propaganda for war'.[267] Iceland has gone no further towards implementing the obligation set forth in Article 20(1) than describing propaganda for war as 'clearly a horrible thing', and has been adamant in its position that to prohibit such would be regarded in Iceland, and also in the other Scandinavian countries, as an infringement of freedom of expression. Despite the Committee's repeated requests that their reservations be withdrawn,[268] Iceland has consistently maintained this position,[269] as have Denmark,[270] Sweden,[271] and Norway.[272]

Although several states have claimed that should they perceive the need to arise they will implement legislation prohibiting propaganda for war, Finland is unique among states which have entered reservations to have actually done so. Finland's first periodic report asserted that a penal sanction was required if the prohibition was to be effective, but that this was not possible since the concept of propaganda for war was 'somewhat vague' and not sufficiently defined, thus making it difficult to draw the line between permissible and impermissible speech.[273] Suggesting that

---

[264] ibid.
[265] CCPR/C/SR.638, para 33.
[266] CCPR/C/46/Add 5, para 328.
[267] CCPR/C/SR.392, para 72: Mr Tomuschat.
[268] CCPR/CO/83/ISL, para 8; CCPR/C/SR.54, 9; CCPR/C/70/DNK, para 9; CCPR/C/SR.1877, para 13; CCPR/C/NOR/CO/5, para 8.
[269] CCPR/C/SR.395, para 31; CCPR/C/94/Add 2, para 74; CCPR/C/ISL/2004/4, paras 32 and 106.
[270] CCPR/C/1/Add 51, 36; CCPR/C/64/Add 11, para 125; CCPR/C/DNK/99/4, para 202.
[271] CCPR/C/58.Add 7, para 244, CCPR/C/SR.1044, CCPR/C/SWE/2000/5, CCPR/C/SR.1456.
[272] CCPR/C/1/Add 52; CCPR/C/32/Add 6; CCPR/C/115/Add 2, para 233, CCPR/C/NOR/2004/5.
[273] CCPR/C/Add 10, 4.

the reservation might not be acceptable since it had the effect 'of removing the need to implement an entire provision of the Covenant',[274] the Committee acknowledged the difficulty in defining penal rules on the matter, yet reiterated that States parties were nevertheless required to implement the provision 'within their constitutions and penal laws'.[275] It was asserted that this problem was not insurmountable 'especially as propaganda for war had been condemned in the Declaration on Principles of International Law Concerning Friendly Relations and the Final Act of the Helsinki Conference'.[276] The government was asked for specific information on the legal difficulties which had been experienced[277] and why a reservation had been deemed necessary to Article 20(1) but not to Article 20(2), 'both of which imposed an obligation on states, and both of which were equally difficult to define and punish'.[278]

Finland's reply stated that whereas the bulk of its reservations were mainly of a technical nature and would be withdrawn as soon as national legislation was brought in line with the Covenant, this was not the case with Article 20(1). The government claimed that to oblige Finland to implement such an obligation was 'absurd' since its Constitution stated, '[d]eclarations of war and peace shall be taken by the president with the consent of Parliament'.[279] According to the government, declaration of war:

[...] was a matter which concerned the State and it was impossible to have an article in the penal Code concerning either the President or Parliament. Any provision in that Code had to be based on practical necessity, whereas any attempt to incite the president and the parliament to start an aggressive war would be a futile attempt.[280]

It is an underlying argument in this study that the responsibility for propaganda for war rests in the main with states themselves rather than private individuals or the media. Refusing to apply Article 20(1) on the grounds that a government cannot be incited to start an aggressive war not only places undue faith in governments, but also acts to exclude from the scope of the provision any consideration that the President or members of Parliament might themselves be responsible for propaganda for war. Moreover, to suggest that the President or Parliament is immune from prosecution is incompatible with the concept of individual responsibility for violations of human rights. Finally, it is incongruous to link the prohibition of propaganda for war with the formality of a declaration of war since

[274] Mr Graefrath, CCPR/C/2/SR.30, 4 and Mr Koulishev, CCPR/C/2/SR.30, 5.
[275] CCPR/C/2/SR.30, 4: Mr Graefrath.
[276] ibid, 5: Mr Koulishev.
[277] ibid 6: Mr Espersen.
[278] ibid: Mr Opsahl. Following submission of Finland's second periodic report (CCPR/C/1/Add 32, 20-1), the Committee stated that since legislative measures had been adopted to give effect to CERD, the government 'should do likewise in order to prohibit propaganda for war, particularly since war constituted the negation of all rights and freedoms, including the right to freedom of expression'. CCPR/C/SR.171, para 40: Mr Movchan.
[279] ibid, para 46.
[280] ibid.

such propaganda is intended to initiate a war regardless as to whether an official declaration is made.

This statement again clearly illustrates the conceptualization by states of propaganda for war being exclusively a tool of private individuals and not of states themselves. Nevertheless, Finland's representative continued to state that since the Penal Code contained provisions on causing offence to states having friendly relations with Finland, he would recommend to his government that the whole question of reservations be reconsidered, adding, 'perhaps even that reservation was unnecessary'.[281]

Finland's second periodic report restated that it would not withdraw the reservation which was described as 'a highly political question'.[282] It claimed to have increased its efforts against war propaganda by means of information, education, and cultural activities rather than having adopted a law on the subject.[283] The government also stated that certain forms of 'war propaganda' were in fact punishable by law. In this respect Article 12 of the Penal Code which made it a punishable offence to appeal to a foreign state to go to war against Finland was cited,[284] as was the Freedom of the Press Act which excluded 'war propaganda against good morals', leading the government to ask 'whether Finland's measures in that field were good enough for the Committee'.[285]

Finland's third periodic report noted that proposals for new provisions on treason in the Penal Code included a prohibition against certain forms of incitement to war.[286] While the government asserted that 'the principle of not banning propaganda for war was so firmly entrenched in the philosophy of all the Nordic countries that the new provision would not be sufficient to remove it',[287] the subsequent periodic report outlined a legislative bill directed towards fulfilling the obligation in Article 20(1). In overcoming its previous opposition to the provision, Finland told the Committee that:

Literally speaking, the criminalization of propaganda for war does not entail banning all war propaganda. However, it criminalizes any propaganda for war which increases the risk of war during a crisis or when a crisis is imminent, in other words, the most dangerous forms of war propaganda.[288]

Finland submitted its fifth periodic report in 2003. This confirmed the establishment of a criminal offence in 1995 of engaging in propaganda for war during

---

[281] ibid.
[282] CCPR/C/32/Add 11.
[283] CCPR/C/SR.646, para 34.
[284] ibid, para 35.
[285] ibid.
[286] CCPR/C/58/Add 5 1989, para 110. Mr Ndiaye of the Committee reiterated that 'condemnation of propaganda for war could contribute effectively to the prevention of war', and requested a more specific explanation as to why, in light of the previous report, Finland's reservation was being maintained. CCPR/C/SR.1016, paras 32–4.
[287] CCPR/C/SR.1016, para 43.
[288] CCPR/C/95.Add 6 (4), para 96.

military action or an international political crisis concerning Finland.[289] In order for such propaganda to be punishable, 'it is required that its purpose is to lead Finland to war or make the country a military target and that it clearly increases such a risk'.[290] The Penal Code provided for the offence, if undertaken at a time of crisis, of:

(a) incitement to aggression; (b) public dissemination of statements designed to influence public opinion to turn in favour of acts of aggression; (c) dissemination of false information about Finland's defence and military policy; or (d) an unlawful act of violence towards a foreign State in such a manner as to increase the risk of Finland becoming a target of military action.[291]

The government explained that these measures had been introduced because of changes in society since the entering into force of the Covenant, resultant from 'the use of freedom of expression by new technological means [which] has brought about a new dimension to the debate on the freedom of expression as a fundamental right'.[292] Although it is difficult to assess how new technology has increased the risk posed by propaganda for war, since developments such as the internet have, if anything, provided a means for combating such propaganda,[293] Finland's revision of its interpretation and application of Article 20(1) is to be welcomed. In overcoming its longstanding opposition to the provision Finland has set an example of how Article 20(1) can be interpreted with due regard both to the right to freedom of expression and to the purpose of the Article and the UN Charter. In providing for additional offences other than 'incitement to aggression' as in paragraph (d) of the provision above, Finland has adopted a somewhat broader offence than that which had been advocated by the liberal democracies during drafting including 'propaganda of the deed'.

Despite affirming that in principle it would be possible to prohibit all kinds of propaganda for war by law, provided the provisions of law concerned were sufficiently precise and bearing in mind the prohibition of interference with the core of the right to freedom of expression, Finland has nonetheless retained its reservation to Article 20(1).[294] While it has expressed its intention to review this position,[295] the Committee was informed that since 'the worst forms of

---

[289] CCPR/C/95.Add 6 (4), paras 95–6.
[290] CCPR/C/FIN/2003/5, para 271.
[291] CCPR/C/95.Add 6, para 95.
[292] CCPR/C/FIN/2003/5, para 272.
[293] Whilst media technology such as the world wide web has provoked much concern regarding other forms of expression long deemed immoral or criminal such as pornography, blasphemy, and hate speech, recent developments also suggest that such technology has provided a crucial tool for challenging state sponsored propaganda for war by facilitating free criticisms and analysis of propaganda for war. See generally Alistair Alexander, 'Disruptive Technology: Iraq and the Internet', in David Miller (ed), *Tell Me Lies*, 277 and Patrick Carmichael, 'Information Interventions, Media Development and the Internet', in Monroe E Price and Mark Thompson (eds), *Forging Peace*, 365–92.
[294] CCPR/C/FIN/2003/5, para 273.
[295] ibid.

propaganda for war had been established as criminal offences, and that there had been no need to extend the scope of application of the relevant provisions, Finland did not currently consider it necessary to take the legislative measures required for the withdrawal of the reservation'.[296]

v. Summary

Finland's enactment of legislation prohibiting propaganda for war is a welcome development which should provide a precedent for the other liberal democracies who retain reservations and declarations to Article 20(1). In General Comment 6 on the right to life—'the supreme right'—as enunciated in Article 6 of the Covenant, the Committee re-emphasized the importance of the prohibition of propaganda for war.[297] Affirming that states had 'the supreme duty' to prevent wars, the Committee stressed the particular connection between Article 6 and Article 20.[298]

In summarizing the manner in which Article 20(1) has drifted out of the collective consciousness in the decades since the adoption of the Covenant, the responsibility of the Committee and States parties must be emphasized. In the first instance, the Committee has rarely accorded the provision as much consideration as it requires, particularly given its widespread violation. The majority of communications between the Committee and States parties on the subject are confined to the decade immediately following the coming into force of the Covenant. The emphasis on the subject at that stage can be ascribed to the action of Committee members from communist or non-aligned States parties who seized on the failure of the liberal democracies to accept the obligation as evidence of their superficial commitments to international law.

When discussing Syria's first periodic report in 1977, the Committee had stressed the necessity, when seeking to apply Article 20(1), of striking 'a balance between the individual's rights and the legitimate interests of the community'.[299] It was affirmed that the task of the Committee in this regard was 'to determine whether national legislation had or had not transgressed the limits set down by the Covenant'.[300] Examples of the Committee exercising this duty have been rare.[301]

---

[296] CCPR/C/SR.2226, para 26. Heyns and Viljoen report that 'according to Arto Kosonen (Legislative council, Ministry of Foreign Affairs) this is the only remaining reservation which might still be withdrawn'. Christof Heyns and Frans Viljoen, *The Impact of the United Nations Human Rights Treaties on the Domestic Level*, 272.

[297] General Comment 6, Article 6 (1982), UN Doc HRI\GEN\1\Rev 1 at 6 (1994), para 1.

[298] ibid, para 2.

[299] CCPR/C/SR.26, 6–7: Mr Tomuschat.

[300] ibid 7. He added that concerning the prohibition of propaganda for war, 'the interests of the community were considered more important than that of the individual'.

[301] The Committee did express concern that Uzbek legislation prohibiting 'the formation and activities of political parties and other public associations disseminating propaganda for war' (Article 57 of the Uzbek Constitution: CCPR/C/UZB/2004/2; ICCPR/C/UZB/99/1(1)) has been abused by the state in order to harass human rights defenders in violation of the Article 22 right

McGoldrick has noted that a proposal had been made during the drafting of General Comment 11 to include 'an express reference to propaganda by States and governments as distinct from individuals and organizations and to forms other than the written or spoken word, for example by threatening demonstrations of armed force'.[302] While such an interpretation of the meaning of the provision by the Committee would not have been strictly consistent with the intentions of the drafters, who had focused primarily but not exclusively on the press, it might well have encouraged many of the liberal democracies to reconsider the basis for their reservations. Nevertheless, since the end of the Cold War the Committee has paid negligible attention to the provision, rarely pausing to elucidate either the significance or the meaning of the provision, a situation which needs to be reversed both in order to ensure the implementation of the provision and to discourage States parties from abusing the principle in order to restrict the enjoyment of other rights.

Article 20(1) has not been dealt with under the optional protocol and no State party has been rebuked by the Committee for engaging in propaganda for war. Given the focus on propaganda for war in recent years, it is perhaps apt that Iraq has been the sole State party to claim in a periodic report to have been subjected to propaganda for war in violation of Article 20(1). Following the 1991 Gulf War Iraq protested to the Committee that the coalition of states which had attacked it had been acting in violation of Article 20, as well as Article 3 of the UNESCO Declaration on Fundamental Principles concerning the Contribution of the Mass Media to Strengthening Peace and International Understanding. It was claimed that 'the western media' urged war against Iraq and incited national hatred and intercommunity sedition: '[t]he mass media contributed to an orchestrated campaign against Iraq which paved the way for war, resulting in the destruction of its infrastructure and interrupting the promotion of human rights.'[303] Meeting with the Committee, Iraq reasserted that it had been 'subjected to an orchestrated campaign of hostility by the western media, in obvious violation of article 20 of the Covenant'.[304] Its subsequent periodic report again claimed that it had been 'the victim of a flagrant and systematic violation of this article'.[305] The Committee made no comment in response to these repeated allegations.

---

to freedom of assembly. The state's response noted that a decision on whether to grant or deny the requisite registration by judicial bodies for non-governmental organizations could depend on whether the organization was held to have the aim of disseminating propaganda for war (CCPR/C/SR.1911, paras 35–7), but that '[i]nvestigative and court practice in Uzbekistan has thus far recorded no cases of anyone being prosecuted for, or convicted of, propaganda for war' (CCPR/C/UZB/2004/2).

[302] Dominic McGoldrick, *The Human Rights Committee*, 486. Citing CCPR/SR.447, para 21 (Mr Vincent Evans).
[303] CCPR/C/64/Add 6, para 65.
[304] CCPR/C/SR.1080, para 7.
[305] CCPR/C/103/Add 2, paras 74–5.

The example set by Finland demonstrates that clearly drafted legislation can be drawn up to give full effect to the provision without negatively impacting on other rights. The repeated assertions by governments that they have no need to apply a prohibition of propaganda for war because no such propaganda is disseminated within their jurisdictions are clearly unacceptable. Such 'general or imprecise' assertions as the claim by the Netherlands that '[i]n reality, no practical difficulties over the issue arose in the Netherlands, since the media did not disseminate war propaganda; on the contrary, they argued in favour of peace and restriction of the use of force'[306] require immediate and unequivocal reappraisal. The Committee must be to the fore on this issue and thus it should reassert its intent to hold states accountable for their duties under Article 20(1). The failure of the Committee to do so is apparent in the Committee's List of Issues document responding to Bosnia and Herzegovina's initial Periodic Report. Therein the Committee requested, under the ambit of Articles 19 and 20, that the government provide 'detailed information on the number and nature of court cases and the sanctions imposed on local politicians and journalists inciting to ethnic discrimination, hostility or violence'.[307] Given that the Periodic Report actually reported on positive measures taken to implement Article 20(1), the Committee's failure to include a specific request on information pertaining to propaganda for war is unacceptable.

B. Regional Human Rights Treaty Systems

i. The American Convention on Human Rights

In the early decades of the twentieth century and particularly in the years preceding the outbreak of the Second World War, American states' concern as to the potential destabilizing effects of subversive and hostile international communications led to several regional agreements and initiatives whose aim was to restrict and control international propaganda. In 1935, the South American Regional Agreement on Radio Communications was signed at Buenos Aires.[308] Contracting states pledged to control the sources and accuracy of information broadcast, to avoid defamatory transmissions, and to abstain from favouritism to political and social parties operating in other adhering states.[309] At the Eighth International Conference of American States held in Lima in 1938, delegates discussed the German government's attempts to organize propaganda in foreign

---

[306] CCPR/C/SR.863, para 49. Colombia's first periodic report had claimed that since propaganda for war was not known to occur in Colombia, the necessity of enacting legislation in accordance with Article 20(1) had not come to the attention of the legislative bodies. CCPR/C/1/Add 50.

[307] CCPR/C/BIH/Q/1, para 21.

[308] Reprinted in 7 International Legislation 47 (1941) 51–2.

[309] John B Whitton, 'Radio Propaganda: A Modest Proposal', 743.

countries 'to a degree hitherto unknown'.[310] Of particular concern was German propaganda which capitalized on the colonial concept of 'indelible allegiance', according to which the Nazis required German emigrants to retain their allegiance to their homeland in all matters and to make 'concerted efforts to influence the policy of the government of their country of residence in favor of the policies which they were instructed by agents to promote'.[311] The Conference adopted a blunt resolution as part of attempts to restrict the effects of subversive activities, including international propaganda, which stated that:

aliens residing in an American State are subject to domestic jurisdiction and any official action, therefore, on the part of the governments of the countries of which such aliens are nationals, tending to interfere with the internal affairs of the country in order to regulate the status or activities of those aliens, is incompatible with the sovereignty of such state.[312]

At the Second Meeting of American Foreign Ministers in Havana in July 1940, several resolutions concerning international propaganda were adopted. Resolution II condemned the use by the German government of its embassies and consulates in foreign countries to subsidize the local press and to organize local support for its policies.[313] Resolution VI, entitled '[a]ctivities directed from abroad against domestic institutions', provided for immediate consultation between the American governments in the event that the peace was menaced by 'activities directed, assisted or abetted by foreign governments, or foreign groups or individuals, which tend to subvert the domestic institutions, or to foment disorder in their internal political life, or to modify by pressure, propaganda, threats, or in any other manner', the free and sovereign right of the American peoples to be governed by their existing democratic systems.[314] Resolution VII forbade foreigners to engage in political activities within the territory of the state in which they reside on the basis that the Second World War 'has revealed the existence of foreign political organizations in certain neutral states with the deliberate purpose of making attempts against public order, the system of government and the very personality of such states'.[315] In the wake of the Second World War the International Conference of American States was to turn its attention to a new threat of subversive propaganda emanating from the 'international communist movement'. The Caracas Declaration of Solidarity for the Preservation of the Political Integrity of the American States against International Communist Intervention, adopted in 1954, recommended that the American states take measures 'to require disclosure of the identity, activities, and sources

---

[310] Charles G Fenwick, 'Intervention by Way of Propaganda', 35 AJIL 626 (1941) 626.
[311] ibid.
[312] Resolution XXVIII cited in Charles G Fenwick, 'Intervention by Way of Propaganda', 627.
[313] Resolution II 'Norms concerning diplomatic and consular functions'. Cited ibid 628.
[314] ibid 628.
[315] ibid 629.

of funds, of those who are spreading propaganda of the international communist movement'.[316]

It was not until the establishment of the Organization of American States (OAS) that American states began to consider the issue of the prohibition of propaganda for war through the lens of human rights. The OAS, a regional organization of states for the western hemisphere, was established in 1948 at the Ninth International American Conference when delegates signed the Organization's Charter[317] and adopted the American Declaration of the Rights and Duties of Man.[318] Article IV of the American Declaration guaranteed the right to freedom of expression, providing that '[e]very person has the right to freedom of investigation, of opinion, and of the expression and dissemination of ideas, by any medium whatsoever'.[319] In accordance with Article XXVIII of the Declaration this right is limited only 'by the rights of others, by the security of all, and by the just demands of the general welfare and the advancement of democracy'. The issue of hostile international propaganda was central to one of the first international disputes which the OAS attempted to adjudicate. In 1949 the government of Haiti claimed that it had been the victim of 'moral aggression' on the grounds that one of its former military colonels, taking refuge in the Dominican Republic, had made 'extremely vulgar and provocative broadcasts', aimed at the overthrow of the Haitian government.[320] Following submission of the dispute to the OAS's Council of Consultation, the two states settled the matter by agreeing 'not to tolerate in their respective territories the activities of any individuals, groups, or parties, national or foreign, that have as their object the disturbance of the domestic peace of either of the two neighboring Republics or of any other friendly Nation'.[321]

a. Drafting History of Article 13(5)

In establishing a regional framework for the protection of human rights the OAS created the Inter-American Commission on Human Rights (Commission)

[316] Section II(1), Declaration of Solidarity for the Preservation of the Political Integrity of the American States against International Communist Intervention Adopted by the Tenth Inter-American Conference, 28 March 1954.
[317] Charter of the Organization of American States, 119 UNTS 3, entered into force 13 December 1951; amended by Protocol of Buenos Aires, 721 UNTS 324, OAS. Treaty Series, no 1-A, entered into force 27 February 1970; amended by Protocol of Cartagena, OAS Treaty Series, no 66, ILM 527, entered into force 16 November 1988; amended by Protocol of Washington, 1-E Rev OEA *Documentos oficiales* OEA/Ser A/2 Add 3 (SEPF), 33 ILM 1005, entered into force 25 September 1997; amended by Protocol of Managua, 1-F Rev OEA *Documentos oficiales* OEA/Ser A/2 Add 4 (SEPF), 33 ILM 1009, entered into force 29 January 1996.
[318] American Declaration of the Rights and Duties of Man, OAS Res XXX, adopted by the Ninth International Conference of American States (1948), reprinted in Basic Documents Pertaining to Human Rights in the Inter-American System, OEA/Ser L.V/II.82 Doc 6 Rev 1 (1992), 17.
[319] ibid, Article IV.
[320] John B Whitton, 'Radio Propaganda: A Modest Proposal', 743.
[321] ibid 744.

in 1959. The American Convention on Human Rights,[322] which opened for signature on 20 November 1969 and came into force in 1978, includes a more substantial provision on the right to freedom of expression than that provided for in the Declaration. Article 13 set forth the right of everyone to freedom of thought and expression, including the freedom to seek, receive, and impart information and ideas of all kinds, regardless of frontiers, either orally, in writing, in print, in the form of art, or through any other medium of one's choice. Article 13(2), whilst stating that the exercise of these rights shall not be subject to prior censorship, allowed for the subsequent imposition of liability as established by law and to the extent necessary to ensure 'respect for the rights or reputations of others' or 'the protection of national security, public order, or public health or morals'. Article 13(4) permits the prior censorship of public entertainments 'for the sole purpose of regulating access to them for the moral protection of childhood and adolescence'. Article 13(5) of the American Convention provides that:

Any propaganda for war and any advocacy of national, racial, or religious hatred that constitute incitements to lawless violence or to any other similar action against any person or group of persons on any grounds including those of race, color, religion, language, or national origin shall be considered as offenses punishable by law.

In 1959, the Inter-American Council of Jurists (IACJ) prepared a Draft Convention on Human Rights which was to set the basis for the final text of the American Convention.[323] The preamble to this draft presupposed the existence of obligations and responsibilities essential to maintain 'the existence and personality of the State against everything that might disturb the peace, security, and public order' and affirmed that '[w]hoever makes use of information media assumes a grave responsibility before public opinion and has the moral duty to respect the truth'.[324] Article XI of the Draft Convention provided for permissible limitations to be placed on the right to freedom of expression on the grounds of 'national security, territorial integrity, public order, or the prevention of crime, to prevent incitement to racial or religious strife', but not propaganda for war.[325]

The IACJ Draft Convention, along with drafts submitted by Uruguay and Chile, was examined by the Second Special Inter-American Conference at Rio de Janeiro in 1965. Whereas the Uruguayan draft contained no reference to propaganda for war,[326] the Chilean draft reflected the views advanced by Chile during the final stages of the drafting of Article 20(1) of the Covenant, and its

[322] American Convention on Human Rights, OAS Treaty Series no 36, 1144 UNTS 123 entered into force 18 July 1978, reprinted in Basic Documents Pertaining to Human Rights in the Inter-American System, OEA/Ser L.V/II.82 Doc 6 Rev 1 at 25 (1992).
[323] Draft Convention on Human Rights prepared by the Inter-American Council of Jurists, OAS Doc 128 (English) Rev, 8 September 1959.
[324] Inter-American Commission on Human Rights Report on the Work Accomplished during its Tenth Session, 15–26 March 1965, OEA/Ser L/V/II.11, Doc 19, 1 July 1965, 13.
[325] ibid.
[326] Doc 49. Inter-American Yearbook on Human Rights 1968, 298.

draft Article 13(1) provided that, '[q]ueda prohibida toda propaganda en favor de la guerra'.[327]

This Conference in turn sent the drafts to the Inter-American Commission which appointed a Rapporteur to undertake a comparative study of the texts.[328] Following examination of the Rapporteur's Report[329] the Inter-American Commission issued recommendations and several amendments[330] to the IACJ draft for consideration by the Council of the OAS,[331] recommending that the Council should take into consideration the 'essential concepts' of the 1965 Draft Inter-American Convention on Freedom of Expression, Information, and Investigation.[332]

The Inter-American Commission also appointed a Rapporteur to prepare a comparative study of the UN Conventions on Civil and Political Rights, Social, Economic, and Cultural Rights, and the Draft Inter-American Conventions on Human Rights. The Rapporteur noted that the IACJ Draft,[333] and the amendments proposed thereto by the Inter-American Commission,[334] were silent on the prohibition of propaganda for war as found in the International Covenant on Civil and Political Rights and suggested that the American Convention ought to take up the theme since the constitutions and the press laws in several American states already included such a prohibition.[335]

Following the Council's examination of the Opinion of the Commission on the Rapporteur's study,[336] it requested the Inter-American Commission to prepare a Preliminary Draft Convention on Human Rights. Article 12(5) of the Inter-American Commission's draft reproduced the text of Article 20(1) of the International Covenant on Civil and Political Rights providing that '[a]ny

---

[327] 'Artículo 13: 1. Queda prohibida toda propaganda en favor de la guerra. 2. Queda prohibida toda apologia del odio nacional, racial o religioso que constituya incitación a la discriminación, la hostilidad o la violencia.' Doc 35. Inter-American Yearbook on Human Rights 1968, 275.

[328] Inter-American Yearbook on Human Rights 1968, 73.

[329] OEA/Ser.L/V/II.14 Doc 7; 15-Doc 2; 15-Doc 3 (Rev 2).

[330] Text of the Amendments Suggested by the Inter-American Commission on Human Rights Regarding the Draft Convention Prepared by the Inter-American Council of Jurists, Appendix to Doc OEA/Ser L/V/II.16, Doc 8.

[331] Opinion of the Inter-American Commission on Human Rights Regarding the Draft Convention Prepared by the Inter-American Council of Jurists (Civil and Political Rights) Part I, OEA/Ser L/V/II.15, Doc 26, 329.

[332] ibid.

[333] Draft Convention on Human Rights (Approved by the Fourth Meeting of the Inter-American Council of Jurists, Santiago, Chile, September 1959) Final Act, Doc CIJ-43. Inter-American Yearbook on Human Rights 1968, 237.

[334] Text of the Amendments Suggested by the Inter-American Commission on Human Rights to the Draft Convention on Human Rights Prepared by the Inter-American Council of Jurists, Appendix to Doc OEA/Ser L./V/II.16. Doc 8.

[335] Comparative Study of the United Nations Covenants on Civil and Political Rights and on Economic, Social, and Cultural Rights and of the Draft Inter-American Conventions on Human Rights, OAS Doc OEA/L/V/II.19 Doc 18, para 67.

[336] Opinion of the Inter-American Commission on Human Rights of the Comparative Study of the United Nations Covenants on Civil and Political Rights and on Economic, Social and Cultural Rights and of the Draft Inter-American Conventions on Human Rights, Doc. OEA/L/V/II.19 Doc 26.

propaganda for war shall be prohibited by law'.[337] The Commission explained that it had included this provision 'in order to coordinate the Preliminary Draft with the Covenant',[338] and the draft as a whole was unanimously approved by the Commission in July 1968 and by the Council of American States in October 1968.[339]

When Article 12(5) came up for discussion at the Conference of San Jose in 1969 the USA recommended that it be deleted since it 'require[d] censorship',[340] reiterating its view that the remedy to the problem at hand was 'more speech, not enforced silence'.[341] Conversely, Argentina (which had voted against Article 20(1) of the Covenant and Article 20 as a whole in 1961) considered the permitted restrictions on the right to freedom of expression to be inadequate,[342] while Brazil disputed the suggestion that the article meant that censorship must be established, 'but rather that the law shall prohibit a certain type of activity'.[343] Stephanie Farrior regards the critical moment in the drafting of paragraph 5 as having been the presentation of the delegate of El Salvador, who 'spoke very powerfully in favor of Article 13(5), particularly on the prohibition on war propaganda'.[344] In advocating the inclusion of the provision he told delegates that if such propaganda were to cease, there would probably be a solution to the then ongoing conflict between Honduras and El Salvador.[345] Following the delivery of this statement, the delegates of both countries embraced to rapturous applause, at which point the US delegate was resigned to the fact that the Conference 'would

---

[337] Draft Inter-American Convention on Protection of Human Rights, OEA/Ser L/V/II.19, Doc 48.

[338] Annotations on the Draft Inter-American Convention on Protection of Human Rights (Documents prepared by the Secretariat of the Inter-American Commission on Human Rights); Doc OEA/Ser L/V/II.19/Doc 53 (21 March 1969).

[339] OEA/Ser G/V-C-d-1631.

[340] Observations of the Governments of the Member States Regarding the Draft Inter-American Convention on Protection of Human Rights, United States (6 October 1969), reprinted in Thomas Buergenthal (ed), 2 *Human Rights: The Inter-American System, Part II: The Legislative History of the American Convention on Human Rights* (ch II, Booklet 13, August 1982), Doc 10, 157. Cited in Stephanie Farrior, 'Molding the Matrix', 78.

[341] ibid.

[342] Draft Inter-American Convention on Protection of Human Rights and Observations and Comments of the American Governments, Working Document Prepared by the Secretariat of the Inter-American Commission on Human Rights, OEA/Ser L/V/II.22/Doc 10 (10 September 1969), reprinted in Thomas Buergenthal (ed), 3 *Human Rights* (Part II, ch II, Booklet 14, August 1982), Doc 13, 32-3. Cited in Stephanie Farrior, 'Molding the Matrix', 79.

[343] Summary Minutes of the Conference of San Jose, (1982) Minutes of the Eighth Session of Committee I Summary Version, Doc 48 (15 November 1969), reprinted in Thomas Buergenthal (ed), 2 *Human Rights* (Part II, ch I, Booklet 12, August 1982), 89. Cited in Stephanie Farrior, 'Molding the Matrix', 79.

[344] Stephanie Farrior, 'Molding the Matrix', 79.

[345] Summary Minutes of the Conference of San Jose, (1982) Minutes of the Eighth Session of Committee I Summary Version, Doc 48 (15 November 1969), reprinted in Thomas Buergenthal (ed), 2 *Human Rights* (Part II, ch I, Booklet 12, August 1982), 89. Cited in Stephanie Farrior, 'Molding the Matrix', 79.

not delete the paragraph entirely'.[346] At this juncture of the drafting, debate on Article 13(5) was declared closed and the following draft approved:

Any propaganda for war shall be prohibited by law, as shall any advocacy of national, racial, or religious hatred that constitutes incitement to discrimination, hostility, crime or violence.[347]

The United States regarded this text to be in conflict with the First Amendment of the US Constitution and persisted in its efforts to have it amended. The language, as finally adopted in the plenary session, was drafted and proposed by the United States whose approach was premised on that year's US Supreme Court decision in *Brandenburg v Ohio*.[348] The US delegation considered paragraph 5 to be consistent with the *Brandenburg* decision in that it required the prohibition only of 'propaganda or advocacy that actually constitutes an incitement to violence'.[349] The final text of Article 13(5) sets forth the Convention's prohibition of propaganda for war. Article 13(5) condenses the principles of paragraphs 1 and 2 of Article 20 of the Covenant into a single provision and provides that:

Any propaganda for war and any advocacy of national, racial, or religious hatred that constitute incitements to lawless violence or to any other similar illegal action against any person or group of persons on any grounds including those of race, color, religion, language, or national origin shall be considered as offenses punishable by law.[350]

b. *Jurisprudence of the Inter-American System*

From the comments of the US delegate, and the formulation of the Convention's prohibition of propaganda for war, which unlike that of the Covenant links the term propaganda for war to 'incitement to violence or any other similar illegal action', it would appear that the meaning of propaganda for war is more restrictive than that of the Covenant, covering only those forms of propaganda which directly incite to war, and thus precludes the obligation to prohibit propaganda which does not directly incite to war. Nowak has further argued that in locating the prohibition

---

[346] Report of the United States Delegation to the Inter-American Conference on Protection of Human Rights, San Jose, Costa Rica, 9-22 November 1969, reprinted in Thomas Buergenthal (ed), 3 *Human Rights* (Part II, ch III, Booklet 15, August 1982), 26. Cited in Stephanie Farrior, 'Molding the Matrix', 80. It is again notable that with regard to the propaganda which was fuelling the conflict between Honduras and El Salvador the US delegate commented that 'the press has exacerbated the tense conditions between the two countries', without any reference to the responsibility of respective governments themselves. ibid.

[347] ibid.

[348] *Brandenburg v Ohio*, 395 US 444 (1969).

[349] Report of the United States Delegation to the Inter-American Conference on Protection of Human Rights, San Jose, Costa Rica, 9–22 November 1969, reprinted in Thomas Buergenthal (ed), 3 *Human Rights* (Part II, ch III, Booklet 15, August 1982), 26. Cited in Stephanie Farrior, 'Molding the Matrix', 80.

[350] Article 13(5), American Convention on Human Rights, OAS Treaty Series no 36, 1144 UNTS 123.

of propaganda for war in the article on freedom of expression, the drafters of the American Convention were restricting its application to that right only and not, as in the Covenant, to other rights such as association and religion.[351]

Whereas both the Commission and the Court have had occasion to consider the meaning of the right to freedom of expression as set forth in Article 13, there has been little direct reference to the requirement that propaganda for war be considered an offence punishable by law.[352] Article 13 has been interpreted by the Court as establishing that those to whom the Convention applies not only have the right and freedom to express their own thoughts but also the right and freedom to seek, receive, and impart information and ideas of all kinds.[353] The freedom of expression provision of the Convention is notable insofar as Article 13(2) explicitly prohibits all prior censorship, and restrictions on expression can only occur *ex post parte* in the form of subsequent liability. In its advisory opinion on Compulsory Membership in an Association Prescribed by Law for the Practice of Journalism, the Inter-American Court compared Article 13 of the American Convention with equivalent provisions in other international human rights instruments to hold that a

comparison of Article 13 with the relevant provisions of the European Convention (article 10) and the Covenant (article 19) indicates clearly that the guarantees contained

---

[351] Manfred Nowak, *U.N. Covenant on Civil and Political Rights*, 468.

[352] A welcome development in the jurisprudence of the Inter-American system concerns the development of the 'right to truth'. To date this right has been concerned with the right to know the fate of family members 'disappeared' under various authoritarian American regimes, and is premised on States parties' obligation under Article 25 of the American Convention to provide victims, or their next of kin, simple and prompt legal recourse for violations of fundamental rights (Case 10.580, Report no 10/95, Ecuador, Manuel Bolaños, 12 September 1995). The Commission's understanding of this right has evolved so that it is understood to be a right that belongs both to victims and family members and to society as a whole. The right to truth was first considered in the context of Article 13 by the Commission's 1998 report in a group of cases from Chile where the Commission also recognized that the right to truth belongs to members of society at large as well as to the families of victims of human rights violations (Cases 11.505, 11.532, 11.541, 11.546, 11.549, 11.569, 11.572, 11.573, 11.583, 11.595, 11.657, 11.705, Report no 25/98, Chile, Alfonso René Chanfeau Orayce, 7 April 1998). The issue of the right to the truth has subsequently arisen in two cases considered by the American Court, but it was held to be unnecessary to consider this as a separate issue since in both cases the issue was addressed as part of the violation of Articles 8 and 25 of the Convention (*Bámaca Velásquez* case, 25 November 2000; *Barrios Altos* case, 14 March 2001). Given that propaganda for war has historically been premised on falsities, manipulation of the truth, and the withholding of information, it may be that the development of the right to truth taken in combination with Article 13(5) may provide an effective means of combating propaganda for war.

[353] The Court has stated that the right protected by Article 13 'has a special scope and character, which [is] evidenced by the dual aspect of freedom of expression. It requires, on the one hand, that no one be arbitrarily limited or impeded in expressing his own thoughts. In that sense, it is a right that belongs to each individual. Its second aspect, on the other hand, implies a collective right to receive any information whatsoever and to have access to the thoughts expressed by others.' Compulsory Membership in an Association Prescribed by Law for the Practice of Journalism (Articles 13 and 29 of the American Convention on Human Rights), Advisory Opinion OC-5/85, 13 November 1985, Inter-Am Ct HR (Ser A) no 5 (1985), para 30.

in the American Convention regarding freedom of expression were designed to be more generous and to reduce to a bare minimum restrictions impeding the free circulation of ideas.[354]

The Court's analysis omitted any discussion of the prohibition of propaganda for war. In the Report on the Situation of Human Rights in Paraguay, the Commission's Special Rapporteur expressed concern with the 'propensity of the media to become political and economic tools of the various power sectors to the detriment of its main function, which is to inform society', and reminded those who would exercise the right to freedom of expression in such a manner that the American Convention 'prohibits all propaganda for war and any advocacy of national, racial, or religious hatred that constitutes an incitement to violence'.[355] The Commission has read the limitation clauses of Article 13 to mean 'that the zone of legitimate state intervention begins at the point where the expression of an opinion or idea directly interferes with the rights of others or constitutes a direct and obvious threat to life in society', and found that, '[c]onsidering the consequences of criminal sanctions and the inevitable chilling effect they have on freedom of expression, criminalization of speech can only apply in those exceptional circumstances when there is an obvious and direct threat of lawless violence', such as set forth in Article 13(5).[356] The Commission's Report on Terrorism and Human Rights stated that whilst propaganda for war is an offence punishable by law, legislation that broadly criminalizes the public defence (*apologia*) of terrorism or of persons who might have committed terrorist acts, without considering the element of incitement 'to lawless violence or to any other similar action', is incompatible with the right to freedom of expression.[357]

It has been argued by Claudio Grossman, former President of the Inter-American Commission on Human Rights, that the regime of prior censorship also applies to any expression that constitutes propaganda for war, if it conforms to the requirements of legality, necessity, reality or imminence, or valid purpose.[358] Similarly, Adeno Addis considers propaganda for war to be 'a candidate for prior censorship' under Article 13(5).[359] The Court's jurisprudence does not directly

---

[354] ibid, para 50.

[355] Third Report on the Situation of Human Rights in Paraguay, OEA/Ser L/V/II.110 Doc 52, 9 March 2001, para 75.

[356] Report on Compatibility between Contempt Laws and the American Convention on Human Rights, OAS/Ser L/VIII.88, Doc 9 Rev (1995), 210–23.

[357] Report on Terrorism and Human Rights, OEA/Ser L/V/II.116, Doc 5 Rev 1 Corr, 22 October 2002, para 323.

[358] Claudio Grossman, 'Freedom of Expression in the Inter-American System for the Protection of Human Rights', 7 ILSA J Int'l & Comp L 619 (2001) 636. De Torres also affirms that Article 13(4) provides the only exception to the rule against prior censorship and, whilst citing Grossman's commentary on this provision, neglects to address his assertion that it also applies to Article 13(5). Amaya Ubeda de Torres, 'Freedom of Expression under the European Convention on Human Rights: A Comparison with the Inter-American System of Protection of Human Rights', 10 Hum Rts Br 6 (2003) 7.

[359] Adeno Addis, 'International Propaganda and Developing Countries', 506.

support this contention, however. In an Advisory Opinion which arose from a request by Costa Rica that the American Court consider the compatibility of its domestic legislation regulating the compulsory licensing of journalists with the Convention, the Court held that 'prior censorship is always incompatible with the full enjoyment of the rights listed in Article 13, but for the exception provided for in subparagraph 4 dealing with public entertainments, even if the alleged purpose of such prior censorship is to prevent abuses of freedom of expression'.[360] Without specifically referring to propaganda for war, the Court continued to state that '[a]buse of freedom of information thus cannot be controlled by preventive measures but only through the subsequent imposition of sanctions on those who are guilty of the abuses'.[361] In order that the imposition of subsequent liability does not itself constitute a violation of Article 13, the Court determined that the following conditions must be satisfied:

a) the existence of previously established grounds for liability;
b) the express and precise definition of these grounds by law;
c) the legitimacy of the ends sought to be achieved;
d) a showing that these grounds of liability are 'necessary to ensure' the aforementioned ends.[362]

The 1998 Report of the Inter-American Special Rapporteur on Freedom of Expression stated that '[p]rior censorship, regardless of its form, is contrary to the system that Article 13 of the Convention guarantees'.[363] The Declaration of Principles on Freedom of Expression,[364] drafted by the Office of the Special Rapporteur for Freedom of Expression and adopted by the Commission in 2000, reaffirms that '[p]rior censorship, direct or indirect interference in or pressure

[360] Compulsory Membership in an Association Prescribed by Law for the Practice of Journalism (Articles 13 and 29 of the American Convention on Human Rights), Advisory Opinion OC-5/85, 13 November 1985, Inter-Am Ct HR (Ser A) no 5 (1985), para 38.

[361] ibid, para 39.

[362] ibid. The appropriateness of subsequent liability was a cause for concern in a Commission Report on the human rights situation in Nicaragua. Article 22 of the Nicaraguan Statute of Rights and Guarantees prohibited speech which manifests itself as 'propaganda against peace and any apology for national, racial or religious hatred', and whilst the Commission held that this restriction was not incompatible with Article 13, it stated that '[p]roblems arise, however with regard to the restrictions imposed by subsequent regulation of the press'. Report on the Situation of Human Rights in the Republic of Nicaragua, OEA/Ser L/V/II.53 Doc 25, 30 June 1981, para 3. In the *Martorell* case, which arose from the finding by Chilean judiciary that the right of the protection of the individual's honour and dignity set forth in Article 11 of the American Convention justified the prior censorship of a book, the Commission held that this was an invalid decision since subsequent imposition of liability was the only restriction authorized by the American Convention to protect society from offensive opinions. Francisco Martorell, Case 11.230, Report no 11/96, Inter-Am Ct HR, para 55, 3 May 1996.

[363] Inter-Am Ct HR, Report of the Office of the Special Rapporteur for Freedom of Expression 1998, OEA/Ser L./V./II.102, Doc Rev 6, at vol iii, ch II, Sec B(5).

[364] Declaration of Principles on Freedom of Expression, Basic Documents Pertaining to Human Rights the Inter-American System, OEA/Ser L/V/I.4 Rev 8 (22 May 2001), 189. The Inter-American Commission on Human Rights adopted the Declaration of Principles on Freedom of Expression at its 108th regular session in October 2000.

exerted upon any expression, opinion or information transmitted through any means of oral, written, artistic, visual or electronic communication must be prohibited by law',[365] since '[p]rior conditioning of expressions, such as truthfulness, timeliness or impartiality, is incompatible with the right to freedom of expression recognized in international instruments'.[366] Thus, the jurisprudence of both the Commission and the Court in no way suggests that an expression constituting propaganda for war may legitimately be made subject to prior censorship even though it must constitute an offence punishable by law.

The Declaration of Principles on Freedom of Expression issued by the Special Rapporteur for Freedom of Expression, drafted with the aim of regulating 'the effective protection of freedom of expression in the hemisphere that would incorporate the principal doctrines set forth in different international instruments',[367] proclaims to have incorporated 'international standards into the inter-American system to strengthen protection of this right',[368] yet again omits any reference to propaganda for war. The Declaration of Principles does however confirm that '[l]imitations on the free flow of ideas that do not incite lawless violence are incompatible with freedom of expression and with the basic principles that form the underpinnings of the pluralistic, democratic way of life in modern societies'.[369]

In light of the trend internationally to overlook the prohibition of propaganda for war in international law, the dearth of comment and analysis of Article 13(5) may not be surprising but it remains a glaring void in the human rights discourse of the Inter-American human rights system. None of the States parties which have ratified the American Convention has entered any reservation or declaration to Article 13, while the USA, the single member state of the OAS to have entered a reservation to Article 20(1) of the Covenant, has not yet signed the Convention. Despite repeated emphasis on the importance of respect for the right to freedom of expression made by all organs of the OAS, the lack of judicial or other guidance on the subject of the prohibition of propaganda for war necessitates further attention.

ii. The European Convention on Human Rights

The final human rights treaty to be considered is the European Convention on Human Rights.[370] The European Convention differs from the International Covenant on Civil and Political Rights and the American Convention in that it does not place any obligation on States parties to prohibit specific forms of

---

[365] ibid, para 5.
[366] ibid, para 7.
[367] Special Rapporteur for Freedom of Expression, *Background and Interpretation of the Declaration of Principles*, para 2.
[368] ibid, para 3.
[369] ibid, para 27.
[370] European Convention for the Protection of Human Rights and Fundamental Freedoms (1950), entered into force 3 September 1953, 213 UNTS 221, ETS 5.

expression dangerous to human rights.[371] Given the persistent opposition of many European states to the prohibition of propaganda for war set forth in the Covenant, the absence of a prohibition of propaganda for war from the European Convention is unsurprising. Nonetheless, in recent years, many states which were once part of the Soviet Bloc and whose national legislation prohibits propaganda for war have acceded to the European Convention, increasing the likelihood that the European Court of Human Rights may have to consider whether such restrictions on freedom of expression are compatible with the Convention.

The Czech Republic, for example, in a periodic report submitted to the Human Rights Committee in 2006, highlighted the Soviet era Act on the Protection of Peace, whereby the 'threatening of peace means the disturbance of peaceful cohabitation among nations by instigating war, promoting war, or by other similar war propaganda, regardless of the manner in which it is carried out'.[372] Noting that '[t]he Czech legal order only contains an explicit prohibition of war propaganda as a rule contained in international treaties which constitute a part of the Czech legal order' the report continues to assert that ongoing recodification of criminal law in the Czech Republic 'also explicitly stipulates the unambiguous culpability of war propaganda', and the intent is that 'the introduction of new criminal offences of instigation of an offensive war and the preparation of an offensive war is to replace the existing definition of a criminal offence against peace under the Act on the Protection of Peace'.[373]

The first issue which the European Court will have to consider in this case, and the standard basis for many European states' opposition to acceptance of Article 20(1) of the Covenant, is likely to be whether the word 'propaganda' can be understood to have a sufficiently precise meaning for an acceptable limitation on the right to freedom of expression. The European Court has already had occasion to consider this question in a series of cases concerning the prohibition of 'separatist propaganda' in Turkey's criminal code. Article 10 of the European Convention provides that everyone has the right to freedom of expression but also sets forth grounds for permissible limitations to the right. Article 10(2) states that since the exercise of the right to freedom of expression carries with it duties and responsibilities, it

may be subject to such formalities, conditions, restrictions or penalties as are prescribed by law and are necessary in a democratic society, in the interests of national security, territorial integrity or public safety, for the prevention of disorder or crime, for the protection of health or morals, for the protection of the reputation or rights of others, for preventing

---

[371] For a comparison of the European Convention on Human Rights and the ICCPR, see generally AH Robertson, 'The United Nations Covenant on Civil and Political Rights and the European Convention on Human Rights', 43.

[372] CCPR/C/CZE/2, para 418: Act on the Protection of Peace (no 165/1950 Coll).

[373] ibid, para 419.

the disclosure of information received in confidence, or for maintaining the authority and impartiality of the judiciary'.[374]

On 8 July 1999, the European Court issued a series of judgments concerning the legality of convictions made under Turkey's Prevention of Terrorism Act (Law no 3713), 1991. Each of the applicants claimed that their convictions for having disseminated 'separatist propaganda' constituted a violation of Article 10.[375] Section 8(1) of the 1991 Act (subsequently amended by Law no 4126 of 27 October 1995) provided that:

Written and spoken propaganda, meetings, assemblies and demonstrations aimed at undermining the territorial integrity of the Republic of Turkey or the indivisible unity of the nation are prohibited, irrespective of the methods used and the intention. Any person who engages in such an activity shall be sentenced to not less than two and not more than five years' imprisonment and a fine of from fifty million to one hundred million Turkish liras.[376]

In determining whether there had been a violation of Article 10, the Court looked to establish whether there had been an interference with the right to freedom of expression before determining whether the interference was prescribed by law and whether it satisfied one or more of the legitimate aims set forth in

---

[374] Article 10. 'Everyone has the right to freedom of expression. This right shall include freedom to hold opinions and to receive and impart information and ideas without interference by public authority and regardless of frontiers. This Article shall not prevent States from requiring the licensing of broadcasting, television or cinema enterprises.

2. The exercise of these freedoms, since it carries with it duties and responsibilities, may be subject to such formalities, conditions, restrictions or penalties as are prescribed by law and are necessary in a democratic society, in the interests of national security, territorial integrity or public safety, for the prevention of disorder or crime, for the protection of health or morals, for the protection of the reputation or rights of others, for preventing the disclosure of information received in confidence, or for maintaining the authority and impartiality of the judiciary.'

[375] *Baikaya and Another v Turkey* (App nos 23536/94, 24408/94) 8 July 1999; *Sürek v Turkey (No. 1)* (App no 26682/95), 8 July 1999; *Gerger v Turkey*, [1999] ECHR 24919/94, 8 July 1999 (App no 24919/94); *Okguoglu v Turkey*, [1999] ECHR 24246/94, 8 July 1999 (App no 24246/94); *Sürek and Another v Turkey* (App nos 23927/94 and 24277/94) 7 BHRC 339; *Arslan v Turkey*, [1999] ECHR 23462/94, (App no 23462/94); *Erdogdu and Another v Turkey* [1999] ECHR 25067/94, 8 July 1999 (App nos 25067/94, 25068/94); *Karata v Turkey*, [1999] ECHR 23168/94, 8 July 1999 (App no 23168/94); *Polat v Turkey* (App no 23500/94), [1999] ECHR 23500/94; *Ceylan v Turkey* (App no 23556/94), 8 July 1999; *Sürek v Turkey (No. 2)* (App no 24122/94), 8 July 1999; *Sürek v Turkey (No. 3)* (App no 24735/94), 8 July 1999; *Sürek v Turkey (No. 4)* (App no 24762/94), [1999] ECHR 24762/94.

[376] Section 8(2): 'Where the crime of propaganda contemplated in the above paragraph is committed through the medium of periodicals within the meaning of s 3 of the Press Act (Law no. 5680), the publisher shall also be liable to a fine equal to ninety per cent of the income from the average sales for the previous month if the periodical appears more frequently than monthly, or from the average sales for the previous month of the daily newspaper with the largest circulation if the offence involves printed matter other than periodicals or if the periodical has just been launched. However the fine may not be less than one hundred million Turkish liras. The editor of the periodical concerned shall be ordered to pay a sum equal to half the fine imposed on the publisher and sentenced to not less than six months' and not more than two years' imprisonment.'

Article 10(2), namely, that the interference was necessary in a democratic society. In each of the cases the Court had found that there had been an interference with the right to freedom of expression, and it was in its determination as to whether the prescription was prescribed by law that the Court considered the meaning of 'propaganda'.

In most cases the applicants did not challenge the government's contention that this requirement had been met since the restrictions at issue had been based on Section 8(1) of the 1991 Act. While the Court accepted this contention without comment in the majority of cases, criticisms of the manner in which Turkey was interpreting and applying the 1991 Act prompted the Court to clarify the issue on several occasions. In *Sürek v Turkey (No 1)*[377] the applicant did not specifically address the compatibility of Section 8(1) of the 1991 Act with the requirement that the interference be prescribed by law, but he claimed that the provision 'was used by the authorities to silence the opposition press and to punish the dissemination of views and opinions including those which do not incite to violence or espouse the cause of illegal organisations or advocate the division of the State'.[378] Similarly, in the case of *Polat v Turkey*,[379] it was contended that the application of Section 8 of the 1991 Act 'gave rise to different results for different defendants, because its interpretation varied from one person to another and from one judge to another, which made its effects unforeseeable'.[380]

In considering whether the interference had in fact been prescribed by law, the Court first noted the observation of the delegate of the European Commission of Human Rights that the wording of Section 8(1) was 'rather vague and that it might be questioned whether it satisfied the conditions of clarity and foreseeability inherent in the prescribed-by-law requirement'.[381] Despite such misgivings, the Commission had nevertheless accepted that Section 8(1) formed a sufficient legal basis for the applicants' conviction and held that the interference had been 'prescribed by law'.[382] Although acknowledging the Commission's concerns, the Court concurred to hold in both cases that since the applicants' convictions were based on the 1991 Act, the interference with the right to freedom of expression could properly be regarded as having been 'prescribed by law'.[383]

---

[377] *Sürek v Turkey (No. 1)* (App no 26682/95), 8 July 1999.
[378] ibid, para 45.
[379] *Polat v Turkey* (App no 23500/94), [1999] ECHR 23500/94.
[380] ibid, para 33.
[381] *Sürek v Turkey (No. 1)* (App no 26682/95), 8 July 1999, para 47; *Polat v Turkey* (App no 23500/94), [1999] ECHR 23500/94, para 35.
[382] ibid. See also *Erdogdu and Another v Turkey*, [1999] ECHR 25067/94, 8 July 1999 (App nos 25067/94, 25068/94), para 38.
[383] *Sürek v Turkey (No. 1)*, (App no 26682/95), 8 July 1999, para 48; *Polat v Turkey* (App no 23500/94), [1999] ECHR 23500/94, para 36. In the case of *Sürek (No. 1)* the Court added that this was 'all the more so given that the applicant has not specifically disputed this'.

In a further two cases, the applicants contended that their convictions under Section 8(1) constituted not only a violation of Article 10 but also of Article 7.[384] The applicants in *Erdogdu and Another v Turkey* claimed that there had been a violation of Article 7 on the grounds that 'acts of mere propaganda cannot constitute an offence under s 8 of that Act unless they incite to terrorist acts'.[385] They further argued that 'the concept of the "crime of propaganda" under s 8 of the 1991 Act was not precise enough to enable them to distinguish between permissible and prohibited behaviour'.[386] Both Turkey and the Commission expressed the view that Section 8 of the 1991 Act had been sufficiently specific to enable the applicants, 'if necessary after taking legal advice, to regulate their conduct in the matter'.[387] The Court approved of these views and found that there had been no violation of Article 7.[388]

In *Baikaya and Another v Turkey*, the applicants claimed that due to the lack of clarity of the wording of Section 8 of the 1991 Act, particularly the vagueness of the notion of 'dissemination of propaganda against the indivisibility of the State', it had not been foreseeable at the material time that the publication in question, which they contended was solely an academic work, constituted a criminal offence.[389] The Court noted that since none of those taking part in the proceedings had submitted any argument in relation to the requirement of 'prescribed by law' under Article 10(2) which substantially differed from those invoked in connection with Article 7,[390] the requirements under both provisions in this regard were largely the same.[391] The Court declared that in accordance with its case-law, Article 7 embodies:

[...] the principle that only the law can define a crime and prescribe a penalty (nullum crimen, nulla poena sine lege) and the principle that the criminal law must not be extensively construed to an accused's detriment, for instance by analogy. From these principles it follows that an offence and the sanctions provided for it must be clearly defined in the law. This requirement is satisfied where the individual can know from the wording of the

---

[384] 'Article 7: 1. No one shall be held guilty of any criminal offence on account of any act or omission which did not constitute a criminal offence under national or international law at the time when it was committed. Nor shall a heavier penalty be imposed than the one that was applicable at the time the criminal offence was committed.

2. This article shall not prejudice the trial and punishment of any person for any act or omission which, at the time when it was committed, was criminal according to the general principles of law recognised by civilised nations.'

[385] *Erdogdu and Another v Turkey*, [1999] ECHR 25067/94, 8 July 1999 (App nos 25067/94, 25068/94), para 57. The applicants did not challenge the requirement under Article 10 that the restriction on the right to freedom of expression be prescribed by law, and the Court was satisfied that this requirement had been met by Section 8 of the 1991 Act, paras 36–9.

[386] ibid.

[387] ibid, para 58.

[388] ibid, para 59.

[389] *Baikaya and Another v Turkey*, [1999] ECHR 23536/94, 8 July 1999, para 34.

[390] ibid, para 48.

[391] ibid, para 49.

relevant provision and, if need be, with the assistance of the courts' interpretation of it, what acts and omissions will make him criminally liable.[392]

The Court further acknowledged that in relation to restrictions on the right to freedom of expression:

> [...] it may be difficult to frame laws with absolute precision and that a certain degree of flexibility may be called for to enable the national courts to assess whether a publication should be considered separatist propaganda against the indivisibility of the State. However clearly drafted a legal provision may be, there is an inevitable element of judicial interpretation. There will always be a need for elucidation of doubtful points and for adaptation to changing circumstances.[393]

In finding no violation of Article 7, the Court dismissed the applicants' suggestion that Section 8 of the 1991 Act conferred an over-broad discretion on the Turkish National Security Courts in interpreting the scope of the offence. According to the Court, it was sufficient that a definition of the offence was contained in the first subsection of Section 8; the second subsection, setting out the penalties, gave pointers as to what kinds of publications were covered by the offence and who might incur liability. Furthermore, it held that the interpretation of the provision by the domestic courts did not go beyond what could reasonably have been foreseen in the circumstances.[394] In holding that a provision of domestic law prohibiting 'separatist propaganda against the indivisibility of the state' was adequately defined to justify the criminalization of speech, the European Court is unlikely to hold that a prohibition of propaganda for war in domestic law is incompatible with Article 10.

C. Summary

Although focusing on the interpretation and application of Article 20(1) of the International Covenant on Civil and Political Rights, this chapter has also considered the prohibition of propaganda for war in Article 13(5) of the American Convention and demonstrated that states may legitimately criminalize 'separatist propaganda', a far less grievous form of speech than propaganda for war, in accordance with Article 10 of the European Convention.

Two clear conclusions can be drawn from this study. The first is that the prohibition of propaganda for war in international law is fully compatible with the right to freedom of expression. This has been repeatedly affirmed by the Committee in the General Comments and in its communications with States parties. The second is that there are adequate resources available upon which states can draw

---

[392] *Baikaya and Another v Turkey*, [1999] ECHR 23536/94, 8 July 1999, para 36.
[393] ibid, para 39.
[394] ibid, para 40.

in order to suitably define 'propaganda for war'. Robertson argued that a large number of rights set out in the Covenant are frequently given more 'liberal or progressive' definitions than in comparable instruments, several of which are 'so general or imprecise that the texts appear to be more statements of political principle or policy than of legally enforceable rights'.[395] More than any other provision of the Covenant, Article 20(1) has laboured under an incorrect assumption that it is legally unenforceable. While it is clear from the *travaux préparatoires* and the comments of States parties that much political controversy surrounds the provision, it appears that the meaning of 'propaganda for war' is only as imprecise as states wish it to be, and that by permitting the provision to be misinterpreted and misapplied without comment or analysis either by the Committee or other States parties, this serves as a self-fulfilling prophecy. Complacency with regard to such a situation represents not only a violation of the obligation upon states to refrain from and prohibit propaganda for war, but an intolerable undermining of the entire international human rights framework.

[395] AH Robertson, *Human Rights in the World* (Manchester: Manchester University Press, 1972) 38.

5

From Nuremberg to The Hague: Towards an International Crime of Incitement to Aggression

Prior to the conclusion of the Second World War, Trainin had asserted that while aggression was clearly criminal under international law, propaganda inciting to aggression was also an international crime:

In the interests of the struggle for peace, the penalty for crime must fall not only on those guilty of carrying out aggression, but also on those who try to fan the flame of war, who prepare aggression. Activities preparing the ground for aggression must comprise [...] the provoking of international conflicts by all kinds of means; the propaganda of aggression.[1]

More than sixty years later, the question of whether direct and public incitement to aggression constitutes a criminal act in contravention of international law has been tabled as part of the drafting of the crime of aggression for inclusion in the Rome Statute of the International Criminal Court.[2] In order to determine the basis for such a crime in the Rome Statute, it is necessary to analyse the approach taken by the International Law Commission in its efforts at drafting a Code of Offences Against the Peace and Security of Mankind from 1947. The jurisprudence of the ad hoc International Criminal Tribunals for the Former Yugoslavia and Rwanda, as had been the case with the International Military Tribunal at Nuremberg, includes many cases in which the impact of propaganda and incitement to international crimes have been examined and analysed, with the Rwandan Tribunal in particular making a strong case for the reappraisal of the manner in which international criminal law addresses propaganda inciting to the most serious international crimes.

---

[1] AN Trainin, *Hitlerite Responsibility under Criminal Law*, 37. As USSR delegate to the second session of the General Assembly in 1947, his editor Vishinski had proposed that criminal propaganda be condemned in what became Resolution 110(II).

[2] Elements of the Crime of Aggression: Proposal by Samoa, PCNICC/2002/WGCA/DP.2, 21 June 2002, paras 16–18. See generally Roger S Clark, 'Rethinking Aggression as a Crime and Formulating its Elements: The Final Work-Product of the Preparatory Commission for the International Criminal Court', 15 Leiden J Int'l L 859 (2002) 884.

A. The International Law Commission

The principles of international law recognized by the Charter and the judgment of the IMT were affirmed in a Resolution of the UN General Assembly in December 1946.[3] The General Assembly also requested the Committee on the Codification of International Law to direct its attention to plans for the formulation 'of a general codification of the offenses against the peace and security of mankind, or of an international criminal code of the principles recognized in the Charter of the Nuremberg Tribunal and in the Judgment of the Tribunal'.[4] This Committee recommended that the International Law Commission (Commission) should undertake 'the actual formulation of these principles', by preparing '[a] draft convention incorporating the principles of international law recognized by the Charter of the Nuremberg Tribunal and sanctioned by the judgment of that Tribunal'.[5] It also recommended that the Commission draft a plan of general codification of offences against the peace and security of mankind that would clearly indicate the place to be accorded to these principles. While the draft convention never materialized, the General Assembly requested the Commission to: (a) formulate the principles of international law recognized in the Charter of the Nuremberg Tribunal and in the judgment of the tribunal; and (b) prepare a draft code of offences against the peace and security of mankind, indicating clearly the place to be accorded to the principles mentioned in (a) above.[6]

Prior to the Commission commencing this work, Wright had assumed that it would doubtless 'consider whether a crime of "war-mongering" exists or should exist in international law'.[7] He was critical that up to that point 'propaganda which instigates or encourages aggression or other crime against international law has been considered a crime, not in itself, but because of its relationship to the international delinquency or crime which it incites'.[8] Advocating a reappraisal of this position he reasoned that when 'propaganda provokes or encourages aggression or other international crime it becomes a crime itself'.[9] Wright considered 'general principles of law, diplomatic discussion, treaties, juristic opinion, national and international legislation, and juridical precedents' to indicate 'that libelous and inflammatory utterances intended to incite, and tending to produce, aggressive war or other crime against the law of nations, and other acts

[3] GA Res 95(I), 11 December 1946.
[4] ibid.
[5] Report of the Committee on the Progressive Development of International Law and its Codification on the Plans for the Formulation of the Nuremberg Charter and Judgment, Doc A/AC.10/52, 17 June 1947, para 2(a): reprinted in 41 AJIL 3 Supplement: Official Documents 18 (1947) 26–7.
[6] GA Res 177(II), 21 November 1947.
[7] Quincy Wright, 'The Crime of "War-Mongering"', 128.
[8] ibid 131.
[9] ibid 132.

short of direct planning or use of military force with the same intention and tendency, are crimes against international law which might well be designated "war-mongering" '.[10] The Fifth International Congress on Penal Law, meeting in Geneva in 1947, had passed a resolution to similar effect, advocating the adoption of 'an international law to give penal protection to peace by scrupulous repression of acts of propaganda for aggressive war'.[11]

The Report of the Committee on the Codification of International Law noted similar assertions which had been made by Poland, and supported by the USSR and Yugoslavia, that 'propaganda of aggressive wars constitutes a crime under international law and falls under the scope of preparation to such wars as listed in Article 6(a) of the Statute of Nuremberg'.[12] Pointing to its national Criminal Code, which had prohibited propaganda for war since 1932, Poland described such propaganda as 'a form of psychological armaments as opposed to the notion of moral disarmament'.[13] It asserted that 'this crime is a dangerous form of preparation, likely to cause and increase international friction and lead to armed conflicts'.[14] These states advocated for a similar provision to be incorporated into the Draft Code and requested that the Commission 'take appropriate action on this matter as one of primary importance'.[15]

i. Draft Code of Offences Against the Peace and Security of Mankind (1954)

Debate on the formulation of a Draft Code of Offences against the Peace and Security of Mankind commenced at the Commission's second session in 1950. Among the documents submitted for discussion was a report by Pella which outlined proposals for a criminal offence of propaganda for war.[16] Under three distinct titles the report made several succinct observations about the role that international criminal law had to play vis-à-vis propaganda for war. The titles were: 'La propagande de guerre';[17] 'La diffusion de nouvelles fausses ou déformées ou de faux documents sachant qu'ils nuisent aux relations internationales';[18] and 'La pression en faveur de la guerre'.[19] Pella argued that since the threat or use of force had been prohibited under Article 2(4) of the UN Charter and constituted a crime against

---

[10] ibid 133.

[11] Revue internationale de droit penal, 18 (1947), 44.

[12] Report of the Committee on the Progressive Development of International Law and its Codification on the Plans for the Formulation of the Nuremberg Charter and Judgment, Doc A/AC.10/52, 17 June 1947, fn 2: reprinted in 41 AJIL 3 Supplement: Official Documents 18 (1947) 27.

[13] ibid.

[14] ibid.

[15] ibid.

[16] A/CN.4/39, [1950] 2 YB ILC, 278.

[17] A/CN.4/39, para 123; [1950] 2 YB ILC, 341. 'Propaganda for war' (author's translation).

[18] ibid, para 129, p 343. 'The dissemination of false or distorted news or documents harmful to international relations' (author's translation).

[19] ibid, para 134, p 345. 'pressure for war' (author's translation).

peace under the Charter and in the judgment of the IMT, then it followed logically that 'l'incitation publique' (public incitement) to these crimes must also be considered a crime. He supported this contention by reference to the fact that all national legislations prohibited direct incitement to crime, and since incitement ('la provocation') to murder was subject to severe punishment, then the prohibition of incitement to war, 'qui représente un meurtre en masse', under international criminal law was a necessity.[20] He noted, however, that such a provision should not be interpreted in a manner that would restrict necessary preparations for self-defence by prohibiting attempts to alert the public to a threat of war.[21] Acknowledging that the drafting and application of a prohibition of propaganda for war in international criminal law would be a complex and difficult task for the Commission, he nevertheless asserted that it should not be omitted from the Draft Code.[22]

Poland reiterated to the Commission that the Draft Code 'should punish not only acts directed immediately toward the commission of the crime, but should also counteract any activity which creates favourable conditions for the commission of those crimes'.[23] On this basis it argued that one of the Draft Code's essential elements should be 'the prevention and suppression not only of incitement to war or to the perpetration of other offences against the peace and security of mankind contained in the future code, but also of all other forms of spreading nationalistic, racial or religious hatred'.[24]

A Draft Code submitted by the Netherlands proposed the inclusion of criminal offences of both incitement to, and propaganda for, war. Under the heading of 'crimes against peace', this draft included the criminal offence of '[d]iffusion in bad faith of evidently false publications likely to endanger the relations with another State'.[25] The draft provided for a stand-alone offence of '[i]ncitement to any of the foregoing crimes' under the title of '[p]lanning, preparation etc', which would have applied to the crime of 'waging a war of aggression'.[26] Additionally, the Dutch draft sought to criminalize '[p]ropaganda of a war of aggression or of a war in violation of international treaties, agreements or assurances',[27] and '[p]ropaganda of one of the other crimes'.[28] The Netherlands considered these offences to be acts which already constituted offences according to international law.[29] An explanatory note stated that while the crime of aggression could only be committed by states, the other crimes could be committed either by a government or private individuals and were suitable for inclusion in national penal codes.[30]

---

[20] A/CN.4/39, para 123, p 341. 'which represents mass murder' (author's translation).
[21] ibid, 'de réveiller un pays ignorant des dangers qui le menacent' (author's translation).
[22] ibid.
[23] Draft Code of Offences against the Peace and Security of Mankind, Docs A/CN.4/19 and Add 1 and 2, Replies from Governments to Questionnaires of the International Law Commission. [1950] 2 YB ILC, 250.
[24] ibid.   [25] ibid, para 8.
[26] ibid, Article 16(a), 252.   [27] ibid, Article 17(a), 252.
[28] ibid, para 17(b), 252.   [29] ibid 252, para 2.
[30] ibid 253, para 9.

As a follow up to his initial report, Pella submitted a short Draft Code to the Special Rapporteur, Jean Spiropoulos.[31] In addition to a proposed offence of 'dissemination of false or distorted news or of forged documents in the knowledge that they are harmful to international relations',[32] he also included the crime of 'war propaganda' under the heading '[t]hreat of unlawful use of force and preparation for such use'.[33] There was little debate on these proposals,[34] other than the assertion by the Commission Chairman that 'the dissemination of false news was an act of propaganda'.[35]

Although the Commission showed little inclination to include an offence of 'propaganda' in the Draft Code, there was general acceptance of the idea that incitement to the offences set forth therein should constitute a distinct offence. The Special Rapporteur proposed a Draft Code in which direct and public incitement to each of the crimes, including aggression, was also to be considered an offence.[36] Crime no X(b) of this Draft Code provided that '[d]irect and public incitement to commit any of the acts under Crimes I–X' was a crime in itself, the crime of aggression having been set forth in Crime no I as '[t]he use of armed force in violation of international law and, in particular, the waging of aggressive war'.[37]

The Special Rapporteur's commentary suggested that direct and public incitement to war crimes should be regarded as an inchoate offence under the Code.[38] He cited as precedent the case of Brigadeführer Kurt Meyer, who 'in violation of the laws and usages of war incited and counselled troops under his command to deny quarter to allied troops',[39] a rare yet notable example of an inchoate war crime (although Meyer's troops went on to kill Canadian prisoners). A brief discussion on the appropriateness of the word 'public' resulted in a distinction being made between Crime no X(b) of the draft and Article III of the Genocide Convention which also contained the term 'direct and public', on the grounds that the 'atmosphere' that needed to be created before the crime of genocide could be committed was not strictly necessary for the crimes set out in the Code.[40] The term 'direct incitement' was thus held to be adequate, and the words 'and public' were deleted from the Draft Code as adopted by the Commission.[41]

---

[31] A/CN.4/R.3; [1950] 1 YB ILC, para 121, p 166.

[32] This proposal was included under the title 'Various acts constituting failure on the parts of States to observe their obligations to respect the dignity of other States and to conform to international usages'. Paragraph VIII(3), A/CN.4/R.3.

[33] Paragraph II(4), A/CN.4/R.3.

[34] [1950] 1 YB ILC, paras 122–7, p 166.

[35] ibid, para 47, p 169.

[36] Doc A/CN.4/25, Report by J Spiropoulos, Special Rapporteur; Docs A/CN.4/19 Add 1, [1950] 2 YB ILC, 253, 278.

[37] ibid 253.

[38] ibid 267.

[39] *The Abbaye Ardenne Case; Trial of S.S. Brigadeführer Kurt Meyer*, Canadian Military Court, Aurich, Germany, 10–28 December 1945, IV *Law Reports of Trials of War Criminals* 97.

[40] [1950] 1 YB ILC, paras 82–8.

[41] [1950] 1 YB ILC, para 88.

At the close of its second session the Commission adopted a formulation of the principles of international law recognized in the London Charter and in the judgment of the IMT which was to be sent to the General Assembly.[42] Principle VI(a) reproduced Article 6(a) of the Charter of the IMT in providing that crimes against peace consisted of:

(i) Planning, preparation, initiation or waging of a war of aggression or a war in violation of international treaties, agreements or assurances;

(ii) Participation in a common plan or conspiracy for the accomplishment of any of the acts mentioned under (i).[43]

That propaganda inciting to aggression constituted a violation of Principle VI(a) was confirmed in discussions at the Commission's next session. In his second report to the Commission the Special Rapporteur noted the opinion of Yugoslavia that:

[...] any propaganda inciting to war carried on in conjunction with plans of aggression constituted preparation for war and as such should be included among the acts condemned under principle VI (crimes against peace). Where such propaganda was not carried on together with plans of aggression, it constituted an act of a particular kind and should be subject to indictment [...] not among the acts indicated at Nuremberg but in a draft code [...][44]

The latter suggestion appears to have been incorporated into the Draft Code submitted to the Commission by the Rapporteur, insofar as Crime no 11(b) provided that acts which constitute '[d]irect incitement to commit any of the offences to defined in Nos. 1–10' were offences against the peace and security of mankind and crimes under international law.[45] In his commentary on the draft, the Special Rapporteur considered the 1948 Genocide Convention and 'certain municipal enactments on war crimes' as providing a precedent for the inclusion of the offence of incitement in the Draft Code.[46] The formula used is largely a reiteration of the offence of incitement as adopted at the Commission's previous session, and would have been applicable to Crime no 1, namely 'the employment or threat of employment, by the authorities of a State, of armed force against another State'. The commentary stated that whereas the offence of aggression could only be committed by the authorities of a state, a penal responsibility of private individuals for

<hr />

[42] Text of the Nürnberg Principles Adopted by the International Law Commission, A/CN.4/L.2: [1950] 2 YB ILC 374.

[43] Principle VII addressed the issue of complicity which was to resurface frequently throughout the drafting: 'Complicity in the commission of a crime against peace, a war crime, or a crime against humanity as set forth in Principle VI is a crime under international law.'

[44] Second Report by Mr J Spiropoulos, Special Rapporteur, Doc A/CN.4/44, para 109; [1951] 2 YB ILC, 54.

[45] ibid 59.

[46] Second Report by Mr J Spiropoulos, Special Rapporteur, Doc A/CN.4/44; *Draft text to be submitted to governments in application of article 16(g) and (h) of the statute of the International Law Commission*, [1951] 2 YB ILC, 59.

acts of incitement to aggression could accrue through Crime no 11(b).[47] This was a clear statement by the Special Rapporteur that propaganda inciting to aggression should be set forth as an offence in the Draft Code.

The Commission Chairman raised doubts as to the necessity of the word 'direct' in the Rapporteur's formulation since he considered it of little matter whether incitement should be direct or indirect.[48] The Rapporteur again cited Article III(c) of the Genocide Convention as the basis for this formulation.[49] The Commission's Assistant Secretary General stated that the words 'and public' had been added to the word 'direct' in the Genocide Convention 'to soften the effect of the word "direct"', since certain states had found ratification difficult on freedom of expression grounds.[50] Although the chairman found it inconsistent to include the word 'direct' given that the word 'public' had been dropped at the previous session, Crime no 11(b) as drafted by the Special Rapporteur was adopted without change.[51]

At this juncture a new proposal saw the discussions turn from direct incitement to aggression to the issue of 'propaganda' constituting a crime of aggression. Two additional articles were proposed by the Colombian delegate for inclusion in Article I of the Draft Code concerning the use of armed force by a state:

i) The dissemination in a State of false reports, or of faked documents falsely attributed to other States, where such dissemination has taken place with evil intent and has actually helped to disturb international relations.

ii) All forms of propaganda, in whatever country, intended or calculated to cause or encourage any threat to peace, or to break that good understanding between peoples on which peace depends.[52]

Precedent cited in support of this proposal included General Assembly Resolution 127(II) of 1947 concerning 'the diffusion of false and or distorted reports likely to injure friendly relations between states', resolutions of the Inter-Parliamentary Union, the judgment of the IMT, and finally 'world opinion [which] expected the Commission to take courageous action for peace through law'.[53] Taking the judgment of the IMT as 'the origin' of the proposal, it was argued that the Code would be incomplete if a provision was not included making propaganda by means of false reports an offence.[54]

Whilst agreeing with the principle and sentiments of the proposal, the Special Rapporteur felt that 'the time had not yet come to insert such crime definitions in the Code'.[55] Describing them as 'very vague', he did not accept that they could fit in with 'the other crimes which were of an entirely different nature'.[56] He then noted that the *Streicher* case concerned a conviction for acts of propaganda which

[47] ibid 58.
[48] [1951] 1 YB ILC, para 89, p 77.
[49] ibid, para 90, p 77.
[50] ibid (Mr Kerno), para 91, p 77.
[51] ibid, para 92, p 77.
[52] (Mr Yepes), [1951] 1 YB ILC, para 112, p 79.
[53] ibid, paras 113–17, p 79.
[54] ibid, para 115, p 79.
[55] ibid, para 118, p 79.
[56] ibid, para 122, p 79.

had provoked a war.[57] Such acts, he said, were covered by Article 1(2) of the Draft Code concerning '[t]he planning of or preparation for the employment by the authorities of a State, of armed force against another State for purpose other than national or collective self-defence or execution of a decision by a competent organ of the United Nations'.[58] Since the proposed crimes were to be included independently of a crime of aggression, he stated that the examples given did not apply.[59]

It is clear therefore that the Special Rapporteur was in no doubt but that propaganda which did not itself directly incite to aggression, but was an element of a plan to commit aggression, could constitute a crime against peace. He was not willing to accept that propaganda which tended to affect friendly relations or peace itself could be a distinct offence under the Draft Code unless it was clearly linked to incitement to one of the other crimes. It is submitted that the Special Rapporteur was mistaken in relying on the precedent set in *Streicher* since the accused had not been convicted for incitement to crimes against peace, but rather for incitement constituting crimes against humanity, an act that was held to be a crime independent of any link to charges of crimes against peace.

As was the case on each occasion that proposals concerning the less clearly defined the term 'propaganda', rather than 'incitement' to aggression, were put to the Commission, criticisms of the suitability of the word were aired. Several delegates, whilst acknowledging the desirability of such provisions in the Draft Code, argued that defining such a crime would be of too great a difficulty.[60] It was also suggested that while the second article of the proposal was too vague, the first, although more precise, was of little potential effect.[61] Taking these views into account the proposal was withdrawn to avoid delaying approval of the Draft Code[62] and Crime no 11, setting forth the offence of direct incitement to crimes including aggression, was subsequently adopted.[63]

The first Draft Code was included in the Commission's report which was submitted to the General Assembly following this session.[64] Article 2 provided that 'any act of aggression, including the employment of armed force against another State', was an offence against the peace and security of mankind and thus an international crime under Article 1. The commentary to the article stated that aggression 'can be committed by acts other than armed force including some of those set out in the other paragraphs of article 2'.[65] The commentary did not detail which other acts could constitute aggression but since Crime no 11 (b), renamed as Article 2(12)(ii), set forth the offence of 'direct incitement to commit any of the

[57] (Mr Yepes), [1951] 1 YB ILC.
[58] ibid.
[59] ibid.
[60] ibid (Mr Amado), para 127, pp 79–80.
[61] ibid (Mr Sandstrom), paras 128–30, p 80.
[62] ibid, para 131, p 80.
[63] ibid, para 41, p 224.
[64] Draft Code of Offences Against the Peace and Security of Mankind, [1951] 2 YB ILC 134.
[65] ibid 135.

offences defined in the preceding paragraphs',[66] it is possible that incitement to aggression may have satisfied as an act of aggression in its own right. Nonetheless, as the Draft Code was not considered by the General Assembly it was referred back to the Commission in 1952.

The Commission then considered a revised Draft Code as submitted by the Special Rapporteur in his third report to the sixth session in 1954.[67] Article 2(12)(ii) reproduced the offence of incitement as adopted at the ILC's 1952 session, providing for the offence of '[l]'incitation directe à commettre l'un quelconque des crimes défins aux paragraphes précédents du présent article'. The commentary noted the assertion by the Netherlands that the offence of 'direct incitement'[68] should be limited to direct incitement to an act of aggression only.[69] The Dutch were opposed to this being an inchoate offence on the basis that it should not apply to the suppression of mere attempts ('tentatives') of incitement to aggression.[70] In contrast, they did not require such a restriction to apply to the offences of direct incitement to genocide, crimes against humanity, or crimes in violation of the laws and customs of war.[71]

This point in the drafting process marks a shift away from discussions of incitement to aggression as a distinct crime, towards incitement being considered alongside the various modes of commission such as conspiracy,[72] preparation,[73] and complicity[74] which were also set forth in Article 2(12). Although the effects of this shift would not become apparent until the debates on drafting of the 1996 Draft Code, it was already evident at this juncture that incitement to the offences set forth in the Draft Code, and particularly incitement to aggression, was no longer being accorded the attention its grievous nature warranted.

Once again the Special Rapporteur explained to the Commission that by including a provision on 'direct incitement' to crimes in the Draft Code, he had followed the example of the Genocide Convention.[75] Noting the criticisms of the United Kingdom and other delegates that Article 2(12) as a whole would create serious difficulties in practice,[76] he made four alternative proposals. His first suggestion was to leave the provision untouched, reasoning that judges applying a reasonable interpretation of the crimes could resolve the criticisms raised. The second option was to retain the provision but to specify that its application be limited by its compatibility with the definition of the crimes set out in Article 12(1)–(11). The third option, '[u]ne solution radicale', would have been to delete

---

[66] ibid 136–7.
[67] Doc A/CN.4/85, [1954] 2 YB ILC, 112.
[68] 'L'incitation directe'.
[69] The crime of aggression was set forth in Article 2(1) : 'Toute acte d'agression, y compris l'emploi, par les autorités d'un Etat, de la force armée contre un autre Etat à des fins autres que la légitime défense nationale ou collective ou, soit l'exécution d'une décision, soit l'application d'une recommandation d'un organe compétent des Nations Unies.' Doc A/CN.4/85, [1954] 2 YB ILC, 115.
[70] ibid 119.   [71] ibid.
[72] ibid, Article 2(12)(i), 118.   [73] ibid, Article 2(12)(iii).
[74] ibid, Article 2(12)(iv).   [75] ibid 119.
[76] ibid.

Article 2(12) in its entirety. By doing so, only those crimes that were already existent in other international conventions would be punishable under the Draft Code. Therefore, the crimes of conspiracy and complicity under international law would derive solely from Article 6 of the Nuremberg Charter. The crimes of incitement and attempt would be restricted to their meaning under Article III of the Genocide Convention, although he also suggested that national legislation might provide a further possible source of criminal responsibility.[77] His final suggestion, and the one which he considered to be the most suitable, was to indicate in Article 2(12) the crimes in Article 2 to which conspiracy, incitement, attempt and complicity were to apply.[78]

Several delegates favoured the deletion of paragraph 12 in its entirety.[79] Others advocated its retention on the grounds that the gravity of the offences enumerated 'made it essential that all forms of criminal activity should be punished, so as to strike at the very roots of aggression'.[80] It was put to the Commission that the only difficulty would be the definition of those 'technical terms' which were not given the same meaning in different legislative systems.[81] Finally, the Special Rapporteur stated that after having 'long hesitated' between the four possible alternatives, his inclination had changed from the fourth alternative to the first, and he proposed the retention of the text of the paragraph as drafted at the third session.[82]

This proposal was accepted and clause (ii) of Article 2(12) was adopted unopposed.[83] In the Draft Code as adopted by the General Assembly[84] Article 2(12)(ii), renumbered as Article 2(13)(ii), provided for the offence of '[d]irect incitement to commit any of the offences defined in the preceding paragraphs of this article'.[85] Thus 'direct incitement' to the crime of aggression was held to constitute a distinct offence against the peace and security of mankind.[86]

---

[77] The crime of aggression was set forth in Article 2(1) : 'Toute acte d'agression, y compris l'emploi, par les autorités d'un Etat, de la force armée contre un autre Etat à des fins autres que la légitime défense nationale ou collective ou, soit l'exécution d'une décision, soit l'application d'une recommandation d'un organe compétent des Nations Unies.' Doc A/CN.4/85, [1954] 2 YB ILC.

[78] ibid.

[79] [1954] 1 YB ILC, paras 17–18, p 137. Mr Pal representing India was amongst these delegates. As a judge at the Tokyo Tribunal Pal had critiqued and rejected Trainin's propositions concerning the crime of 'propaganda of aggression'. BVA Roling and CF Ruter (eds), *The Tokyo Judgement*, 605.

[80] ibid, para 19, p 137.

[81] ibid. Mr Scelle echoed the Rapporteur's first option when he asserted that the paragraph should stand since any competent court could overcome potential difficulties by means of a reasonable interpretation (at para 20, p 137), an opinion seconded by Mr Amado (at para 21, p 137).

[82] ibid, para 22, p 137.

[83] ibid, para 23, p 137. Both Article 2(12)(ii) and Article 2(12) as a whole were adopted 9 : 0 with 4 abstentions.

[84] GA Res 897 (IX), 4 December 1954.

[85] [1954] 2 YB ILC 150.

[86] 'Article 2 The following acts are offences against the peace and security of mankind:
(1) Any act of aggression, including the employment by the authorities of a State of armed force against another State for any purpose other than national or collective self-defence or in pursuance of a decision or recommendation of a competent organ of the United Nations.
(2) Any threat by the authorities of a State to resort to an act of aggression against another State.

ii. Draft Code of Crimes Against the Peace and Security of Mankind (1996)

The General Assembly decided to postpone consideration of the 1954 Draft Code until the submission of a report by the Special Committee charged with preparing a draft definition of aggression.[87] In 1981, several years subsequent to the General Assembly's adoption by consensus of the 'Definition of Aggression' Resolution in 1974,[88] the International Law Commission was invited to begin work on a new Draft Code.[89]

In 1984 the new Special Rapporteur, Doudou Thiam, submitted his second report to the Commission.[90] He recalled that as part of Pella's efforts to broaden the scope of the first drafts of the Code to cover all international offences, it had been proposed that 'the dissemination of false or distorted news or forged documents in the knowledge that they are harmful to international relations' should be considered an offence against the peace and security of mankind.[91] The Special Rapporteur acknowledged that whilst the dissemination of false news was undoubtedly an international offence which 'can certainly disturb international public order',[92] the question as to whether it should be included in the Draft Code must be left to the Commission. He also stated, perhaps over-confidently, that given 'the current state of international awareness and the opportunities for immediate corrective reaction and denial', it was doubtful that the dissemination of false news as defined by Pella could be a source of armed conflict.[93] Drawing on the records of the Sixth Committee and on General Assembly Resolutions,

(3) The preparation by the authorities of a State of the employment of armed force against another State for any purpose other than national or collective self-defence or in pursuance of a decision or recommendation of a competent organ of the United Nations.
    [...]
(5) The undertaking or encouragement by the authorities of a State of activities calculated to foment civil strife in another State, or the toleration by the authorities of a State of organized activities calculated to foment civil strife in another State.
(6) The undertaking or encouragement by the authorities of a State of terrorist activities in another State, or the toleration by the authorities of a State of organized activities calculated to carry out terrorist acts in another State [...].'

[87] GA Res 897 (IX), 4 December 1954.
[88] GA Res 3314 (XXIX), 14 December 1974. See further Nicolaos Strapatsas, 'Rethinking General Assembly Resolution 3314 (1974) as a Basis for the Definition of Aggression under the Rome Statute of the ICC', in Olaoluwa Olusanya (ed), *Rethinking International Criminal Law: The Substantive Part* (Groningen: Europa Law, 2007) 155–90.
[89] GA Res 36/106, 10 December 1981.
[90] Second report on the Draft Code of Offences against the Peace and Security of Mankind by Mr Doudou Thiam, Special Rapporteur, UN Doc A/CN.4/377; [1984] 2 YB ILC, 99.
[91] [1984] 2 YB ILC, 295–6; UN Doc A/CN.4/39, paras 40–1. Citing Pella at [1950] 2 YB ILC, 343–6, 354–5.
[92] Second report on the Draft Code of Offences against the Peace and Security of Mankind by Mr Doudou Thiam, Special Rapporteur, UN Doc A/CN.4/377, para 74; [1984] 2 YB ILC (Part 1), 99.
[93] ibid.

he asserted that this offence should not be included in the Draft Code[94] since it did not reach the level of other offences which constituted 'attacks [on] the very foundations of contemporary civilization and the values on which it is based'.[95] He argued that such an offence should not be covered by the codification but that it would be more appropriately dealt with in domestic penal codes.[96]

Although the Special Rapporteur stated that the 1954 Draft Code remained the basis of the Commission's consideration of the topic,[97] his report omitted any reference to direct incitement to aggression and did not refer to Article 2(13) at all.[98] Responding to an assertion by Lebanon that such acts were 'as much criminal acts as the offences themselves',[99] the Special Rapporteur stated that 'the general part would of course deal with some aspects of the questions of conspiracy, direct incitement, complicity or attempts to commit criminal offences'.[100] Another delegate went even further in asserting that Article 12(13) was not 'an exhaustive list of the general principles of general criminal law applicable in international law', and that it required further clarification.[101]

In the Commission's report on its work at this session it was noted with regard to Article 12(13) of the 1954 Draft Code that the offences contained therein would be examined in due course but that regard must first be had to the study of the particular offences to which they related.[102] The report included a Draft Code, the first section of which comprised offences covered by the 1954 Draft Code. The second section concerned offences which had arisen in the intervening period, and referred for guidance to relevant international instruments adopted during that time, including the International Covenant on Civil and Political Rights which prohibited any propaganda for war, and the Outer Space Treaty and the Declaration of Principles on Friendly Relations, each of which condemns propaganda for war. The Commission also affirmed that it had been decided to exclude from future consideration any offence of the dissemination of false information or distorted news, reasoning that it would weaken the overall draft since it did not reach a level of gravity commensurate with the purpose of the Code.[103]

The question of whether direct incitement to aggression would be included as a separate crime in the Draft Code was not to be revisited by the Special

---

[94] Second report on the Draft Code of Offences against the Peace and Security of Mankind by Mr Doudou Thiam, Special Rapporteur, UN Doc A/CN.4/377, para 74; [1984] 2 YB ILC (Part 1), paras 77–8, p 99.

[95] ibid, para 77, p 99.

[96] ibid, para 78, p 99.

[97] [1984] 1 YB ILC, para 1, p 4.

[98] Second report on the Draft Code of Offences Against the Peace and Security of Mankind by Mr Doudou Thiam, Special Rapporteur, UN Doc A/CN.4/377, para 79; [1984] 2 YB ILC (Part 1), 100.

[99] [1984] 1 YB ILC, para 24, p 8.

[100] ibid, para 37, p 10.

[101] ibid (Mr Razafindralambo), para 39, p 11.

[102] [1984] 2 YB ILC (Part Two), p 14, para 48.

[103] ibid 17, para 63.

Rapporteur. His third report omitted any reference to incitement or any modes of commission of crimes.[104] His fourth report addressed the offences of complicity, attempt, and conspiracy only, as set forth in draft Article 14, with the offence of incitement to any of the crimes set forth in the Draft Code having been subsumed into the offence of 'complicity'. This was evidenced by his statement that complicity should mean 'any act of participation prior to or subsequent to the offence, intended either to provoke or to facilitate it'.[105] Introducing the report to the Commission, he stated that '[w]ith regard to "other offences", the 1954 Draft code referred to such concepts as conspiracy, complicity and attempts, but did not analyse or define them'.[106] The omission of incitement, which had been a core element in the 1954 Draft Code, was not explained.

Responding to this omission, Boutros Ghali noted that the Draft Code should attend to 'press and radio campaigns that were waged before the outbreak of a conflict and [which] were a major element in subversive activities'.[107] Suggesting that such activity could be covered in draft articles on either aggression, the threat of aggression, or terrorism, he asserted that '[t]he crux of the matter was that it should be included in the draft code'.[108] The Special Rapporteur dismissed this proposal on the grounds that 'subversion [. . .] was not one offence in itself [and] a distinction had to be made between subversion and criminal acts'.[109] Given the weight attached to propaganda for war and incitement to aggression both in the judgment of the IMT and in the 1954 Draft Code, it is submitted that this was an inadequate response from the Special Rapporteur. While Ghali's proposal might have carried more weight had it specifically addressed 'incitement to aggression', the failure of the Special Rapporteur to address incitement at any level is regrettable.

The absence of any discussion on the criminal nature of incitement to international crimes was noted by the representatives of India[110] and Sudan[111] who submitted that since such was present in both the 1954 Draft Code and the Genocide Convention, direct incitement to commit any of the crimes set forth in the Draft Code should be included as separate offences.[112] The United Kingdom

---

[104] The exception being a statement that complicity as a method of commission of the crime of mercenarism deserved closer attention. [1985] 2 YB ILC (Part One), p 66, para 14. On the subject of fomenting civil strife in another state, the Special Rapporteur spoke candidly of the provocation by one state of civil war, riots, and other disturbances in another state as constituting an offence. [1985] 1 YB ILC, p 8, paras 20–1. In a similar vein the United Kingdom advocated the inclusion of an offence of incitement of terrorist acts against another state. [1985] 1 YB ILC, p 67, para 43.

[105] [1986] 2 YB ILC (Part One), 86.

[106] ibid 89, para 18.

[107] [1986] 1 YB ILC, 116, para 50. Boutros Ghali had initially raised the subject of the offence of subversion at the 37th session of the ILC. [1985] 1 YB ILC, 11, paras 41–4.

[108] [1986] 1 YB ILC, Para 50.

[109] ibid 116, para 53.

[110] ibid 126, para 82.

[111] ibid 132, para 56.

[112] ibid 126, para 84.

stated that in order that the scope of the Genocide Convention would not be limited by the draft, an offence of 'direct and public incitement to genocide' should be considered for inclusion.[113] Nevertheless, the Commission's report on this session omitted any reference to incitement to any of the crimes.[114]

In 1987 the General Assembly agreed with the Commission's recommendation to amend the title of the Draft Code to read 'Draft Code of Crimes against the Peace and Security of Mankind'.[115] In his sixth report, the Special Rapporteur stated that the acts set out as crimes against peace in the 1954 draft were set forth in Article 2, paragraphs 1–9, thereby omitting paragraphs 10–13, including 'direct incitement to commit any of the offences', which had been an integral part of that text.[116] He added that he was not in favour of a separate offence of preparation of aggression on the grounds that the content of the concept was not sufficiently precise.[117] The retention of this crime, which had been a core element of crimes against peace at Nuremberg, and which had been understood to include incitement to aggression, was nevertheless favoured by many members of the Commission. The Commission's report on its work at this session noted that many delegates believed 'a distinction could be drawn between preparation of aggression and defensive measures on the basis of existing military, technical, legal and political criteria'.[118] It was stated that aggression required sophisticated planning, 'which would be carried out by the entire State apparatus. It was a fairly long-term undertaking and, at every stage, it involved particular persons who occupied key posts in the State military or economic apparatus.'[119] It was noted that the necessary elements of the crime of preparation of aggression were criminal intent and the material element of preparation, and the report highlighted a widely held view that '[i]n general, preparation would not consist simply of military measures [. . .] which would be difficult to distinguish from a country's preparation of its defence', but that it would also consist of more specific military manoeuvres and planning as well as 'persistent refusal of peaceful settlement of disputes'.[120] Given the weight attached to the gravity of the role played by propaganda inciting to wars of aggression by the IMT, it is submitted that incitement to aggression would constitute a key factor in an offence of preparation of aggression premised on the above considerations.

Part 1 of the Special Rapporteur's eighth report once again omitted any reference to incitement when discussing the 'related offences' of conspiracy, complicity, and attempt, set forth in Article 12(13) of the 1954 Draft Code.[121]

[113] [1986] 1 YB ILC, 106, para 22.
[114] [1986] 2 YB ILC (Part Two), 47–9.
[115] GA Res 42/151, 7 December 1987.
[116] [1988] 2 YB ILC (Part One) 198, para 4.
[117] [1988] 1 YB ILC, 60, para 1.
[118] [1988] 2 YB ILC (Part Two) 58–9, paras 224–8.
[119] ibid.
[120] ibid.
[121] [1990] 2 YB ILC (Part One), 28.

It has been shown that in the debates on the 1954 Draft Code it was agreed that judges exercising a reasonable interpretation of the crimes would be best suited to decide which methods of commission were applicable to a given offence on a case-by-case basis. Nevertheless, the discussions on the modes of commission, and particularly with regard to attempt, were again to attract much controversy and debate. The draft provision concerning complicity as proposed by the Special Rapporteur read:

The following constitute crimes against the peace and security of mankind: 1. Being an accomplice to any of the crimes defined in this Code. [2. within the meaning of this Code, complicity may mean both accessory acts prior to or concomitant with the principal offence and subsequent acts.][122]

The commentary explains that complicity may be either physical (aiding, abetting, provision of means, etc), or intellectual/verbal (counsel, instigation, incitement, ordering, etc), on which grounds incitement to commit a crime which actually occurs may constitute the offence of complicity under the Draft Code.[123] There was much discussion as to the wisdom of including an offence of complicity in the Draft Code, particularly in relation to the crimes of aggression and apartheid,[124] and it was suggested that the Draft Code should be elaborated upon to explicitly set forth acts such as aiding and abetting, instigating, and directing.[125] Following these discussions, the Special Rapporteur submitted a revised draft Article 15 which stated that '[p]articipation in the commission of a crime against the peace and security of mankind constitutes the crime of complicity'. Article 15(2)(b) considered the following to be acts of complicity: 'inspiring the commission of a crime against the peace and security of mankind by, inter alia, incitement, urging, instigation, order, threat [. . .].'[126]

The Commission's report on its work at this session shows that there was general support for this draft. One delegate displayed satisfaction that the draft covered incitement, 'which was closely related to propaganda', emphasizing

---

[122] ibid 28, para 5.

[123] ibid 29, paras 7–9, 13.

[124] The Commission's report noted that some members thought that the application of a category of traditional criminal law such as complicity which had been unequivocally characterized as an international crime in the Nürnberg Principles, would be easier in the case of war crimes than crimes against peace, since the former are generally committed by individuals or groups on their own initiative, without the knowledge or participation of their superiors, while crimes such as aggression and apartheid involved governments, and often the people as a whole; thus it was feared that its application would unduly widen the circle of offenders, when 'what was needed was to strike at the leaders and organizers, since it was impossible to prosecute a whole people'. [1990] 2 YB ILC (Part Two), 13, para 47.

[125] ibid 13, para 49.

[126] ibid 12, fn 34; [1990] 1 YB ILC para 23, p 52. As regards the definition of the 'perpetrator' of a crime, the Special Rapporteur, drawing on criminal codes such as in France and Germany, said that the absence of a definition was of little concern since in his view it was for the competent courts to decide. He further stated that the link between the act and perpetrator was also for the judge to decide, with which the Commission concurred. [1990] 2 YB ILC (Part Two), 14, para 53.

that 'it would be wrong to underestimate the control which belligerent and racist propaganda could exert over the masses or to invoke freedom of expression, information or the press in tolerating such activities'.[127] There was broad agreement that complicity could consist either of physical acts or intellectual acts such as incitement. Incitement was also discussed with regard to the crime of conspiracy, with one delegate stating that preparatory acts, 'such as participation in a plan to incite or carry out a war of aggression, were punishable and called for an appropriate penalty'.[128] Nevertheless, the discussion centred on whether conspiracy, complicity, and attempt should be dealt with in the section of the Draft Code dealing with general principles, as separate offences as suggested by the Special Rapporteur, or by a case-by-case approach, with minimal analysis or consideration of incitement as a distinct method of commission.[129]

At its forty-third session in 1991, the Commission provisionally adopted on first reading draft articles of the Draft Code of Crimes Against the Peace and Security of Mankind.[130] Article 3(2) on responsibility and punishment explicitly included incitement as a means of commission, providing that '[a]n individual who aids, abets or provides the means for the commission of a crime against the peace and security of mankind or conspires in or directly incites the commission of such a crime is responsible therefore and is liable to punishment'.[131] The draft articles were transmitted to governments for their comments and observations but responses tended to be limited to comments on the draft provision on attempt to commit a crime, rather than incitement.[132]

The Special Rapporteur's twelfth report was intended to provide the basis for the second reading of the Draft Code. The text of Article 3(2) as found in the 1991 Draft Code was retained, and in keeping with the trend during negotiations, the Special Rapporteur's explanatory remarks were limited to attempt as a means of commission of a crime.[133] The Commission's report on this session noted that some members found its wording too vague and 'likely enormously to expand

---

[127] Report of the ILC on the work of its 42nd session (1990) A/CN.4/L.456 p 25, para 77.

[128] ibid 29, para 90.

[129] ibid 23–33, paras 69–103.

[130] [1991] 2 YB ILC (Part Two), para 173.

[131] Text of the Draft Code of Crimes Against the Peace and Security of Mankind, Adopted on First Reading by the Commission at its Forty-Third Session, A/CN.4/448, 4–15.

[132] Comments and Observations of Governments on the Draft Code of Crimes Against the Peace and Security of Mankind Adopted on First Reading by the International Law Commission at its Forty-Third Session A/CN.4/448 (1 March 1993), 16. At its forty-fourth and forty-fifth sessions in 1992 and 1993 the Commission devoted its attention to the question of the possible establishment of an international criminal jurisdiction, culminating with the adoption of a draft statute of an international criminal court at its forty-sixth session in 1994. Report of the International Law Commission on the work of its 46th session, 2 May–22 July 1994, GAOR Supp no 10 (A/49/10), p 43, para 91.

[133] Twelfth Report on the Draft Code of Crimes Against the Peace and Security of Mankind, A/CN.4/460 (1994), 8–9.

the category of persons who could be punished under the Code'.[134] Whilst this may have been true of the first part of the paragraph concerning aiding and abetting, such concerns were unlikely to have been as relevant with regard to 'directly inciting the commission of such a crime', yet the issue of attempt remained the overriding subject of discussion.

The subject of incitement did arise with regard to the crime of 'threat of aggression', which had been included in each of the drafts up to and including the 1991 Draft Code. Article 16 of the 1991 draft defined 'threat of aggression' as constituting 'declarations, communications, and demonstrations of force or any other measures which would give good reason to the Government of a State to believe that aggression is being seriously contemplated against that State'. Given that a distinct crime of incitement to aggression had not been considered in this phase of drafting, this provision was perhaps the closest the Commission came to dealing with the subject. Several delegates considered the provision to be superfluous on the grounds that it concerned a mode of commission of aggression which was already covered by Article 15 and furthermore criticized it for providing too wide a scope for subjective appraisal and political manipulation by others.[135] Others supported the inclusion of the provision on the grounds that 'incitement, including propaganda, should be mentioned in the text as it often preceded the commission of the crime concerned', an observation also made in relation to Articles 19, 20, and 23.[136]

Several commentators have suggested that propaganda for war should be included within the definition of aggression on the grounds that such incitement constitutes 'ideological' or 'indirect' aggression. Whilst critical of broad definitions covering 'fleabites as well as plagues',[137] Murty, having reference to the efforts made by the USSR to have ideological aggression recognized as a crime,[138] considered that any propaganda activity which 'is capable of creating a reasonable expectation on the part of the government of the attacked state that deprivation of the state's territorial integrity or political independence is fairly imminent, unless the coercive process is stopped or substantially reduced in its intensity [constitutes] ideological aggression'.[139]

---

[134] Report of the International Law Commission on the work of its 46th session, 2 May–22 July 1994, GAOR Supp no 10 (A/49/10), p 169, para 127.

[135] Report of the ILC on the work of its 43rd session (1991) A/CN.4/L.469, p 47, para 167.

[136] ibid 47, para 166.

[137] BS Murty, *Propaganda and World Public Order*, 163.

[138] For example the USSR submitted the following definition of aggression to the twelfth session of the General Assembly in 1957: 'That State shall be declared to have committed an act of ideological aggression which: (a) Encourages war propaganda; (b) Encourages propaganda in favour of using atomic, bacterial, chemical and other kinds of mass extermination weapons; (c) Stimulates propaganda of fascist-nazi views, racial or national superiority, hatred and disdain for other peoples.' A/AC.77/L.4. See generally Yuri Bobrakov, 'War Propaganda: A Serious Crime against Humanity', 473.

[139] BS Murty *Propaganda and World Public Order*, 166. John Novogrod argued that 'hostile propaganda', particularly the external fomentation of support for rebel groups and civil strife in

Advocacy of such views was absent from the Commission debates and at its forty-seventh session in 1995 many members of the Commission endorsed the Special Rapporteur's proposal to delete the crime of the threat of aggression because of 'the nebulous character of the underlying concept and the lack of rigour required by criminal law'.[140] In summing up the debate the Special Rapporteur suggested abandoning the notion in view of the difficulty of producing a suitable definition that would be acceptable to governments, adding that no strong arguments had been advanced in its favour.[141]

The Special Rapporteur also proposed a new text of Article 19 on the crime of genocide, paragraph 3 of which stated that '[a]n individual convicted of having engaged in direct and public incitement to genocide shall be sentenced to ...'.[142] Delegates questioned whether the term 'direct and public incitement' was intended to refer to an independent crime of incitement, which would not require the actual commission of genocide, or to 'abetment' as an accessory to a principal crime.[143] While emphasis was placed on the exceptional nature of the independent crime of 'incitement' as a consequence of the need to avoid encroaching on freedom of expression, other members drew attention to the role of incitement in the Rwandan Genocide as evidence of the need to include both 'attempt' and 'incitement' to commit genocide as punishable offences.[144]

At its forty-eight session in 1996 the Commission adopted the Draft Code of Crimes Against the Peace and Security of Mankind and commentaries thereto.[145] In the interest of obtaining support for the Draft Code from governments its scope was considerably reduced from the text adopted at the first reading in 1991.[146] Given the difficulties experienced during the drafting with regard to the forms of commission which could apply to the crimes set forth in the Draft Code, the final approach taken was to distinguish the means of commission between the crime of aggression and other crimes.

Article 2 set forth the principle of individual responsibility for crimes, ensuring that individuals who commit such crimes incur responsibility and are liable

---

target states, could constitute an act of aggression. He considered a definition of aggression limited to the direct use of physical force to be 'dangerously restrictive', and drew on Article 1 of the Broadcasting Convention 1936, as well as the writings of publicists such as Lauterpacht, von Glahn, Martin, and Murty, to assert that impermissible coercion need not involve the direct use of physical force, since the use of hostile propaganda 'for the purpose of undermining the political independence of the target state [...] is a delict of international law'. John C Novogrod, 'Civil Strife and Indirect Aggression', in M Cherif Bassiouni and Ved P Nanda (eds), *International Criminal Law*, 198–238, 218.

[140] Report of the International Law Commission on the work of its 47th session, 2 May–21 July 1995, GAOR Supp no 10 (A/50/10), 40, para 74.

[141] ibid 65–6, para 134.

[142] ibid, Article 19(3), p 44, para 80, fn 37.

[143] ibid 44, para 80.

[144] ibid.

[145] A/48/10, [1996] 2 YB ILC (Part Two).

[146] Report of the International Law Commission on the work of its 48th session, 6 May–26 July 1996, GAOR Supp no 10 (A/51/10), p 13, para 46.

to punishment,[147] paragraph 1 stating the general principle that '[a] crime against the peace and security of mankind entails individual responsibility'. Article 2(3) addressed the various ways in which an individual can incur responsibility for participating in, or otherwise contributing significantly to, the crimes of genocide, crimes against humanity, crimes against United Nations and associated personnel, and war crimes which are set forth in Articles 17 to 20. Whilst the Commission's commentary describes 'incitement' as a form of complicity,[148] the 1996 Draft Code went beyond the earlier drafts and accorded incitement a specific subparagraph distinct from the other methods of commission, although it was not to be viewed as an inchoate offence.

Concerning Article 2(3)(d) which provided for criminal responsibility for an individual who 'knowingly aids, abets or otherwise assists, directly and substantially, in the commission of such a crime, including providing the means for its commission', William Schabas has noted that whereas the offence of 'abetting' means the same as incitement, 'when the underlying crime occurs', the Commission had described it as 'providing assistance' although 'it also connotes encouragement or incitement to commit a crime [and] is derived from old French, *à beter*, meaning to bait or to excite'.[149] Similar language is to be found in resolutions of several non-governmental organizations, which, in the inter-war years had advocated the adoption of penal sanctions targeting 'une propagande dans le but d'exciter publiquement à la guerre d'agression'.[150]

Article 2(3)(f) provided that an individual shall be responsible for any one of these crimes if that individual 'directly and publicly incites another individual to commit such a crime which in fact occurs'. The commentary to subparagraph (f)

---

[147] 'Article 2 Individual responsibility
1. A crime against the peace and security of mankind entails individual responsibility.
2. An individual shall be responsible for the crime of aggression in accordance with article 16.
3. An individual shall be responsible for a crime set out in article 17, 18, 19 or 20 if that individual:
   (a) intentionally commits such a crime;
   (b) orders the commission of such a crime which in fact occurs or is attempted;
   (c) fails to prevent or repress the commission of such a crime in the circumstances set out in article 6;
   (d) knowingly aids, abets or otherwise assists, directly and substantially, in the commission of such a crime, including providing the means for its commission;
   (e) directly participates in planning or conspiring to commit such a crime which in fact occurs;
   (f) directly and publicly incites another individual to commit such a crime which in fact occurs;
   (g) attempts to commit such a crime by taking action commencing the execution of a crime which does not in fact occur because of circumstances independent of his intentions.

[148] Report of the International Law Commission on the work of its 48th session, 6 May–26 July 1996, GAOR Supp no 10 (A/51/10), p 21, para 6.
[149] William A Schabas, 'Hate Speech in Rwanda: The Road to Genocide', 46 McGill LJ 141 (2000) 156.
[150] *Union internationale des avocats, doc. No. 8 du Congrès tenu à Luxembourg du 14 au 17 mai* 1931, 13 & 50. A/CN.4/39; [1950] 2 YB ILC, p 342, para 125. 'Propaganda with the goal of publicly inciting to a war of aggression' (author's translation).

notes that '[s]uch an individual urges and encourages another individual to commit a crime and thereby contributes substantially to the commission of that crime'.[151] According to the commentary, the 'direct' element of incitement requires 'specifically urging another individual to take immediate criminal action rather than merely making a vague or indirect suggestion'. The 'public' element requires 'communicating the call for criminal action to a number of individuals in a public place or to members of the general public at large [...] such as by radio or television'.[152] Highlighting the role of modern mass communications technology which enabled individuals in Rwanda to reach a large number of people and to repeat the message of incitement to genocide,[153] the commentary states that the principle of individual criminal responsibility for incitement was recognized in Article 6 of the Nuremberg Charter, Article III(c) of the Genocide Convention, Article 7(1) of the Statute of the ICTY, Article 6(i) of the Statute of the ICTR, and by the Commission itself in Article 2(13)(ii) of the 1954 Draft Code.[154] Nevertheless, the application of the means of incurring individual responsibility set out in Article 2, including commission, incitement, attempt, and complicity, is limited by the requirement either that the crime did in fact occur or, in the case of attempt, that the crime was not completed because of circumstances independent of the intentions of the person attempting the crime.[155]

Article 2(2) deals with individual responsibility for the crime of aggression separately from responsibility from the other crimes, providing that '[a]n individual shall be responsible for the crime of aggression in accordance with article 16'. The Commission's commentary provides little guidance on the question of whether an individual can incur individual responsibility for acts constituting incitement to aggression, explaining that 'it was not necessary to indicate [the] different forms of participation which entail the responsibility of the individual, because the definition of the crime of aggression in Article 16 already provides all the elements necessary to establish the responsibility'.[156] Article 16 provides that '[a]n individual who, as leader or organizer, actively participates in or orders the planning, preparation, initiation or waging of aggression committed by a State shall be responsible for a crime of aggression'. The Commentary notes that under the Draft Code aggression can only be committed by individuals who are agents of the state and who use their power to give orders and the means this power

---

[151] Report of the International Law Commission on the work of its 48th session, 6 May–26 July 1996, GAOR Supp no. 10 (A/51/10), p 26, para 16.

[152] Private incitement was stated to be covered by the principle of participation in conspiracy to commit a crime as set forth in subparagraph (e). ibid 26–7, para 16.

[153] ibid 27, para 16, fn 34.

[154] ibid 27, para 16.

[155] Article 2(3), Draft Code of Crimes Against the Peace and Security of Mankind, 1996 (A/48/10), [1996] 2 YB ILC (Part 2).

[156] Report of the International Law Commission on the work of its 48th session, 6 May–26 July 1996, GAOR Supp no 10 (A/51/10), pp 20–1, para 5.

makes available in order to commit this crime.[157] It further asserts that all the situations listed in Article 2(3) which would have application in relation to the crime of aggression are already found in the definition of that crime contained in Article 16, '[h]ence the reason to have a separate paragraph for the crime of aggression in article 2'.[158]

iii. Summary

The failure of the Commission to consider in any depth the crime of incitement to aggression when drafting the 1996 Draft Code appears to have been not only a grave oversight, but also a deliberate one. The progress made in developing the jurisprudence of the Second World War trials to include a distinct offence of direct incitement to aggression in the 1954 Draft Code was completely reversed by the drafters of the 1996 Draft Code. Although the final text of the Code included a specific provision for the non-inchoate offence of incitement to each of the crimes except for aggression, there had been minimal discussion of this offence during drafting. It has been suggested that since there had been little advance made since the establishment of the Commission in defining the crime of aggression, its removal from the common regime of responsibility under Article 2(3) of the 1996 Draft Code was 'probably the only logically supportable [formulation]'.[159] Although the definition of aggression had prolonged the work of the Commission by many decades, this should not have precluded any consideration being given to a distinct and inchoate crime of incitement to aggression.

Allain and Jones considered the 1996 Draft Code to have rejected all the past work of the Commission[160] and suggested that it would be 'better for the administration of international criminal law if the Code is simply not adopted at all'.[161] They are particularly critical of the restriction of incitement to genocide to a non-inchoate crime since the events of Rwanda had demonstrated that 'incitement may very well be the most odious of crimes, even if the offence incited does not take place at all or on the scale indicted'.[162]

Nonetheless, the history of the drafting of the Code contains a salient warning as to the danger of failing to comprehensively examine the formulation of crimes of incitement in international criminal law. Whilst the manner in which the Commission approached the issue of incitement to aggression is illustrative of the marginal position accorded to this immensely important provision over recent

---

[157] ibid.

[158] ibid.

[159] Rosemary Rayfuse, 'The Draft Code of Crimes Against the Peace and Security of Mankind: Eating Disorders at the International Law Commission', 8 Crim LF 43 (1997) 58–9.

[160] Jean Allain and John RWD Jones, 'A Patchwork of Norms: A Commentary on the 1996 Draft Code of Crimes against the Peace and Security of Mankind', 8 EJIL 100 (1997) 117.

[161] ibid 101.

[162] ibid 110.

decades, the development of international criminal law has seen the significance of the Commission's Draft Code being overtaken by the jurisprudence of the ad hoc International Criminal Tribunals and the adoption of the Rome Statute which led to the establishment of an International Criminal Court.

B. The ad hoc International Criminal Tribunals

Contrary to the simplistic myths of primordial 'tribal' hatred, the conflicts in the former Yugoslavia and Rwanda were not expressions of spontaneous blood lust or inevitable historical cataclysms. Both conflicts resulted from the deliberate incitement of ethnic hatred and violence by which ruthless demagogues and warlords elevated themselves to positions of absolute power. At a volatile transition stage, the calculated manipulation of fears and tensions unleashed a self-perpetuating spiral of violence in which thousands of citizens became the unwitting instruments of unscrupulous political elites questing after supremacy.[163]

Martin stated one exception to his belief that international propaganda had little chance of being controlled or adjudicated at the international level: '[s]hould we ever be involved in another international war, it is almost certain that propaganda cases will come before a war crimes tribunal for adjudication.'[164] In contrast to the attention accorded to incitement to international crimes by the International Law Commission, the fundamental role that propaganda played in inciting to violence and genocide in Rwanda and the Balkans has been repeatedly emphasized in the jurisprudence of the ad hoc International Criminal Tribunals for the Former Yugoslavia and Rwanda. While neither has jurisdiction over the crime of aggression and therefore has not had occasion to deliberate upon a crime of incitement to aggression, the jurisprudence with regard to the criminalization of certain forms of speech and of incitement to international crimes provides a welcome indicator as to how the International Criminal Court may proceed in a case concerning direct and public incitement to aggression should such a crime be included in the Rome Statute.

i. The International Criminal Tribunal for the Former Yugoslavia

The International Criminal Tribunal for the Former Yugoslavia[165] (ICTY) was established by the UN Security Council in 1993.[166] The ICTY's judgment in the *Tadic* case was the first determination of individual guilt or innocence in

---

[163] Payam Akhavan, 'Beyond Impunity: Can International Criminal Justice Prevent Future Atrocities?', 95 AJIL 7 (2001) 7.

[164] L John Martin, *International Propaganda*, 4.

[165] Statute of the International Criminal Tribunal for the Prosecution of Persons Responsible for Serious Violations of International Humanitarian Law Committed in the Territory of the Former Yugoslavia since 1991, UN Doc S/25704, Annexe (1993).

[166] UN Doc S/RES/808 (1993), 22 February 1993; UN Doc S/RES/827 (1993), 25 May 1993.

connection with serious violations of international humanitarian law by a truly international tribunal, given that its predecessors at Nuremberg and Tokyo were multinational in nature and represented only part of the world community.[167] As with the Rwandan conflict and genocide, conflict in the Former Yugoslavia was characterized by ethnic stereotyping and the use of mass media to incite to ethnic violence:

The mobilization of political will through ethnic hysteria, and the elimination of rival leaders or ideologies, required the destruction of any belief that multiethnic coexistence was a viable alternative to ethnic partition. The indoctrination of the Serb public was accomplished in part through state-controlled media, the dismantling of multiethnic governmental structures, and their replacement with 'crisis committees'.[168]

Mark Thompson notes that prior to the conflicts in the Former Yugoslavia, '[r]egime-controlled media helped create the conditions for war by attacking civic principles, fomenting fear of imminent ethnic assault, and engineering consent'.[169] Although the ICTY has not had occasion to analyse the role of propaganda and incitement in as comprehensive a manner as the Rwanda Tribunal, the impact of propaganda on the commission of war crimes and crimes against humanity has been the subject of several judgments. In the *Tadic* case[170] the ICTY reflected on the role which propaganda had played in fomenting ethnic discord in the Former Yugoslavia. One aspect of this propaganda campaign was the recollection of the atrocities of the Croat *Ustasa* during the Second World War.[171] The Tribunal found that once the Former Yugoslavia began to disintegrate, Serb-dominated media played on fears of subjugation of Serbs in areas in which Serbs were minority communities, adopting the theme that Serbs had 'no choice but a full-scale war against everyone else'.[172] Serbian political leaders were found to have engendered fear to create support for their nationalist policies through speeches and public rallies. An example cited by the Tribunal is that of Radoslav Brdanin, President of the Crisis Staff of the Serb Autonomous Region of the Banja Luka area, who declared at a public rally in 1992 that 2 per cent was the upper tolerable limit on the presence of all non-Serbs in that region.[173] Serbian control over the media was ensured through the takeover by Serbian armed forces of television transmitters resulting in the broadcast of Serb-only programming in many areas.[174] Serb forces also used 'mirror politics' to create the impression that each and every member of other ethnic

[167] *Prosecutor v Dusko Tadic a/k/a/ 'Dule'* IT-94-1-T, 7 May 1997, para 1.

[168] Payam Akhavan, 'Beyond Impunity: Can International Criminal Justice Prevent Future Atrocities?', 10.

[169] Mark Thompson and Dan De Luce, 'Escalating to Success? The Media Intervention in Bosnia and Herzegovina', in Monroe E Price and Mark Thompson (eds), *Forging Peace*, 201.

[170] *Prosecutor v Dusko Tadic a/k/a/ 'Dule'*, Opinion and Judgment, 7 May 1997, Case no IT-94-1.

[171] ibid, para 87.

[172] ibid, para 88.

[173] ibid, para 89.

[174] ibid, para 92.

groups was aligned with opposition military groups. The *Tadic* judgment details
examples of print articles, television programmes, and public proclamations in
which Serbs were told that they needed to protect themselves 'from a fundamen-
talist Muslim threat' and were encouraged to arm themselves since 'the Croats
and Muslims were preparing a plan of genocide against them'.[175] Similarly, in the
Sentencing Judgment of Milan Babic, the ICTY noted 'there was a media campaign directed by Belgrade that portrayed the Serbs in Croatia as being threatened
with genocide by the Croat majority'.[176] As noted by the Trial Chamber in *Tadic*,
such tensions as existed in the Former Yugoslavia were exacerbated by the use of
propaganda and political manoeuvres, 'the twin tools advocated by Slobodan
Milosevic to shift the balance of power in the former Yugoslavia to Serbia'.[177] The
role of propaganda in the Balkan conflicts has also arisen in relation to the bomb-
ing of the Serbian TV station *RTS* by NATO forces in 1999, an incident which led
to attempts to expand the extraterritorial jurisdiction of the European Convention
on Human Rights in the *Bankovic* case, and which was premised on the belief that
RTS propaganda was contributing to the perpetration of war crimes.[178]

The indictment in *Kordic and Cerkez* charged Dario Kordic with having
committed the crime of persecution as a crime against humanity as set forth in
Article 5 of the ICTY Statute through the use of hate propaganda.[179] It alleged that
by 'encouraging, instigating and promoting hatred, distrust and strife on political,
racial, ethnic or religious grounds, by propaganda, speeches and otherwise' as part
of a campaign of widespread or systematic persecutions, he should be held individually criminally responsible under Article 5.[180] The Chamber noted that this was the
first instance of such a charge before the ICTY, and that it was not enumerated as a
crime in the ICTY Statute. It then proceeded to review the international case-law
in order to determine whether the criminal prohibition of hate speech falling short
of incitement to violence had attained the status of customary international law.[181]

[175] *Prosecutor v Dusko Tadic a/k/a/ 'Dule'*, Opinion and Judgment, 7 May 1997, Case no IT-94-1, para 91.
[176] *Prosecutor v Milan Babic*, Sentencing Judgment, Case no IT-03-72-S, para 24(g).
[177] *Prosecutor v Dusko Tadic a/k/a/ 'Dule'*, Opinion and Judgment, 7 May 1997, Case no IT-94-1, para 130.
[178] *Bankovic and Others v The Contracting States also Parties to the North Atlantic Treaty* (Admissibility), App no 52207/99, 11 BHRC 435 (12 December 2001). See further Michael Kearney, 'The Extraterritorial Jurisdiction of the European Convention on Human Rights', 5 TCL Rev 158 (2002); Andreas Laursen, 'NATO, the War over Kosovo, and the ICTY Investigation', 17 Am U Int'l L Rev 765 (2002); Helen Darbishire, 'Non-Governmental Perspectives: Media Freedom versus Information Intervention?', in Monroe E Price and Mark Thompson (eds), *Forging Peace*, 329–64.
[179] 'Article 5: Crimes against humanity: The International Tribunal shall have the power to prosecute persons responsible for the following crimes when committed in armed conflict, whether international or internal in character, and directed against any civilian population: (a) murder: (b) extermination: (c) enslavement: (d) deportation: (e) imprisonment: (f) torture: (g) rape: (h) perse-cutions on political, racial and religious grounds: (i) other inhumane acts.'
[180] *Prosecutor v Dario Kordic & Mario Cerkez*, Amended Indictment, 30 September 1998, paras 37(c) and 39(c).
[181] *Prosecutor v Dario Kordic & Mario Cerkez* [2001] ICTY 3 (26 February 2001), para 209.

This review, set forth in a footnote to the judgment, commenced by noting that in *Streicher* the IMT had convicted the accused of persecution because he 'incited the German people to active persecution' which amounted to 'incitement to murder and extermination'. It also noted that in the *Akayesu* case the International Criminal Tribunal for Rwanda had found the accused guilty of direct and public incitement to commit genocide. In stating that the only speech act explicitly criminalized under the statutes of the IMT, Control Council Law No 10, the ICTY, ICTR, and the ICC, is direct and public incitement to commit genocide, the Trial Chamber erred in fact since incitement was not mentioned in either the Charter of the IMT or in Control Council Law No 10.

The Trial Chamber continued to note the 'sharp split' in treaty law in this area as indicative that such speech may not be regarded as a crime under customary international law. It was stated that while initial drafts of Article 20 of the ICCPR made incitement to racial hatred a crime, only the obligation to provide for a prohibition by law prevailed, as was the case with Article 4 of the International Convention on the Elimination of Racial Discrimination.[182] The Trial Chamber also highlighted the fact that 'significant number of States have attached reservations or declarations of interpretations to these provisions' but does not appear to have distinguished between reservations and declarations submitted with regard to paragraph 1 or paragraph 2 of Article 20.

Finally the Chamber noted the broad spectrum of legal approaches to the prohibition of 'encouraging, instigating and promoting hatred, distrust and strife on political, racial, ethnic or religious grounds, by propaganda, speeches or otherwise' as indicating that there is no international consensus on the criminalization of this act that rises to the level of customary international law. In holding that the speech in question was not a criminal act in customary international law and that to convict the accused for such an act would violate the principle of legality,[183] the Trial Chamber may have come to the correct conclusion, but its analysis of national legislation is bereft of context and unduly biased towards the protection of hate speech provided for in the US Constitution.

Although it considered several other jurisdictions with more stringent criminal prohibitions of such hate speech,[184] the cumulative weight of such jurisprudence

---

[182] Nowak was cited in support of the idea that this formulation does not require a prohibition by criminal law. Manfred Nowak, *U.N. Covenant on Civil and Political Rights: CCPR Commentary* (Kehl: NP Engel, 1993) 361.

[183] *Prosecutor v Dario Kordic & Mario Cerkez* [2001] ICTY 3 (26 February 2001), para 209.

[184] ibid, fn 272. The Chamber noted that: 'Germany and the United States mark the opposite ends of this spectrum, although various other countries, including the former Yugoslavia, have provided for some form of regulation of hate speech. See, e.g, South Africa Constitution 1996, Art. 16(c) (excluding "advocacy of hatred that is based on race, ethnicity, gender and religion, and that constitutes incitement to cause harm"), Canadian Criminal Code, section 319(2) (prohibiting the communication of statements that wilfully promote hatred against any identifiable group distinguished by colour, race, religion or ethnic origin), and French Criminal Code, article 32 ("Those, who by publication by any of various means, provoke discrimination, hatred, or violence with regard to a person or a group of persons by reason of their origin or their membership or

was found to be inferior to that of the USA. Thus it was held that since this act was not enumerated as a crime in the Statute, nor was it of the same level of gravity as the other acts set forth in Article 5, it would not be considered by the ICTY.[185] It is unlikely, however, that international criminal tribunals will not have to reconsider this finding as the international law on the criminalization of hate speech, speech which is necessarily antecedent to direct incitement to violence, continues to develop.[186] With regards the understanding of propaganda for war in the judgment of the IMT and the other Second World War Tribunals, as constituting both propaganda intended to create a warlike spirit generally in addition to propaganda which directly incites to wars of aggression—a formulation which found expression also in Article 20(1) of the Covenant—similar cases may in future be considered with regard to a crime of direct and public incitement to aggression.

Nevertheless, Kordic was found responsible for the commission of the crime of persecution by means of instigation which was premised on the prosecution's argument that he had incited such crimes.[187] The ICTY will have to revisit a similar issue as regards the former Serbian Prime Minister Vojislav Seselj, whose case is currently before the Tribunal.[188] Seselj had previously come to the attention of the ICTY in the *Tadic* case where the Trial Chamber stated that he had publicly supported militant Serb nationalism on television and radio, by stating that, 'for the Serbs, the Second World War had not ended'.[189]

---

nonmembership in an ethnic group, nation, race, or particular religion, shall be punished by a term of imprisonment of one year and by a fine"). Article 133 of the Yugoslav Federal Criminal Code prohibited the publication of information that could "disrupt the brotherhood, unity and equality of nationalities." The German Criminal Code provides for the punishment of those who incite hatred, or invite violence or arbitrary acts against parts of the population, or insult, maliciously degrade, or defame part of the population, in a manner likely to disturb the public peace (StGB, § 130). The United States, in contrast, is exceptional in the extent of its free speech guarantees. Hate speech finds protection in the United States constitutional regime provided it does not rise to the level of "incitement", a very high threshold in American jurisprudence. See United States Constitution, 1st amendment.'

[185] *Prosecutor v Dario Kordic & Mario Cerkez* [2001] ICTY 3 (26 February 2001), para 209.

[186] For a compelling argument that virulent hate propaganda should be accorded the status of an international crime since incitement, in the sense of instigation, is insufficient with regard to the crime of genocide, see Wibke Kristin Timmermann, 'The Relationship between Hate Propaganda and Incitement to Genocide: A New Trend in International Law towards Criminalization of Hate Propaganda?', Leiden J Int'l L 18 (2005) 257.

[187] The prosecutor submitted that instigation is essentially defined 'by the fact that the accused prompted another person or persons to commit a crime, and may take a variety of forms including incitement (forms of promises of financial or other advantage)'. In his role as political leader he was found to be individually criminally responsible under Article 7(1) for planning, instigating and ordering the crimes and was thus held liable on these charges. *Prosecutor v Dario Kordic & Mario Cerkez*, [2001] ICTY 3 (26 February 2001), paras 380 and 834.

[188] *Prosecutor v Vojislav Seselj*, Modified Amended Indictment, Case no IT-03-67, 15 July 2005.

[189] *Prosecutor v Dusko Tadic a/k/a/ 'Dule'*, Opinion and Judgment, 7 May 1997, Case no IT-94-1, para 91. Human Rights Watch had also condemned Seselj for 'incitement to violence' on account of his threats to human rights and independent media groups in the Federal Republic of Yugoslavia which were reporting on the crisis in Kosovo in 1998. 'Serbian Deputy Prime Minister

The prosecutor of the ICTY alleges that Seselj had participated in a joint criminal enterprise to commit crimes within the Statute by espousing and encouraging the creation of a homogeneous 'Greater Serbia' by violence and that he
'thereby participated in war propaganda and incitement of hatred towards non-
Serb people'.[190] The facts in *Seselj*—as set forth in the indictment—primarily
relate to the accused's own speech in public places rather than his influence
over mass media, and have clearly linked the 'war propaganda' and incitement
to hatred to specific acts of violence. Counts 2–4 of the indictment allege that
Seselj aided and abetted in the planning, preparation, or execution of the extermination and murder of Croat, Muslim, and other non-Serb civilians. Specific
allegations include that in November 1991 Seselj visited Vocin and addressed
volunteers under his control who, incited by his speeches, engaged in the burn-
ing of houses of Croat citizens and killing of Croat civilians.[191] The indictment further alleges that also in November 1991, while Serb forces fought to
take over Vukovar, Seselj visited the town and publicly announced that '[n]ot
one Ustasha must leave Vukovar alive', thus instigating the killing of Croats.[192]
The significance of the defendant's alleged acts of incitement is further raised in
relation to Counts 5–9 regarding imprisonment, torture, and other inhumane
acts where the indictment alleges that volunteer units recruited and/or incited
by Seselj captured and detained hundreds of Croat, Muslim, and other non-Serb
civilians[193] in detention facilities which were characterized by inhumane treatment.[194] While this case remains under way at The Hague, the prosecutor's continued emphasis on the role of incitement and propaganda in the commission of
war crimes is welcome.

It is crucial at this point to highlight the distinction between the textually
similar terms 'war propaganda' and 'propaganda for war'. Although variations
of these terms have been employed in a loose and confusing manner by all parties including the Human Rights Committee, clarification of their meaning and
consistency in their application is critical for the purposes of international criminal law. The former, as used in the *Seselj* indictment, relates to propaganda inciting war crimes or crimes against humanity during a conflict, whereas the latter
concerns propaganda inciting to wars of aggression.

The influence of 'war propaganda' in encouraging the commission of criminal
acts by several of those found guilty of war crimes or crimes against humanity

Seselj Threatens Journalists and Human Rights Organizations', Human Rights Watch (New York,
2 October 1998).

[190] *Prosecutor v Vojislav Seselj*, Modified Amended Indictment, Case no IT-03-67, 15 July 2005,
para 10(c). See also *Prosecutor v Vojislav Seselj*, Indictment, Case no IT-03-67, 14 February 2003,
para 10(c).

[191] ibid, para 19.

[192] ibid, para 22.

[193] ibid, para 25.

[194] ibid, para 26. Allegations of further incitement to crimes of deportation and forced transfer
are also included in the indictment. Para 28.

has been considered by the ICTY. The Trial Chamber in *Tadic* found that the defendant had 'responded' to such propaganda, noting that 'the virulent propaganda that stoked the passions of the citizenry in Opstina Prijedor was endemic and contributed to the crimes committed in the conflict and, as such, has been taken into account in the sentences imposed on Dusko Tadic'.[195]

In the Sentencing Judgment of Milo Babic, the Trial Chamber noted the defendant's admission that during his participation in a campaign of persecutions, he 'had made ethnically based inflammatory speeches during public events and in the media that added to the atmosphere of fear and hatred amongst Serbs living in Croatia and convinced them that they could only be safe in a state of their own'.[196] The defence had argued that Babic's responsibility for such incitement was resultant from the fact that 'during the events and in particular at the beginning of his political career, he was strongly influenced and misled by Serbian propaganda, which repeatedly referred to an imminent threat by the Croatian regime against the Serbs in Croatia'.[197] On appeal the defence argued that the Trial Chamber should have stated whether it accepted this statement as true and made a finding or reasoned opinion as to the impact of this influence on the ethnically motivated speeches he made.[198] In dismissing this ground of appeal, the Appeals Chamber held that the Trial Chamber's reference to the undisputed fact that Babic had fallen prey to the media campaign directed by the Serbian government was indicative that it had accepted it,[199] and reiterated that a Trial Chamber is not obliged to make specific findings on facts agreed upon by the parties or on undisputed facts.[200]

In the *Banovic* case the defendant had pleaded guilty to the crime of persecution.[201] His defence had argued that the effects of war propaganda should be considered when assessing the gravity of the crime, and that the role of the accused and his participation in crimes should be put into the broader context 'of the aggressive wartime propaganda that was prevalent in the whole territory', to which, as a young, uneducated, and immature person, he had succumbed.[202] The Chamber rejected this argument, stating that the role of war propaganda 'clearly does not affect the gravity of the criminal conduct of the Accused and is more appropriately considered in relation to mitigating factors'.[203]

---

[195] *Prosecutor v Dusko Tadic a/k/a/ 'Dule'*, Sentencing Judgment, 14 July 1997, para 72.
[196] *Prosecutor v Milan Babic*, Sentencing Judgment, Case no IT-03-72-S, para 24(g).
[197] ibid.
[198] *Prosecutor v Milan Babic*, Judgment on Sentencing Appeal, Case no IT-03-72-A, 18 July 2005, para 20.
[199] ibid, para 22.
[200] ibid, para 21.
[201] *Prosecutor v Predrag Banovic*, Sentencing Judgment, Case no IT-02-65/1-S, 28 October 2003, para 13.
[202] ibid, para 44.
[203] ibid, para 48.

A report submitted in evidence by the defence to demonstrate mitigating factors to be considered in sentencing claimed that with his low education and modest intellectual capabilities, Banovic easily succumbed to the war propaganda which spread collective hatred and rumours about the enemy's brutality.[204] According to this report 'the combined effect of the war propaganda and authoritarian behaviour help to explain why, psychologically, the accused did not understand the criminality of his behaviour'.[205] These claims were rejected by the Trial Chamber, which did not fully accept the findings of the report and expressed severe reservations about its accuracy.[206] In holding that the accused had voluntarily participated in the beatings and killings at Keraterm Camp, the Chamber refused to accept the argument that the accused did not have the strength of character to resist the war propaganda.[207]

Jose Alvarez has stated that Tadic received a lenient sentence partly on account of the fact that he had been a 'low-level culprit' and thus susceptible to propaganda which raised ethnic tensions, a decision made 'on the basis of a rationale that buttresses the international legal paradigm's premises that high-level perpetrators are more culpable than a low-level culprit'.[208] The contrast between the weight attached to the influence of propaganda in the cases of *Tadic* and *Banovic* suggests that international criminal tribunals may face a dilemma in such circumstances, since by recognizing the reality of the power of propaganda to shape attitudes and affect people's actions, international criminal law faces the possibility of accepting that individuals committed crimes under an 'air of reality'[209] in which they believed that their actions were justified.

ii. The International Criminal Tribunal for Rwanda

The International Criminal Tribunal for Rwanda (ICTR) was established by the Security Council in 1994 pursuant to Chapter VII of the UN Charter, on the basis of UN reports indicating that genocide and other systematic, widespread, and flagrant violations of international humanitarian law had been committed in Rwanda.[210] The international community had been forewarned of the impending genocide in Rwanda by, amongst others, a coalition of international NGOs which published a report after a fact-finding mission to the country in 1993 citing acts of genocide and warning of the violence which was to ensue.[211] One of the primary indicators that genocide was likely in Rwanda was the after-effect of a speech

---

[204] ibid, para 78.   [205] ibid, para 78.
[206] ibid, para 80.   [207] ibid, para 81.
[208] Jose E Alvarez, 'Crimes of States/Crimes of Hate: Lessons from Rwanda', 24 Yale J Int'l L 365 (1999) 428–9.
[209] ibid.
[210] Statute of the International Criminal Tribunal for Rwanda, adopted by UN Doc S/RES/955 (1994), 8 November 1994.
[211] Fédération Internationale des Droits de l'Homme, Union Interafricaine des Droits de l'Homme et des Peuples, Africa Watch, and Centre International des Droits de la Personne et du

given by Leon Mugesera, a confidant of the Rwandan President. According to Schabas, who had been a member of the NGO coalition:

We arrived to find a country in a state of turmoil and agitation provoked by a speech suggesting that ethnic hatred had taken a new and genocidal turn [...] One of our first stops in Kigali should have been a visit with the minister of justice. But he resigned out of frustration days before our arrival when he learned that his attempts to prosecute Mugesera for incitement to racial hatred were thwarted by the man's powerful friends.[212]

The exacerbation of pre-existing ethnic tensions had been identified by the Rwanda Tribunal as the goal of Rwandan President Habyarimana and the Rwandan army. In the years preceding 1994 the military had 'persistently launched propaganda campaigns which often consisted of fabricating events'.[213] On 2 September 1998 the Trial Chamber of the ICTR found Jean-Paul Akayesu guilty of direct and public incitement to genocide. This was the first occasion that an international criminal tribunal had convicted an individual of the crime of direct and public incitement to genocide, and the decision has provided a precedent for several further cases, both at the ICTR and the ICTY. In the *Akayesu* judgment the Tribunal highlighted the testimony of expert witness Dr Alison Des Forges, which addressed the phenomenon of 'mirror politics', whereby a person accuses others of what he or she does, or wants to do.[214] Among the examples cited in the judgment was the stimulation of an attack on Kigali, the Rwandan capital, orchestrated by the government in order to claim that the city had been infiltrated by the RPF (a Tutsi army in exile), with the assistance of local Tutsi accomplices. The following day some 8,000 Tutsi and members of the Hutu opposition were arrested and several dozens of them died in jail.[215]

Développement Démocratique, *Rapport de la commission internationale d'enquête sur les violations des droits de l'homme au Rwanda depuis le 1er octobre 1990* (1993).

[212] William A Schabas, 'Hate Speech in Rwanda: The Road to Genocide', 141.

[213] *Prosecutor v Jean-Paul Akayesu*, Case no ICTR-96-4-T, Judgment, 2 September 1998, para 99.

[214] Alison Des Forges has highlighted the power which the state and government exercised over radio in Rwanda. She notes how in 1992 the national radio station—Radio Rwanda—broadcast excerpts from a diatribe by Mugesera which incited to violence, noting how '[g]iven the unity between state and the governing party, the National Democratic Republican Movement (MRND), it is not surprising that the national radio promoted the party just as vigorously as it served the state'. She further notes how after RTLM was established in 1993, 'it was allowed to broadcast on the same frequencies as the national radio when Radio Rwanda was not transmitting, a measure which encouraged listeners to see the station as also enjoying the support of the government.' Alison Des Forges, 'Silencing the Voices of Hate in Rwanda', in Monroe E Price and Mark Thompson (eds), *Forging Peace*, 236–58, 238–40.

[215] ibid, para 99. This phenomenon was again highlighted in the *Nahimana* judgment, where the Trial Chamber noted that a document found in the Butare prefectural office advocated such propaganda: 'Drawing also on Lenin and Goebbels, he advocated the use of lies, exaggeration, ridicule and innuendo against the adversary and suggests that the public must be persuaded that the adversary stands for war, death, slavery, repression, injustice and sadistic cruelty. He stressed the importance of linking propaganda to events and suggested simply "creating" events, if necessary. He proposed the use of what he called "Accusation in a mirror", meaning that one would impute to the adversary one's own intentions and plans. "In this way", he wrote, "the party which is using

The Chamber asserted that the purpose of such propaganda was in part to make the economic, social, and political conflict in Rwanda appear more as an ethnic conflict, an interpretation which may equally be applied to many of the world's conflicts.[216] It was further held that the conflict between the armed groups in Rwanda was exploited in order to facilitate genocide, noting that:

[T]he fighting against the RPF forces was used as a pretext for the propaganda inciting genocide against the Tutsi, by branding RPF fighters and Tutsi civilians together, through dissemination via the media of the idea that every Tutsi was allegedly an accomplice of the Inkotanyi.[217]

Another method of propaganda employed by those seeking to incite genocide in Rwanda was the advocacy of the systematic rape of Tutsi women. The Trial Chamber in *Akayesu* found that '[a]s part of the propaganda campaign geared to mobilizing the Hutu against the Tutsi, the Tutsi women were presented as sexual objects'.[218] Lezlie Green's study of the hate propaganda specifically targeted at women on the basis of the intersection of gender and race concludes that the widespread sexual violence perpetrated against Tutsi women resulted from propaganda campaigns 'in which an atmosphere of tension and hate in which genocidal acts that might normally seem unimaginable, benefited from the support of the military, local authorities, and the general population'.[219] The sexualized representation of ethnic identity incited sexual violence against Tutsi women and was a crucial step towards the destruction of the Tutsi group as a whole. The identification of all Tutsi as a 'Fifth Column' of the RPF and the propaganda which capitalized on such aspersions to incite people to genocide, combined with the obscene representation of Tutsi women as sexual objects, are recurring themes in the jurisprudence of the Tribunal.

Such hate propaganda was disseminated in speeches at public meetings as well as through the media of radio and the printed press. Rwandan Prime Minister during the genocide, Jean Kambanda, was charged with the crime of direct and public incitement to genocide in 1997 and in his guilty plea to the Tribunal described how 'in his particular role of making public engagements in the name of the government, he addressed public meetings, and the media, at various places in Rwanda directly and publicly inciting the population to commit

---

terror will accuse the enemy of using terror". Such a tactic could be used to persuade honest people that attack by the enemy justifies taking whatever measures are necessary for legitimate defense.' *Prosecutor v Ferdinand Nahimana, Jean-Bosco Barayagwiza, Hassan Ngeze*, Case no ICTR- 99-52-T, Judgment and Sentence, 3 December 2003, para 111.

[216] *Prosecutor v Jean-Paul Akayesu*, Case no ICTR-96-4-T, Judgment, 2 September 1998, para 99.

[217] ibid, para 127.

[218] ibid, paras 731–4.

[219] Lezlie L Green, 'Gender Hate Propaganda and Sexual Violence in the Rwandan Genocide: An Argument for Intersectionality in International Law', 33 Colum Hum Rts L Rev 733 (2002) 774. See further Nicoletta F Gullace, 'Sexual Violence and Family Honor', 714–47 and Jose E Alvarez, 'Crimes of States/Crimes of Hate: Lessons from Rwanda', 365.

acts of violence against Tutsi and moderate Hutu'.[220] Kambanda stands amongst several individuals convicted by the Rwanda Tribunal in relation to the infamous radio station RTLM that began broadcasting in Rwanda in July 1993. In a plea agreement with the Office of the Prosecutor,[221] Kambanda admitted that he had used the mass media as part of a plan to mobilize and incite Hutu to commit massacres of the civilian Tutsi population.[222] He further acknowledged that on or about 21 June 1994, in his capacity as Prime Minister, he had encouraged RTLM staff to continue to incite the massacres of the Tutsi civilian population, describing it as 'an indispensable weapon in the fight against the enemy'.[223] The Trial Chamber in the *Ruggiu* judgment noted that:

The media, particularly RTLM radio, was a key tool used by extremists within the political parties to mobilize and incite the population to commit the massacres. RTLM had a large audience in Rwanda and became an effective propaganda instrument [...] In his broadcasts at the RTLM, [Ruggiu] encouraged setting up roadblocks and congratulated perpetrators of massacres of the Tutsis at these roadblocks.[224]

Although the role of propaganda and incitement in fomenting and shaping the course of the Rwandan Genocide has resurfaced in many of the ICTR's decisions, the Tribunal's 2003 judgment in the *Nahimana* case, commonly referred to as 'the Media Judgment',[225] is of particular significance as it represents the most comprehensive analysis undertaken by an international criminal tribunal of 'incitement to crimes of an international dimension'.[226] The three accused, Nahimana, Barayagwiza, and Ngeze, were charged with the crime of direct and public incitement to genocide.[227] All were found to have acted with genocidal intent, the *mens rea* necessary for the crime of direct and public incitement

---

[220] *Prosecutor v Jean Kambanda*, Case no ICTR 97-23-S, Judgment and Sentence, 4 September 1998, para 39(x).

[221] ibid, para 39.

[222] ibid, para 39(vi).

[223] ibid, para 39(vii). In the light of these admissions the Chamber accepted his plea and found him guilty of direct and public incitement to genocide and sentenced him to life imprisonment. *Prosecutor v Jean Kambanda*, Case no ICTR 97-23-S, Judgment and Sentence, 4 September 1998, IV, Verdict. Upheld on appeal, *Jean Kambanda (Appellant) v Prosecutor (Respondent)*, Case no ICTR 97-23-A, Judgment, 19 October 2000, para 126.

[224] *Prosecutor v Georges Ruggiu*, Case no ICTR-97-32-I, Judgment and Sentence, 1 June 2000, para 50. The *Ruggiu* case concerned a Belgian national employed by RTLM who pleaded guilty to charges of direct and public incitement to commit genocide. In the plea agreement submitted to the Tribunal, Georges Ruggiu stated that RTLM broadcasters, managerial, and editorial staff 'bear full responsibility' for the 1994 massacre of Tutsis and Hutu opposition party members. *Prosecutor v Georges Ruggiu*, Case no ICTR-97-32-I, Judgment and Sentence, 1 June 2000, para 44(xii).

[225] *Prosecutor v Ferdinand Nahimana, Jean-Bosco Barayagwiza, Hassan Ngeze*, Case no ICTR-99-52-T, Judgment and Sentence, 3 December 2003.

[226] *Prosecutor v Jean-Paul Akayesu*, Case no ICTR-96-4-T, Judgment, 2 September 1998, para 550.

[227] Count Three, Amended Indictment, 15 November 1999, ICTR-96-11-I; Count Four, Amended Indictment, 14 April 2000, ICTR-97-19-I; Count Four, Amended Indictment, 10 November 1999, ICTR-97-27-I.

to genocide,[228] and each was found guilty of direct and public incitement to genocide under Article 6(1) of the ICTR Statute on account of their roles with the radio station Radio Télévision Libre des Mille Collines (RTLM), the weekly tabloid *Kangura,* and the political party Coalition for the Defence of the Republic (CDR).[229] A substantial section of the *Nahimana* judgment is concerned with the responsibility of RTLM for inciting acts of violence and genocide in Rwanda. The Chamber found that RTLM broadcasts engaged in ethnic stereotyping in a manner that promoted contempt and hatred for the Tutsi population. RTLM broadcasts called on listeners to seek out and take up arms against the enemy, which was identified as the RPF, the *Inkotanyi*, the *Inyenzi*, and their accomplices, all of whom the broadcasts effectively equated with the Tutsi ethnic group. The Chamber found that after 6 April 1994 RTLM broadcasts 'called explicitly for the extermination of the Tutsi ethnic group',[230] and held that RTLM had broadcast:

[…] messages encouraging Tutsi civilians to come out of hiding and to return home or to go to the roadblocks, where they were subsequently killed in accordance with the direction of subsequent RTLM broadcasts tracking their movement […] RTLM broadcasts exploited the history of Tutsi privilege and Hutu disadvantage, and the fear of armed insurrection, to mobilize the population, whipping them into a frenzy of hatred and violence that was directed largely against the Tutsi ethnic group. The *Interahamwe* and other militia listened to RTLM and acted on the information that was broadcast by RTLM. RLTM actively encouraged them to kill, relentlessly sending the message that the Tutsi were the enemy and had to be eliminated once and for all.[231]

The Trial Chamber also considered evidence regarding the newspaper *Kangura* and the political party the Coalition for the Defence of the Republic (CDR). *Kangura* was published from May 1990 until 1995, although 1994 saw a hiatus in publication.[232] The Chamber found that articles published in *Kangura* such as 'The Ten Commandments' of the Hutu and the '19 Commandments' of the Tutsi, were complementary efforts to the same end, namely, 'the promotion of fear and hatred among the Hutu population of the Tutsi minority and the mobilization of the Hutu population against them'.[233] The Chamber further held that this appeal to the Hutu was visibly sustained in every issue of *Kangura* from February 1991 to March 1994 by the title 'The Voice that Awakens and Defends the Majority People'.[234] Articles and editorials portrayed the Tutsi as inherently wicked and

[228] *Prosecutor v Ferdinand Nahimana, Jean-Bosco Barayagwiza, Hassan Ngeze*, Case no ICTR-99-52-T, Judgment and Sentence, 3 December 2003, para 969.
[229] ibid, paras 1033–9.
[230] ibid, paras 486.
[231] ibid, paras 487–8.
[232] ibid, para 122. The newspaper had two versions, one primarily in Kinyarwanda and another primarily in French, referred to as the international version.
[233] ibid, para 245.
[234] ibid, para 245.

ambitious, using language 'clearly intended to fan the flames of resentment and anger, directed against the Tutsi population'.[235] *Kangura* no 26 was singled out for particular attention. The front page of this issue answered the question '[w]hat weapons shall we use to conquer the *Inyenzi* once and for all?' with the depiction of a machete. The Chamber held that the message meant by *Kangura* and understood by the public by the depiction of the machete and the reference to *Inyenzi* was that all Rwandans of Tutsi origin should be conquered through violence.[236]

The Chamber found the CDR party to have equated political interest with ethnic identity and thereby equated the RPF with the Tutsi, effectively defining the enemy as the Tutsi ethnic group. The Tribunal referred as an example of CDR policy to a communiqué issued by the CDR in November 1993, following massacres it attributed to the RPF, which called on the Hutu population to 'neutralize by all means possible its enemies and their accomplices', having defined the enemies as the Tutsi ethnic group.[237] The Chamber held that the CDR was a Hutu party and that membership was not open to Rwandans of Tutsi ethnicity, a policy explicitly communicated to members and the public by the defendants Barayagwiza and Ngeze.[238] The methods of propaganda which Barayagwiza was found to have employed varied from his role in the mass media to appearances at public meetings and rallies of the CDR. The Chamber describes for example how '[h]e was present at and participated in demonstrations where CDR demonstrators armed with cudgels chanted "*Tubatsembatsembe*" or "let's exterminate them", and the reference to "them" was understood to mean the Tutsi. Barayagwiza himself said "*tubatsembatsembe*" or "let's exterminate them" at CDR meetings.'[239] Similarly, Ngeze was found to have incited Hutus against Tutsis on the streets of Rwanda by driving around with a megaphone in his vehicle mobilizing the population to come to CDR meetings 'spreading the message that the *Inyenzi* would be exterminated, *Inyenzi* meaning, and being understood to mean, the Tutsi ethnic minority'.[240]

The incitement to genocide for which each of the three defendants in the *Nahimana* case was responsible interwove to form a 'propaganda framework' which magnified the effect of their individual speech. Nahimana and Barayagwiza worked together in the management of RTLM, and Barayagwiza worked closely with Ngeze in the CDR. Barayagwiza and Ngeze discussed CDR, *Kangura*, and RTLM as all playing a role in the Hutu struggle against the Tutsi.[241] Significant incidents reported in the judgment include the promotion of RTLM 'to fight against the *Inyenzi*' at an MRND[242] meeting of 15,000 people where the platform was shared by the three accused.[243] Ngeze was held to have used *Kangura* to

---

[235] *Prosecutor v Ferdinand Nahimana, Jean-Bosco Barayagwiza, Hassan Ngeze*, Case no ICTR-99-52-T, Judgment and Sentence, 3 December 2003, para 246.

[236] ibid, para 246.   [237] ibid, para 301.

[238] ibid, para 339.   [239] ibid, para 719.

[240] ibid, para 837.   [241] ibid, para 889.

[242] Mouvement Révolutionnaire National pour le Développement.

[243] *Prosecutor v Ferdinand Nahimana, Jean-Bosco Barayagwiza, Hassan Ngeze*, Case no ICTR-99-52-T, Judgment and Sentence, 3 December 2003, para 907.

support the CDR and the Chamber found that 'through editorials, photographs, and the publication of letters and communiqués, *Kangura* endorsed and actively promoted the CDR'.[244] The Chamber's summary of the interactions among the accused and their respective organizations demonstrates the success which they had in organizing a 'propaganda framework' capable of inciting the population to genocide:

Kangura and RTLM functioned as partners in a Hutu coalition, of which CDR was also a part. *Kangura* and RTLM presented a common media front, publicly interacting and promoting each other through articles, broadcasts, and the joint initiative represented by the *Kangura* competition in March 1994. *Kangura* portrayed all three of the Accused in a common undertaking relating to RTLM. The purpose of the coalition was to mobilize the Hutu population against the Tutsi ethnic minority.[245]

Although a comprehensive analysis of the crime of direct and public incitement to genocide is beyond the scope of this book,[246] it is apt to focus on several key features of the jurisprudence of the Rwanda Tribunal with respect to this crime which are of great significance in considering whether the crime of direct and public incitement to aggression should be included in the Rome Statute of the International Criminal Court. The Tribunal's jurisprudence, with its emphasis on the power of words and the media to kill, particularly when such propaganda is state sponsored, highlights the dangers posed to international peace by propaganda and incitement whilst affirming that international criminal law must, and can, play an important role in combating such threats.

The meaning of 'direct and public' was first considered by the Tribunal in the *Akayesu* case where the defendant had been charged with direct and public incitement to genocide under Article 2(3)(c) of the Tribunal's Statute.[247] The Trial Chamber found that he had led a gathering of over 100 people in the area where he was *bourgmestre*, urging the population to unite in order to eliminate 'the sole enemy', that is, all Tutsi, and that he had read names from a list to the crowd stating that they were RPF accomplices, knowing that to label anyone in public as an accomplice of the RPF would put them in danger.[248] The Chamber relied upon the *Streicher* case, common law and civil law rules, as well as proceedings at the International Law Commission and the Genocide Convention, to define 'direct and public incitement' as:

directly provoking the perpetrator(s) to commit genocide, whether through speeches, shouting or threats uttered in public places or at public gatherings, or through the sale or dissemination, offer for sale or display of written material or printed matter in public

---

[244] ibid, para 930.
[245] ibid, para 943.
[246] See William A Schabas, *Genocide in International Law* (Cambridge: Cambridge University Press, 2000) 266–80.
[247] Statute of the International Criminal Court for Rwanda, SC Res 955, UN SCOR, 49th Sess, 3453d mtg, UN Doc S/RES/955 (1994).
[248] *Prosecutor v Jean-Paul Akayesu*, Case no ICTR-96-4-T, Judgment, 2 September 1998, para 673.

places or at public gatherings, or through the public display of placards or posters, or through any other means of audiovisual communication.[249]

The meaning of the 'direct' element of the crime has often been the most controversial. The Trial Chamber in Nahimana noted that incitement may be 'direct' yet implicit, citing the observation of the Polish delegate during the drafting of the Genocide Convention that 'it was sufficient to play skilfully on mob psychology by casting suspicion on certain groups, by insinuating that they were responsible for economic or other difficulties in order to create an atmosphere favourable to the perpetration of the crime'.[250] With regard to such concerns the Chamber held that it would consider on a case-by-case basis 'whether, in light of the culture of Rwanda and the specific circumstances of the instant case, acts of incitement can be viewed as direct or not, by focusing mainly on the issue of whether the persons for whom the message was intended immediately grasped the implication thereof'.[251]

The Trial Chamber also considered whether the crime of direct and public incitement to commit genocide could be punished even where such incitement was unsuccessful. Reviewing the *travaux préparatoires* of the Genocide Convention the Chamber noted that whereas the delegates decided against explicitly stating that incitement to genocide could be punished even where unsuccessful, in light of the overall *travaux* it could not be inferred that the intent of the drafters was not to punish unsuccessful acts of incitement.[252] The Chamber further considered the regime of inchoate crimes under the common law system and their civil law counterparts, *infractions formelles*, found in the Rwandan Penal Code and asserted that acts such as incitement to genocide are in themselves particularly dangerous because of the high risk they carry for society. Thus, even if they fail to produce results, they should be punished as an exceptional measure. The Chamber held therefore 'that genocide clearly falls within the category of crimes so serious that direct and public incitement to commit such a crime must be punished as such, even where such incitement failed to produce the result expected by the perpetrator'.[253] It should be noted, however, that the question of unsuccessful incitement in this case was really obiter dictum since Akayesu's exhortation to the local population was in fact shown to be successful.[254] The Trial Chamber in

---

[249] *Prosecutor v Jean-Paul Akayesu*, Case no ICTR-96-4-T, Judgment, 2 September 1998, para 559.
[250] ibid, para 557.
[251] ibid, para 558. This factor was subsequently taken into account by the Canadian Supreme Court of Justice in a June 2005 decision concerning Leon Mugesera. It was found that a lower court had erred in law in finding that Mugesera's speech did not constitute an incitement to murder, genocide, or hatred since it had 'failed to take account of the nature of the target audience, which is an important contextual factor, and consequently erred in relying on an abstract "reasonable listener"'. *Mugesera v Canada* (*Minister of Citizenship and Immigration*) [2005] SCJ no 39, para 111. For a history of these proceedings see William A Schabas, 'International Decision: Mugesera v Minister of Citizenship and Immigration. Nos. M96-10465, M96-10466. Immigration and Refugee Board (Appeal Division) of Canada, November 6, 1998', 93 AJIL 529 (1999).
[252] ibid, para 561.   [253] ibid, para 562.
[254] William A Schabas, 'Hate Speech in Rwanda: The Road to Genocide', 157.

Nahimana confirmed that the crime of direct and public incitement to commit genocide is an inchoate offence that continues in time until the completion of the acts contemplated,[255] and noted that the causal relationship between expression and subsequent massacres is not requisite to a finding of incitement, since '[i]t is the potential of the communication to cause genocide that makes it incitement [...] when this potential is realized, a crime of genocide as well as incitement to genocide has occurred'.[256]

The temporal jurisdiction of the ICTR is limited by its Statute to acts committed between 1 January and 31 December 1994. Given that the indictments in the *Nahimana* case frequently referred to acts of the accused prior to 1994, the Trial Chamber had to consider what weight could be attached to such evidence. This question is of importance since the most effective propaganda is often that which is shaped around the 'propaganda framework' and which has been gradually introduced into the circulation of a society as evidenced in the judgments of the IMT and the Tokyo Tribunal. The ICTR was faced with the task of responding to this phenomenon.

The *Nahimana* Trial Chamber highlighted the Joint Separate Opinion of Judges Vohrah and Nieto-Navia in the decision of the Appeals Chamber on an interlocutory appeal, that, '[w]ith inchoate crimes in particular, it can be difficult to ascertain when all of the constituent elements of the offence exist so that a potential problem arises if it is intended that a conviction will be based upon not just one defined event occurring on a specific date but upon a series of events or acts which took place over an extended period of time'.[257]

In holding that with regard to the commission of crimes in 1994, pre-1994 material 'may constitute evidence of the intent of the Accused or a pattern of conduct by the Accused, or background in reviewing and understanding the general manner in which the Accused related to the media at issue',[258] the Chamber considered that the adoption by the Security Council of 1 January 1994 rather than 6 April 1994—the date the genocide commenced—as the commencement of the Tribunal's temporal jurisdiction, expressly for the purpose of including the planning stage:

[...] indicates an intention that is more compatible with the inclusion of inchoate offences that culminate in the commission of acts in 1994 than it is with their exclusion. It is only

---

[255] *Prosecutor v Ferdinand Nahimana, Jean-Bosco Barayagwiza, Hassan Ngeze*, Case no ICTR-99-52-T, Judgment and Sentence, 3 December 2003, para 1017.

[256] ibid, para 1015.

[257] ibid, para 102. Citing 'Decision on the Interlocutory Appeals', *Hassan Ngeze and Ferdinand Nahimana v Prosecutor*, 5 September 2000, 'Joint Separate Opinion of Judge Lal Chand Vohrah and Judge Rafael Nieto-Navia', para 7. A Separate Opinion of Judge Shahabuddeen suggested more specifically that evidence dating to a time prior to 1 January 1994 could provide a basis from which to draw inferences, for example with regard to intent or other required elements of crimes committed within the limits of the temporal jurisdiction of the Tribunal. 'Decision on the Interlocutory Appeals', *Hassan Ngeze and Ferdinand Nahimana v Prosecutor*, 5 September 2000, 6.

[258] ibid, para 103.

the commission of acts completed prior to 1994 that is clearly excluded from the temporal jurisdiction of the Tribunal.[259]

Accordingly, it was held that the publication of *Kangura*, from its first issue in May 1990 to its March 1994 issue, the impact of which culminated in events that took place in 1994, fell within the temporal jurisdiction of the Tribunal, particularly since a competition in the March 1994 issue had 'effectively and purposely brought these [pre-1994] issues back into circulation'.[260] Similarly, the Chamber considered that the entirety of RTLM broadcasting, from July 1993 to July 1994, the effects of which culminated in events that took place in 1994, also fell within the temporal jurisdiction of the Tribunal.[261] This 'broader and more fluid'[262] approach appears correct in light of the reality of propaganda inciting to genocide, which, as understood by the IMT in the *Streicher* case, manifested itself in the manner of a 'poison'. Endorsing this approach, Gregory Gordon considers the *Nahimana* judgment as representing 'a more appropriate understanding of "mass media" incitement to genocide, which could be seen as proceeding in fits and starts and building to a genocidal crescendo'.[263]

Introducing its legal findings relating to individual criminal responsibility for direct and public incitement to genocide, the Trial Chamber noted that unlike in the case of Akayesu, who engaged in incitement through his own speech, the accused in the *Nahimana* case used organs of the mass media for communication. Thus the Chamber stated that it would examine not only the content of particular broadcasts and articles but also 'the broader application of these principles to media programming, as well as the responsibilities inherent in ownership and institutional control over the media'.[264] The parallels which can be drawn between incitement to genocide and incitement to aggression—both of which represent 'incitement to commit crimes of an international dimension'—suggest that the jurisprudence of the ICTR in this case may be of immense value in determining what approach an international court could take in considering the responsibility of individuals charged with a crime of incitement to aggression. Prior to making its legal findings, the Chamber reviewed international jurisprudence on issues related to the crimes of incitement to violence and discrimination. Drawing on the freedom of expression provisions of the Universal Declaration and the International Covenant on Civil and Political Rights, as well as the jurisprudence of the IMT and the ECtHR,[265] the Trial Chamber directed its attention towards

---

[259] *Prosecutor v Ferdinand Nahimana, Jean-Bosco Barayagwiza, Hassan Ngeze*, Case no ICTR-99-52-T, Judgment and Sentence, 3 December 2003, para 104.

[260] ibid, para 257.   [261] ibid, para 1017.

[262] Gregory S Gordon, ' "A War of Media, Words, Newspapers, and Radio Stations": The ICTR Media Trial Verdict and a New Chapter in the International Law of Hate Speech', 45 Va J Int'l L 139 (2004) 195.

[263] ibid.

[264] *Prosecutor v Ferdinand Nahimana, Jean-Bosco Barayagwiza, Hassan Ngeze*, Case no ICTR-99-52-T, Judgment and Sentence, 3 December 2003, para 979.

[265] ibid, paras 978–99.

three central principles which it considered to serve as a useful guide to the factors to be considered in defining elements of 'direct and public incitement to genocide' as applied to mass media, namely: purpose, context, and causation.[266]

In determining the scope of editors' and publishers' responsibility for the media under their control, the Chamber stressed the importance of intent, 'the purpose of the communication they channel',[267] which is to a great extent reliant on the bona fide nature of the communication in question. The Chamber drew on the international jurisprudence to cite historical research, the dissemination of news and information, and the public accountability of governmental organizations as legitimate objects of expression. The actual language or text used in an impugned communication was seen as providing an important indicator of intent and the Chamber cited the case of *Faurisson v France* in which the Human Rights Committee held that by using terms such as 'magic gas chambers', Faurisson was motivated by anti-Semitic intentions rather than any pursuit of historical truth, and thus his speech was not protected by Article 19 of the Covenant.[268] Regarding the responsibility of editors and publishers for impugned communications, the Chamber stated that the content of the communication was of greater importance than the identity of the author, citing the ECtHR's decision in *Sürek v Turkey, (No. 1)*[269] which found that readers' letters were to be treated without distinction as subject to liability and that editors and publishers were to be held as equally responsible with the authors, given that they are providing a forum for expression and continuously retain 'the power to shape the editorial direction'.[270] The Chamber adopted the approach taken by the ECtHR in the Turkish cases on 'separatist propaganda', which distinguished between language which sought to explain the motivation of those who used illegal violence and language which was intended to promote terrorist activities, emphasizing that the question as to whether the expression was intended to 'incite or inflame to violence' was of vital importance in determining intent.[271]

---

[266] ibid, para 1000.

[267] ibid, para 1001.

[268] *Faurisson v France* (Communication 550/1993), UN Human Rights Committee, 2 BHRC 1, 8 November 1996. Similarly the Chamber approved the decision of the European Court of Human Rights in *Jersild v Denmark* (23 September 1994, Series A no 298), where the comments of an interviewer in a television programme distancing himself from the opinions expressed by the subjects of the programme were found to be critical in establishing that the communication was motivated by the bona fide dissemination of news rather than any racist intent.

[269] *Sürek v Turkey (No. 1)* (App no 26682/95), 8 July 1999.

[270] *Prosecutor v Ferdinand Nahimana, Jean-Bosco Barayagwiza, Hassan Ngeze*, Case no ICTR 99-52-T, Judgment and Sentence, 3 December 2003, para 1003. In a Partly Dissenting Opinion, Palm J of the European Court of Human Rights disagreed with the majority, stating that letter-writing by readers is by its very nature of limited influence and that some allowance must be made for the fact that members of the public expressing their views in letters for publication are likely to use a more direct and vehement style than professional journalists. *Sürek v Turkey (No. 1)* (App no 26682/95), 8 July 1999.

[271] ibid, para 1002.

The Chamber also stressed the importance when considering the potential impact of any communication of the context in which it was made. The Chamber approved the ECtHR decision in the case of *Zana v Turkey*,[272] where a former Mayor's 'general statement' concerning massacres had to be considered in the light of the fact that massacres of civilians were actually taking place at the time, and thus was 'likely to exacerbate an already explosive situation'.[273] A further consideration to be taken into account when establishing the context of an expression was that of text which may 'conceal objectives and intentions different from the ones it proclaims'.[274] The actual intent of the expression, the Chamber held, can only be determined on the question of evidence, taking the context into account. The *Arslan* decision of the ECtHR,[275] in which the Court distinguished between the potential impact of a book from the mass media, finding that a book, as a literary work, would be of less impact, was cited by the Chamber as an example of a court taking context into account when determining the potential of a text impacting on public order and national security.[276]

The Rwanda Tribunal previously had occasion to consider the meaning of certain expressions in the particular context of the Rwandan Genocide. The *Niyitegeka* judgment of May 2003 concerned Eliézer Niyitegeka, a journalist and a news presenter on Radio Rwanda and Minister of Information of the Interim Government from 9 April until mid-July 1994, who had been charged with direct and public incitement to genocide.[277] The Trial Chamber held that the accused had told armed attackers to go back to 'work', finding that 'work' referred to the killings of Tutsi and that pursuant to Niyitegeka's instructions the attackers launched an attack

[272] *Zana v Turkey* (69/1996/688/880), 25 November 1997.

[273] *Prosecutor v Ferdinand Nahimana, Jean-Bosco Barayagwiza, Hassan Ngeze*, Case no ICTR-99-52-T, Judgment and Sentence, 3 December 2003, para 1004.

[274] ibid, para 1005.

[275] *Arslan v Turkey* [1999] ECHR 23462/94, 8 July 1999.

[276] *Prosecutor v Ferdinand Nahimana, Jean-Bosco Barayagwiza, Hassan Ngeze*, Case no ICTR-99-52-T, Judgment and Sentence, 3 December 2003, para 1006. A similar issue had arisen in the case of *Karata v Turkey* where the majority of the European Court laid particular emphasis on the fact that the applicant was a private individual, 'who expressed his views through poetry—which by definition is addressed to a very small audience—rather than through the mass media, a fact which limited their potential impact on "national security", "[public] order" and "territorial integrity" to a substantial degree. Thus, even though some of the passages from the poems seem very aggressive in tone and to call for the use of violence, the Court considers that the fact that they were artistic in nature and of limited impact made them less a call to an uprising than an expression of deep distress in the face of a difficult political situation.' *Karata v Turkey*, [1999] ECHR 23168/94, 8 July 1999, para 52. In a Joint Partly Dissenting Opinion, however, four judges expressed criticism of the fact that the Court 'saw the poetic form as being more important than the substance, that is to say the tone and content. We consider that the Court should be wary of adopting an ivory tower approach. One only has to think of words of the "Marseillaise" as an example of a poetic call to arms.' Joint Partly Dissenting Opinion, Judges Wildhaber, Pastor Ridruejo, Costa, and Baka, *Karata v Turkey*, [1999] ECHR 23168/94, 8 July 1999, See also *Okguoglu v Turkey*, [1999] ECHR 24246/94, 8 July 1999 (App no 24246/94), para 48 and *Polat v Turkey* (App no 23500/94), [1999] ECHR 23500/94, para 48.

[277] *Prosecutor v Eliezer Niyitegeka*, Case no ICTR-96-14-T, Prosecutor's Submission of the Harmonised Amended Indictment, 25 November 2002.

against Tutsi from a specific location.[278] In particular by 'urging the attackers to work, thanking, encouraging and commending them for the "work" they had done', Niyitegeka was using the word 'work' as a reference to killing Tutsi.[279] The Chamber held that, 'in urging attackers to work, and to eat meat so that they would be strong to return the next day to continue the "work", the Accused is individually criminally responsible, pursuant to Article 6(1) of the Statute, for inciting attackers to cause the death and serious bodily and mental harm of Tutsi refugees'.[280]

Establishing context requires an examination of all the circumstances that are relevant to the expression in question. The Chamber noted that this involves considering the potential impact of an impugned expression on the basis of all possible evidence, taking into account factors as diverse as the historical truth of a statement, the position in society of both those who have published a communication and those who are the target or subject of a communication, and the actual intent and potential impact of the expression.[281]

The Trial Chamber in *Nahimana* first had occasion to consider the issue of causation in relation to the charges of genocide brought against each of the defendants, when it noted that '[t]he nature of media is such that causation of killing and other acts of genocide will necessarily be effected by an immediately proximate cause in addition to the communication itself'.[282] It stressed that 'this does not diminish the causation to be attributed to the media, or the criminal accountability of those responsible for the communication'.[283] In this instance the Chamber held that the downing of the Rwandan President's plane in April 1994 served as a trigger for the genocide that followed but asserted that causation could clearly be attributed to acts of the media outlets in question:

[…] if the downing of the plane was the trigger, then RTLM, *Kangura* and CDR were the bullets in the gun. The trigger had such a deadly impact because the gun was loaded. The Chamber therefore considers the killing of Tutsi civilians can be said to have resulted, at least in part, from the message of ethnic targeting for death that was clearly and effectively disseminated through RTLM, *Kangura* and CDR, before and after 6 April 1994.[284]

In relation to the charges of direct and public incitement to genocide, the Chamber was satisfied that under the international jurisprudence, including the decision of the IMT with regard to *Streicher*, there is no 'specific causation requirement linking the expression at issue with the demonstration of a direct effect'.[285]

---

[278] *Prosecutor v Eliezer Niyitegeka*, Case no ICTR-96-14-T, Judgment and Sentence, para 238.
[279] ibid, para 436.
[280] ibid, para 437.
[281] See further Donna E Arzt, 'Nuremberg, Denazification and Democracy', 753.
[282] *Prosecutor v Ferdinand Nahimana, Jean-Bosco Barayagwiza, Hassan Ngeze*, Case no ICTR-99-52-T, Judgment and Sentence, 3 December 2003, para 952. See further Joshua Wallenstein, 'Punishing Words: An Analysis of the Necessity of the Element of Causation in Prosecutions for Incitement to Genocide', 2 Stanford L Rev 54 (2001) 351.
[283] ibid, para 952.
[284] ibid, para 953.
[285] ibid, para 1007.

In the series of 'separatist propaganda' cases which the European Court has heard with regard to Turkey, and which are cited with approval in *Nahimana*, the state was accorded a wide margin of appreciation to restrict the right to freedom of expression despite repeated dissenting opinions criticizing the majority's tendency to allow the state great power.[286] Whereas Turkey asserted that the relevant legislative measures were necessary since 'separatist propaganda inevitably incites to violence and provokes hostility among the various groups in Turkish society thus endangering human rights and democracy',[287] Kerim Yildiz of the Kurdish Human Rights Project argues that such restrictions on publishing and the media:

[...] have long been a central tenet of Turkish determination to maintain the *status quo* of the monolithic, unaccountable state [with] non-violent expression which would be considered perfectly acceptable in a pluralist, democratic society being punished under the heads of 'inciting separatism' or 'terrorism', insulting the organs of the state, inciting racial hatred or aiding an illegal organization.[288]

The Trial Chamber in *Nahimana* made what may be its defining comment when it elaborated upon the role which international law has to play in protecting the individual and the community from the state's propensity to use propaganda to incite to violence. The Tribunal acknowledged that the protection of freedom of political expression has 'historically been balanced in the jurisprudence against the interest in national security', and that the emphasis of much freedom of expression jurisprudence has focused on the role of censorship in the suppression of minorities including opponents of the government.[289] While noting that this approach sought to protect the freedom of expression of those vulnerable to the exercise of power by majority groups or by the government, the Chamber found

[286] *Baikaya and Another v Turkey* (App nos 23536/94, 24408/94), 8 July 1999; *Sürek v Turkey (No. 1)* (App no 26682/95), 8 July 1999; *Gerger v Turkey*, [1999] ECHR 24919/94, 8 July 1999 (App no 24919/94); *Okguoglu v Turkey*, [1999] ECHR 24246/94, 8 July 1999 (App no 24246/94); *Sürek and Another v Turkey* (App nos 23927/94 and 24277/94) 7 BHRC 339; *Arslan v Turkey*, [1999] ECHR 23462/94, (App no 23462/94); *Erdogdu and Another v Turkey*, [1999] ECHR 25067/94, 8 July 1999 (App nos 25067/94, 25068/94); *Karata v Turkey*, [1999] ECHR 23168/94, 8 July 1999 (App no 23168/94); *Polat v Turkey* (App no 23500/94), [1999] ECHR 23500/94; *Sürek v Turkey (No. 4)* (App no 24762/94), [1999] ECHR 24762/94; *Ceylan v Turkey* (App no. 23556/94), 8 July 1999; *Sürek v Turkey (No. 2)* (App no 24122/94), 8 July 1999; *Sürek v Turkey (No. 3)* (App no 24735/94), 8 July 1999.
[287] *Sürek v Turkey (No. 1)* (App no 26682/95), 8 July 1999, para 55.
[288] Kerim Yildiz, *The Kurds in Turkey: EU Accession and Human Rights* (London: Pluto Press, 2005) 49–50. Applicants to the European Court have claimed that the purpose of the legislation was to silence all ideas which were incompatible with the official views of the state, asserting that media which communicate ideas contradicting the official position of the authorities in Turkey 'are accused of disseminating propaganda in favour of terrorist organisations and are punished on the pretext of protecting national security and territorial integrity'. *Erdogdu and Another v Turkey*, [1999] ECHR 25067/94, 8 July 1999, para 44. See also Edel Hughes, 'Hate Speech: A Restriction on Freedom of Expression', 4 KHRP LR 66 (2003).
[289] *Prosecutor v Ferdinand Nahimana, Jean-Bosco Barayagwiza, Hassan Ngeze*, Case no ICTR-99-52-T, Judgment and Sentence, 3 December 2003, para 1008.

that the reality in the immediate case was that the primary issue was the speech of the so-called 'majority population' in support of the government of Rwanda. The Trial Chamber noted that the international jurisprudence on the right to free-dom of expression, and particularly its development 'in the American tradition of free speech', had to be realigned in order that 'ethnically specific expression would be more, rather than less, carefully scrutinized to ensure that minor-ities without equal means of defence are not endangered'.[290] In conclusion, the Chamber stressed that 'the wider margin of appreciation' given by the ECtHR to government discretion in its restriction of expression constituting incitement to violence should therefore be adapted in the circumstances of the immediate case. Asserting that what was at issue was 'not a challenged restriction of expression but the expression itself',[291] the Chamber stated that:

[…] the expression charged as incitement to violence was situated, in fact and at the time by its speakers, not as a threat to national security but rather in defence of national secur-ity, aligning it with state power rather than in opposition to it. Thus there is justifica-tion for adaptation of the application of international standards, which have evolved to protect the right of the government to defend itself from incitement to violence by others against it, rather than incitement to violence on its behalf against others, particularly as in this case when the others are members of a minority group.[292]

The judgment, which is of quite a different tone from the ICTY's pronounce-ments on similar issues, has been widely welcomed as a significant development of international criminal law with regard to hate speech and incitement to geno-cide for its approach to issues such as the causality between words and violence, the inchoate nature of incitement to genocide, and the emphasis on examin-ing speech by reference to the context in which it was made.[293] The Tribunal's recognition of the need for international law to be realigned in order to ensure the protection of individuals and communities from the propaganda of the state itself locates it as a successor to the judgments of the Nuremberg and Tokyo Tribunals. The Trial Chamber in *Akayesu* cited the conviction of Streicher by the IMT at Nuremberg as an example of a famous case of 'incitement to commit crimes of an international dimension'.[294] The approach of the Rwanda Tribunal in cases such as *Akayesu* and *Nahimana* has provided a contemporary basis for the necessity of

---

[290] ibid, para 1008.
[291] ibid, para 1009.
[292] ibid.
[293] Wibke Kristin Timmermann, 'The Relationship between Hate Propaganda and Incitement to Genocide', 257; Catharine A MacKinnon, 'Prosecutor *v* Nahimana, Barayagwiza, & Ngeze. Case no ICTR 99-52-T', 98 AJIL 2 (2004) 325–30; Gregory S Gordon, 'A War of Media, Words, Newspapers, and Radio Stations', 139. Cf Alexander Zahar who contends that the *Nahimana* judg-ment is indicative of the Trial Chamber judges' 'drift into legal activism, at worst legal absurd-ity'. Alexander Zahar, 'The ICTR's "Media" Judgment and the Reinvention of Direct and Public Incitement to Commit Genocide', 16 Crim LF 1 (2005) 33, 48.
[294] *Prosecutor v Jean-Paul Akayesu*, Case no ICTR-96-4-T, Judgment, 2 September 1998, para 550.

the consideration of inclusion in the Rome Statute of a distinct offence of incitement to aggression, the gravest of all international crimes.

C. The Rome Statute of the International Criminal Court

Article 5 of the Rome Statute provides that the jurisdiction of the Court shall be limited to the most serious crimes of concern to the international community as a whole, namely genocide, crimes against humanity, war crimes, and the crime of aggression.[295] Given the failure of the drafters to agree on a definition of the crime of aggression before the adoption of the Statute in 1998, and in response to the strong advocacy of the view that the Statute should include this most serious crime, Article 5(2) provides that the Court may only exercise jurisdiction over the crime of aggression once an acceptable definition is adopted in accordance with Articles 121 and 123 of the Statute.[296] The Preparatory Commission for the International Criminal Court has been charged with the responsibility of formulating a definition of aggression for the Statute.

In light of the development and application of the crime of direct and public incitement to genocide, and a reappraisal by the ad hoc Tribunals of the role which international criminal law has to play in regard to incitement to crimes of an international dimension, significant consideration needs to be given as to whether the formulation of the crime of aggression in the Rome Statute of the International Criminal Court should explicitly provide for a distinct and inchoate crime of direct and public incitement to aggression.[297]

Whereas neither the ICTY nor the ICTR has had jurisdiction over the crime of aggression, the Tribunals' jurisprudence illustrates the centrality of propaganda and incitement to the commission of serious international crimes, and it is not unlikely that in future the International Criminal Court will have to consider also the 'antecedent crime' of incitement to aggression. Murty considered the judgments and charters of the Second World War military tribunals, and the response of the world community thereto, to:

lead us reasonably to expect that in future trials for crimes against peace [...] a person who, having power to shape or influence the policies of his state, plans or conspires to use a strategy of violence for purposes of aggression, or joins such conspiracy, and participates in the ideological strategy—whether to make the necessary psychological preparations at home, or to undermine the will to resist of the people of the state which is intended to be or is actually the victim—will be held guilty of a crime against peace.[298]

---

[295] A/Conf 183/9 (17 July 1998).
[296] Article 5(2), Statute of the International Criminal Court, 17 July 1998, 37 ILM 999.
[297] Rome Statute of the International Criminal Court (1998), UN Doc A/Conf 183/9, entered into force 1 July 2002, 2187 UNTS 90.
[298] BS Murty, *Propaganda and World Public Order*, 151.

The Rome Statute of the International Criminal Court provides the means whereby such expectations may come to be realized. In light of the emphasis placed on incitement as a mode of commission throughout the development of international criminal law a brief consideration of incitement as provided for in Article 25 of the Rome Statute is useful in order to place the need for a distinct crime of incitement to aggression in context with the rest of the Statute.

Article 25 sets forth the grounds for individual criminal responsibility for the crimes within the Court's jurisdiction. Unlike the 1996 Draft Code of Crimes Against the Peace and Security of Mankind, the modes of commission set forth in Article 25(3) (a)–(d) and (f) were intended to apply to all the crimes set forth in the Rome Statute, including aggression, with the exception of Article 25(3)(e) which applies only to the crime of genocide. Kai Ambos has noted that Article 25(3) stands in marked contrast to the International Law Commission's 1996 Draft Codes of Crimes against the Peace and Security of Mankind and the Statutes of the ad hoc International Criminal Tribunals insofar as it distinguishes between perpetration in subparagraph (a), and other forms of participation in subparagraphs (b) and (c).[299] He considers this approach to confirm 'the general tendency in comparative criminal law to reject a pure Unitarian concept of perpetration (*Einheitstätermodell*) and to distinguish, at least on the sentencing level, between different forms of participation'.[300] The International Criminal Court, like its predecessors, is likely to focus not on the actual perpetrators of crimes such as low-ranking soldiers, but rather on those who ordered, organized, planned, and incited genocide, crimes against humanity, war crimes, and aggression.

Article 25(3)(a) of the Statute provides that a person can commit a crime 'as an individual, jointly with another or through another person, regardless of whether that other person is criminally responsible'. Albin Eser notes that the Rome Statute is probably the first international statute in which this mode of indirect perpetratorship of using another person as a tool is explicitly regulated.[301] According to Ambos, such perpetration normally refers to innocent persons who, though they commit the crime, are not responsible as they, in the case of a minor for example, have been used as an instrument or tool by the mastermind, the indirect perpetrator.[302] The scope of this provision may be greatly expanded when considering the field of 'macrocriminality', described by Ambos as the 'systematic or mass criminality organised, supported or tolerated by the State [whereby] the direct perpetrator or executor normally performs the act with the

[299] Kai Ambos, 'Article 25: Individual Criminal Responsibility', in Otto Triffterer (ed), *Commentary on the Rome Statute of the International Criminal Court: Observers' Notes, Article by Article* (Baden-Baden: Nomos Verl, 1999) 475–92, 476–7.

[300] ibid 477.

[301] Albin Eser, 'Individual Criminal Responsibility', in Antonio Cassese, Paolo Gaeta, and John RWD Jones (eds), *The Rome Statute of the International Criminal Court: A Commentary* (Oxford: Oxford University Press, 2002) 767–822, 793.

[302] Kai Ambos, 'Article 25: Individual Criminal Responsibility', 479.

necessary *mens rea* and is fully aware of its illegality'.[303] Eser notes in this regard that whilst committing a crime through a person requires more than soliciting or inducing a person to commit a crime, 'any means of instrumentalising another person to commit a crime, be it the use of force or the exploitation of an error or any other handicap on the tool's side, may suffice, provided that it is the exercise of some controlling predominance on the indirect perpetrator's side'.[304] It may be that 'war propaganda', as considered above in relation to cases before the ICTY, may provide the basis for future convictions for perpetration of crimes under Article 25(3)(a).

Article 25, subparagraphs (b) and (c) set forth the various forms of complicity by which an individual can be held criminally responsible under the Statute. Subparagraph (b) provides individual criminal responsibility for anyone who '[o]rders, solicits or induces the commission of such a crime which in fact occurs or is attempted', while subparagraph (c) imposes responsibility on the person who, '[f]or the purpose of facilitating the commission of such a crime, aids, abets or otherwise assists in its commission or its attempted commission, including providing the means for its commission'.

The 1996 Report of the Preparatory Committee on the Establishment of an International Criminal Court understood 'soliciting' to include 'incitement'.[305] With regard to the 'responsibility of other persons in the completed crimes of principals', Proposal no 1 on 'Participation/Complicity' stated that:

[a] person solicits the commission of a crime if, with the purpose of encouraging another person [making another person decide] to commit [or participate in the commission of] a specific crime, the person commands, [orders], requests, counsels or incites the other person to engage [or participate] in the commission of such crime, and the other person commits a crime [or is otherwise criminally responsible for such crime] as a result of such solicitation.[306]

The Preparatory Committee acknowledged that the definition of incitement for the purposes of the provision on individual criminal responsibility would require that 'the terms of incitement would have to be carefully worded so as to avoid any violations of free speech'.[307] They included a note stating that this proposal recognized 'the importance of being able to punish the planners', and affirmed that it was to be a non-inchoate offence since 'planners are punishable only if a

---

[303] Kai Ambos, 'Article 25: Individual Criminal Responsibility'.

[304] Albin Eser, 'Individual Criminal Responsibility', 794. Ambos states that 'perpetration by means requires a sufficiently tight control by the "Hintermann" over the direct perpetrator, similar to the relationship between superior and subordinate in the case of command responsibility'. Kai Ambos, 'Article 25: Individual Criminal Responsibility', 480.

[305] Report of the Preparatory Committee on the Establishment of an International Criminal Court vol ii (Compilation of proposals) GAOR Supp no 22A (A/51/22), 13 September 1996, 83.

[306] ibid. The words bracketed were specifically highlighted for further discussions.

[307] Report of the Preparatory Committee on the Establishment of an International Criminal Court vol i (Proceedings of the Preparatory Committee during March–April and August 1996), GAOR Supp no 22 (A/51/22), 13 September 1996, 45, para 203.

principal actually committed a crime as a result of such planning or soliciting'.[308] Nevertheless, the Preparatory Committee also suggested for consideration the idea 'that the statute, perhaps in a new and separate article, should also criminalize and punish a person in the situation where that person solicits another person to commit or criminally participate in a crime, but the other person does not commit the crime'.[309]

This latter suggestion was not accepted, and the provision on soliciting, as finally adopted in Article 25(3)(b) of the Rome Statute, required either commission or an attempt at the commission of a crime. According to *Black's Law Dictionary*, soliciting a crime means to command, encourage, request, or incite another person to engage in specific conduct to commit the crime,[310] whilst inducing means to influence another person to commit a crime.[311] Ambos considers soliciting to include incitement[312] and describes inducing as a 'kind of umbrella term covering soliciting which, in turn, has a stronger more specific meaning than inducing. Inducing is broad enough to cover any conduct which causes or leads another person to commit a crime, including soliciting that person.'[313] He surmises that both these forms of complicity are applicable to cases in which a person is influenced by another to commit a crime, noting that 'such influence is normally of psychological nature but may also take the form of physical pressure within the meaning of *vis compulsiva*'. Unlike a case of ordering, however, 'a superior–subordinate relationship is not necessary'.[314]

Eser uses the term 'instigation' to summarize the elements of this provision, stating that this can be done by inducing various persons in a chain provided the first instigator knows and wishes his influence on the first person to be carried on via other persons to the final perpetrator.[315] He considers the mental requirements with regard to the instigator to be reliant on Article 30 of the Rome Statute as no special *mens rea* requirements are referred to in Article 25, other than in relation to the case of aiding and abetting and acting with a common purpose.[316] Thus a double intent is required on behalf of the instigator, who must exert his influence with intent and knowledge of his own conduct and furthermore presuppose that the principal will carry out the crime in a state of mind required by the Statute.

With regard to subparagraphs (b) and (c), Schabas has noted 'a certain redundancy [...] perhaps because of an unfamiliarity of the drafters with the common law term "abets" which, while in paragraph (c), in reality covers everything

---

[308] ibid.
[309] Report of the Preparatory Committee on the Establishment of an International Criminal Court vol ii (Compilation of proposals), GAOR Supp no 22A (A/51/22), 13 September 1996, 83.
[310] *Black's Law Dictionary* (6th edn, 1990) 1392.
[311] ibid 774.
[312] Kai Ambos, 'Article 25: Individual Criminal Responsibility', 486.
[313] ibid 481.
[314] ibid.
[315] Albin Eser, 'Individual Criminal Responsibility', 795.
[316] ibid 797.

described in paragraph (b)'.[317] The International Law Commission's 1996 Draft Code required the act of aiding and abetting to entail assistance to the perpetrator by the accomplice, of a kind which 'contributes *directly* and *substantially* to the commission of the crime'.[318] The Rome Statute omits such requirements, however, and has been considered by the ICTY Trial Chamber in *Furundzija* to be 'less restrictive', since it does not limit aiding and abetting to assistance 'which facilitate[s] in some significant way', or 'directly and 'substantially' assists the perpetrator.[319]

Whereas 'ordinary' incitement, that is, 'incitement as a form of participation in the commission of a consummated crime', undoubtedly applies to all three crimes within the Court's subject-matter jurisdiction,[320] the inchoate crime of 'direct and public incitement' is limited in its application to the crime of genocide. Article 6 of the Rome Statute reproduces almost verbatim the definition of the crime of genocide as set forth in the Genocide Convention, while Article 25(3)(e) provides that anyone 'who directly and publicly incites others to commit genocide' shall be criminally responsible and liable for punishment. The International Law Commission's 1996 Draft Code had provided for a general offence of direct and public incitement, applicable to all crimes in the *Code* including genocide. In spite of citing Article III(c) of the Genocide Convention[321] as the *raison d'être* of the provision, the Commission nonetheless

---

[317] William A Schabas, 'General Principles of Criminal Law in the International Criminal Court Statute (Part III)', 6 Eur J Cr, Crim L & Crim J 4 (1998) 84–112, 95. Schabas also notes that under the statutes of the ad hocs 'instigating' and 'abetting', which are equivalent to incitement, are also criminalized in the general provision dealing with individual responsibility. William A Schabas, 'Hate Speech in Rwanda: The Road to Genocide', 157.

[318] UN Doc A/51/10, Article 2(3)(f), [1996] 2 YB ILC (Part Two) para 11, p. 24.

[319] ibid, para 1, p. 73. The Trial Chamber of the ICTY referred to these criteria in the *Tadic* case where it found that 'substantial' means that the contribution has an effect on the commission of the crime. *Prosecutor v Tadic*, Case no IT-94-1-T, 7 May 1997, paras 674, 688–92 and *Prosecutor v Delalic et al*, Case no IT-96-21-T, 16 November 1998, paras 325–9. In the *Furundzija* judgment the ICTY distinguished between the nature of assistance and its effect on the act of the main perpetrator, finding that the acts of assistance must 'make a significant difference to the commission of the criminal act by the principal'. According to the Trial Chamber, aiding and abetting requires 'practical assistance, encouragement, or moral support which has a substantial effect on the perpetration of the crime'. *Prosecutor v Anto Furundzija*, Case no IT-95-17/1-T, 10 December 1998, paras 190–249. Schabas has suggested that the absence of words like 'substantial' in the Rome Statute, and the failure to follow the International Law Commission draft, may suggest that the Diplomatic Conference meant to reject the higher threshold of the recent case law of The Hague. William A Schabas, 'General Principles of Criminal Law in the International Criminal Court Statute (Part III)', 96. Both Ambos and Eser agree that the 'substantial effect' requirement, as the limiting element of the provision, is a factor which can only be determined on a case-by-case method whereby certain modern theories of imputation and attribution may be taken into consideration by the International Criminal Court. Kai Ambos, 'Article 25: Individual Criminal Responsibility', 482; Albin Eser 'Individual Criminal Responsibility', 801.

[320] William A Schabas, 'National Courts Finally Begin to Prosecute Genocide, the "Crime of Crimes"', 1 J Int'l Crim Just 39 (2003) 53.

[321] Convention on the Prevention and Punishment of the Crime of Genocide New York, 9 December 1948, 78 UNTS 277, Can TS 1949 no 27 (entered into force 12 January 1951).

displayed a 'serious misunderstanding'[322] in specifying that this applied only to inciting a crime that 'in fact occurs'.[323]

There had been some consideration given during the drafting of the Rome Statute to enlarge the inchoate offence of incitement so as to cover the other core crimes. Article 23(7)(f) of the Draft Statute proposed by the Preparatory Committee in April 1998 reproduced Article 17(7)(f) of the Draft Statute in the Report of the Inter-Sessional Meeting of January 1998 in Zutphen.[324] It accorded individual criminal responsibility to anyone who '[directly and publicly] incites the commission of [such a crime] [genocide] [which in fact occurs], [with the intent that such crime be committed]'.[325] It is significant that at this stage of the drafting there remained the possibility that inchoate 'direct and public' incitement would be applicable to each crime included in the Statute. However, the June 1998 Report of the Working Group on General Principles of Criminal Law recommended the inclusion in draft Article 23 on individual criminal responsibility of subparagraph 7(f), which read '[i]n respect of the crime of genocide, directly and publicly incites others to commit genocide',[326] ensuring that the inchoate crime of direct and public incitement related solely to genocide and 'could not be extended to war crimes, crimes against humanity, and aggression'.[327]

It has been shown that in accordance with subparagraphs (b) and (c) of Article 25(3), non-inchoate incitement, that is even indirect and private incitement, may be considered to be a form of commission of the crime of aggression but that 'direct and public incitement', which is narrower than the broader concepts of soliciting or abetting, is applicable only to the crime of genocide.

Roger Clark has argued that since the crime of aggression, by its very nature, 'is a leadership crime involving purposive activity', the structure of Article 25(3) and particularly subparagraphs (a) to (d) do not 'fit' it.[328] He further noted that any attempt to mesh the verbs 'orders' and 'participates' and the nouns 'planning', 'preparation', 'initiation', or 'execution' in the crime of aggression as currently formulated, with the verbs in Article 25(3)(a) to (d), 'would only be a recipe for confusion'.[329] In light of the commentary to the International Law Commission's

---

[322] William A Schabas, 'International Conference: Hate Speech in Rwanda: The Road to Genocide', 156–7.
[323] UN Doc A/51/10, Article 2(3)(f), [1996] 2 YB ILC (Part Two), 15.
[324] Report of the Inter-Sessional Meeting from 19 to 30 January 1998 in Zutphen, the Netherlands, A/AC.249/1998/L.13, 4 February 1998, 53.
[325] Report of the Preparatory Committee on the Establishment of an International Criminal Court (A/Conf 183/2/Add 1, 14 April 1998) 50.
[326] Report of the Working Group on General Principles of Criminal Law, A/Conf 183/C.1/WGGP/L.4 (18 June 1998) 3.
[327] William A Schabas, 'International Conference: Hate Speech in Rwanda: The Road to Genocide', 156. Eser suggests if subparagraph (e) is not to lose its meaning that it must be less understood with regard to a certain individual to be influenced but rather in terms of expressions which not by themselves, 'but by means of misleading interpretations of ill-intentioned mediators are used for provoking genocidal activities'. Albin Eser, 'Individual Criminal Responsibility', 805.
[328] Roger S Clark, 'Rethinking Aggression as a Crime and Formulating its Elements', 883.
[329] ibid.

1996 Draft Code concerning methods of commission of aggression, this observation appears judicious, as does his conclusion that Article 25(3)(a) to (d) should
be specifically excluded from applying to the crime of aggression.[330]

Clark has also raised the question as to whether there should be liability under
the Rome Statute for direct and public incitement to aggression.[331] In a June
2002 proposal by Samoa, for which Clark was largely responsible, this question
was formally suggested for consideration to the Working Group on the Crime
of Aggression.[332] Although the document merely sought 'to flag the issue', it is
extremely significant that the question is a live one in the ongoing drafting process.
The proposal's final comments revisit the jurisprudence of the IMT at Nuremberg
suggesting that where aggression in fact takes place, one who incites to aggression is probably guilty of one or other version of the offence set forth in Samoa's
draft Article 6, namely, that '[t]he perpetrator ordered or participated actively
in the planning, preparation, initiation or waging of the act of aggression'.[333]
Nevertheless, the key aspect of the document is its query as to whether the same
principle that applies in the case of the crime of genocide, namely that direct and
public incitement thereto is a separate offence from participation in a completed
act of genocide and may therefore be prosecuted even though the genocide does
not occur, should apply in the case of the crime of aggression.[334]

While Clark acknowledged that 'weighty free speech arguments', similar to
those made concerning the prohibition of propaganda for war in the International
Covenant on Civil and Political Rights, might be made about penalizing an
incitement to an aggression that does not occur, he stressed that 'a decision needs
to be made'.[335] To date little progress has been made on this subject. The Special
Working Group on the Crime of Aggression failed to discuss the elements of the
crime of aggression in Samoa's proposal,[336] prompting the Working Group's Chair
to state that in light of intervening changes made to the draft provisions, they be
considered 'as a mere placeholder and used for reference purposes only'.[337]

D. Summary

Should the Rome Statute provide for an offence of direct and public incitement
to aggression? It has been noted that the Trial Chamber of the Rwanda Tribunal

---

[330] Roger S Clark, 'Rethinking Aggression as a Crime and Formulating its Elements'.
[331] ibid 884.
[332] Elements of the Crime of Aggression: Proposal by Samoa, PCNICC/2002/WGCA/
DP.2, 21 June 2002.
[333] ibid, para 13.
[334] ibid, paras 16–18.
[335] Roger S Clark, 'Rethinking Aggression as a Crime and Formulating its Elements', 884.
[336] Informal inter-sessional meeting of the Special Working Group on the Crime of Aggression,
23 November to 1 December 2006, ICC-ASP/5/SWGCA/INF.1, 21, fn 11.
[337] Discussion paper proposed by the Chairman, 29 January–1 February 2007, ICC-ASP/5/
SWGCA/2, para 7.

in the *Akayesu* judgment held that 'genocide clearly falls within the category of crimes so serious that direct and public incitement to commit such a crime must be punished as such, even where such incitement failed to produce the result expected by the perpetrator'.[338] It is beyond doubt that aggression must be accepted as falling within this 'category of crimes'. The primary goal of those who established the IMT was not only to hold to account those responsible for the Holocaust, but rather to condemn before the peoples of the world those individuals who had prepared and launched the wars of aggression which provided the setting within which the execution of such immense atrocities was possible. The judgment of the IMT was explicit in this regard, asserting that aggressive war is 'the supreme international crime differing only from other war crimes in that it contains within itself the accumulated evil of the whole'.[339]

Considered in this light, direct and public incitement to aggression must be set forth as a distinct inchoate crime in the Rome Statute. Support for this assertion can be found in several sources. Article 2 of the 1936 Convention on Broadcasting in the Cause of Peace required States parties to prevent the broadcast of material which constituted 'an incitement either to war against another high contracting party or to acts likely to lead thereto'.[340] The offence of direct incitement to aggression was included in the International Law Commission's 1954 Draft Code of Offences Against the Peace and Security of Mankind, its subsequent omission from the 1996 Draft Code, without satisfactory explanation or justification, should not be permitted to prejudice the inclusion of such a crime in the Rome Statute.

Several notable legal publicists have argued that incitement to aggression constitutes a criminal offence in and of itself. Wright considered that customary international law required states to prevent within their territory the incitement of offences against the law of nations including 'warmongering' or incitement of aggressive war; and instigation of filibustering, piracy, or genocide.[341] He asserted that if an act is an offence against the law of nations, either under customary law or by treaty, then so too is incitement 'intended and likely to lead to that act'.[342] Whitton has argued on the basis of the UN Charter that 'when aggressive war becomes illegal, it was only natural that ideological pressures to that end should become illegal as well [hence] war propaganda is held to be illegal by virtue of the general principle of law recognized by all nations that incitement to crime

---

[338] *Prosecutor v Jean-Paul Akayesu*, Case no ICTR-96-4-T, Judgment, 2 September 1998, para 562.

[339] International Military Tribunal (Nuremberg), Judgment and Sentences, 1 October 1946, 186.

[340] Convention Concerning the Use of Broadcasting in the Cause of Peace, Registered no 4319. LON TS, vol 186, 301; vol 197, 394, and vol 200, 557; 17 LON OJ 1438 (1936). Reprinted in 'International Convention Concerning the Use of Broadcasting in the Cause of Peace' 32 AJIL Sup 119 (1938).

[341] Quincy Wright, 'Freedom and Responsibility in Respect of Trans-National Communication', 105.

[342] ibid.

is itself a criminal act'.[343] Soviet jurists had also distinguished between inchoate incitement as a kind of complicity and 'war propaganda' which 'entails criminal responsibility also in the case where aggression did not take place'.[344]

Propaganda for war constituting incitement to war of aggression is prohibited under the International Covenant on Civil and Political Rights and the American Convention on Human Rights, and a large number of states have penal legislation giving effect to this prohibition. Incitement to aggression has also been condemned in many Resolutions and Declarations of the General Assembly including the Declaration on Friendly Relations. In the wake of the Rwandan Genocide, Jamie Metzl asserted that it was imperative that 'traditional Cold War concepts' relating to the response of the international community to incitement to armed conflict and genocide be reconsidered in the light of the threat which they hold for peace.[345] In the *Nahimana* judgment, the Trial Chamber of the ICTR provided an authoritative basis for these suggestions. In finding that 'there is justification for adaptation of the application of international standards, which have evolved to protect the right of the government to defend itself from incitement to violence by others against it, rather than incitement to violence on its behalf against others',[346] contemporary international criminal tribunals have followed the lead taken by the Second World War military tribunals. In the wake of the Second World War the international community declared that it was committed to preventing a repeat of the horrors perpetated during the war. In order to take a belated step towards fulfilling this commitment it is apparent that not only does the crime of direct and public incitement to aggression warrant inclusion in the Rome Statute of the International Criminal Court, but that in the interests of peace and justice, as well as the continued development of international criminal law, such a move is imperative.

---

[343] John B Whitton, 'Hostile Propaganda and International Law', in L John Martin (ed), *Propaganda in International Affairs* 398 Annals of the American Academy of Political and Social Science (1971) 14–25, 21.

[344] *Sovetskoe Ugoluvnie Pravo* [Soviet Criminal Law], Special Part, ed. VD Men'shagin and PS Romashkin (Moscow, 1957) 536–7. Cited in John B Whitton and Arthur Larson, *Propaganda*, 157, fn 120.

[345] Jamie F Metzl, 'Rwandan Genocide and the International Law of Radio Jamming', 172.

[346] *Prosecutor v Ferdinand Nahimana, Jean-Bosco Barayagwiza, Hassan Ngeze*, Case no ICTR-99-52-T, Judgment and Sentence, 3 December 2003, para 1009.

6

Conclusion

The fact that delicts such as aggressive war or abusive propaganda are exceedingly difficult to define, that treaties prohibiting such acts are not easily accepted, and that enforcement against the wrongdoer may not prove feasible in time of crisis, should not discourage the jurist in his effort to establish salutary norms for such unsocial conduct among the nations. Even where these defects are patent, the formulation of the concepts may nevertheless prove to be of great value.[1]

This book has sought to outline the meaning and scope of the prohibition of propaganda for war in international law. Given that it is a subject which has not been analysed in detail for several years, it was necessary to draw on many detailed historical and primary sources in order to contextualize the rationale behind the inclusion of such a prohibition in international law and to determine its meaning.

Whether or not states continue to disregard their obligations to refrain from propaganda for war or to prohibit such as required in accordance with Article 20(1) of the Covenant, it is likely that civil society and human rights campaigners, acting on the national, regional, and international scale, will increasingly seek to have these obligations enforced against states. Similarly, should the crime of aggression, as formulated for the Rome Statute, omit any reference to an inchoate crime of direct and public incitement to aggression, it will nonetheless be likely that the International Criminal Court, as with each of its predecessors, will have to deliberate upon charges of individual criminal responsibility for propaganda which has incited wars of aggression.

In short, propaganda for war has had a grievous impact upon the peace and security of mankind in the age of democracy, and there is little to suggest that in future its exercise will be muted. The challenge remains, therefore, to draw upon both existent and developing provisions of the international law framework in order to reduce and eliminate its impact.

Michael Howard perceived the development of mass society in the early twentieth century and the possibility of government control of communications to have made 'total alienation between belligerent societies, their mutual perceptions as figures of total evil, all too easy'.[2] He identified the intersection of mass participation and

---

[1] John B Whitton, 'International Propaganda', 72 Harv L Rev 396 (1958) 400.
[2] Michael Howard, *'Temperamenta Belli*: Can War be Controlled?' in Michael Howard (ed), *Restraints on War: Studies in the Limitation of Armed Conflict* (Oxford: Oxford University Press, 1979) 1–16, 7.

mass propaganda as having facilitated the 'fundamental tragedy' by which the First World War was transformed from an old style 'war of policy to readjust the balance of power in Europe' to 'a total war between incompatible and mutually exclusive cultures, when in fact it need have been nothing of the kind'.[3]

At the beginning of the twenty-first century propaganda plays a similar role in the planning of further wars within the context of the 'war on terror': directed towards the perpetuation of the idea of an existential conflict in which the opposing parties are intractably divided and there is no partner for peace. Lauterpacht noted that '[i]n the formative period of International Law, the characteristic feature of which is the frequent absence of a clear line of demarcation between the state of war and the state of peace between nations, recourse by Governments to revolutionary propaganda abroad was not an uncommon occurrence'.[4] The absence of such a line of demarcation between the states of war and peace is again a characteristic of contemporary international relations, with governments frequently having recourse to propaganda for war, directed both towards domestic and foreign audiences, which serves to perpetuate the idea that war is inevitable by drawing on heightened fears to keep the world in a constant state of preparation for wars of aggression.

There are three distinct aspects of the prohibition of propaganda for war in international law, each of which overlaps to a significant extent. State responsibility to refrain from propaganda for war, first set forth in the 1936 Broadcasting Convention, has been affirmed in repeated Resolutions and Declarations of the General Assembly, as well as under the International Covenant on Civil and Political Rights which obliges States parties to enact legislation which not only prohibits individuals from engaging in propaganda for war but also governments themselves. The international responsibility of states to refrain from the threat or use of force as set forth in Declaration of Principles of International Law Concerning Friendly Relations includes the requirement that '[i]n accordance with the purposes and principles of the United Nations, states have the duty to refrain from propaganda for wars of aggression'.[5] As with acts of aggression, the prohibition of which the ICJ has ruled to be an erga omnes obligation which states hold to the international community as a whole,[6] there would appear to be a strong case to be made that there is a similar, if less developed, obligation upon states to prohibit propaganda for wars of aggression.

International human rights law prohibits propaganda for war, most notably in the Covenant but also in the American Convention. Although the scope of the meaning of 'propaganda for war' is more comprehensive in the former, the

---

[3] Michael Howard, '*Temperamenta Belli*: Can War be Controlled?' in Michael Howard (ed), *Restraints on War: Studies in the Limitation of Armed Conflict* (Oxford: Oxford University Press, 1979).

[4] Hersch Lauterpacht, 'Revolutionary Propaganda by Governments', 155.

[5] GA Res 2625 (XXV), 24 October 1970, para 3.

[6] Case Concerning the Barcelona Traction, Light and Power Company, Limited, Second Phase (*Belgium v Spain*), ICJ Rep [1970] para 33.

common feature is that States parties are obliged to prohibit by law incitement to wars of aggression. The Covenant additionally requires that a second element of propaganda for war, namely, 'the repeated and insistent expression of an opinion for the purpose of creating a climate of hatred and lack of understanding between the peoples of two or more countries, in order to bring them eventually to armed conflict', be also prohibited by law.[7] Nowak understands this element to constitute intentional actions, 'whereby it is sufficient when intent merely creates or reinforces a willingness to go to war, even if there is no objective, concrete threat of war [and] the propaganda must be specific enough for evaluating whether it relates to war of aggression or not'.[8] Whereas this latter element has rarely been invoked in national legislation or courts, the former element has tended to be interpreted both by States parties and academics as requiring a criminal prohibition.

International criminal law, although not currently containing an explicit crime of incitement to aggression (even if one may be read into 'preparation, planning etc' on the basis of the judgement of the IMT), has a history of such, which in light of the jurisprudence of the ad hoc International Criminal Tribunals, and the increasing awareness of the role which international criminal law has to play as regards crimes of propaganda and incitement, may yet be formulated for inclusion in the Rome Statute. As for the second, 'non-direct' element of propaganda for war, such propaganda had been regarded by the IMT at Nuremberg in the cases of Hess, Keitel, and Rosenberg as constituting an element of Crimes against Peace, and whereas the current development of international criminal jurisprudence towards the criminalization of hate speech or other propaganda which falls short of incitement to crimes may as yet be confused and underdeveloped, it would be incorrect to suggest that significant steps in this direction will not be taken as the international jurisprudence continues to develop.

One of the defining characteristics of the location of the prohibition of propaganda for war in international law to date has been the fact that the discourse on the meaning and scope of the prohibition has been almost exclusively dominated by states. Very little analysis of the sources of international law prohibiting propaganda for war has been undertaken by academics, while human rights activists and non-governmental organizations have accorded little attention to the potential which it presents for the realization of the goal of peace.

This phenomenon takes on a particular significance if it is considered that it is governments themselves, rather than any non-state actor, that are primarily responsible for propaganda for war. They possess not only the means and resources to direct effective propaganda campaigns, but in light of the continuing recourse to wars of aggression in violation of international law, it is apparent that they also have the motive. Having been accorded the opportunity to interpret

---

[7] A/C.3/SR.1079, para 2 (Mr Mello).
[8] Manfred Nowak, *U.N. Covenant on Civil and Political Rights*, 473.

the obligation to prohibit propaganda for war as they see fit, without any input by civil society, states have rejected the prohibition, ostensibly on the grounds of their commitment to protecting human rights. In so doing, states have perpetuated the 'legal vacuum' by which they remain free to engage in such propaganda without any fear of being held to account.

One contributory element to this situation may be as a consequence of the historical perception that the Soviet states had advocated the prohibition of propaganda for war with the primary intention of suppressing legitimate dissent within their territories. To continue to overlook the prohibition on this basis is an error which would vindicate the oppressive nature of the Soviet regimes. Indeed states such as the Czech Republic, as noted above, whilst enthusiastic about their future within the European Union have chosen not to simply reject Soviet era legislation on propaganda for war, but rather to seek to adapt such legislation in light of their nation's development both within the region and internationally.

States have taken several distinct approaches to undermining the prohibition of propaganda for war in international law, the most obvious—and effective—having been to simply ignore it. This has been particularly evident in the failure of the General Assembly to refer to the prohibition in any Resolution since the end of the Cold War. Among those states that have not rejected the Covenant's obligation in an outright manner, two distinct trends emerge. The first is that, rather than give full effect to the obligation by the enactment of domestic legislation, states have relied on general commitments to the cause of peace as evidence of their respect for the principle. In General Comment 11, the Human Rights Committee clearly affirmed that such general commitments were inadequate, asserting that '[f]or article 20 to become fully effective there ought to be a law making it clear that propaganda and advocacy as described therein are contrary to public policy and providing for an appropriate sanction in case of violation'.[9]

The prohibition has been further undermined by the tendency of states to take measures under the guise of prohibiting propaganda for war which are in fact concerned with threats of internal violence. This trend has come to the fore in recent years, and while the Committee has been slow to comment upon its appropriateness, it is clear that the prohibition of propaganda for war relates to wars of aggression and not to other manifestations of violence such as civil war, rebellion, or terrorism. By applying the prohibition to these latter forms of violence states are failing to give effect to the purpose of the provision. In abeyance of their duty to prohibit propaganda for war, states are shifting the purpose of the provision from one which has as its aim the protection of individuals from the state, solely to the protection of the state from perceived threats to its security. Such a development is not only inconsistent with the purpose of the principle, but constitutes a threat to the right to freedom of expression. States are permitted under Article 19(3) of the International Covenant on Civil and Political Rights to restrict the

---

[9] General Comment 11, Article 20 (1983), UN Doc HRI\GEN\1\Rev 1 at 12 (1994), para 2.

right to freedom of expression on grounds of national security or public order, and a move towards taking such measures under Article 20(1) may be interpreted as an attempt to achieve under that provision that which may not be permitted under Article 19.

A significant impediment to the application of the prohibition of propaganda for war in international law, and the primary reason that developments such as these have been permitted to unfurl without comment or criticism, has been the impact of the many reservations to Article 20(1). The primary justification for these reservations has been that since propaganda for war is not defined, it is not possible to respect the obligation to prohibit it by law without violating the right to freedom of expression. The failure to enforce these norms, the lack of state practice or opinio juris on the subject, and the large number of reservations and declarations to Article 20(1) provide little support to suggest that the prohibition of propaganda for war is a prohibition under customary international law.

The challenge facing the application of the prohibition of propaganda for war is not a matter of inadequate norms, but rather an issue of failure to enforce these norms. Continued opposition to the prohibition on the grounds that it cannot be defined adequately so as to be justiciable, and thus is incompatible with guarantees of the right to freedom of expression, require immediate reappraisal. Given the European Court's finding in the Turkish 'separatist propaganda' cases that the word propaganda may be construed as providing for a legitimate restriction on expression, and decisions such as *R v Jones*, wherein the House of Lords held that it was willing and capable of pronouncing on a question of responsibility for the crime of aggression, it would appear that both national and international tribunals are satisfied that they can consider cases concerning the prohibition of propaganda for war, having due regard to the right to freedom of expression, thus negating perhaps the primary arguments of those states which retain reservations to Article 20(1).

Suggestions that legislation based on this definition of propaganda for war would constitute a prima facie violation of the right to freedom of expression often appear to be disingenuous. In General Comment 11 the Committee confirmed that the obligations set forth in Article 20 'are fully compatible with the right of freedom of expression as contained in article 19, the exercise of which carries with it special duties and responsibilities'.[10] The same states which justify their reservations on grounds of respect for freedom of expression nevertheless recognize that that right is not absolute, and have accepted the prohibition in Article 20(2) which requires the obligation to prohibit incitement to hatred and violence, as well as the obligation in Article 4 of the International Convention for the Elimination of Racial Discrimination to prohibit the dissemination of hate propaganda. In condemning the large number of reservations to Article 20(1), the Committee described the provision as 'an achievement of modern international

---

[10] General Comment 11, Article 20 (1983), UN Doc HRI\GEN\1\Rev 1 at 12 (1994), para 2.

law which States parties should regard as a positive development'.[11] In recent years, however, the Committee has shown little initiative in ensuring that Article 20(1) is enforced.

Reservations to Article 20(1) are characterized by the absence of any bona fide intention on behalf of states to overcome concerns regarding the right to freedom of expression by working towards a suitable definition. As demonstrated in the analysis of the *travaux préparatoires* to Article 20(1), a definite meaning of propaganda for war had been suggested by the drafters. At the very least, Article 20(1) requires the prohibition of 'incitement to war'. Whitton and Larson had identified this as constituting the 'hard-core minimal offense in the propaganda field that could and should be prohibited by domestic legislation and that would involve no increase in the threat to the freedom of speech'.[12]

No State party has entered an objection to any of the reservations to Article 20(1). The International Court of Justice, in a Joint Separate Opinion in the *Case Concerning Armed Activities on the Territory of the Congo,* was highly critical of States parties to international human rights treaties, including the International Covenant on Civil and Political Rights, tolerating without question reservations that are 'often of a nature that gives serious concern as to compatibility with the object and purpose of the treaty concerned'.[13] The Opinion noted that when international treaties such as the Covenant were being drafted, it had been envisaged that the vast majority of states would 'scrutinize and object'[14] to any inappropriate reservations, particularly if there were a large number. This has not been realized, however, since '[f]or the great majority, political considerations would seem to prevail'.[15]

Given the failure to date of the Human Rights Committee to hold to account states responsible for violating Article 20(1), the International Court of Justice may provide an effective avenue for consideration of a case on propaganda for war as there had been several suggestions that the ICJ would be a suitable forum to hear cases concerning the 'most damaging and threatening propaganda'.[16] Commenting on the proceedings at the 1948 UN Conference on Freedom of Information and the Press, Whitton had proposed that the regulation of propaganda under international law would be strengthened 'if the treaty obligations against propaganda were accompanied by an agreement to submit all disputes

[11] CCPR/C/SR.391, para 44: Mr Vallejo.

[12] John B Whitton and Arthur Larson, *Propaganda,* 256.

[13] Case Concerning Armed Activities on the Territory of the Congo (New Application: 2002) (*Democratic Republic of the Congo v Rwanda*), Jurisdiction of the Court and Admissibility of the Application, 3 February 2006, General List no 126, para 10.

[14] Joint Separate Opinion of Judge Higgins, Judge Kooijmans, Judge Elaraby, Judge Owada, and Judge Simma, Case Concerning Armed Activities on the Territory of the Congo (New Application: 2002) (*Democratic Republic of the Congo v Rwanda*), Jurisdiction of the Court and Admissibility of the Application, 3 February 2006, General List no 126, para 10.

[15] ibid, para 11.

[16] Adeno Addis, 'International Propaganda and Developing Countries', 536.

over the interpretation and application of the treaty to the International Court of Justice'.[17] The ICJ's judgment in the case of *Democratic Republic of the Congo v Uganda* confirmed that it had jurisdiction over alleged violations of the Covenant. On the basis of a submission by the Congo that Uganda had violated the Covenant,[18] the ICJ accepted that it was relevant to the case,[19] and found that Uganda had violated Article 6(1) and Article 7 thereof.[20] Whitton and Larson considered acceptance of the jurisdiction of the ICJ to be 'a tangible action important to the solution of the propaganda problem'.[21] Given that it is the state which holds most responsibility for engaging in propaganda for war, the ICJ would be an appropriate forum for a case on propaganda for war.

State claims that legislation giving effect to Article 20(1) of the Covenant is unnecessary on the grounds that propaganda for war is not a matter of concern within their jurisdictions or that even if it were then public order legislation would be adequate to deal with offenders are untenable. In the first instance the prohibition of propaganda for war in international law represents an international obligation of concern to the peace and security of the international community at large, with the comprehensive application of the prohibition signifying a crucial step towards ensuring global adherence to the goals and purposes of the UN Charter. Furthermore, it would be unwise for states, particularly in an age of global media and communications, to assume that even if propaganda for war is not an issue of concern within their societies, such will always remain the case.

Suggestions that public order legislation will be adequate to deal with propaganda for war should it arise fail to give sufficient regard to the nature and context of the most egregious manifestations of propaganda for war, as it is engaged in by the representatives of the state itself including government ministers, presidents, army chiefs, and so forth. Propaganda for war is at its most effective when a populace in fear of an alien threat which it does not fully comprehend can be convinced that war is necessary on the basis of the speech of those state representatives framing their propaganda for war in defence of national security. On such occasions public order legislation is unlikely to be adequate to hold to account state officials who are claiming to be acting in defence of public order and national security, thus the need for specific legislation by which any individual may be taken to account for violation of Article 20(1).

[17] John B Whitton, 'UN Conference on Freedom of Information and the Movement against International Propaganda', 87. Article 5 of the Convention on the International Right of Correction (435 UNTS 191, entered into force 24 August 1962) and Article 287(1) of the UN Convention on the Law of the Sea (United Nations Convention on the Law of the Sea, adopted 10 December 1982, 1833 UNTS 397) provide that disputes concerning propaganda can be submitted for settlement to the ICJ.
[18] Case Concerning Armed Activities on the Territory of the Congo (*Democratic Republic of the Congo v Uganda*), Judgment, 19 December 2005, General List no 116, para 190.
[19] ibid, para 217.
[20] ibid, para 219.
[21] John B Whitton and Arthur Larson, *Propaganda*, 265.

During the drafting of the International Covenant on Civil and Political Rights, the delegate of Lebanon was initially opposed to the inclusion of propaganda for war as a permissible limitation to the right to freedom of expression, warning the General Assembly that the real danger 'was not anarchy or individual licence, from which governments required protection, but the excessive development of the modern State, from which the individual required protection'.[22] In the final phase of debates, Lebanon, along with the majority of delegations, supported the inclusion of the prohibition of propaganda for war in the Covenant. This shift in position resulted from the recognition that if the individual and the community at large were to be protected from war, then it was necessary that a comprehensive obligation, independent of the right to freedom of expression, be placed on all states to prohibit propaganda for war under international law.

A clear opportunity for the reinvigoration of the principle at hand, notwithstanding the difficulties involved in achieving consensus on the definition of aggression, pertains to the Rome Statute. In presenting the case that 'warmongering propaganda' should be recognized as an international crime, Wright had displayed a prescient understanding of the challenges which the implementation of the prohibition of propaganda for war in international law would encounter, considering an international crime of incitement to aggression to be necessary because '[s]ecurity from war is a fundamental interest of states protected by international law and national tribunals can not be trusted to penalize propaganda inimical to the security of other states when such propaganda corresponds to national policy'.[23]

International criminal tribunals have provided the clearest analysis of the methods and techniques of propaganda and incitement to international crimes. Indeed, the concept which the drafters of the Covenant spent many years attempting to identify and define had been described in detail in the judgments of both the Nuremberg and Tokyo Tribunals. One of the striking aspects of the overview of the historical development of the crime of incitement to aggression was the manner by which the International Law Commission omitted the crime of direct incitement to aggression, which had been included in the 1954 Draft Code of Offences Against the Peace and Security of Mankind, from its 1996 Draft Code of Crimes Against the Peace and Security of Mankind. Such a retrogressive step may be understood by reference to the negative attitude which many states held towards the prohibition of propaganda for war in international human rights law at this time, and the wish to avoid adding lengthy debates to the Commission's workload.

The lack of emphasis placed on crimes of propaganda and incitement by the International Law Commission stands in marked contrast to the experiences of conflict which the ad hoc International Criminal Tribunals for the Former

---

[22] A/C.3/SR.575, para 18 (Mr Azkoul, 5 November 1954).
[23] Quincy Wright, 'The Crime of "War-Mongering"', 133.

Yugoslavia and Rwanda have had to confront. The likelihood is that as the Tribunals continue their work, ever greater emphasis will be placed on crimes of incitement and the criminalization of speech aimed at fomenting international crimes. This is evidenced by the indictment of an individual for engaging in 'war propaganda' at the ICTY,[24] and the stance taken by the ICTR in the *Nahimana* case.[25] In stressing the significance of the IMT at Nuremberg examining not only previously recognized crimes such as war crimes, but additionally the planning and preparation of aggression, Peter Calvocoressi maintained that '[t]he root of the evil is the antecedent crime and to have ignored it at Nuremberg would have been ostrich-like futility'.[26] Similarly, propaganda for war is an invariable factor in the build-up to wars and acts of aggression, and for the international community to continue to permit Article 20(1) of the Covenant to lapse in the recesses of the international human rights framework, or to exclude an inchoate crime of direct and public incitement to aggression from the Rome Statute of the International Criminal Court, will be contradistinctive to the progressive development of international criminal justice and the cause of peace.

[24] *Prosecutor v Vojislav Seselj*, Modified Amended Indictment, Case no IT-03-67, 15 July 2005, para 10(c).

[25] *Prosecutor v Ferdinand Nahimana, Jean-Bosco Barayagwiza, Hassan Ngeze*, Case no ICTR-99-52-T, Judgment and Sentence, 3 December 2003.

[26] Peter Calvocoressi, *Nuremberg: The Facts, the Law and the Consequences* (New York: Macmillan, 1948) 44.

Bibliography

Ackerman, Carl W, 'The Prelude to War' 192 *Annals of the American Academy of Political and Social Science: The United States and World War* 38 (1937).

Addis, Adeno, 'International Propaganda and Developing Countries' 20 *Vanderbilt Journal of Transnational Law* 491 (1988).

—— 'The Thin State in Thick Globalism: Sovereignty in the Information Age' 37 *Vanderbilt Journal of Transnational Law* 1 (2004).

Aguirre, Mariano, and Ferrandiz, Francisco (eds), *The Emotion and the Truth: Studies in Mass Communication and Conflict* (Bilbao: University of Deusto, 2002).

Aisenberg, Elizabeth A, and Eppenstein, Madeline, 'Radio Propaganda in the Contexts of International Regulation and the Free Flow of Information as a Human Right' 5 *Brooklyn Journal of International Law* 154 (1979).

Akhavan, Payam, 'Beyond Impunity: Can International Criminal Justice Prevent Future Atrocities?' 95 *American Journal of International Law* 7 (2001).

Allain, Jean, and Jones, John RWD, 'A Patchwork of Norms: A Commentary on the 1996 Draft Code of Crimes against the Peace and Security of Mankind', 8 *European Journal of International Law* 100 (1997).

Alsdorf, Robert H, 'The Sound of Silence: Thoughts of a Sitting Judge on the Problem of Free Speech and the Judiciary in a Democracy' 30 *Hastings Constitutional Law Quarterly* 197 (2003).

Alvarez, Jose E, 'Crimes of States/Crimes of Hate: Lessons from Rwanda' 24 *Yale Journal of International Law* 365 (1999).

Amann, Diane Marie, 'International Decisions: Prosecutor v. Akayesu. Case ICTR-96-4-T. International Criminal Tribunal for Rwanda, September 2, 1998' 93 *American Journal of International Law* 195 (1999).

Antkowiak, Thomas M, 'Truth as Right and Remedy in International Human Rights Experience' 23 *Michigan Journal of International Law* 977 (2002).

Arcia, Omar Javier, 'War over the Airwaves: A Comparative Analysis of U.S. and Cuban Views on International Law and Policy Governing Transnational Broadcasts' 5 *Journal of Transnational Law and Policy* 199 (1996).

Arzt, Donna E, 'Nuremberg, Denazification and Democracy: The Hate Speech Problem at the International Military Tribunal' 12 *New York Law School Journal of Human Rights* 3 (1995) 689.

Bailey, James Edwin, 'Current and Future Legal Uses of Direct Broadcast Satellites in International Law' 45 *Louisiana Law Review* 701 (1985).

Bassiouini, M Cherif, *A Draft Criminal Code and Draft Statute for an International Criminal Court* (Dordrecht: Martinus Nijhoff, 1987).

—— 'Observations Concerning the 1997–98 Preparatory Commission's Work' 25 *Denver Journal of International Law and Policy* 397 (1996–7).

—— 'Negotiating the Treaty of Rome on the Establishment of an International Criminal Court' 32 *Cornell International Law Journal* 443 (1999).

Bassiouini, M Cherif and Nanda, Ved P (eds), *International Criminal Law,* vol i (Springfield, Ill: Charles C Thomas, 1974).

Bayer, Stephen D, 'The Legal Aspects of TV Marti in Relation to the Law of Direct Broadcasting Satellites' 41 *Emory Law Journal* 541 (1992).

Beinin, Joel, 'Money, Media and Policy Consensus: The Washington Institute for Near East Policy' 180 *Middle East Report* (January–February 1993) 10.

Biddle, Francis, 'The Nurnberg Trial' 33 *Virginia Law Review* 6 (1947) 679.

Bloed, Arie, and van Dijk, P, *Essays on Human Rights in the Helsinki Process* (Dordrecht: Martinus Nijhoff, 1985).

Bobrakov, Yuri, 'War Propaganda: A Serious Crime against Humanity' 31 *Law and Contemporary Problems* 473 (1966).

Boegli, Urs, 'A Few Thoughts on the Relationship between Humanitarian Agencies and the Media' 325 *International Review of the Red Cross* 627 (1998).

Bossuyt, MJ, *Guide to the 'Travaux Préparatoires' of the International Covenant on Civil and Political Rights* (Dordrecht: Martinus Nijhoff, 1987).

Boyle, A, 'Political Broadcasting, Fairness and Administrative Law' [1986] *Public Law* 562.

Brownling, Gary, Halci, Abigail, and Webster, Frank (eds), *Understanding Contemporary Society: Theories of the Present* (London: Sage, 2000).

Buergenthal, Thomas, 'The Revised OAS Charter and the Protection of Human Rights' 69 *American Journal of International Law* 929 (1975).

—— and Kiss, Alexandre, *La Protection internationale des droits de l'homme: précis* (Kehl: NP Engel, 1991).

—— Norris, Robert, and Shelton, Dinah (eds), *Protecting Human Rights in the Americas: Selected Problems* (3rd edn, Kehl: NP Engel, 1990).

Burkitt, Ian, 'Powerful Emotions: Power, Government and Opposition in the "War on Terror"' 39 *Sociology* 4 (2005) 679.

Butler, WS, 'The Teaching of International Law in the USSR' 8 *Review of Socialist Law* 183 (1982).

Calvocoressi, Peter, *Nuremberg: The Facts, the Law and the Consequences* (New York: Macmillan, 1948).

Carey, Alex, *Taking the Risk out of Democracy: Corporate Propaganda Versus Freedom and Liberty* (Urbana: University of Illinois Press, 1997).

Caron, David D, 'War and International Adjudication: Reflections on the 1899 Peace Conference', 94 *American Journal of International Law* 4 (2000).

Casey, Ralph D, 'The Press, Propaganda, and Pressure Groups' 219 *Annals of the American Academy of Political and Social Science: The Press in the Contemporary Scene* 16 (1942).

Cassese, Antonio, *Violence and Law in the Modern Age* (Princeton: Princeton University Press, 1988).

—— *International Criminal Law* (Oxford: Oxford University Press, 2003).

—— Gaeta, Paolo, and Jones, John RWD (eds), *The Rome Statute of the International Criminal Court: A Commentary* (Oxford: Oxford University Press, 2002).

Chapman, James, 'The Power of Propaganda' 35 *Journal of Contemporary History* 4 (2000) 679.

Chomsky, Noam, *Media Control: The Spectacular Achievements of Propaganda* (2nd edn, New York: Seven Stories Press, 2002).

Christol, Carl Q, 'The 1974 Brussels Convention Relating to the Distribution of Program-Carrying Signals Transmitted by Satellite: An Aspect of Human Rights' 6 *Journal of Space Law* 19 (1978).

Clark, Roger S, 'Rethinking Aggression as a Crime and Formulating its Elements: The Final Work-Product of the Preparatory Commission for the International Criminal Court' 15 *Leiden Journal of International Law* (2002) 859.

Codding, George A, 'Jamming and the Protection of Frequency Assignments' 49 *American Journal of International Law* 384 (1955).

Collins, Antoine L, 'Caging the Bird Does Not Cage the Song: How the International Covenant on Civil and Political Rights Fails to Protect Free Expression over the Internet' 21 *Marshall Journal of Computer and Information Law* 371 (2003).

Commonwealth Secretariat, *Freedom of Expression, Assembly and Association: Best Practice* (London, 2002).

Cull, Nicholas J, *Selling War: The British Propaganda Campaign against American 'Neutrality' in World War II* (New York: Oxford University Press, 1995).

Dale, Alexander C, 'Countering Hate Messages that Lead to Violence: The United Nations's Chapter VII Authority to use Radio Jamming to Halt Incendiary Broadcasts' 11 *Duke Journal of Comparative and International Law* 109 (2001).

Dalfen, CM, 'Direct Satellite Broadcasting: Towards International Agreements to Transcend and Marshal the Political Realities' 20 *University of Toronto Law Journal* 366 (1970).

Delgado, Richard, 'The Language of the Arms Race: Should the People Limit Government Speech?' 64 *Boston University Law Review* 961 (1984).

de Vattel, Éméric, *The Law of Nations or the Principles of Natural Law: Applied to the Conduct and to the Affairs of Nations and of Sovereigns* 3, trans Charles G Fenwick (Washington: Carnegie Institution of Washington, 1916).

De Zayas, A, Moller, J, and Opsahl, T, 'Application by the Human Rights Committee of the International Covenant on Civil and Political Rights under the Optional Protocol' *Canadian Yearbook of International Law* 101 (1986).

Dinstein, Yoram, *War, Aggression and Self-Defence* (3rd edn, Cambridge: Cambridge University Press, 2001).

Dixon, Rod, 'Developing International Rules of Evidence for the Yugoslav and Rwanda Tribunals' 7 *Transnational Law and Contemporary Problems* 81 (1997).

Dolgoff, Sam (ed), *Bakunin on Anarchy* (London: George Allen & Unwin, 1973).

Douglas, Roger, 'Law, War and Liberty: The World War II Subversion Prosecutions' 27 *Melbourne University Law Review* 65 (2003).

Downey, Elizabeth A, 'A Historical Survey of the International Regulation of Propaganda' 5 *Michigan Yearbook of International Legal Studies* 341 (1984).

Eftekhari, Shiva, 'France and the Algerian War: From a Policy of "Forgetting" to a Framework for Accountability' 34 *Columbia Human Rights Law Review* 413 (2003).

Ehard, Hans, 'The Nuremberg Trial against the Major War Criminals and International Law' 43 *American Journal of International Law* 2 (1949) 223.

Erlich, Reese, and Solomon, Norman, *Target Iraq: What the News Media Didn't Tell You* (New York: Context Books, 2003).

Falk, Richard A, 'On Regulating International Propaganda: A Plea for Moderate Aims' 31 *Law and Contemporary Problems* 622 (1966).

Farer, Tom J, 'Political and Economic Coercion in Contemporary International Law' 79 *American Journal of International Law* 405 (1985).

Farrior, Stephanie, 'Molding the Matrix: The Historical and Theoretical Foundations of International Law Concerning Hate Speech' 14 *Berkeley Journal of International Law* 3 (1996).

Feldbrugge, FJM, and Simons, William B (trans), 'Constitution (Fundamental Law) of the Union of Soviet Socialist Republics' 4 *Review of Socialist Law* 57 (1958).

Fenwick, Charles G, 'The Use of the Radio as an Instrument of Foreign Propaganda' 32 *American Journal of International Law* 339 (1938).

—— 'Intervention by Way of Propaganda' 35 *American Journal of International Law* 626 (1941).

—— 'Freedom of Communication across National Boundaries' 44 *American Society of International Law Proceedings* 107 (1950).

—— 'Proposed Control over the Radio as an Inter-American Duty in Cases of Civil Strife' 48 *American Journal of International Law* 289 (1954).

Fischer, Hugo, 'The Human Rights Covenants and Canadian Law' 15 *Canadian Yearbook of International Law* 42 (1977).

Fish, Stanley, *There's No Such Thing as Free Speech (and it's a Good Thing Too)* (Oxford: Oxford University Press, 1994).

Ford, Nick Aaron (ed), *Language in Uniform: A Reader on Propaganda* (New York: The Odyssey Press, 1967).

Freeman, Jennifer, 'Toward the Free Flow of Information: Direct Television Broadcasting via Satellite' 13 *Journal of International Law and Economics* 359 (1978–9).

Freeman, Mark, and Van Ert, Gibran, *International Human Rights Law* (Toronto: Irwin, 2004).

Fridemaan, W, 'Hostile Propaganda' 50 *American Journal of International Law* 498 (1956).

Fugh, John L, 'DAJA-ZX: Memorandum for Staff and Command Judge Advocates: SUBJECT: Relations with News Media—Policy Memorandum 91–2' *Army Law* 4 (1991).

Fulbright, J William, *The Pentagon Propaganda Machine* (New York: Vintage, 1971)

Gearty, Conor, *Principles of Human Rights Adjudication* (Oxford: Oxford University Press, 2005).

Giles, OC, 'Judge-Made Crimes in Eastern Germany' 19 *Modern Law Review* 3 (1956) 313.

Glueck, Sheldon, *The Nuremberg Trial and Aggressive War* (New York: AA Knopf, 1946).

Goldberg, David, 'Transnational Communication and Defamatory Speech: A Case for Establishing Norms for the Twenty-First Century' 50 *New York Law School Law Review* 146 (2005–6).

Goldstone, Richard J, 'Do Judges Speak Out?' 111 *South African Law Journal* 258 (1994).

—— 'The South African Bill of Rights' 32 *Texas International Law Journal* 451 (1997).

—— 'The Role of International Criminal Law in the Prosecution of War Crimes' 16 *Temple International and Comparative Law Journal* 371 (2002).

Gordon, George N, Falk, Irving, and Hoddap, William, *The Idea Invaders* (New York: Hastings House, 1963).

Gordon, Gregory S, ' "A War of Media, Words, Newspapers, and Radio Stations": The ICTR Media Trial Verdict and a New Chapter in the International Law of Hate Speech' 45 *Vanderbilt Journal of International Law* 139 (2004).

Graefrath, B, 'How Different Countries Implement Standards on Human Rights' *Canadian Yearbook of International Law* 3 (1984–5).

Graubart, Jonathan, 'What's News: A Progressive Framework for Evaluating the International Debate over the News' 77 *California Law Review* 629 (1989).

Gray, Christine, *International Law and the Use of Force* (2nd edn, Oxford: Oxford University Press, 2004).

Green, Lezlie L, 'Gender Hate Propaganda and Sexual Violence in the Rwandan Genocide: An Argument for Intersectionality in International Law' 33 *Columbia Human Rights Law Review* 733 (2002).

Greenawalt, Alexander KA, 'Rethinking Genocidal Intent: The Case for a Knowledge-Based Interpretation' 99 *Columbia Law Review* 8 (1999) 2259.

Grossman, Claudio, 'Freedom of Expression in the Inter-American System for the Protection of Human Rights' 7 *ILSA Journal of International and Comparative Law* 619 (2001).

Grzybowski, Kazimierz, 'Propaganda and the Soviet Concept of World Public Order' 31 *Law and Contemporary Problems* 479 (1966).

Gullace, Nicoletta F, 'Sexual Violence and Family Honor: British Propaganda and International Law during the First World War' 102 *American Historical Review* 3 (1997) 714.

Gutman, Roy W, 'Spotlight on Violations of International Humanitarian Law: The Role of the Media' 325 *International Review of the Red Cross* 619 (1998).

Haack, Susan, 'Truth, Truths, "Truth", and "Truths" in the Law' 26 *Harvard Journal of Law and Public Policy* 1 (2003) 17.

Hannum, Hurst, and Fischer, Dana D, *U.S. Ratification of the International Covenants on Human Rights* (New York: Transnational, 1993).

Harris, David J, and Livingstone, Stephen (eds), *The Inter-American System of Human Rights* (Oxford: Clarendon Press, 1998).

Hawthorn, Jeremy (ed), *Propaganda, Persuasion and Polemic* (London: Edward Arnold Publishers, 1987).

Hazard, John N, 'The Position of the Soviet Union in Respect to Trans-National Communication' 14 *American Society of International Law Proceedings* 109 (1950).

Henkin, Louis, 'International Human Rights as Rights' 1 *Cardozo Law Review* 425 (1979).

—— (ed), *The International Bill of Rights: The Covenant on Civil and Political Rights* (New York: Columbia University Press, 1981).

Herman, Edward S, and Chomsky, Noam, *Manufacturing Consent: The Political Economy of the Mass Media* (London: Vintage, 1994).

Heyns, Christof, and Viljoen, Frans, *The Impact of the United Nations Human Rights Treaties on the Domestic Level* (The Hague: Kluwer, 2002).

Holtman, Robert B, *Napoleonic Propaganda* (Baton Rouge: Louisiana State University Press, 1950).

Hopkin, Deian, 'Domestic Censorship in the First World War' 5 *Journal of Contemporary History* 4 (1970) 151.

Howard, Michael (ed), *Restraints on War: Studies in the Limitation of Armed Conflict* (Oxford: Oxford University Press, 1979).

Hudson, Manley O, 'The Development of International Law since the War' 22 *American Journal of International Law* 330 (1928).

Hughes, Edel, 'Hate Speech: A Restriction on Freedom of Expression' 4 *Kurdish Human Rights Project Law Review* 66 (2003).

Jackall, Robert, *Propaganda* (London: Macmillan, 1995).

Jakobsen, Peter Viggo, 'National Interest, Humanitarianism or CNN: What Triggers UN Peace Enforcement after the Cold War?' 33 *Journal of Peace Research* 205 (1996).

—— 'Focus on the CNN Effect Misses the Point: The Real Media Impact on Conflict Management Is Invisible and Indirect' 37 *Journal of Peace Research* 2 (2000) 131.

Jay, William, *War and Peace: The Evils of the First and a Plan for Preserving the Last* (New York: Wiley & Putnam, 1842) (reprinted, New York: Oxford University Press, 1919).

Jayawickrama, Nihal, *The Judicial Application of Human Rights Law: National, Regional and International Jurisprudence* (Cambridge: Cambridge University Press, 2002).

Jewett, Arno, 'Detecting and Analyzing Propaganda' 29 *English Journal* 2 (1940) 105.

Johnson, DHN, 'International Control of Propaganda; Propaganda and World Public Order: The Legal Regulation of the Ideological Instrument of Coercion' 17 *International Comparative Law Quarterly* 3 (1968) 790.

Johnson, Loch K, 'On Drawing a Bright Line for Covert Operations' 86 *American Journal of International Law* 284 (1992).

Joseph, Sarah, Schultz, Jenny, and Castan, Melissa, *The International Covenant on Civil and Political Rights: Cases, Materials and Commentary* (Oxford: Oxford University Press, 2000).

Kearney, Michael, 'The Extraterritorial Jurisdiction of the European Convention on Human Rights' 5 *Trinity College Law Review* 158 (2002).

—— 'The Prohibition of Propaganda for War in the International Covenant on Civil and Political Rights' 23 *Netherlands Quarterly of Human Rights* 4 (2005) 551.

Kearney, Richard, *Strangers, Gods and Monsters* (London: Routledge, 2003).

Kellogg, Tom, 'Legislating Rights: Basic Law, Article 23, National Security, and Human Rights in Hong Kong' 17 *Columbia Journal of Asian Law* 307 (2003–4).

Kirsch, Philippe, and Holmes, John T, 'The Rome Conference on an International Criminal Court: The Negotiating Process' 93 *American Journal of International Law* 2 (1999).

Kittichaisaree, Kriangsak, *International Criminal Law* (New York: Oxford University Press, 2001).

Komarov, Gary, 'Individual Responsibility under International Law: The Nuremberg Principles in Domestic Legal Systems' 2 *International and Comparative Law Quarterly* 1 (1980) 21.

Kong, Stephen, 'The Right of Innocent Passage: A Case Study on Two Koreas' 11 *Minnesota Journal of Global Trade* 373 (2002).

Krsticevic, Viviana, 'How Inter-American Human Rights Litigation Brings Free Speech to the Americas' 4 *Southwestern Journal of Law and Trade in the Americas* 209 (1997).

Kuner, Christopher B, 'Linguistic Equality in International Law: Miscommunication in the Gulf Crisis' 2 *Indiana International and Comparative Law Review* 175 (1991).

Lane, Robert E, and Sears, David O, *Public Opinion* (Englewood Cliffs, NJ: Prentice-Hall, 1964).

Larson, Arthur, 'The Present Status of Propaganda in International Law' 31 *Law and Contemporary Problems* 439 (1966).

Lasswell, Harold D, 'Psychology of Propaganda', in *Proceedings of the Sixth Conference of Teachers of International Law and Related Subjects* (Washington: Carnegie Endowment for International Peace, 1938), 52.

—— 'The Conditions of Security in a Bi-Polarizing World' 44 *American Society of International Law Proceedings* 3 (1950).

—— *Politics: Who Gets What, When, How* (New York: Meridian Books, 1958).

—— *Propaganda Techniques in World War I* (Cambridge, Mass: MIT Press, 1971).

Laursen, Andreas, 'NATO, the War over Kosovo, and the ICTY Investigation' 17 *American University International Law Review* 765 (2002).

Lauterpacht, Hersch, 'Revolutionary Activities of Private Persons against Foreign States' 22 *American Journal of International Law* 105 (1928).

—— 'Revolutionary Propaganda by Governments' 13 *Transactions of the Grotius Society* 143 (1928).

Lee, Jennifer, 'Peace and the Press: Media Rules during U.N. Peacekeeping Operations' 30 *Vanderbilt Journal of Transnational Law* 135 (1997).

Lerner, Nathan, *The UN Convention on the Elimination of All Forms of Racial Discrimination: A Commentary* (Leiden: Sijthoff, 1970).

LeShan, Lawrence, *The Psychology of War: Comprehending its Mystique and its Madness* (New York: Helios, 2002).

Linarelli, John, 'An Examination of the Proposed Crime of Intervention in the Draft Code of Crimes against the Peace and Security of Mankind' 18 *Suffolk Transnational Law Review* 1 (1995).

Lippman, Matthew, 'The Recognition of Conscientious Objection to Military Service as an International Human Right' 21 *California Western International Law Journal* 61 (1990–1).

—— 'Crimes against Humanity' 17 *Boston College Third World Law Journal* 171 (1997).

—— 'The Good Motive Defense: Ernst Von Weizsaecker and the Nazi Ministries Case' 7 *Touro International Law Review* 57 (1997).

Lippmann, Walter, *Liberty and the News* (Harcourt: Brace & Howe, 1920).

Lisann, Mavry, *Broadcasting to the Soviet Union: International Politics and Radio* (New York: Praeger, 1975).

Lumley, Frederick E, *The Propaganda Menace* (New York: D. Appleton–Century Company, 1933).

Lurie, Jonathan, 'Andrew Jackson, Martial Law, Civilian Control of the Military, and American Politics: An Intriguing Amalgam' 126 *Military Law Review* 133 (1989).

Luther, LF, *The United States and the Direct Broadcasting Satellite: The Politics of International Broadcasting in Space* (New York: Oxford University Press, 1988).

McDougal, Myres S, and Feliciano, Florentino P, 'International Coercion and World Public Order: The General Principles of the Law of War' 67 *Yale Law Journal* 5 (1958) 771.

McGoldrick, Dominic, *The Human Rights Committee: Its Role in the Development of the International Covenant on Civil and Political Rights* (Oxford: Clarendon, 1991).

McGoldrick, Dominic, 'The Interface between Public Emergency Powers and International Law' 2 *International Journal of Constitutional Law* 2 (2004) 380.

MacKinnon, Catharine A, 'Prosecutor v. Nahimana, Barayagwiza, & Ngeze. Case No. ICTR 99-52-T' 98 *American Journal of International Law* 2 (2004) 325.

Macksey, Kenneth, and Woodhouse, William, *The Penguin Encyclopaedia of Modern Warfare: From the Crimean War to the Present Day* (London: Viking, 1991).

McWhinney, Brian, 'The "New" Countries and the "New" International Law: The United Nations' Special Conference on Friendly Relations and Co-operation amongst States' 60 *American Journal of International Law* 1 (1966).

Marcus, Maria L, 'Policing Speech on the Airwaves: Granting Rights, Preventing Wrongs' 15 *Yale Law and Policy Review* 447 (1997).

Martin, L John, *International Propaganda: Its Legal and Diplomatic Control* (Minneapolis: University of Minnesota Press, 1958).

Matsuda, Mari J 'Public Response to Racist Speech: Considering the Victim's Story' 87 *Michigan Law Review* 2320 (1989).

Melvern, Linda, *Conspiracy to Murder: The Rwandan Genocide* (London: Verso, 2004).

Meron, Theodor, 'The Meaning and Reach of the International Convention on the Elimination of All Forms of Racial Discrimination' 79 *American Journal of International Law* 283 (1985).

Metzl, Jamie F, 'Rwandan Genocide and the International Law of Radio Jamming' 91 *American Journal of International Law* 628 (1997).

Mgret, Fredric, 'War? Legal Semantics and the Move to Violence' 13 *European Journal of International Law* 361 (2002).

Miller, David (ed), *Tell Me Lies: Propaganda and Media Distortion in the Attack on Iraq* (London: Pluto Press, 2004).

Mitchell, Mairín, *Storm over Spain* (London: Secker, 1937).

Moller, Jakob, and de Zayas, Alfred, 'Optional Protocol Cases Concerning the Nordic States before the United Nations Human Rights Committee' 55 *Nordic Journal of International Law* 398 (1986).

Moore, John Norton, 'The Secret War in Central America and the Future of World Order' 80 *American Journal of International Law* 43 (1986).

Morsink, Johannes, *The Universal Declaration of Human Rights: Origins, Drafting, and Intent* (Philadelphia: University of Pennsylvania, 1999).

Murty, BS, *Propaganda and World Public Order: The Legal Regulation of the Ideological Instrument of Coercion* (New Haven: Yale University Press, 1968).

Ni Aolain, Fionnuala, 'The Emergence of Diversity: Differences in Human Rights Jurisprudence' 19 *Fordham International Law Journal* 101 (1995).

Nordenstreng, Kaarle, and Schiller, Herbert I (eds), *National Sovereignty and International Communication* (Norwood, NJ: Ablex, 1979).

Novick, Ben, *Conceiving Revolution: Irish Nationalist Propaganda during the First World War* (Dublin: Four Courts Press, 2001).

Nowak, Manfred, *U.N. Covenant on Civil and Political Rights: CCPR Commentary* (Kehl: NP Engel, 1993).

—— *U.N. Covenant on Civil and Political Rights: CCPR Commentary* (2nd edn, Kehl: NP Engel, 2005).

—— *Introduction to the International Human Rights Regime* (Leiden: Martinus Nijhoff, 2003).

Nuttal, Colby C, 'Defining International Satellite Communications as Weapons of Mass Destruction: The First Step in a Compromise between National Sovereignty and the Free Flow of Ideas' 27 *Houston Journal of International Law* 389 (2005).

O'Brien, William V, 'International Propaganda and Minimum World Public Order' 31 *Law and Contemporary Problems* 589 (1966).

Office of United States Chief of Counsel for Prosecution of Axis Criminality, *Nazi Conspiracy and Aggression: Opinion and Judgement* (Washington: United States Government Printing Office, 1947).

Olusanya, Olaoluwa (ed), *Rethinking International Criminal Law: The Substantive Part* (Groningen: Europa Law, 2007).

O'Malley, Eric S, 'Destabilization Policy: Lessons from Reagan on International Law, Revolutions and Dealing with Pariah Nations' 43 *Vanderbilt Journal of International Law* 319 (2003).

Overy, Richard, *Interrogations: The Nazi Elite in Allied Hands, 1945* (London: Penguin Press, 2001).

Pasqualucci, Jo M, *The Practice and Procedure of the Inter-American Court of Human Rights* (Cambridge: Cambridge University Press, 2003).

Patrick, Jack B, 'Trial Defense Service Notes: The Case of the Famous Client: Effects of the Media on Ethics, Influence, and Fair Trials' *Army Law* 24 (1988)

Paul, Joel R, 'Images from Abroad: Making Direct Broadcasting by Satellites Safe for Sovereignty' 9 *Hastings International and Comparative Law Review* 329 (1986).

Pella, Vespasien, 'Un nouveau délit: la propagande pour la guerre d'agression' *Revue de droit international* 174 (1929).

—— 'La protection de la paix par le droit interne' *Revue générale de droit international public* 40 (1933) 401.

Peterson, HC, *Propaganda for War: The Campaign against American Neutrality, 1914–1917* (Norman: University of Oklahoma, 1939).

Plate, Christoph, 'Journalists' Reports Cannot Prevent Conflict' 839 *International Review of the Red Cross* 617 (2000).

Poltak, Celeste, 'Humanitarian Intervention: A Contemporary Interpretation of the Charter of the United Nations' 60 *University of Toronto Faculty of Law Review* 1 (2002).

Powell, John T, 'Towards a Negotiable Definition of Propaganda for International Agreements Related to Direct Broadcast Satellites' 45 *Law and Contemporary Problems* 3 (1982).

Preuss, Lawrence, 'International Responsibility for Hostile Propaganda against Foreign States' 28 *American Journal of International Law* (1934) 649.

Prevost, Ann Marie, 'Race and War Crimes: The 1945 War Crimes Trial of General Tomoyuki Yamashita' 14 *Human Rights Quarterly* 3 (1992) 303.

Price, Monroe E, 'Part II. The Bill and Comparative Media Law: Conclusion' 5 *Cardozo Journal of International and Comparative Law* 541 (1997).

—— and Thompson, Mark (eds), *Forging Peace: Intervention, Human Rights and the Management of Media Space* (Edinburgh: Edinburgh University Press, 2002).

Ramcharan, BG (ed), *The Right to Life in International Law* (Dordrecht: Martinus Nijhoff, 1985).

Rawls, John, *A Theory of Justice* (Cambridge, Mass: Harvard University Press, 1971).

Rayfuse, Rosemary, 'The Draft Code of Crimes against the Peace and Security of Mankind: Eating Disorders at the International Law Commission' 8 *Criminal Law Forum* 43 (1997).

Richstad, Jim, and Anderson, Michael H (eds), *Crisis in International News: Policies and Prospects* (New York: Columbia University Press, 1981).

Robertson, AH, 'The United Nations Covenant on Civil and Political Rights and the European Convention on Human Rights' 43 *British Yearbook of International Law* 21 (1968–9).

—— *Human Rights in the World* (Manchester: Manchester University Press, 1972).

Robinson, Piers, 'The Policy–Media Interaction Model: Measuring Media Power during Humanitarian Crisis' 37 *Journal of Peace Research* 5 (2000) 613.

Rockwood, Frederick W, '1973, the United Nations 27th Session: Direct Satellite Broadcasting' 14 *Harvard International Law Journal* 604 (1973).

Roling, BVA, and Ruter, CF (eds), *The Tokyo Judgement: The International Military Tribunal for the Far East (IMTFE) 29 April 1946–12 November 1948,* vol. ii (Amsterdam: APA—University Press, 1977).

Roosevelt, Franklin Delano, 'Four Human Freedoms' 6 *Human Rights Quarterly* 3 (1984) 384.

Rosenstock, Robert, 'The Declaration of Principles of International Law Concerning Friendly Relations: A Survey' 65 *American Journal of International Law* 4 (1971) 713.

Rowson, Richard C, 'The American Commitment to Private International Political Communications: A View of Free Europe, Inc.' 31 *Law and Contemporary Problems* 458 (1966).

Rusk, Dean, 'The 25th U.N. General Assembly and the Use of Force' 2 *Georgia Journal of International and Comparative Law* 19 (1972).

Ryan, Kevin, 'Rights, Intervention and Self-Determination' 20 *Denver Journal of International Law and Policy* 55 (1991–2).

Sadurska, Romana, 'Threats of Force' 82 *American Journal of International Law* 239 (1988).

Sagues, Nestor Pedro, 'Judicial Censorship of the Press in Argentina' 4 *Southwestern Journal of Law and Trade in the Americas* 45 (1997).

Sakr, Naomi, *Satellite Realms: Transnational Television, Globalization and the Middle East* (London: IB Tauris, 2001).

Sandoz, Yves, 'Is There a 'Droit d'Ingérence' in the Sphere of Information? The Right to Information from the Standpoint of International Humanitarian Law' 325 *International Review of the Red Cross* 633 (1998).

Sarkin, Jeremy, 'The Drafting of South Africa's Final Constitution from a Human-Rights Perspective' 47 *American Journal of Comparative Law* 1 (1999) 67.

Schabas, William A, 'General Principles of Criminal Law in the International Criminal Court Statute (Part III)' 6 *European Journal of Crime, Criminal Law and Criminal Justice* 4 (1998) 84.

—— 'International Decision: Mugesera v. Minister of Citizenship and Immigration. Nos. M96-10465, M96-10466. Immigration and Refugee Board (Appeal Division) of Canada, November 6, 1998' 93 *American Journal of International Law* 529 (1999).

—— *Genocide in International Law* (Cambridge: Cambridge University Press, 2000).

—— 'International Decision: Barayagwiza v. Prosecutor (Decision, and Decision (Prosecutor's Request for Review or Reconsideration)). Case No. ICTR-97-19-AR72' 94 *American Journal of International Law* 563 (2000).

—— 'International Conference: Hate Speech in Rwanda: The Road to Genocide' 46 *McGill Law Journal* 141 (2000).

—— 'Editorial: International Criminal Court: The Secret of its Success' 12 *Criminal Law Forum* 3 (2001) 415.

—— 'Mens Rea and the International Criminal Tribunal for the Former Yugoslavia' 37 *New England Law Review* 1015 (2003).

—— 'National Courts Finally Begin to Prosecute Genocide, the "Crime of Crimes"' 1 *Journal of International Criminal Justice* 39 (2003).

—— *An Introduction to the International Criminal Court* (2nd edn, Cambridge: Cambridge University Press, 2004).

Schenone, Christine M, 'Jamming the Stations: Is There an International Free Flow of Information?' 14 *California Western International Law Journal* 501 (1984).

Schwelb, Egon, 'International Conventions on Human Rights' 9 *International and Comparative Law Quarterly* 654 (1960).

—— 'The International Convention on the Elimination of All Forms of Racial Discrimination' 15 *International and Comparative Law Quarterly* 996 (1966).

Schwenk, James, 'Military Justice and the Media: The Media Interview' 12 *USAFA Journal of Legal Studies* 15 (2002/3).

Shaw, Malcolm N, *International Law* (5th edn, Cambridge: Cambridge University Press, 2003).

Short, KRM (ed), *Film and Radio Propaganda in World War II* (London: Croom Helm, 1983).

Sieghart, Paul, *The International Law of Human Rights* (Oxford: Clarendon Press, 1983).

Smith, Bradley F, *Reaching Judgment at Nuremberg* (New York: Basic Books, 1977).

Smith, Jaqueline M, 'Acceptance of Prior Consent as a Means of Regulating Direct Broadcast Satellites' 3 *Emory Journal of International Dispute Resolution* 99 (1988–9).

Smith, Kevin A, 'The Media at the Tip of the Spear' 102 *Michigan Law Review* 1329 (2004).

Smith, Rhona, *Textbook on International Human Rights* (2nd edn, Oxford: Oxford University Press, 2005).

—— and van den Anker, Christien (eds), *The Essentials of Human Rights* (London: Hodder Arnold, 2005).

Sobel, Richard, 'Public Opinion and American Foreign Policy; Getting to War: Predicting International Conflict with Mass Media Indicators' 93 *American Political Science Review* 4 (1999) 1017.

Sohn, Louis B, 'The New International Law: Protection of the Rights of Individuals Rather than States' 32 *American University Law Review* 1 (1982).

Stiglmayer, Alexandra (ed), *Massenvergewaltigungen: Krieg gegen Frauen* (Frankfurt am Main: Fischer Verlag, 1993).

Stockwell, John, *In Search of Enemies: A CIA Story* (London: WW Norton, 1978).

Stone, Geoffrey, 'Free Speech in World War II: "When are you Going to Indict the Seditionists?"' 2 *International Journal of Constitutional Law* 2 (2004) 334.

Strapatsas, Nicolaos, 'The Crime of Aggression' 16 *Criminal Law Forum* 1 (2005) 89.

Strubel, Michael (ed), *Film und Krieg: Die Inszenierung von Politik zwischen Apologetik und Apokalypse* (Opladen: Leske + Budrich, 2002).

Symonides, Janusz (ed), *Human Rights: New Dimensions and Challenges* (Dartmouth: Ashgate, 1998).

Tarnopolsky, WS, 'A Comparison between the Canadian Charter of Rights and Freedoms and the International Covenant on Civil and Political Rights' 8 *Queens Law Journal* 211 (1982–3).

Taylor, Philip M, *Global Communications, International Affairs and the Media since 1945* (London: Routledge, 1997).

Taylor, Porcher L, 'The Installation Commander Versus an Aggressive News Media in an On-Post Terrorist Incident: Avoiding the Constitutional Collision' *Army Law* 19 (1986).

Taylor, Telford, *The Anatomy of the Nuremberg Trials: A Personal Memoir* (New York: Knopf, 1992).

Terry, James P, 'Press Access to Combatant Operations in the Post-Peacekeeping Era' 154 *Military Law Review* 1 (1987).

Thomas, Daniel C, *The Helsinki Effect: International Norms, Human Rights, and the Demise of Communism* (Princeton: Princeton University Press, 2001).

Thompson, Seymour D, 'Andrew Jackson and his Collisions with Judges and Lawyers' 31 *American Law Review* 801 (1897) 810.

Timmermann, Wibke Kristin, 'The Relationship between Hate Propaganda and Incitement to Genocide: A New Trend in International Law towards Criminalization of Hate Propaganda?' *Leiden Journal of International Law* 18 (2005) 257.

Tomlinson JD, *The International Control of Radio Communications* (Ann Arbor, Mich: Edwards Bros., 1945).

Tomuschat, Christian, 'National Implementation of International Standards on Human Rights' *Canadian Yearbook of International Law* 31 (1984–5).

Torres, Amaya Ubeda de, 'Freedom of Expression under the European Convention on Human Rights: A Comparison with the Inter-American System of Protection of Human Rights' 10 *Human Rights Brief* 6 (2003).

Trainin, AN, *Hitlerite Responsibility under Criminal Law*, ed AY Vishinski, trans Andrew Rothstein (London: Hutchinson, 1945).

Triffterer, Otto (ed), *Commentary on the Rome Statute of the International Criminal Court: Observers' Notes, Article by Article* (Baden-Baden: Nomos Verl, 1999).

Turley, Jonathan, 'Presidential Papers and Popular Government: The Convergence of Constitutional and Property Theory in Claims of Ownership and Control of Presidential Records' 88 *Cornell Law Review* 651 (2003).

Udombana, Nsongurua J, 'Articulating the Right to Democratic Governance in Africa' 24 *Michigan Journal of International Law* 1209 (2003).

Unger, Toby R, 'The Status of the Arts in an Emerging State of Palestine' 14 *Arizona Journal of International and Comparative Law* 193 (1997).

Van Alstyne, William W, 'The First Amendment and the Suppression of Warmongering Propaganda in the United States: Comments and Footnotes' 31 *Law and Contemporary Problems* 530 (1966).

van der Heijden, Barend, and Tahzib-Lie, Bahia, *Reflections on the Universal Declaration of Human Rights: A Fiftieth Anniversary Anthology* (The Hague: Martinus Nijhoff, 1998).

van der Vyver, Johan D, 'Personal and Territorial Jurisdiction of the International Criminal Court' 14 *Emory International Law Review* 1 (2000).

Van Dyke, Vernon B, 'Responsibility of States for International Propaganda' 34 *American Journal of International Law* 58 (1940).

Verduce, Valerie M, 'Meese v. Keene: An Attempt to Keep the First Amendment from Raining on the Congressional Parade' 17 *Southwestern University Law Review* 373 (1987).

Viswanathan, Gauri (ed), *Power, Politics and Culture: Interviews with Edward W. Said* (London: Bloomsbury, 2004).

Von Glahn, Gerhard, 'The Case for Legal Control of "Liberation" Propaganda' 31 *Law and Contemporary Problems* 553 (1966).

Wallenstein, Joshua, 'Punishing Words: An Analysis of the Necessity of the Element of Causation in Prosecutions for Incitement to Genocide' 2 *Stanford Law Review* 54 (2001) 351.

Waluchow, Wilfred (ed), *Free Expression: Essays in Law and Philosophy* (Oxford: Clarendon Press, 1994).

Weis, George, 'International Criminal Justice in Time of Peace' 28 *Transactions of the Grotius Society* 27 (1942).

White, Amber Blanco, *The New Propaganda* (London: Victor Gollancz, 1939).

Whitton, John B, 'Radio after the War' 22 *Foreign Affairs* 309 (1943–4).

—— 'Efforts to Curb Dangerous Propaganda' 41 *American Journal of International Law* 899 (1947).

—— 'UN Conference on Freedom of Information and the Movement against International Propaganda' 43 *American Journal of International Law* (1949) 73.

—— 'Cold War Propaganda' 45 *American Journal of International Law* 151 (1951).

—— 'Radio Propaganda: A Modest Proposal' 52 *American Journal of International Law* 739 (1958).

—— 'International Propaganda' 72 *Harvard Law Review* 396 (1958).

—— 'Subversive Propaganda Reconsidered' 55 *American Journal of International Law* 120 (1961).

—— 'The Problem of Curbing International Propaganda' 31 *Law and Contemporary Problems* 601 (1966).

—— 'Propaganda and World Public Order: The Legal Regulation of the Ideological Instrument of Coercion' 6 *American Journal of International Law* 3 (1968) 793.

—— and Larson, Arthur, *Propaganda: Towards Disarmament in the War of Words* (New York: Oceana Publications, 1964).

Wilcox, Francis O, 'The Use of Atrocity Stories in War' 34 *American Political Science Review* 6 (1940) 1167.

Winkler, John K, *William Randolph Hearst: A New Appraisal* (New York: Hastings House, 1955).

Woolsey, Theodore S, 'The Effect of the Unfriendly Act or Inequitable Conduct of the Citizen upon the Right to Protection' *American Society of International Law Proceedings* 99 (1910).

Wright, Quincy, 'The Law of the Nuremberg Trial' 41 *American Journal of International Law* 1 (1947) 38.

—— 'The Crime of "War-Mongering"' 42 *American Journal of International Law* 1 (1948) 128.

Wright, Quincy, 'Freedom and Responsibility in Respect of Trans-National Communication' 44 *American Society of International Law Proceedings* 95 (1950) 104.

—— 'Proposal for an International Criminal Court' 46 *American Journal of International Law* 60 (1952).

—— 'Subversive Intervention' 54 *American Journal of International Law* 521 (1960).

Yildiz, Kerim, *The Kurds in Turkey: EU Accession and Human Rights* (London: Pluto Press, 2005).

Zahar, Alexander, 'The ICTR's "Media" Judgment and the Reinvention of Direct and Public Incitement to Commit Genocide' 16 *Criminal Law Forum* 1 (2005) 33.

Index

Lightning Source UK Ltd.
Milton Keynes UK
UKHW021813170622
404595UK00003B/140